Random, incomprehensible violen[ce] ... a peeping Tom crouching excitedly [beside] lovers' cars ... Blackburn's meticu[lous ...] frightening times is a masterly pie[ce ...] not for bedtime reading ... step by [step she has uncovered the] terrible details of Cooke's murders ... an outstanding work of investigative journalism.
Reg Harrison, *The Australian*

A painstakingly researched book that throws new light on Cooke's crimes and points to what may be one of the worst miscarriages of justice in Australia ... Blackburn's image of Perth in the 1960s and her account of the impact of Cooke's reign of terror is compelling ... that the story she tells is true – and the fact that mild-mannered John Button and deaf-mute Darryl Beamish remain legally convicted of murder – makes an extraordinary story.
Kelly Ryan, *Herald Sun,* **Melbourne**

Graphic and gripping ... magnificent ... one of the greatest works I have ever read on crime, courts and police ... amazed at the detail ... the Australian literary equivalent of *In Cold Blood* (Truman Capote) and *Executioner's Song* (Norman Mailer). Estelle Blackburn is one hell of a brilliant author.
Ken Pedersen, *Innisfail Advocate,* **Queensland**

The extent of Blackburn's research and forensic analysis is staggering. She has left no stone unturned and in my opinion she is a brilliant investigative journalist.
Wendy Page, *Australian Story,* **ABC**

The significance of Estelle's work, which has unearthed a good deal of fresh evidence relative to John Button, may be that it destroys what I have called the entrenched judicial belief. It may be that it compels one to say that when Cooke said that he ran down Anderson he WAS telling the truth.
Sir Francis Burt, former Chief Justice and Governor of Western Australia

Brilliant reconstruction of the crimes of Perth's hare-lipped serial killer ... this six-year reinvestigation leaves no room to doubt that Darryl Beamish did 15 years for a murder committed by Cooke in 1959 and that John Button did five years for a 1963 murder by Cooke. Why do the guilty get off while innocent people such as Beamish, Button and Lindy Chamberlain go to prison?
Evan Whitton, *The Australian*

Broken Lives is compulsive and fascinating reading.
Susan Hewitt, *Sound Telegraph*, **Perth**

First ever detailed study of serial killer Eric Edgar Cooke; a must-read.
Former Commissioner of Police, Brian Bull

Exceptional; a flaming sword for justice.
Dr Greg Blackburn, psychiatric doctor, Brisbane

Broken Lives brilliantly exposes a system that in all likelihood shafted a cowering 19-year-old 35 years ago.
Post Newspapers

Blackburn ... has done enough to point to the possibility of a miscarriage of justice ... it can never be to late to rectify an injustice.
The West Australian

This book presents evidence that Eric Edgar Cooke confessed to committing other crimes which were never made known to the community of Western Australia but which were accepted by the police and authorities.
Tom Stephens, Leader of the Opposition in the Western Australian Legislative Council.

I support Mr Button's cause. An inquiry ... should at least have the status of a down-scaled Royal Commission.
Michael Chamberlain, former husband of Lindy Chamberlain

BROKEN LIVES

The end of **Estelle Blackburn**'s childhood saw the end of innocence for her safe home city of Perth — all because of one man. Estelle went on to gain a Bachelor of Arts degree from The University of Western Australia and become a newspaper journalist for *The West Australian*, then a radio and television journalist for the Australian Broadcasting Corporation, and later a publicist for two police ministers and a premier. A chance social meeting with the convicted killer's brother sent her back in time and started an exhaustive search for the facts about the death of Rosemary Anderson, one of Cooke's victims.

Broken Lives has won numerous awards, including the 1999 WA Premier's Book Award for Historical and Critical Studies and the 2001 Ned Kelly Crime Writing Award for Best Non-fiction Australian Crime Book.

BROKEN LIVES

ESTELLE BLACKBURN

Revised and updated edition published in 2002
by Hardie Grant Books
12 Claremont Street
South Yarra
Victoria 3141
www.hardiegrant.com.au

First published in 2001
Copyright © Estelle Blackburn, 2001

All rights reserved. No part of this publication may be reproduced, stored in a retrieval system or transmitted in any form by any means, electronic, mechanical, photocopying, recording or otherwise, without the prior written permission of the publishers and copyright holders.

National Library of Australia Cataloguing-in-Publication Data:
Blackburn, Estelle.
Broken lives.

ISBN 1 74064 073 X.

1. Cooke, Edgar. 2. Serial murders – Western Australia.
3. Serial murderers – Western Australia – Biography. I.
Title.

364.1523092.

Cover design by David Rosemeyer
Text design by Phil Campbell
Typeset by J & M Typesetting
Map by Karena Holden
Photographs courtesy of WA Newspapers
Printed and bound in Australia by Griffin Press

Note All measurements in use at the time of the events were imperial measures, and currency was in pounds, shillings and pence. As a guide, 5 miles is about 8 kilometres; 1 inch is 2.5 cm; 1 foot is 30 cm and 1 yard is about 1 metre.

Weight converts roughly to 2 pounds per kg.

A pound is worth around two dollars today. There were 20 shillings in a pound and 12 pence in a shilling.

All temperatures are in Fahrenheit.

Contents

Preface	ix
Acknowlegements	xiii
Map: Crime as the City Slept	xvi
Gallows Confession	1
Lover Come Back (I)	5
Wednesday's Child Is Full Of Woe	17
A Father's Influence	27
A Powerful New Urge	46
Violent Nightmare	58
The Season of Goodwill	62
A Fight to the Death	74
The Australian Way of Life	80
Like Father, Like Son	86
The Marker Boy	91
The Brookwood Flats Prowler	94
The Other Side of Mr Nice Guy	104
Life's a Ball	114
Black Friday	117
A Powerful Car to Match a Powerful Urge	133
The City of Light	149
Love in the Air	158
Happy New Year	164
Australia Day Bloodletting	172
Fear City	199
Lover Come Back (II)	206
Death and Defeat	234

Tears on My Pillow	237
Evil Valentine	255
Death Row	264
Circumstantial Evidence	281
Ten Years' Hard Labour	304
A Smart Cookie	314
Attack on a Little Lovely	324
Another Gun, Another Unlocked Door	328
The Geraldton Wax Trap	337
'We've Had a Visitor'	343
A Cooke's Tour	358
Defence of the Nedlands Monster	384
A Beggared Imagination	402
The Highest Judges in the Land	429
Before the Executioner	438
Epilogue	450
The Verdict	459

Preface

Broken Lives is factual, a result of my investigations over six years involving original research and interviews with more than 160 people. At points where I have found conflicting evidence, I have chosen the version that I find to be most acceptable. Source material consists of:

- Police files of Eric Edgar Cooke and John Button: Police Service Records and State Archives WAS: 1473 pt01
- Prison file of Eric Edgar Cooke: State Archives WAS: 511
- Prison file of John Button: Ministry of Justice file 63/00303
- Legal file of Eric Edgar Cooke: Minter Ellison
- Occurrence Books – Condemned Cells: State Archives WAS: 707
- Regulations – Public Executioner and Flagellation – Appointment of: State Archives WAS: 511
- Instructions for Carrying Out an Execution: State Archives WAS: 511
- Government Gazettes, 24/1/1964 and 30/10/1964: Battye Library
- *Legal Executions in Western Australia* by Brian Purdue, Foundation Press 1993: The Library and Information Service of WA
- Tape recording of John Button's trial: The Supreme Court of Western Australia
- Transcript of Counsels' addresses to the jury and Judge's summing up, Button's trial: Director of Public Prosecutions
- Papers for the Judges in the High Court of Australia No. 9 of 1964: Statutory Declaration by the Reverend George Arthur Jenkins 12/11/64: Godfrey Virtue & Co.

- Hansard Reports of the Western Australian Parliamentary Debates 1964: Parliament House Library
- Ministers' biographies, Cooke's wedding certificate: Uniting and Anglican Church archives; Don Jenkins
- Western Australian Police Reports and Record and Service of police officers: Western Australia Police Service
- Records of Karrakatta and Fremantle Cemeteries
- *The Beamish Case* by Prof. Peter Brett, Professor of Jurisprudence, University of Melbourne, Melbourne University Press, 1966
- *University of Western Australia Law Review*, Vol.7 – Book Review, *The Beamish Case*, Prof. Douglas Payne; Vol. 8 – *The Beamish Case: A Rejoinder*, Prof. Peter Brett; *A Comment on Professor Brett's Rejoinder*, Prof. Douglas Payne: Law Library, The University of Western Australia
- Unpublished autobiography of John Button
- Unpublished manuscript on the Cooke murders by Ralph Wheatley
- Judgment *Darryl Raymond Beamish v The Queen. Judgments of the Supreme Court of WA*, Vol.1 1964: Law Library, The University of Western Australia
- Newspaper articles: Battye Library and the *West Australian* library
- Television specials: *Manhunt*, TVW 7, February 1964; 'Capital Punishment in Western Australia', *Four Corners*, ABC 1964; 'The Sins of the Father', *Australian Story*, produced by Wendy Page, ABC, 24 July 1998
- Letters from John Wiley and Denis McLeod
- Interviews conducted either face-to-face and tape-recorded or recorded by shorthand notes, or conducted by telephone, recorded by shorthand notes. Personal interviews were conducted in the UK, New Zealand, Queensland, Cue, Koorda, Mandurah and Perth.
- Visits to John Button's home and schools in Brixton, UK, Fremantle Prison, Karnet Rehabilitation Centre, former homes of victims and surviving victims, former Perth homes of John Button and Rosemary Anderson, the site of Rosemary's hit–run, graves of Cooke and victims.

The section in Chapter 2 on the attempted running down of Doug Wilkie and his pillion passenger on a scooter comes from Cooke's confession and an interview with Wilkie. I was the first person to interview Wilkie about it, more than 30 years after the event. With such time lapse, he could not definitely remember the date or time of the incident. He recalls it as in the morning and the offending vehicle as a utility. I take it to have been Cooke because Cooke's and Wilkie's descriptions of the unpublicised event match perfectly. I therefore place it on the night of 9 February 1963, according to Cooke's confession made ten months after the event.

I have contained references to the police interview in Chapter 22 to the evidence given in court. I was not able to further question John Wiley or Jack Deering because these retired detectives refused my requests for interviews. Mr Deering wrote to me that he did not wish to be involved in my project; Mr Wiley replied that he was unable to add or subtract from the evidence presented to the court and concluded: 'I have retired from public life after 38 years of faithful and diligent police service to the public and prior to that, three years overseas on active service in World War 2. Therefore I think I have earned a well gained rest in my retiring years.'

The only sections that are not factual are those relating to the thoughts and emotions of Lilly Button, who died in 1989.

My reconstruction of Eric Edgar Cooke's complex personality, his thinking and motives is entirely my interpretation. I formed my opinion through my research and discussions with his family, psychiatrists and a psychologist who examined him and surviving victims.

Acknowledgements

I am indebted to the Western Australia Police Service, Ministry of Justice, Minter Ellison and *The West Australian* for access to files and to the Supreme Court and the Director of Public Prosecutions for access to court proceedings. I am grateful for the provision of photographs by *The West Australian*, the Western Australia Police Service, Bret Christian and interviewees.

My sincere gratitude goes to the Cooke family – Sally Cooke and her five surviving children – for their generosity in allowing this work, and their genuine concern for the victims' families, despite the repercussions for them and their families. I share the Cookes' feelings for the families of those who died and warmly thank those who told me about the lives of their loved ones.

I respect and feel for Denis McLeod in his 'despair at the injustice of the situation; Cooke stole the life of my sister, and even now, he owns her identity in the sense that she is remembered in the public mind as his victim, his possession', and I thank Denis for his blessing and acknowledgement that I had 'clearly attempted to be respectful of the feelings and susceptibilities of the damaged people littering the path of degradation that Cooke drove through the community'.

To the women who survived Cooke's attacks, I owe immeasurable thanks for allowing me to delve into their old emotional wounds. Only because of their willingness to relive their horror can we now understand Cooke's complete range of modus operandi, shedding previously hidden light on his two contentious confessions.

I regret the intrusion into the grief of Rosemary Anderson's family and thank Jack Anderson for his interview. I acknowledge that all references to the romance between Button and Rosemary are one-sided, as told by Button, and that Rosemary may have had a different point of view about events and emotions.

References to *The West Australian*'s police roundsman of the time, the late Ralph Wheatley, come from his unpublished manuscript and I thank his widow, Nancy Blackburn, for access to it.

My thanks go to Jill Murdoch, one of the late Ken Hatfield's daughters, and his friend Dr Mercy Sadka, for some understanding of Hatfield's unique character and of his unwavering certainty as to Button's innocence.

I thank all those people who responded to my requests for information, who volunteered information and who helped in so many ways. They are too many to mention but include Trish Pepper, who enthusiastically believed in the project from the start; Simon Kennedy, who directed me to the prison Occurrence Books; Chris Olney, Allan Hale and Lucille Fisher, who volunteered proofreading; Wendy Page, whose belief in the cause and in me gave it national prominence; and Post Newspapers staff involved in the original edition – Philip Powell for desktop publishing, Karena Holden for the cover design, Sean Conway and Karena for the map, Sharon Itzstein, Karena and Sean for the plates, and all Post staff for their friendliness.

People who went out of their way to help and give me interviews include Sir Frank Burt, John Hughes OAM APM, Heath McLeod, Barry Hansen, Doug Wilkie, Kathy Bellis and others who have since died: Kathleen James, Phil Bellis, Alan Dodd, Leila Keehner, Flora Bunning, Dr Frank Prendergast, Dr William Laurie and the Reverend Ralph Thomas.

A big thanks to all my dear friends who listened, supported, enthused and empathised, who were faithful constants through the exciting highs and the difficult lows of this long journey.

I very much enjoy the fact that my group of friends has grown because of this work and now includes many of Cooke's victims and their families, as well as the Beamish family and Sally Cooke. I value the close friendship that has developed with John and Helen Button, their children Gregory and Naomi and their spouses Marie Button and Gordon Shattock, and appreciate John Button's references in his book *Why Me, Lord*.

Broken Lives would not be as it is without Zoltan Kovacs, my original editor. My deepest appreciation goes to him for his huge contribution to this work, including his excellent guidance, integrity, knowledge, wisdom, attention to detail, lateral thinking, ideas and generosity. This book needed him and I needed his confidence in the project, his encouragement to boldness, his patience and the friendship of him and his wife Kelcey.

I owe an inestimable debt to Bret Christian for his enthusiasm, friendship and moral and financial support, and to his wife Jane for the intrusion into their family time. Bret created the original version of *Broken Lives*, including help with the foreword, epilogue and promotional material, and helped to put together the map and photographs. He generously funded its publication and the gathering of vital further evidence, particularly the recreations carried out by American collision reconstructionist Rusty Haight. My heartfelt thanks to Bret for enabling my six years' effort to see the light of day and for taking up the torch in the effort to overturn two terrible injustices and strengthen the justice system by giving it the opportunity to acknowledge and rectify its mistakes.

Since publication of the original version, I have been overwhelmed with support and appreciation from so many people throughout Australia and overseas. My thanks go to all of them – particularly Hardie Grant Books for their belief in it, Foong Ling Kong for her sensitive and consultative editing, Trevor Condren for his courage, Trevor and Mary Cross for their care and generosity, Trish Lake for her help, the Australian Journalists Association, the Perth Press Club and the Library and Information Service of WA for their awards, Paul B. Kidd for his enthusiasm and acknowledgment in *Australia's Serial Killers*, Malcolm Brown for his acknowledgment in *Bombs, Guns and Knives* and the Western Australian Government for granting new appeals to John Button and Darryl Beamish.

The Court of Criminal Appeal is the next step for Button and Beamish in their efforts to overturn their convictions. They and I appreciate so much the support of Jon Davies and Tom Percy QC, who are representing them pro bono. Thanks to Jon and Tom for the music, the friendship and the time, effort and legal expertise they are donating to Button, Beamish and the cause of justice.

ESTELLE BLACKBURN
Perth, Western Australia
February 2001

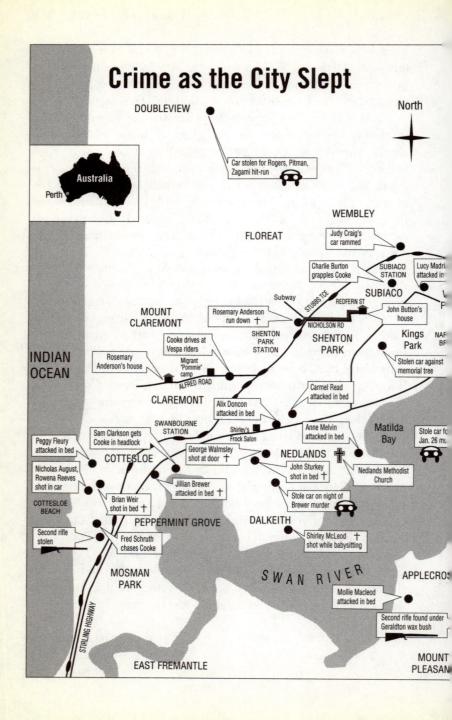

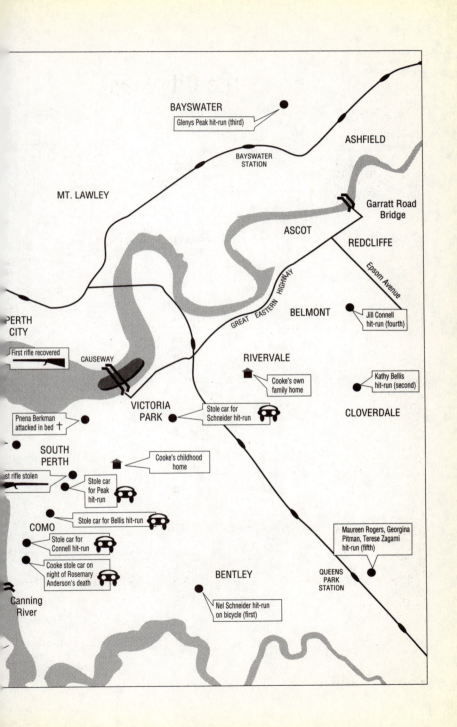

Gallows Confession

26 OCTOBER 1964

The hangman is ready. The noose has been prepared and tested, the witnesses are gathered and the cornermen are standing in position on planks over the trapdoors. It's just before 8 o'clock on a cool, cloudy morning in Perth, Western Australia.

A short, slight man with dark, wavy hair and a twisted mouth has watched the first streaks of light herald the day through the small slit window high up in a narrow cell in the punishment block at the back of Fremantle Prison. It's the bare segregated block of cells where the Swan River settlement's convicts were punished by solitary confinement on bread and water and flogging in the courtyard.

It's still used for solitary confinement and as a last holding cell before execution. The gallows is only ten yards away. The small man was led to the holding cell at 6 a.m. from Death Row, further away in New Division, where he'd spent the past thirteen months. He now waits out his final two hours with the prison chaplain and his spiritual adviser.

He is Eric Edgar Cooke, 33 years old, a married truck driver of seven children. He has murdered at least five people, blasted away the useful life of another and injured at least a further ten. Through random shootings in the elite western suburbs, he held Perth in the grip of fear for seven months in 1963. The small city with a population of 518,000 previously had ways of a friendly, easy-going big country town where people left their doors unlocked and their car keys in the ignition of unlocked cars. They trusted each other. Cooke turned it into a city of suspicion and terror.

The prison chaplain asks Cooke if he has a last wish.

The condemned man responds firmly and calmly. The last wish, a present for his eldest son, is clear to the minister, who swears to honour it.

Then Cooke voluntarily reaches for the Bible, taking it out of the Methodist minister's hand. Holding it fervently, Eric Edgar Cooke states: 'I swear before Almighty God that I killed Anderson and Brewer.'

His gallows confession repeats a confession he has made several times. He is referring to the hit–run murder of seventeen-year-old Rosemary Anderson and the hatchet and scissors slaying of 22-year-old Melbourne heiress Jillian McPherson Brewer.

Before Cooke was caught and confessed to these murders and other crimes, two young men had been arrested. They had confessed to the murders after hours of intense questioning. John Button, a nineteen-year-old brickie's labourer from England, had been charged with the wilful murder of his girlfriend Rosemary Anderson in February 1963, found guilty of the lesser crime of manslaughter and jailed.

Darryl Beamish, a twenty-year-old deaf-mute, was convicted in 1961 of the wilful murder of Jillian Brewer in December 1959. His death sentence had been commuted to life imprisonment. Appeals initiated by the two men on the fresh evidence of Cooke's confessions were rejected by the Court of Criminal Appeal and the High Court.

The hangman arrives at the holding cell. He shackles Cooke's legs and places a hood over his head. Forty-two steps to the scaffold, the flap of the hood pulled down over his face, the lever pushed. In less than a minute from leaving the holding cell, Eric Edgar Cooke is dead.

Out in the prison yards, prisoners know the exact moment of execution. There is a great flurry of pigeons from the gallows roof, unsettled from their regular perch by the crash of the trap doors. As he sees the pigeons rise, John Button knows that any hope that Cooke can ever convince the judiciary that he, not Button, really had run down Rosemary has come to an end.

The next day, while Cooke was being buried, Button was living through another day of prison routine.

When the cell was opened at 7 a.m., he went out to the yard to wash at the tap. He went back to his cell to have his breakfast of porridge and tea, which had been left at the cell door. At 7.30 he went back to the yard to empty his sanitary bucket. At 8 he was lined up and marched to the carpentry shop to work.

At lunchtime he lined up for parade, collected his dixie and was locked in his cell to eat. He went back to work. At 4 p.m. he lined up for parade again and then took his dixie lid of soup and mug of tea into his cell. He was locked in at 4.30. The lights went out at 8. Imprisoned in the small cell in total darkness, he was left to battle his demons – for hours through the night, monotonously pacing up and down his cell, filled with grief, anger, confusion and frustration.

The twenty-year-old was facing a further eight-and-a-half years of this.

Cooke's initial confession had brought Button much relief. At last there would be an end to his nightmare. Button believed that everyone – even the police and the judiciary – would understand that his own confession was given in a moment of trauma, on learning that his beloved girlfriend, Rosemary, had lost her fight for life in hospital. He hadn't cared about anything then, and he was sure the two detectives weren't going to leave him alone until they got what they wanted. But with Cooke's confession the injustice would be recognised and his wrongful conviction overturned. But no-one would believe Cooke.

Button was nonplussed. Two men had confessed to Rosemary's murder – he, the loving boyfriend whose only prior brush with the law had been one speeding fine; the other, Cooke, a known murderer who had tried to kill seven women in exactly the same way as Rosemary was killed, and who remained insistent that he had done it. Yet the highest judges in the land decided Button was the culprit.

More than three decades later, Button has finished his sentence and is leading a normal life as a bricklayer and Elder of the Westminster Presbyterian Church. He is married to a retired police sergeant's daughter and has two married children: Gregory, a qualified medical doctor and veterinary surgeon and Naomi, a social worker. He has a grand-daughter called Amy. He is still battling to have his name cleared.

This is his story.

Lover Come Back (I)

9 February 1963

John Button sat on the hard ground of a prison yard while the post-execution formalities were carried out. It would be another half an hour or so before they would be escorted off to their work stations. He closed his eyes in utter defeat and despair, giving in to the rush of memories and reliving every moment of the fateful day that had started out so happily and ended with his becoming Prisoner No. 29050.

It was Saturday, 9 February 1963, the day of his nineteenth birthday. John woke up to a perfect hot summer's day with no other birthday wish than to spend it with Rosemary. He woke early so that he could spend some time with his family and be at Rosemary's with most of the day before him. She was all he could think of; he was in love and was still consumed by the beautiful night at the Skyline Drive-in. He could smell her hair, feel her as they clung together across the front seat.

He sat at the breakfast table with his parents and Jimmy, his younger brother. But with his mind elsewhere, he wasn't very interested in his father talking about the day's headlines – the police drawing a blank on the latest tip-off in the murder hunt, or the cyclone devastating Onslow on the northwest coast, its 144 mph winds the highest ever recorded in Australia. He just wanted to talk about Rosemary while he tucked into his mother's generous serve of bacon and eggs. He was happy to answer his parents' questions about how he'd enjoyed his evening and what movies they'd seen. He could tell them a fair bit about the first one, *Wild and the Innocent*, and though he could name the second movie, *Lover Come Back*, and had noticed that Rock Hudson and Doris Day were in it, he was glad to be relieved of any detail by sixteen-year-old Jimmy interrupting with something about his latest ballroom competition.

John was in a hurry, but his parents didn't mind. They were used to him spending more time at the Andersons' place than at home and they happily saw this as a step towards his setting up his own home. John's six-month romance with Rosemary Anderson had blossomed and, although they were young – Rosemary had turned seventeen three weeks back and John was now nineteen – it appeared to be leading towards marriage. John's mother was quietly anticipating the joys of having John settled and grandchildren around her.

John left as soon as he could, driving from his home in Subiaco to Rosemary's home in Mt Claremont. Rosemary lived with her parents, younger sister Helen and younger brother Jim at 145 Alfred Road, a big brick house on the corner of Strickland Street. Ten minutes later, John was pulling up on the gravel drive in the side street and running across the huge backyard to knock on the kitchen door. It was always the back door for him – he was part of the family now. Rosemary was just up, greeting him in her shortie pyjamas and leaving him in the kitchen while she ran to her bedroom to get dressed. Also pleased at having all day together, she was in a hurry, too, not bothering to put on her panties and bri-nylon petticoat, but quickly throwing her pink cotton dress over her pyjama pants.

The young couple had no plans. They didn't care what they did, as long as they were together. It was the best birthday John could have, just doing nothing in particular with Rosemary.

Her present for him was small. She had no money, because she'd finished up at the newsagency the week before. She'd been working at Dymock's Newsagency in Waratah Avenue, Dalkeith, but was frightened to tell her parents she'd lost her job and left home each day as though she was going to work. John didn't care about the present – she was his present. But he worried again about not having given her a friendship ring for her birthday in January. She'd been disappointed and he again wished he'd given her that tangible proof of love that girls seemed to attach so much importance to. It was a regret, and while it crossed his mind a few times that her special day hadn't been as special as she'd hoped, he didn't let it tarnish his. They'd since agreed to get engaged on her eighteenth birthday the following year. He'd make sure that ring would be what she wanted.

Brian William Robinson, a 23-year-old labourer from Belmont, had also left home early this Saturday morning. He went with his brother, Edward, to the Railway Hotel in the city, where he spent the morning drinking. At 2 p.m. he returned to the Epsom Avenue home that he shared with his parents and brothers and sisters, and went to bed.

The good-looking young man with fair wavy hair had recently left a surveying job at Southern Cross in the Eastern Goldfields. Often unemployed, he complained about his father picking on him for it. They'd had an argument about it the previous night and that morning, his father had again questioned him about leaving the last job. George Robinson, a 70-year-old pensioner, went into Brian's room a while later that afternoon. Now another fight broke out. Brian confronted his father about a rumour he'd heard from his friend Dick Hutchinson – that he was the product of incest between his father and a daughter, so that his mother Shirley was also his sister.

George had known of this incest rumour for a long time. His wife Violet had a two or three-year-old illegitimate daughter, Shirley Mucklow, when they were married in 1922. Shirley's paternity was never spoken of, but the rumour had persisted that George was the father. Violet suffered from a rare inherited mental disease, Huntington's Chorea. She was hospitalised long-term, and when Shirley was about nineteen, George started living with her as man and wife. They had Brian a year later when Shirley was twenty, followed by three more children.

Brian demanded to know if the rumour was true. In the midst of the fighting Brian managed to get hold of his father's shotgun. After unsuccessfully trying to wrestle the gun from his son, George Robinson announced he was calling the police. Despite Brian's warning that he'd shoot the policeman, George left the house and spoke to his neighbour, whose seventeen-year-old son ran to the petrol station over the road and called the Belmont Police Station. George waited outside for the police and Brian put the gun on the lounge-room window sill pointing outwards. His mother, Shirley, now also mentally ill with Huntington's Chorea, was with him.

Constable Noel Iles was just coming off duty at Belmont when the call came through for him to attend a domestic dispute at 160 Epsom Avenue, Belmont, four houses up from the shopping centre. The 29-year-old father of four volunteered to call in on his way home. Iles pulled up outside the house and was about to walk in when he was hit by a shot from the inside. He slumped to the footpath beside his green Ford Consul. Brian Robinson ran from the house, vaulted the cyclone fence and shot the off-duty officer at point blank range.

Leaving Iles dead on the footpath, Robinson ran towards a man driving a yellow Holden. The terrified driver pulled the keys from the ignition and ran for his life. That left a blue open-topped Goggomobil carrying three people stranded in the middle of the road, the driver unable to get around the abandoned Holden. John Monger, Joan Templeton and Andy McDougall in the Goggomobil saw Robinson run towards them pointing a gun. When Robinson told the one in the back seat to get out, McDougall said: 'Ah, you're kidding,' and went to brush away the gun.

Robinson fired.

Andrew Gurvan McDougall, a 36-year-old father of two, was killed instantly by a bullet to the head. Robinson ran off, leaving his second victim's body slumped over the side of the car.

Taxi driver Arthur Smith had witnessed the second shooting as he was leaving the nearby betting shop. He ran to his taxi to send a Mayday call over the radio when the gunman appeared at the back door: 'Right, drive or I'll blow your brains out.' He sat in the back seat with the shotgun resting over the back of the front seat, pointing it at the terrified 54-year-old who drove along Great Eastern Highway at 70 miles per hour, towards the Gnangara Pine Plantation on the northern edge of suburban Perth.

Rosemary put on her stockings, collected her yellow cardigan and her clutch bag and left home with John about 6 p.m. to drive to his place at 8 Redfern Street. Her parents, Jack and Joan, were going out that night to a barbecue at the Swanbourne–Nedlands Surf Life Saving Club, where her father was secretary.

His parents, Charlie and Lilly, were surprised to see the youngsters, presuming that John would be out all day and evening, only arriving home late to fall into bed as he'd done almost every night these past six months. Not expecting the birthday boy to be home, they'd planned to visit friends after dinner, but decided instead to stay in for a family evening. They kept to their arrangements only on John's insistence. He assured them that he and Rosemary were happy to stay in and watch the Channel 7 movie *Dark Command*, reluctantly accepting Jimmy's insistence on staying home with them and his parents' approval of the sixteen-year-old seeing the A-rated movie.

Lilly set an extra two places at the kitchen table, pleased to have Rosemary with them. Over dinner they talked about their day and Charlie filled them in on the afternoon's drama at Belmont.

In the Gnangara Pine Plantation, Arthur Smith, searching for a way to save his life from this gun-wielding madman, purposely bogged his taxi on a sand track. He was forced to walk deeper into the forest with the gun at his back. Robinson knew the police would be out in force. In another effort to get away, Smith pretended to hurt his ankle, lamely dropping behind the gunman who was trying to get away fast. The ruse worked when a police spotter plane flew over, the desperate gunman running off into the trees, allowing the taxi driver to escape.

The Cessna aircraft was sent to the plantation after a sighting of the taxi, and the spotter pilot saw it abandoned on a dirt track just after 6 p.m. Police converged on the plantation, as did taxi drivers trying to help their kidnapped colleague. Smith was finally found and rescued by a newspaper photographer. Road blocks were set up and the hunt was on for the murderer hiding out in the State pine forest.

In the Button household in Subiaco, Charlie played penny poker with the three youngsters while his wife got ready. They were sitting around the kitchen table, Rosemary joining in the boys' game after John tossed her a few pennies. Young Jimmy lost most hands, despite mastering the poker face and frustrating the efforts of the young lovers to distract him with their tomfoolery. They won several hands, even though they were far more interested in each other than in the game.

When Lilly emerged from the bedroom, Charlie finished the hand and left John to deal as he and his wife walked out amidst a chorus of goodbyes, reassurances they'd be OK and good wishes for a pleasant evening.

John, Rosemary and Jimmy shifted around the table a bit and kept playing. After a while, Jimmy tired of losing and suggested they play something different. John knew of a game that added a touch of spice, and explained how to play strip jack naked. Dealing out four hands, he told them to hold the cards face down in a pile and take turns to pick up the top one and place it face up on the table. They each did that until someone turned over the same number card as the previous one. That person picked up the whole central pile. The one who ran out of cards was the loser and the one with the most cards was the winner. After a game to get the hang of it, John explained the next bit – the loser had to take off an item of clothing.

Rosemary, suspicious at first, agreed to play after checking that she could lose several hands without causing herself any embarrassment. She was the first to lose, and kicked her shoes off under the table. To the delight of the boys, she lost again and her stockings had to go. But to their dismay, they didn't get a strip tease – Rosemary went into the sleepout off to the side of the living room, returning bare-legged but sedate, revealing under her skirt far less leg than they'd seen many a time at the beach. Another couple of games and it was John's turn to disrobe. Like Rosemary, his shoes were first to go, then his socks. Rosemary again, her suspender belt this time. She disappeared into the sleepout and returned looking no different, her stockings and suspender belt left on the bed out of sight. Next was John, who lost his shirt. Young Jimmy, triumphant at only losing his shoes, was looking forward to the consequences of the next few games, now that the preliminaries were over. But spoilsport John called it quits once he was down to his trousers, packing up the cards and putting them back on the sideboard after just a half an hour of play. They didn't bother retrieving their clothing, after all it was a very hot night, they were decent and they were cooler and more comfortable without it.

Jimmy was mumbling about the game being over before the fun had started, when he was cheered up by the suggestion of fish and chips. They were watching television when John announced that he and Rosemary would take a spin down to the local fish-and-chip shop. They weren't really hungry – it wasn't long since dinner – it was just something to do and a means of getting away from the kid brother for a short time. Rosemary collected her things from the sleepout and put them on the back seat in readiness for later. She snuggled up to John on the front seat as they drove a couple of blocks to Nicholson Road.

Eric Edgar Cooke was out and about again, doing what he did every Friday and Saturday night: prowling dark suburban streets, breaking into houses and stealing, watching unsuspecting girls and couples through their bedroom windows, stealing cars – and killing and injuring.

Tonight was the first time he could relax in the two weeks since that hot night when he'd shot five people, killing two of them, seriously wounding another and slightly wounding two more. The people of Perth were terrified, locking themselves in their hot houses and calling the police at every small sound. The street lights were left on all night in the western suburbs; police were everywhere, under pressure and desperate to catch the perpetrator of the random shootings. It was harder for Cooke to sneak around now, but he was cunning, he loved outwitting the police and he basked in the power to triumph against all those people out there who scorned him. But tonight was easier for him. Tonight the police were chasing someone else.

It was quite early in the evening as he toured his old haunts in South Perth and Como, not far from his parents' home. It was an area he knew well and one in which he did well. After a while he was back in Norton Street, the road alongside the Como Hotel. Remembering his luck at finding the rifle at No. 5 two weeks earlier, he headed in that direction, checking out the houses along the way, looking for dark accessible ones. He'd made the most of that rifle. And what a shot he was – right in the forehead each time.

Further up the street from No. 5, he noticed a window open at the front of a dark house. Putting on his white-coloured women's gloves, he niftily climbed through it, dropping into the lounge room of No. 21. He looked for money in the bedroom and found a bank book with two £10 notes inside.

As he continued, he wondered if the fugitive on the other side of town would be as clever as he was at evading the police.

A few minutes later John and Rosemary were in the fish-and-chip shop next to the Shenton Park Hotel in Nicholson Road. They placed the minimum order – one piece of fish and two shillings worth of chips, just enough for a snack.

Driving back home along Derby Road John found a dark spot, where trees covered the street lights. He pulled over. Rosemary put the newspaper-wrapped parcel on the floor in front of her as John drew her close to him. Not even the overpowering smell of fish and chips could counter the romance of the balmy summer's night and his desire for her. As they cuddled and kissed he reached for the lever and lowered the seat. Savouring the snatched moments on their own, conscious of Jimmy waiting for them back at the house, John made love to his beloved – quickly and furtively, just as it had to be each time, always aware of society's censure and the attendant danger. But his need for her overwhelmed his conscience. What a birthday, to have spent it with Rosemary and to hold her and have her close like this.

Kathleen and Arthur James wound down their windows and enjoyed the breeze over the river as they drove along Canning Beach Road. Their son John was at a Festival of Perth concert at the Supreme Court Gardens with his friend Michael Wood, who was staying with them during the school holidays. About

7 o'clock, they decided to go for a quick run in the car they'd just bought. They could collect the rent from the flats they owned in Melville Parade, and while over the other side of Canning Bridge in Como, they could drop in on their friends Ernest and Pearl Head. The two couples had met in 1954 after the Heads came to Perth from New Guinea. Kath's brother, who'd worked with Ernest in New Guinea, had introduced them and the four had become firm friends. The Heads lived near the James' flats and so it would be easy to stop by and show them the new car.

After collecting the rent, they pulled in at 1 Leonora Street. The Heads were pleased to see Kath and Jim, as Arthur was called, and to have a look at the car. Yes, they'd love to go for a test run around the block in the shiny new demonstration-model FB Holden. Not bothering to turn off the lights or television for the few minutes it would take, they pulled the front door shut and admired the car before getting into the back. They drove over the bridge to the Raffles Hotel and came back. It didn't take much longer than five minutes, just enough for Ernest to see for himself that it ran as well as the proud new owner claimed, with the girls going along for the ride.

Back at the Heads', they parked in the driveway and went inside. The Jameses hadn't planned to intrude for long, but agreed to a quick cup of tea and a chance to catch up. As Pearl headed into the kitchen to turn on the kettle and the others settled in the lounge, conversation was quickly stopped short by the television bulletin. They were all amazed to see live coverage of the hunt for the man who'd killed the policeman. They'd heard about the murders on the news, now they were watching the drama unfold as the police hunted down the killer. The four friends were as engrossed as the rest of the Perth population. There were horrifying television pictures of the policeman's body, covered with a blanket, lying on the footpath, and the Goggomobil down the road with a man's blanket-covered body slumped across the back seat and out over the side. The woman driver was still sitting at the wheel, nervously smoking through a long cigarette holder. To have something like this happen just two weeks after the last outbreak of shootings was adding to the shock and the growing awareness that Perth wasn't the safe, sane place everyone had taken it for. So much for a quick cup of tea. They couldn't tear themselves away, expecting the fugitive to be caught any minute. The Jameses were at the Heads' house much longer than expected.

But the telecast finished without the anticipated climax. The excitement over for the night, Kath and Jim said goodbye to the Heads, who saw them out at about 11 p.m. The car wasn't there. The driveway where he'd left it an hour or so earlier was bare. They couldn't believe it – his brand-new car, taken virtually from under their noses. The lounge room was only a few feet from the driveway. They were certain the thief couldn't have started up the car, because Jim had extremely good hearing. Kath was convinced that the fugitive Robinson had rolled it down the drive – she'd heard he'd stolen cars to get out to the pine plantation.

'That's my little darling, always a drama,' Jim laughed as he accepted the Heads' offer of a lift home. He was sure Robinson hadn't taken his car, but he was puzzled at who could have.

Cooke wandered down Leonora Street, Como. He was near the flats on the corner of Henley Street, at No. 46 where he'd stolen a Morris Minor three years previously. He walked on and when he reached the end of the road, he saw some people get into a car and drive away. An empty house, an easy target. But when he got closer he found lights on and the television blaring. He had to be careful to find out who was still in the house before going in. He took his time, peering in the windows, trying the door and checking the windows for an entry point.

He was at the side windows when a car turned in. They were back! Just five minutes or so after they'd left. He ducked behind the bushes at the side of the house, and watched as two men and two women went inside. He lay low for a little while until he was sure it was safe. Then, deprived of a house break by their unexpected arrival home, he took the opportunity of a car instead. It wasn't locked and the keys were in the ignition. Removing the interior light globe, he drove away in the new two-tone green Holden, UKN 547.

The Grey Simca, UKA 547, moved slowly along Derby Road. John cuddled Rosemary as he drove and she patted down her hair. They arrived back at 8 Redfern Street with a cold parcel of fish and chips. Jimmy was watching television, seemingly unaware of the time the errand had taken. It wasn't the advertised film but live coverage of the manhunt. The dark pine forest was swarming with police, spectators' cars were lined up along the road to the area and there were people, spotlights and guns everywhere. The three young people were transfixed.

John, Rosemary and Jimmy sat on the floor and watched the drama. It was bedlam, police everywhere and hundreds of onlookers milling around, out with their children for a night's entertainment. The air was electric with the suspense of when and where they would find the killer. This was the sort of thing you only saw in the movies, not in safe suburban Perth. While the police were hot and weary at Gnangara, the rest of Perth was wide awake, waiting for the shoot-out. For the first time in a fortnight they forgot their fear of the sniper.

There was no thought of sitting at the table and eating their fish and chips while this was going on. Still sitting on the floor, John unwrapped the parcel and divided the fish into three. Despite announcing that the food was cold, Jimmy picked at the snack with the others. John's eyes were fixed on the set when out of the corner of his eye he saw a hand come across to take his piece of fish. Without looking, he assumed it was Jimmy pinching his share and he was annoyed. He liked his brother enough, but he thought his mother spoilt her youngest child. He got away with a lot and John didn't want him to get away with this impudence, too.

'Get your own.'

The words were snapped at Jimmy in a short, harsh way that was out of character for mild-mannered John. It wasn't that he was hungry and needed the fish, it was just Jimmy, thinking he could do whatever he liked and get away with it, as usual. Only it wasn't Jimmy. He wasn't even there, having briefly gone into the kitchen. It was Rosemary. Not Jimmy, whose cheekiness needed tempering, but Rosemary, who needed constant reassurance of his love for her. The words were already out when he turned and saw his terrible mistake. Rosemary! He would have given her the piece of fish if he'd known it was her.

Rosemary's eyes were brimming with tears. He stammered his explanation and apology, reaching out to hold her and comfort her. But it was too late. Rosemary ignored his efforts and took her shoes from under the table and her bag from the sideboard, announcing that she was going home. John rushed after her, catching her as she was just out the front, beside the car parked on the verge. He took her by the arm, apologising again and begging her to come back inside. She pulled away, refusing to listen, insisting that she would walk home. Realising he couldn't win her over, John tried a compromise, offering to drive her home. No. Then he was begging. No, she was walking.

He reached into the car to get her girdle and stockings and called out: 'Aren't you going to take these, too?' She said no, he could bring them to her the next day, it was up to him.

Bring them to her – maybe there was a chance later. But he needed to make it better now. His birthday couldn't end like this.

She started along the road, oblivious to any danger, forgetting there was a man out there killing people. Nor did John think about the murderer of a fortnight ago. He was too upset about his stupidity to think of anything else.

He called desperately, 'Rosemary, come back,' as she kept going, walking towards her fate – a fate that would entwine the lives of John Button and Eric Edgar Cooke.

Wednesday's Child is Full of Woe

1931–48

John Button was heralded into the world by air-raid sirens. Lillian Button bore her third child on the kitchen floor, under the table. The thick wood was Lilly's best protection against the bombs that were expected to fall on Liverpool. Air raids were common in war-torn England, especially since the Allies had started their daylight air offensive seventeen days earlier.

As the sirens warned of the Luftwaffe's arrival and John Button took his first breath on Wednesday, 9 February 1944, Allied planes were penetrating their farthest yet from English bases. Waves of RAF and USAAF medium bombers, light bombers and fighter bombers swept across the Channel, blasting targets in the Reich and occupied France.

More bombs were falling on the Italian battlefront that day, as both sides prepared for a big battle for the Nettuno bridgehead south of Rome. The Luftwaffe was bombing the Anzio beachhead as the hard-pressed Anglo-American forces landed reinforcement troops and equipment and Allied bombers were shelling enemy troops on and behind the beachhead front. On the Baltic front, Russian air support was bombing ten German divisions trapped in the Kanev pocket. They were trying to annihilate the encircled retreating Germans after the Allies had captured the mining centre of Nikopol. While shelling was adding to the numbers of dead, Russian soldiers were spending the day removing tens of thousands of corpses piled three feet high, blocking ravines and roads and totally covering parts of the Dnieper River around Nikopol.

In the West Derby area of Liverpool, the newborn slept and suckled through the day's strife, and 36-year-old Lilly and 45-year-old Charlie quietly celebrated the addition to their family of five-year-old Margaret and three-year-old Peter.

Thirteen years earlier, on the other side of the world, another Wednesday's child was born.

In February 1931 the international arts world was grieving the loss of two big stars: 46-year-old Russian ballerina Anna Pavlova and the Australian queen of song, Dame Nellie Melba. On Wednesday, 25 February 1931, Dame Nellie Melba's coffin was railed to Melbourne in a draped wagon with one end reserved for flowers. The train from Albury to Spencer Street stopped at the twelve major stations en route to receive hundreds of floral tributes from the mourning population. While it was making its slow, sad journey, Christine Veronica Cooke was giving birth to her first child in Perth.

It was a moderate summer's day of 74°F when Eric Edgar Cooke took his first breath in the suburb of Victoria Park. His mother loved the little baby she held to her breast, giving him her maiden name for a middle name. But there was no announcement of the happy event in the 'Births' column on the front page of *The West Australian*. Vivian Thomas Cooke loathed his son at first sight.

The baby had a hare lip and cleft palate. Operations on the hare lip two months after his birth and on the cleft palate three-and-a-half years later made some improvement, but not enough. Nor was speech therapy particularly successful. The little boy's face was deformed and he spoke in a mumble. His nineteen-year-old alcoholic, violent father took it out on him with hatred and brutal treatment.

Charles Button, John's father, was too old to go to war. A tough, hard-working man, he moved the family to London because of the lack of employment opportunities in the north of

England. When the blitzing of London became too regular, he sent the family to the relative safety of Bath in the west country.

Charles wasn't worried for himself – he'd seen plenty of action and danger during World War I, when he'd lied about his age to join the army, becoming a drummer boy in France. His wife was a solid no-nonsense woman. They'd been engaged for nine years – Lillian Davis had been unable to marry while she cared for her mother in the family home in Fountains Close, Anfield. She was 30 before she was free, Charles was 39. She saw it as her duty to raise their three children as safely as possible and his to earn enough to feed them.

There was plenty of work in London, rebuilding the parts of the city demolished by bombs and fires. When the destruction finally ended, Charlie prepared for his family's peacetime reunion by buying half of a former inn that had been newly renovated and turned into semi-detached houses. He managed to get it cheaply, though it was a place of note. It was three storeys, designed by Prince Albert and previously owned by a theatre company to house famous people. The Buttons settled into the big old house in Tulse Hill and Jimmy's arrival in January 1947 completed the family.

The children loved the huge house, with its many fruit trees in the overgrown backyard, a wonderful wild playground large enough for an all-weather cricket pitch. There was also a big weeping willow in which they built a tree house. From the attic, they could look across London and see the dome of St Paul's Cathedral.

Charlie was doing very well with his building business in the post-war reconstruction. But conditions in the north of England during the Depression had taken a toll on his health, which prompted a decision to move to a drier climate. They decided on Australia, with Charlie going first to establish himself. He left in 1954, sailing from Southampton to start a new life, despite being 56. Lilly was left to manage the four children on her own – Margaret aged fifteen, Peter thirteen, John ten and Jimmy seven. There was some income from renting out rooms of their big house, and Lilly supplemented their income by cooking for the

Stork Club, leaving the children alone more than she would have liked.

Domestic violence was a way of life in the Cooke home. Eric was left alone and neglected because of his father's loathing and abuse. He soon considered himself to be the freak of the family. Raised by a violent, alcoholic father and farmed out on occasions to an orphanage or a foster home, Vivian Cooke understood no other way of life. His wife Christine, son Eric and two daughters were subject to their father's violence and depravity. But it was young Eric who was the target of most of the beatings. The boy was regularly thrashed with his father's belt, with his fists and with sticks. Sometimes it was because Eric had done something wrong – he was often in trouble – but generally it was for nothing, and sometimes it was for trying to protect his mother from Vivian's beatings.

Vivian Cooke, known as Snowy, was a fitter at J. & E. Ledger in Pier Street, just over the railway line from the central city. It was a general engineering company with a foundry and a machine shop, making mostly farm machinery. The big tough man who ended up as leading hand was known to his workmates as a big drinker with a lousy temper. It was generally known that he went straight to the pub after work and took it out later on his wife and family who lived in a little workers' cottage down the road from the works.

Apprentice fitter and turner Jack Marks was one who detested the violent leading hand and felt sorry for Eric, the neglected son who roamed the streets and often hid under the house. Marks would sometimes buy an extra pie at lunchtime, calling over the shy child, who took it with his face lowered to hide his disfigurement. Neighbours, too, would sometimes give food to this boy who always seemed hungry.

The loathing Vivian Cooke openly felt for his son was soon returned equally. Escaping the unhappy home whenever he could, Eric wandered the streets. He lied and stole – just small amounts, nothing that would really worry anybody. After eight months, the six-year-old first grader was expelled from Subiaco State School for stealing money from a teacher's purse, and was transferred to Newcastle Street Infants' School.

He was an outcast at school and at play. The children were cruel to the kid with the scar from his lip to his nose. He looked funny, he spoke in a comical mumble and he snuffled and sniffed with chronic sinus trouble. They constantly mocked him, humiliated him and played cruel jokes – they'd say they were going to catch tadpoles in one direction and sneak off in the other. Eric learnt to stand up for himself over these cruel games and torments, and he learnt to be nasty and revengeful in return.

He always had a caring, adoring ear from his mother, his only solace and source of love and security. She did her best with the neighbouring kids. Like many in the pre-war Depression years, the family didn't have much, but she gave the kids their favourite bread, dripping and salt whenever they came by. Her kindness worked sometimes. Just occasionally they would let him join their fun. There were the fry-ups in the paddock down the road, when they would chop up potatoes, get some fat and light a fire. And there were the wonderful games of cowboys and Indians with play guns from the furniture store just up the road. Its off-cuts made perfect pistols for the weekend entertainment of the Pier Street kids.

Any fun Eric had with the neighbouring kids when they included him was offset by coming home to a beating from his drunk father. It was generally for no reason at all, and Vivian was usually remorseful next morning, and could even be quite nice when he was sober. But not to Eric – this unattractive child wasn't like other children and Vivian Cooke couldn't accept this. His caring mother was unable to protect him.

Eric was tormented at every school – Highgate Primary School, Forrest Street Primary School and Newcastle Street Junior Technical School – and was regularly in trouble, often getting the cane. Despite this, and despite a lot of time away from class through illness, he did well at all subjects but maths. He passed eighth standard, testament to his natural intelligence. But as soon as he reached the minimum school-leaving age of fourteen, his father sent him out to work.

John Button also left school to start work at fourteen – because he wanted to. He, too, had missed a lot of his schooling. A passive, nervous boy with a stutter, he didn't fit in at high school and played truant as much as he could, rejoicing when he was able to leave and get a job.

He was a sickly child, suffering regular boils and sties. The slight boy with the tussled thatch of curly hair had done well through primary school in Brixton despite his delicacy. He'd been given special encouragement by the women teachers at Christ Church Primary School, a private school his mother had chosen to help with his stutter. He'd responded well to their interest and extra attention.

The attitude of the men teachers at Dunraven High School was different. High school was a grown-up domain, and students were expected to be more mature and independent. But eleven-year-old John did not fit the mould. He was missing the male guidance and role model of a father – his father having been too old to have much in common with the children and then leaving for the other side of the world a year previously. John's elder brother Peter was doing well, scoring top marks in the Eleven Plus and qualifying for Battersea Grammar School. But John needed careful coaching and the extra understanding and help were not forthcoming.

Unable to keep up, the nervous boy became more so, developing a stutter and a twitch, squeezing both eyes closed at the same time when he felt under pressure. He was teased at school, called 'Button and his 40 Blinks' for his involuntary twitch and a sissy for running out the back gate to avoid the regular playground fights.

Just as he ran away from the fights, he soon started running away from school. Without a strict father around to keep a firm grip on the children, it was easy to wag school and escape the pain and humiliation. School attendance became a game of heads or tails for John and his friend Mickey: heads they went to school, tails they didn't.

His mother was too busy to be able to do much about it. Lilly Button was coping with four children, working and managing the tenants renting the spare rooms. She did her best to control John, chaperoning him as far as the school's front gate. But she didn't have the authority over the children that her husband had, and John, in no fear of punishment from her, quickly ran out the back gate to idle the day away.

At thirteen John discovered girls – the one advantage of school. That's where he and Mickey could see Penelope Baker and Carol Brown, who lived in flats near Clapham Common. At school they could organise to meet the girls on the Common on Saturday. John loved Saturdays and the freedom of rollerskating with Mickey to their rendezvous. The shy youngster even managed to sneak a kiss once – surprising Penny, the policeman's daughter and a real little lady. She was the pick of the eleven-year-olds, the fancy of all the boys, but John and Mickey were the only ones privileged enough to walk her and Carol home.

When Tulse Hill Comprehensive opened closer to home, Lilly transferred John to the trade school, hoping the hands-on education might rekindle John's interest. Her efforts were in vain. It was a ten-storey, dull, grey building attended by some of the toughest boys in South London. John felt more intimidated and he didn't have Penny and Carol as a reason to go to school.

With the authority figure away in Australia, John was able to get up to other mischief as well. There was the odd snuck cigarette, and good marksmanship with a sling shot, knocking out street lights. Jimmy Button reacted in much the same way to their father's absence. Mickey was starting to take his education more seriously at Tulse Hill, so John started spending more time with his younger brother, who also started wagging school. The Button boys became renowned – not for being troublesome, but for being so often absent. The schools did their best to control the boys, but it got to the point with John that they needed to bring in the authorities.

Fourteen-year-old Eric Edgar Cooke started his working life as a delivery boy for Central Provision Stores in Newcastle Street, on the northern side of the city, where his grandmother lived. He lived with his parents at 31 Pitt Street, Como, on the other side of the river, and each week he gave his wages to his mother who struggled to raise the children on a pittance from her kitchen and cleaning work.

Christine Cooke was generally able to get low-paid unskilled jobs in places such as the Como Hotel kitchen, Plaistowes confectionery factory, West Australian Newspapers' canteen and the Perth Dental Hospital. Her husband did not maintain the family, despite his current job as a spare parts salesman for the car firm Sydney Atkinson. Vivian Cooke's wages went to the Como and Hurlingham Hotels, both on Canning Highway not far from their home. It was a battle for Christine to work, care for three children and manage her husband, but sometimes work also provided a haven. Many nights she slept in the staff room of the Como Hotel instead of going home to a beating. Her son's wages helped the family's survival, and she gave Eric a few shillings for pocket money. He supplemented his pocket money through petty pilfering of money and food.

In an effort at some social life, Eric joined the Scarborough Junior Surf Life Saving Club, where he made some friends. But he wanted more. He stole a watch and had it engraved 'To Cookie from the boys of the SJLSC', showing it to people and saying it was for good service to the club – until he was found out and the watch returned to the owner. Despite being small in size and suffering constant headaches and occasional blackouts, he did beach training with the club. He had little hope of ever being able to swim or row out to save the lives of swimmers in trouble in the surf – twice he had be to be pulled out of the water himself, unconscious from blackouts. This gave the club an excuse for dismissing him, but their real reason was the number of reports of missing money and other items from the club rooms. They suspected that Eric was the culprit.

Eric knew it was dangerous for him to be in the surf, but didn't try to avoid dangerous situations. He even sought them out at times to gain the attention and admiration he so badly craved. One daredevil act landed him in hospital with serious headaches and neck pain – to show off, he had dived off a rock ledge into the Serpentine River 50 feet below. He staggered out of the water semiconscious and after four days of pain was admitted to hospital. He spent five days in Royal Perth Hospital, or RPH as it was commonly known. Spine and chest X-rays revealed that nothing was broken, but while hospitalised, he was treated for his sinus trouble. A month later he was back in hospital with a suspected frontal-lobe abscess or infection, having fallen unconscious for three-quarters of an hour. Besides his sinusitis, X-rays showed a possible calcified blood clot under the lining of the tissue covering the brain. In February 1947 a craniotomy was performed at RPH, followed by further investigations, including an encephalogram. No abnormalities were detected.

A trip to Noggerup for a couple of months of farm-work convalescence resulted in his return to RPH with a snakebite. Back in the city, he found a job in the factory of Harris, Scarfe and Sandover. It wasn't long before the accident-prone sixteen-year-old was in RPH again, suffering from the effects of being struck on the nose by a winch.

On 25 August 1947 Cooke started a new job with the Western Australian Government Railways as a hammer boy in the blacksmith section of the workshop at Midland Junction. To the blacksmiths and sub-foreman he was just another young worker. There was only one oddity the staff noticed about him. In the morning each worker wrote out his lunch order on a brown paper bag, adding his name and number for easy identification of lunch bags when the pies and pasties were delivered to the workshops. Young Eric always signed his lunch bag 'Al Capone'.

His fantasy didn't reflect the reality of the tragedy at home as his father's drinking, cruelty and violence continued. He'd been in his new job just two months when he tried to stop his drunken father beating his mother. His father hit him so hard that his head was smashed against a light switch on a wall, fracturing his skull. Eric was hospitalised for three weeks. Too ashamed to admit he had a violent father, he said he'd been in a fight. It was nine weeks before Eric could return to work.

He lasted a month before he was off for another week. He was put on workers' compensation after burning his face with steam and suffering second-degree burns. Just over two months later he was off on workers' compensation again for another three weeks. Tired of young Cooke throwing carbide in the water trough for the fun of making a bad smell, the blacksmith grabbed him and tried to stick his head in the trough. Cooke's head struck the side of the trough, rendering him unconscious for ten minutes.

He'd been back at work for seven weeks when he jarred his right hand and was off on workers' compensation for a month because an abscess formed. He was back at work for a month, then off on workers' compensation again for a week after jarring the thumb of his other hand.

On 24 September 1948, while he was off work with his injured left hand, he joined the army. He enlisted in the 16-28 battalion of the Citizens Military Forces. Finally he had found something he really loved, was earnest about and succeeded in. He joined the non-commissioned-officers' class and was promoted to lance corporal. Even when he was told that his speech impairment would prevent him attaining higher rank, he maintained his enthusiasm and attended training on a regular basis.

On the rifle range he was taught how to handle firearms. He learnt quickly and proved to be a very good shot.

A Father's Influence

1948–58

On Friday 15 October 1948 a short, slim youth with dark wavy hair broke into a flat in the city, looking for food and other items to steal. John Birman, the assistant director of Adult Education, was out, giving the intruder plenty of time to look around flat 3 at 170 Adelaide Terrace. The burglar found something to help him with this and future break-ins – a torch. He took this and a small travelling clock.

Eric Edgar Cooke was seventeen-and-a-half years old when he started a series of serious break-ins. He'd been petty-thieving for a long time. Why not? Wandering the streets to avoid his father's beltings and abuse at home, it was easy to take things here and there to provide some pleasure in life. A bit of food, a few coins – people who had so much more than him wouldn't even notice most of the time.

But now he felt vengeful, too. He wanted to spoil things a little for those happy people who didn't have to suffer like he did. They didn't have funny faces or cruel, drunken fathers who beat them for no reason. Their home life wasn't miserable. They had nice houses and flats, with lots of things in them. They were treated kindly by everyone. They weren't beaten, abused and shunned. He was angry and bitter, and hated everyone who was better off than him. Before he left Birman's flat, he opened several bottles of wine and poured the contents over clothing in the linen cupboard.

Police combing the flat next day found the evidence they

needed. Detectives Owen Leitch and Max Blight found fingerprints on the empty wine bottles and a thumbprint on the wireless on the mantelpiece. There were no matching fingerprints on file. But they would wait.

Three weeks later young Cooke broke into another flat in Adelaide Terrace, 3 Hampton Court. He broke a glass panel in the front door to get in and searched the flat but found nothing to steal. He could destroy, though. He pulled all the clothes out of the wardrobe and slashed the men's and women's clothing with a knife. He went on to slash a pillow and bedspread. Checking the fridge for food, he found some chocolate which he fed to the goldfish in a bowl on top of the fridge. He then found a bottle of shellite and started a fire, sitting there watching it burn until the heat overpowered him. When the fire brigade arrived, he walked home to Como, savouring the memory of the destructive flames. Harold Hender arrived home at 11.30 p.m. to find his living room ablaze. The place was full of smoke, the dressing table was burning and furniture was ruined by the heat. Total damage was estimated at £525.

Two weeks later Cooke was at nearby Burtway flats. There was nobody home at flat No. 3 in block 5. Looking for a way in, Cooke saw a side window he could open, but it was too high. He found a box in the washhouse and stood on it. The effort of getting into lawyer Philip Sharp's flat was worth it. On the dressing table in the bedroom he found 20 shillings, an engagement ring, a wrist watch and a fountain pen in a top drawer. He was short of money and thought he could sell the jewellery. He was looking for more when he was noticed by a woman from the flats. She gave chase as he dashed out. He got away, running across the Causeway, but threw the jewellery into the Swan River from the Causeway in case he was caught with it. When Mrs Sharp arrived home from the theatre at 11 p.m., she found police in the flat.

A month later at Christmas, his friend went away for a few days. Mrs Mason, two houses from his, was kind and friendly to him and he spent a lot of time at her place. She gave him a key to look after her home while she and her police officer husband Thomas were away. Thanks to her trust and the key, he didn't need to break in, but he cunningly smashed a window to avoid detection. He wanted to steal the officer's pistol. However, once inside, that anger at the comfortable people overcame him again, despite her great kindness to him. He piled Mrs Mason's clothing in the bedroom and poured fly spray all around, intending to set fire to it. But he was thwarted when he couldn't find any matches.

On New Year's eve he made his way into the city about 8 p.m. and went to the pictures, alone. Afterwards he wandered up through the city. Starting up the Mount Street hill, he found flat 10 at 40 Mount Street in darkness. He searched around the flat with his torch, but found only fruit to steal. He took the fruit and, lighting a candle by the bed, set fire to cellophane in a drawer. When the heat became too much, he left and watched the fire from Kings Park near the Mount Hospital. Laura Watkins, a widow who lived there with her son, returned at 12.45 a.m. from seeing in the New Year, to find her bedroom destroyed by fire.

On 21 January 1949 Cooke, who was about to turn eighteen, was given a change of job in the Western Australian Government Railways. From blacksmith striker in the Midland Workshops, the youth was transferred to the East Perth locomotive shed as a cleaner.

The first day at the new job he tripped and fell down an engine pit, badly hurting his back. He was sent to RPH and admitted under neurosurgeon Ross Robinson. Mr Robinson found that the youth's back wasn't fractured, but the abdominal injury required continued treatment. So the new cleaner was put on sick leave and paid workers' compensation.

Around this time, Cooke moved in with his grandmother in the north of the city to escape his father's brutal treatment. On workers' compensation, he had time on his hands, and he needed more money. From his new base at 51 Lindsay Street, North Perth, he moved his breaking and entering activity to the local area.

The first was on 8 February 1949 at 113 Parry Street, three blocks away from his grandmother's house. He looked for something to eat but didn't steal anything. Collecting clothing into three heaps on the cement floor of the vestibule, he set it alight with kerosene and lit the gas stove. Running from the flat, he walked home to Lindsay Street. WA Newspapers proofreader Harold Montefiore arrived home at 11.30 p.m. to find his furniture and clothing alight. Nothing was missing, but the damage amounted to £30. The next day, police looking for fingerprints had some luck. They found right and left thumb prints and a right index fingerprint on a bottle.

Prowling around ten days later Cooke saw a handbag on a dressing table near an open window at 265 Stirling Street. He leaned in and grabbed the handbag belonging to Nellie Hasleby. He hid in the washhouse at the rear while he looked through it, taking £32 before neatly returning it to the dressing table.

The following Friday was his eighteenth birthday. He celebrated by lighting a fire, this time in a flat in the northern part of the city. He broke into flat 10 in St James Flats on the corner of Aberdeen and Museum streets, the home of Ernest Williams and his wife. He took seven dresses from a wardrobe in the sleepout and set fire to them in the bedroom. But before he lit the fire and watched it cause £400 damage, he added to his insult by leaving excreta in a doll's cot – underneath and on top of the pillow. That showed them what he thought of them and everyone like them.

The flat fires worried the police. But a week later, the elusive young burglar and arsonist finally slipped up and was apprehended. He was in his local area, north of the city, again. He knew the house, 55 Nash Street, Perth, from delivering groceries there eighteen months previously. After getting in through the back door not long after midnight, he took off his shoes, tucked them under his arm, and searched for money by torchlight. Finding a handbag in the bedroom, he took it into the bathroom to fossick through it. While he was doing this, labourer Ivan Yelcic was creeping around the house looking for him. Mr Yelcic's wife had woken him telling him there was someone in the kitchen. He found the back door open and soon discovered the intruder hiding behind the bathroom door.

The eighteen-year-old came up with a quick story: 'I'm Eric next door. I was drunk and lying outside, and when I got up I went to go home but missed the door.'

Mr Yelcic wasn't so easily fooled. A bit of a fight followed and Cooke collected a punch before running off, dropping the torch on the way.

It took the police a week to find him. He was interviewed on Friday, 12 March 1949, at his grandmother's house. He was caught with some evidence. Detective Bert Burrows found the clock he'd taken from the Adelaide Terrace flat. Cooke also still had the £32 he'd stolen from the handbag he'd grabbed a month ago. The police could now identify the fingerprints from the earlier two break-ins.

Cooke admitted his crimes, telling police that he was short of money because he'd received only two workers' compensation payments, about £11 in all. He'd given all of that to his mother, as he'd always done with his wages, getting back only five shillings a week pocket money from her. He said he'd also given £1 of the money he'd stolen to the Red Cross the previous day when he donated 500 cc of blood.

Cooke was arrested and held in custody. He made no application for bail. The short slim youth with dark wavy hair and a hare lip faced the first of the charges before a magistrate in the Children's Court on 23 March 1949.

With Cooke in custody, the spate of incidents ended. For some time, police had received numerous complaints of prowlers from people living in Adelaide Terrace and South Perth – prowlers who stole clothes from clotheslines or slashed them, leaving them hanging in shreds. Cooke was never charged for this use of his sharp army knife.

Years later, in London, another slight youth with wavy hair was before a magistrate. John Button's so-called crime was truancy.

The thirteen-year-old blinked and stammered when he tried to answer the magistrate's questions about why he was wagging school. His mother, a plucky, determined woman, spoke for him. She said she felt John's failure to attend his high school classes was caused by the lack of his father's authority and influence. Lilly told the court that she and her husband had planned to send the eldest two children to join him in Australia soon, but she would be prepared to send this boy to his father in place of his elder brother. His hard-working father would provide the necessary guidance that he'd been missing.

The magistrate accepted Lilly's proposal. John Button was placed on probation with the condition that he attend school until embarkation.

John had been terrified of going to the Children's Court and of the thought of what might happen to him. He was so glad to have his mother there speaking for him and coming up with an idea that put an end to his nightmares about his punishment. He loved the idea of going to Australia. Not only would he be free from the last year of compulsory schooling in England, but also there would be the adventure of the high seas and the brave new world of sunshine and beaches. And, best of all, compulsory schooling ended a year earlier in Australia. At fourteen, John would be over this age when he arrived. First, though, there were six months of forced school attendance and weekly reports to his probation officer.

One case against Eric Edgar Cooke was heard in the Children's Court and he was committed for trial in the Criminal Court. He was similarly committed for trial on the others after an initial hearing in the Perth Police Court. After two months in custody, he appeared in the Criminal Court on 24 May 1949 and was convicted on two charges of stealing, seven of breaking and entering and four of arson.

The arresting officer, Detective Burrows, had interviewed the young offender and investigated his life for a character report. It outlined the social circumstances contributing to Cooke turning to crime. The detective wrote of the youth's miserable life at home and school, his accident-proneness that could be a sign of a deeply hidden suicidal tendency and his numerous admissions to hospital. He ended the report: 'I consider that from a perusal of Cooke's medical history and from my knowledge of his home life, gained through inquiries made, that Cooke can be classed as one of life's unfortunates.'

The Inspector General of Mental Hospitals, Dr E. J. Thompson, examined Cooke at Fremantle Prison on 13 May and reported to the Crown Prosecutor.

I am of the opinion that:
1) Cooke is not certifiably insane.
2) He is of normal intelligence but is emotionally undeveloped and has been unable to adjust himself in his adolescence to an adult social world.
3) This maladjustment is the result of a series of factors, mainly resultant from a deformity at birth (cleft palate and hare lip) which has brought about:
   a) Psychological trauma – by rejection by his father (which was apparently made known to him at an early age) and consequent natural over-indulgence by a protecting mother.
   b) A series of physical illnesses (mainly states of infection) which required regular hospital attendance from the age of 3 weeks.
   c) The onset of a psycho-neurotic state – probably hysterical – after leaving school.
   d) The onset of delinquent behaviour.

As the latter is of immediate concern to His Honour, the Chief Justice, the following comment may be of assistance in Cooke's disposal.

Despite long periods of illness as a child, Cooke appears to have maintained a normal educational standard in which the best subjects were those requiring a retentive memory and manual dexterity, but he admits that he did not like, and was poor at, science subjects – maths etc. which required deductive reasoning. While good at sports, he does not appear to have had any real companions and being hypersensitive to his physical deformity, became a 'butt' amongst his school mates, from which his teachers to some extent shielded him. Post-school employment as a grocer's boy does not appear to have been conducive to development and satisfying of natural aptitudes and he admits to two petty thefts (a wristlet watch from a customer and 10/– from his employer, both of which were returned). During this period he became a member of a Surf Club but apparently was not able to satisfy his desires for companionship and was again amongst the 'rejected' by his fellows. It was during this period that he developed a series of blackouts which were investigated at RPH. Though there were indications of organic disease (following high diving), operation (craniotomy) revealed no organic pathology. These blackouts were probably purely functional in origin and of an hysterical nature. He states he has had no 'blackouts' since his operation in 1946.

Employment following hospitalisation appears to have been more congenial to his talents – but he again met with disappointment when he was rejected for an apprenticeship in carpentry for which he had a keen desire. The physical disability, in his own appreciation of it, still prevented him from gaining the friendships which he desired. The weekly wage (about £3/7/–) was given to his mother who returned him 5/– per week. This he appears to have given willingly, but at the same time, as a youth with a desire to find companionship, he found the allowance of 5/– too small to do what his few acquaintances did or to join with them in their activities.

It is at this stage that his reasoning appears to have become bizarre and somewhat fantastic and his conduct antisocial. The entry into crime appears primarily to have been to obtain money, or its equivalent, as a means to establish friendships and the companionship he craved for (without injuring a mother to whom he retained special attachment). He wanted money to be able to go out with his mates. The bizarre reasoning is shown by his thinking that notoriety would gain him friendship, and with this in view he used to cut out the paper accounts of his criminal episodes and show them to his mates, claiming them as his doing – claims which were naturally rejected and pooh-poohed by his mates. While displaying a certain cunning for carrying out the crimes, there are certain irrational features in his actions. The fact that he 'got away with' his first episodes appears to have led to the belief that he would never be caught. The burning of clothes etc. as a means of 'covering up his tracks' so that nobody would know what actually had been stolen and the lack of appreciation of the possibility of starting a large conflagration are quite bizarre and fantastic. He denies the memory of tearing women's clothing but in reading the depositions, the destruction appears to have been of a fairly general nature and not in the nature of a fetish often associated with repressed sexual content. Cooke also denies the correctness of the statement that he sat and watched the fires or that he watched them from a distance – he states that he left immediately and went home.

Cooke is well aware of the acts he has committed and that they are wrongful acts, he does not, however, appear to have appreciated at the time he committed them, the seriousness.

It would not be possible at the present stage to say that he was not criminally responsible in the terms of Section 27 of the Criminal Code, but his whole medical (physical and psychological) history and background is such that the dice appears to have been loaded heavily against him in making a normal adjustment into the social community.

If His Honour thinks fit, I would suggest that an attempt should be made to rescue this youth from either
1) a life of crime or
2) from an incipient mental state of schizophrenia of which his antisocial conduct, his bizarre and somewhat fantastic reasoning and his emotional maladjustment may be merely early symptoms.

There is no place in this State ideally suited for Cooke's treatment which would involve discipline under modified prison conditions, psychotherapy (and possibly physical methods of treatment) and training rehabilitation. In my opinion it is imperative, for his and the community's future good, that he should not be allowed to gain the impression that he has 'got away with anything' or that he is 'not responsible for his acts'. I would suggest that he might receive sentence and be released on parole provided he is willing to submit himself for further investigation and, if necessary, treatment, as an inpatient of Heathcote and that at a later date a further medical report be submitted to the Court for subsequent action.

On 24 May 1949 the Chief Justice sentenced Cooke to three years' jail, accepting the Head of Mental Health's suggestion to give the first offender a chance to rehabilitate himself: 'After undergoing two or three months confinement as an experience of punishment, he should be released on parole. The conditions should be on the lines set by Inspector General Thompson.'

The worst punishment for Cooke was his dismissal from the CMF under defence force rules precluding anyone with a conviction.

Cooke was considered for release on probation after three months; the Deputy Comptroller-General of Prisons, Alexander MacKillop, agreeing that it was desirable 'to allow the lad to leave the prison before any possible contamination by hardened criminals took place, while handing him to the jurisdiction and supervision of some responsible authority'.

Dr Thompson visited Cooke at Fremantle Prison on 2 August, noting him to be a little uncooperative and rather apprehensive about going to Heathcote Reception Hospital for a month's assessment, a condition of parole. Cooke was frightened he would be detained for a long time, certified and sent to Claremont Mental Hospital. Dr Thompson assured him it was for tests and rehabilitative training. He reported: 'What we want is to help the young man from relapse into crime. If he were allowed to "paddle his own canoe" as it were, I think we should set the course for him to follow and in the event of any deviation from the course through unforeseen elements, step in and "take the helm" and assist him from being wrecked on the "shores of disaster".'

The Indeterminate Sentences Board visited Cooke and formed the opinion that 'he was not of criminal habits but had committed the acts which led to his incarceration out of a foolish desire for notoriety, which he had hoped would gain him friendships'. The members found that 'the taste of imprisonment had been quite enough for him and the Board believes he will honestly endeavour to overcome his past failings'.

The Board was unanimous in its recommendation for release on parole. Cooke willingly agreed to the conditions, including regular reporting to Mr MacKillop and voluntary admission to Heathcote for observation. When his parents took him to the mental hospital where his father had spent some time ten years earlier, staff noted that his mother was subdued and his father was bluffing and jocular. At Heathcote, Cooke was seen by psychiatrist Frank Prendergast, the superintendent of Claremont Mental Hospital. Dr Prendergast wanted to follow up on information the young offender had given him when he saw him in Fremantle Prison that he was the accomplice of a 40-year-old man whose control he was under and whom he feared. At Heathcote, the psychiatrist dismissed it as a lie that suffered from Cooke's fault of continuing to embroider and develop a story even when it didn't help his case. He decided Cooke was a liar beyond help.

However, Cooke seemed to respond to the chance he was given. He was sent to the Commonwealth Employment Service for tests and on discharge from Heathcote on 30 September, he was instructed to report to the Rehabilitation Service Centre for suitable employment in carpentry. Unable to get an apprenticeship because of his age, he agreed to his mother's suggestion of a job with her at Plaistowes, although he would have preferred to have become a hospital orderly. Within a fortnight he was employed at the confectionery factory as a storehand, earning £5/6/6 a week – giving £2 to his mother and banking £2.

He also gained a happier social life than he'd ever had when the Reverend George Jenkins volunteered to help rehabilitate the wayward youth by taking him into the fold of the South Perth Methodist Church. Cooke warmed to the Methodist minister who was tough and manly, who called a spade a spade, but was sympathetic and understanding. The minister's father, Sydney Arthur Jenkins, had also been a Methodist minister and a miner at Kalgoorlie. The family was poor and the father suffered the miner's disease, silicosis. He died suddenly after cycling 30 miles and back to do a church service when George was just eight. His mother and the three children moved to Fremantle, where she took in washing to eke out a living. George left school at thirteen to help the family by getting a job in a menswear shop. He was eighteen when he and three friends formed a preaching group and took services throughout the metropolitan area, leading to his study for theological qualifications and ordination.

Cooke could relate to this minister whom he'd met at Heathcote; he wasn't a part of the easy society that didn't want the likes of a deformed, poor boy with a father to be ashamed of. Cooke had been given a religious upbringing from his Catholic mother and easily adapted to a new religious path, becoming Methodist, regularly attending services and Bible studies, and reading the Bible so much that it concerned his mother.

The members of the youth group were people raised with the Christian ethic of acceptance of people who were different and sympathy for people not as fortunate as themselves. They went out of their way to include Cooke in their activities. Cooke gained spiritual guidance and a social life. Now he was a part of tennis afternoons, hockey matches at which he played goalkeeper, movie nights, teas and get-togethers, as well as summer camps at Watermans Beach and Bible-study Easter camps in the bush at Glen Forrest. He was quiet and kept to himself a lot, but took advantage of his new social acceptance.

MacKillop was pleased with his charge's attitude to probation. On 21 October he reported to the Parole Board that Cooke had visited him after finishing work and told him of his job and joining the Methodist youth movement. 'He is now determined to do the right thing by his mother and himself,' MacKillop reported. 'General demeanour appears calm and clear and provided he continues as at present and keeps away from his former bad associates, the indications are he will be all right.' He advised that Cooke was to report to him in person every two weeks and that 'the Board may rest assured that I will spare no effort to try and keep him on the straight and narrow path'.

Cooke soon expanded his Methodist circle beyond the Reverend Jenkins' South Perth church by attending the Tuesday tea and Bible study at the Central Methodist Mission in the city and joining the Nedlands Methodist Church. Cooke's membership of this church, on the corner of Princess Road and Bruce Street, Nedlands, took him into an older affluent area of the western suburbs.

With the Nedlands youth group he expanded his social circle further, finding acceptance among young people from a completely different area from the one in which he grew up. He even made a special friend of a girl who came from a well-to-do family in Louise Street, Nedlands. Although much younger than him, she became his close friend and confidant.

He kept out of trouble during his probation, living at home and reporting that 'everything is rosy'. He had work, his mother's care, religious training and guidance and a broad social outlet. But he needed to show off to improve his status and was known in the group for such daredevil acts as walking along the narrow top of the high dam wall at Mundaring Weir.

He still suffered headaches and fainting spells – the first within weeks of leaving prison, as a result of being hit on the cheek with a rifle butt just before he went to jail. It was at least three months back, but his eye had been swollen for three days, and he was fainting, vomiting and suffering bad headaches. He was admitted to the observation ward and Dr Mercy Sadka checked out his skull again, finding no fresh fracture or other abnormality. He was treated for his sinusitis and after a week in hospital was discharged for further treatment at the ear, nose and throat clinic.

He was accident prone, too, managing to get stung by a stingray, requiring another trip to RPH, and there were other hospital treatments during the time for ailments such as acute appendicitis, a boil on his neck and another infected lump. As well, he had an operation to remove all his teeth, which were replaced with dentures.

At the end of June 1951, he left Plaistowes to work as an orderly at the tuberculosis sanitorium in the bush east of Perth at Wooroloo. He wanted to do nursing training, but after just two weeks he had to be rushed to RPH for an appendectomy and was in hospital for a week.

Cooke's probation period and obligation to report to the board ceased on 15 August 1951. He promised to continue to call on Mr MacKillop and look to him for advice and guidance. He received a glowing report from the Board:

> I would like to congratulate you on the manner in which you have carried out the conditions required of you and assure you that the Board is very happy to know that its high regard of you has not been misplaced. I am glad that you intend to keep in touch with Mr MacKillop as he will be able to advise

me from time to time of your continuing example to those less fortunate than yourself.

The day after his twenty-first birthday, Cooke caught the train to Melbourne with money he'd saved at Wooroloo. He spent a week sight-seeing in the big, bright city, staying at Scott's Hotel. After a week he went to the Central Methodist Mission to enquire about places to board and was put onto Mrs Mac, staying the rest of the time with her in Dundas Road, Albert Park, and working as a bench hand at the Karri Timber Company.

Cooke enlisted in the army in Melbourne, hoping they wouldn't know of his discharge from the CMF in Perth. He got away with it for fourteen weeks, during which he did more basic training, and where again he shone in weapon-training. He got so proficient with the .303s, Bren guns and Owen guns that he could shoot a blackboy spear from 10 to 15 yards, firing any one of them from the hip. With the .303 he could shoot a magazine of ten in something like eight seconds and still hold his accuracy.

It was the best time of his life. He loved the regimentation, the companionship and the fellowship. It ended again when Captain Parson called him in and discharged him because of his former crimes.

Back in Perth just before his twenty-second birthday, Cooke was charged with breaking and entering with intent. On 19 February 1953 he'd broken into the home of one of the South Perth Methodist Church people and stolen a money box. He was caught because of his fingerprints. But the loyal Methodists just couldn't believe it.

Two detectives from Victoria Park Police Station, Max Baker and Gordon Moorman, collected Cooke and took him to the station, their passenger warning them 'you'll be sorry' during the short journey. That caused a little concern to Moorman, still a rookie as a probation detective and a little unsure of himself and the possible retribution from his accused.

The authorities again looked kindly on him and gave him a second chance, placing him on a £50 good behaviour bond.

Cooke took a job as a truck driver at the Metropolitan Markets in West Perth, and it was there that he met a pretty, wholesome waitress in the staff canteen. Sally Lavin (who was never called by her real name Sarah) was seventeen, and lived with her mother and sister in Rivervale. She had come from Liverpool with her mother and two sisters in 1942 to escape the bombings after suffering the privations of the Depression. Sally and Eric met in July 1953 and she was charmed, deeply in love with the kind and polite boy with the magnetic personality. Her mother was equally pleased with her catch, not minding that the daughter she'd sent to St Patrick's Convent in West Perth was mixing with a Protestant.

Cooke introduced Sally to his social circle. The strict young Methodists were shocked when Cooke informed them that they needed to get married. But Sally was clearly in love and the Nedlands group offered their Christian support, giving her a traditional kitchen tea.

Eric Edgar Cooke and Sally Lavin were married in the Cannington Methodist Church on 14 November 1953 by the Reverend Prestage Lucas Sullivan. The Reverend Sullivan joined his colleague George Jenkins, who'd been posted to Albany on the south coast, in his special interest in the bridegroom with the troubled background. The couple had a son, Michael Peter, on 11 May 1954, and another son a year later.

Cooke enjoyed the love and security of family life, but he had great difficulty adapting to the responsibility. His father had been no role model. It wasn't long before he was wandering the streets again, looking for houses to rob and for new conquests. In 1955, two months after the birth of his second son, a girl he fancied was playing in a hockey tournament in Bunbury. He decided to follow her, stealing a car for the two-hour drive south.

He didn't make it to Bunbury. He rolled the car on the way, managing to crawl out a smashed window. He was taken to Yarloop District Hospital for emergency treatment of a broken sternum, face and knee injuries, and later transferred to RPH. Repairs to the car cost £400. Constable Gordon Moorman, now a detective, charged Cooke with assuming control of a motor vehicle.

The authorities called for another psychiatric report and Dr Prendergast was called in. The psychiatrist reported that Cooke was definitely unreliable: 'He was given a chance to rehabilitate himself, and a further chance in 1952. He is very plausible in playing as much as possible on sympathy for his disability. I don't think this is any ground for psychiatric intervention as regards the present charge.'

The faithful Methodist Church still supported their lost sheep. One of his friends from the Nedlands Youth Group was a lawyer by profession, but was now the Methodist minister in Mullewa. Neville Watson travelled to Perth to represent Cooke. Assuring the judge that the defendant had stayed out of trouble for the past two years and was making a definite attempt to rehabilitate himself, the lawyer had no comeback for Mr Justice Virtue's response: 'Perhaps he has just been lucky, Mr Watson.'

In September 1955 Cooke, father of two babies, was jailed for two years with hard labour for stealing a car. He was also given a six-month sentence, to be served concurrently, for breaking his personal bond on the 1953 conviction. Mr Justice Virtue said he was not disposed to leniency given Cook's record and his squandering of previous chances when he had been extremely leniently dealt with.

A Justice of the Peace who knew Cooke and his wife from the Metropolitan Markets visited Sally and offered to help her annul her marriage, telling her she knew from experience that Cooke would never change. Sally had now seen the other side of her husband, carefully hidden until after the first child was born. She was miserable, totally controlled by a violent man, but she declined the offer – she couldn't desert him when he was down and she believed he should be given a chance to change. During her husband's imprisonment, she managed her two sons on her own and caught the bus to Fremantle Prison on visiting days. She hoped things would be better when he was released.

Cooke was released three months earlier than expected, thanks to the centenary of Fremantle Prison and a sympathetic Comptroller-General. To mark the centenary, Cooke was given 60 days special remission. That made his discharge date 6 January 1957. But the Comptroller-General thought he should be out for Christmas and suggested a further remission of a month because Cooke had been 'an exemplary inmate' and his wife and a number of church associates were prepared to help with his rehabilitation. Cooke had studied in prison, and would be able to be a bookkeeper. His local Federal Member of Parliament and Methodist church man, Richard Cleaver, made representations to the Minister for Justice on Cooke's behalf: 'While the wife has been treated rather badly, in the interests of her family she has resolved to make a new start and to assist in a practical way her husband upon his release.'

Cooke was home for Christmas.

At sea, John Button was glad about being sent to Australia to overcome his truancy. Life on board was even better than he had expected. Through a chance change in an elderly couple's arrangements, he ended up with a first-class cabin all to himself, giving him unexpected luxury and freedom, and a class barrier against sister Margaret's motherly eye. After a few miserable days of homesickness and seasickness, he found a group of boys his own age. They were too young to drink, but they managed to talk the barman into selling them Pimms under the guise of Coke with fruit and John took up smoking. One night his friends dared him to ask the prettiest girl on board for a dance. He chose a Maltese girl sitting with her parents. From then on, a fledgling shipboard romance with Tessie added to the newfound thrills of alcohol and cigarettes, along with foreign ports and crossing the equator.

It was a glorious four weeks. After having endured Britain's worst Easter weather for more than 50 years, he soaked up the sunshine on board. He was blissfully unaware of the troubles going on in the world around him: France was on the verge of civil war in Algeria, Britain was ignoring protests and testing its fifth hydrogen bomb in the central Pacific, there was a rebellion in Indonesia with fighting on five major islands, Britain was sending ships to riot-torn Lebanon and Malta called a state of emergency after protests against British policy. John's dream cruise ended at 7.30 a.m. on Thursday, 22 May 1958, when the tugs pushed the *Stratheden* up against the wharf by G Shed at

Victoria Quay. Despite the wind and squalls, John and Margaret stood on deck, watching the tugs and the building work on a new passenger terminal on the wharf in front of them. Coming down the gangplank later, they spotted the father they hadn't seen for four years waving up at them. Charlie had done well in his new life, bricklaying on country and city jobs and batching in boarding houses. For the children's arrival, he'd rented a house in the northern Perth suburb of Innaloo. John and Margaret had their first view of their new city through the Ford Prefect's rain-splashed windows as they drove along Stirling Highway into Perth and home along Scarborough Beach Road.

It was a wet May after Perth's driest summer for fourteen years. It brought John back to earth after the sunny days on deck, but he and Margaret set about getting into their new life, adapting to the difference between London and this small city of only 450,000 people. Margaret soon found work as a shorthand typist for a tool-maker in Milligan Street and naturally fell into the role of mother, looking after the house, her father and young brother. But after a few months, the nineteen-year-old wanted to make a life of her own and she moved out into the women's boarding house run by the Young Women's Christian Association in West Perth.

John was homesick and unsettled for about a year. Besides having to get used to a new country, he had to get used to life without his mother and with his previously estranged father. Daily newspaper reports of the Empire Games in Cardiff took his mind and his heart back to the UK. How he missed his mother and her warming breakfast of bacon and home-made bread. She gave him a sense of security and was always there for him. It felt strange to be living with his father, a distant figure in his youth and absent since John was ten, and such a grandfather-like figure. John had watched from the second-storey window as Charlie Button had set out for the other side of the world.

John's first job was as the junior for Supa Furn, a furniture factory on Scarborough Beach Road, not far from home. Freed from the horrors of school, his stutter and twitch abated, reappearing only when he was nervous or under pressure He cycled to work each day on the bike his father had bought him, spending the day sweeping the floor and polishing the chrome legs of the laminex tables. By September 1958 John Button was looking forward to spending weekends on the beach in his first Australian summer.

A Powerful New Urge

12 September 1958

In September 1958 Jan and Nel Schneider were also immigrants making a new life in Australia. They had been in Perth for three years, having left the chronic post-war shortages of Holland to find opportunity in New Holland, the land the Dutch seafarers had discovered centuries earlier. The quiet couple lived a simple life in a state housing commission house in McKay Street, Bentley, 33-year-old Jan working as a spray painter and his 26-year-old wife Nel caring for their two small children.

Establishing themselves in Perth had not been easy, but they were contented despite the difficulties. Their peace and happiness, born out of their love for each other and their deep faith, did not reflect the horrors they had lived through during the time their neutral homeland was held to ransom by the Nazis.

Nor did their work and lifestyle reflect their talents and expertise which they were unable to use in their new country. Jan, the man who spray-painted cars for a living, was a fine-art technician, an expert who had trained at the Amsterdam Museum and who'd been technical assistant to the Professor of Art at Leiden University. Nel was an accomplished organist, with a Diploma in Pipe Organ, and an experienced bilingual office clerk. The couple who had met at a youth gospel camp in Belgium just after the war had sacrificed their professional careers and status to start anew. Now they lived in a small asbestos house in outer Perth and scraped a living, happy just to be alive.

The newlyweds had left Holland for brighter shores because no housing was available in what was left of their country. So, with sponsorship by the Reformed Church, they set out for the opportunities promised by Australia.

They sailed from Amsterdam on the *Fairsea* in September 1955, just a fortnight after their trip to the registry office for the legal ceremony required by the State, followed by their wedding service in the Oosterkerk church in Delft. Even the misery of Nel's incessant seasickness couldn't blight their exultation at leaving behind the fear, the cold and the starvation of the occupation years. The Hunger Winter would be forever etched on their memories, the freezing winter of 1944-45 when the Nazis cut off the western cities from the farming hinterland. More than 16,000 people starved to death in the cities, and Nel only just survived, thanks to her father's heroism at getting her through the blockade to a farm foster home.

They arrived in Perth during a very wet October, battling wind and rain to learn their way around and find work. The Reformed Church looked after them, organising lodgings. But getting work was more difficult.

Jan's artistic talents, so sought-after in Europe, were wasted in Perth and he couldn't get a job in his specialised field, despite references from Leiden University. He moved from one labouring job to another; his hands, used to dealing with fine art, were now put to cleaning, maintenance and farmwork while he searched for something in his beloved profession. Nel couldn't put her skills to use either. She was rejected at each attempt at an office job because her typing wasn't fast enough. She was exasperated. Her English was polished, but she couldn't get a job because of her typing speed in her second language. And newly pregnant, the slight-framed mother-to-be couldn't resort to cleaning jobs or anything that required exertion.

With Jan's odd-job income they were eventually able to move out of the lodgings to a place of their own in Riverton. Nel was very happy to be in what she regarded as her very first home, and was very proud of it. In fact, it was a big brick garage that they ingeniously divided into rooms – one part became their bedroom, a big middle section the lounge and a small part at one end the kitchen.

Eight months after their arrival, their son Tony was born, followed sixteen months later by a daughter and the news that their turn had come on the state housing commission list. Two years after making do with what they could afford, in October 1957 they were able to bring baby Judy home from St Ives Hospital to the comparative luxury of a three-bedroom house at 4 McKay Street, Bentley. It was a simple asbestos house and they had no furniture, but they were happy. Jan had become resigned to working as a spray painter, cycling each day to Albany Highway and leaving his bicycle behind the Charlie Carters shop to take the bus to the panel beaters Malone & Co. in Murray Street, West Perth. Nel cared for the children, walking to Tom the Cheap Grocer nearby or getting home deliveries from their Riverton grocer, and making close friends with their Australian-born neighbour. They had an income, a house and their little family of a chubby two-year-old boy and a sweet baby girl.

As well, they had their worship and the companionship of compatriots in the Reformed Church. Nel's musical abilities were welcomed there and she was quickly appointed church organist. The couple caught the bus to church and Nel played for the service each Sunday. She also joined the choir and took on the task of choir treasurer. They were both active and admired members of the church community. They were free, safe, healthy and happy.

Eleven months later, on 12 September 1958, their lives were changed again. Cooke, now 27, had been out of jail for nearly two years and in that time, his family had doubled with the arrival of twins. The responsibility of four young children didn't keep him home on Friday and Saturday nights. They were his nights, when he dressed immaculately in his suit and highly polished shoes and went out. No low-status clothes of the working man at night – he was the smart man-about-town, with money to spend and women to woo. He often didn't get home till the early hours of the morning – sometimes not for a few days – but Sally was not allowed to ask any questions. Nor did she see the women's gloves he kept hidden up behind the lavatory cistern and donned to avoid fingerprints at his crime scenes. She never saw any of the hats he wore at night, stealing them from the first house he broke into each evening, or the small torch he always used during his break-ins.

He spent the early hours of these evenings leading the life of a single man – playing ten-pin bowls, going to pubs and the movies, partying and meeting his girlfriends. When he'd had his fun, he put on the gloves for a different kind of fun – prowling and stealing. That way he made enough money to play the dapper single man, and he got his own back against the society that ignored and rejected a misfit with a speech impediment and a twisted mouth. He invaded their privacy, watched their most intimate moments through windows, and entered their castles, taking their money and goods. Clumsy and accident-prone as he was at his job, late at night he turned into the most skilful cat burglar. People who knew him during the day would never guess the other side of him.

It was a fine evening as Nel cycled to choir practice. She hummed her favourite hymn 'Great is Thy Faithfulness' on the way to the church just opened in Colombo Street near the Causeway.

When the practice finished she decided to go to St Joachim's a little further on. It would add only an extra half-mile to the couple of miles she had to cycle home and while she was in the area, she wanted to fix the rent. Before it had finished building its own church, the Reformed Church had used St Joachim's hall for choir practice and another church in King Street for its services. The choir owed the Catholic Church the final hall rent. The choir treasurer set off just after 10 p.m., pushing hard up the steep hill in Shepperton Road to St Joachim's. At the presbytery next to the church, she knocked on the door and handed the rent to Father Kearn.

Then she set off for home along Albany Highway and right into Hill View Terrace. She rode along the street she knew well, unperturbed by the distance, the coolness of the light spring breeze, the occasional passing car, or the hour. A short hill took her to Berwick Street, where she could see the outline of the trunks of the burnt-out pine trees in the distance. Then she could freewheel down as far as Devenish Street. Hill View Terrace was undulating from there and she rode easily past houses on the left and bush and a park to her right. As she reached the Collier Pine Plantation at Jarrah Road, she pedalled a little faster, preparing for the short sharp rise taking her to the Y-junction at Marquis Street, where she started an easy downward run home – a few hundred yards along Marquis Street before she would turn into McKay Street.

She noticed two young boys on the footpath, but they didn't see her roll past – they were too engrossed in the adventures of Clark Gable they'd seen at the Hurlingham Picture Theatre. Nel didn't know the boys' names but recognised them as coming from homes around the corner from hers and, straining her eyes ahead a few houses in the dimly lit street, she could see the boys' parents in their front gardens.

Cooke was in Hill View Terrace, watching Nel Schneider cycling along from behind the wheel of a blue Consul. His eyes were fully focused on the cyclist he'd spotted as he turned out of Berwick Street. He'd stopped the car especially to watch her.

He'd spent the evening prowling in the Victoria Park area, ending up in Mackie Street, just three blocks from where Nel was singing in the Colombo Street church. He'd walked down Mackie Street, checking out the possibilities at each house. Maybe he'd be lucky at No. 71 where that attractive young woman lived. He'd gone there before and hidden behind the pepper tree in the street outside her house, hoping to catch a glimpse of her. It was by chance he knew where she lived. Hanging around the fish-and-chip shop in Albany Highway one night, he had seen her get off a bus at the stop a few yards away and set off along Mackie Street. He'd followed her, matching her pace as she quickened it, waiting for the right moment to catch her attention. He'd been close behind her when, two-and-a-half blocks later, she turned in at No. 71. It had been his last opportunity to make contact, so he said hello.

Eighteen-year-old Jennifer Cleak had walked home extra

quickly after noticing the fellow outside the shop over the road turn and look at her. She heard the stranger stay behind her, catching up as she turned into home. She returned his greeting politely, though she was uneasy. That encouraged him to go on and ask her if she lived there. She thought quickly, not wanting to give anything away to this unusual-looking man who behaved so strangely. 'No, I live in Nedlands, I'm just staying the night with my aunt.' And she disappeared inside.

Cyril, Cliff and Fred Head didn't live at 67 Mackie Street any more, but visited their parents each Friday night. The boys heard about the number of peeping Tom and other incidents in their parents' street, and about Jennifer, next door but one, who was having a problem with a peeping Tom. Their parents, Fred and Nellie Head, had been surprised to see a policeman they knew arrive next door on his BSA motorbike with another in the sidecar. Their friend told Fred he was checking on a complaint of a man hanging around.

They thought of the night, too, some time previously, when the youngest Head boy, 23-year-old Fred, was having a drink with the Italian family over the road and the girl in the next house screamed. Fred and his mate ran across and tackled a man, getting a few punches in before the prowler jumped the fence.

There was also the Friday night when their friend from Rockingham was visiting after his wife's funeral. When 32-year-old Cliff went out to get some cigarettes from his car parked in the street outside the house, he discovered someone had raided the yellow Vauxhall. The glove box was open and all its contents had been pulled out. Their friend's Morris Minor had also been broken into, but Cyril's Singer sports car hadn't been touched. Cliff was happy for Cyril, but surprised that the sports car with just an unlockable canvas top was the only one to escape the thief's attentions. Cliff ran back inside to tell the others and his father came out with a powerful torch, looking up and down the street. They saw someone walking quickly into Washington Street. The two ran after him, catching up with him not far down that street. Fred shone the torch in his face and took a good look at him, both Fred and Cliff noting a hare lip. Asked gruffly whether he'd been going through their cars, he denied it. A few more questions and he would admit only that he had been wandering down Mackie Street. Warning him to stay away, the Heads went back home to their grieving friend.

A week or so later, Cliff was visiting over the road when he recognised the same man walking slowly down the street. Cliff approached him again, asking him where he lived and what he was doing in Mackie Street. The man replied that he lived in Belmont, and had been having a few drinks in the tavern around the corner and got lost. Cliff warned him he'd call the police if he saw him in the area again.

Cooke did walk down Mackie Street again, on 12 September 1958. He walked to No. 71. There was no sign of the lovely young woman. But there was a car in the drive at the front of the house, with the keys in the ignition.

Dick Cleak had bought his Ford Consul sedan on hire purchase three years earlier, and was still paying it off monthly to Traders Finance Corporation. It was the Gallipoli veteran's only concession to consumer society and he looked after it with the same combination of precision and tenderness that he lavished on his steed as a Tenth Lighthorseman 40 years ago. He had spent hours on it this Friday, putting in a new set of rings and doing other maintenance on the motor.

Cooke never wore a watch, since he'd been caught wearing the one he'd stolen from a customer when he was fourteen. He guessed it was about 10 p.m. when he put on his gloves and pushed the Consul out of the driveway before starting it and driving off. He went slowly along Mackie Street and turned left into Berwick Street.

He drove into Hill View Terrace and when he saw Nel, he pulled over for a couple of minutes, turning off the ignition and watching her as she rolled down the hill then pedalled easily along the gentle rise and fall of the road. She was very slim. As he watched her, he thought of the good time she must have had that night. She was no doubt going home from a date after sharing the carefree laughter of attractive friends, those happy sort of people who ignored him.

A powerful new urge stole over him. He felt a surge of irresistible excitement as the idea took shape. It was more than his usual need to mock the mockers by taking the things they held dear. This was more – this was an urge for more power and a realisation that he had more power. He had the power to hurt the people themselves. And there was a lone woman on a bicycle and nobody else around. He wanted to hurt someone – anyone. And she was it.

When he decided Nel had gone far enough, he drove after her. The street was deserted. At the Jarrah Road junction he accelerated, the car roaring as he followed her into Marquis Street and bore down on her at full speed.

Nel Schneider was tossed into the air, crashing headfirst on to the road. Her bicycle was caught on the grille. Cooke sped on, enraged and excited.

The two boys walking home from the pictures saw the car speed past and heard the thud up ahead as metal hit metal. But in the dark they couldn't make out exactly what had happened. They ran down the hill, calling to their parents standing on the front lawn that the car had hit something.

It was about 11.15 p.m. when Joy and Mick Hurley saw a car speed past with a bicycle attached to the grille. Minutes later, their eldest son Glen reached them, excitedly telling them that the car had hit something. Yes, they'd seen it, the car had collected a bicycle that someone must have left lying on the road.

They took Glen inside as the neighbours took Billy next door. Then they went to bed, thinking no more of the abandoned bicycle. It wasn't until next day that they learnt to their horror that someone had been riding the bicycle when it was hit. They woke up to find police everywhere along the street. While they had slept oblivious to the attack, Nel had been lying unconscious in a pool of blood, her skull fractured and a part of her brain permanently damaged. She, too, was oblivious to her plight, saved from the agony by the black nothingness of a coma.

Cooke had intended to stop and remove the bike from the grille, but as he sped around a corner, it fell off. He drove on and found a dark spot to leave the car, abandoning it about half a mile away from his hit–run. Nobody was following him. Thanks to the gloves, there would be no fingerprints. His first real act of violence and he'd be safe from being found out. He'd had his revenge and was satisfied; the urge left him. But the knowledge of the his new-found power stayed with him.

Nel lay on the road for maybe 45 minutes before a passing motorist noticed a buckled bicycle. Seeing it in the beam of his headlights, his curiosity was roused. The back wheel was crushed. Stopping to examine it more closely, he became more curious and explored the area further. Two hundred yards away, around the corner, he found Nel.

Just after midnight, Jan Schneider became a little worried at Nel's lateness, but he had no reason to be concerned for her safety, even when he heard an ambulance scream to a halt just fourteen houses away around the corner, and a few minutes later take off again, its siren sounding the urgency. Jan turned back to the task at hand, concentrating on the negatives laid out in the spare room. He was intensely interested in his hobby of photography and lost track of the time. It was maybe 2 a.m. when he looked up again and realised Nel should be home. He went outside. There were people in the street and they asked if he was looking for somebody. 'Yes, my wife.' He was told there had been an accident. Then he learnt more from the patrolling police car. The driver hadn't stopped after the accident. Nel was in hospital, in a serious condition.

Jan ran around the corner to his friends, who were very willing to help despite being woken up in the middle of the night. Jan's friend drove him to RPH while his wife went to mind the children. It was a silent trip into the city. Jan was in shock, unable to believe that someone could accidentally run into a cyclist and not stop to help. He was allowed to see Nel briefly before being advised to go home and wait. Jan had seen a lot of death and injury during the war. Now he saw his dear wife unconscious, her head heavily bandaged, and heard the grim news that she might not make it.

There had been two hit–runs in the area that night and a special squad of accident inquiry police worked during the night in an intensive hunt for the drivers involved.

They had no clues in the case of a teenage motorcyclist who was hit by a car leaving the Balmoral Hotel parking area at 6.15 p.m. The driver of the green Holden had reversed into seventeen-year-old Murray McKeon as he rode along Westminster Street, crushing his leg, before driving off without stopping.

Nor did they have much to go on in the more serious case. Early on Saturday morning Constables George Fancourt and Alf Gregson interviewed Jan and examined Nel's wrecked bicycle. They found what appeared to be the pattern of a vehicle bumper on it and scrape marks. It looked as if it had been jammed upright and pushed along for some distance by the vehicle. They also found traces of light blue paint on the bicycle, giving them the colour of the car they were looking for. A squad of special uniformed and plainclothes police combed Bentley and Victoria Park for a car of matching colour. Later that day they found a vehicle abandoned near the intersection of Walpole and Gladstone streets in Bentley. Marks on the front of the Ford Consul sedan corresponded to the blue paint on the bicycle. The registration number, 2638, was in the name of Richard Augustine Cleak, of 71 Mackie Street, Victoria Park, who had reported it stolen that morning.

When Cleak reported the theft of his car to the police, they added it to the list of 842 other cars stolen in Perth that year. *The West Australian* reported that the theft and hit–run had been put down to joyriders. Police investigations continued and the file was sent to Inspector Johnston by a young detective, Jack Deering, informing him that Ford Consul sedan licence number 2638, the property of Richard Augustine Cleak, which was reported stolen on 13/9/58 had been recovered. Deering's report went on that particulars of this file had been retained for future reference and inquiries would be continued.

Five years to the day after this offence, Deering met the target of the continued inquiries. On 12 September 1963, when Cooke confessed to running down another woman in Shenton Park in much the same way, Deering drew Cooke's attention to some differences between his memory and the facts and Cooke withdrew his confession.

Nel lay in a deep coma in RPH. At 7.30 the next morning her condition deteriorated sharply and Jan prepared for the worst. But Nel hung on tenaciously despite the odds, just as she had done during the Hunger Winter. Jan sat by her bed, one hand gripping his wife's, the other supporting his head. It was bowed, his eyes closed as he prayed and struggled against the possibility of her death now after surviving all the traumatic war years.

For two long weeks, Jan would catch a bus into the city and walk to RPH to wait by Nel's bedside for a sign that she would survive yet another test of her strength and faith. Finally, after fourteen days, his prayers were answered. Nel's eyes slowly fluttered open and she whispered: 'I want my children.' Her first words were greeted with relief and joy and thanks to God. Jan quickly handed Tony to her, too choked up to speak and not knowing what to say. Finally he came up with something offhand, belying the emotion of the moment. 'I didn't know he was so heavy,' he said about the chubby boy he'd carried all the way from the bus stop so often during the past fortnight.

Nel's head wounds were extremely serious and she was under the care of a brain surgeon, Mr John Lekias. She floated in and out of deep sleep and confusion, fighting to work out what had happened. Unaware of the extent of her injuries, her main worry was not having her own nightie or dressing gown with her. It took another two weeks of specialised care before she could leave hospital to continue her recuperation at home, in a bed made up for her in the lounge room, her children in the care of people from the church.

Nel gradually recovered and could resume her life. But she wasn't the same. Sometimes a funny feeling came over her. The doctor tried to dismiss it as nerves, but occasionally the feeling engulfed her, and she blacked out. The blackouts occurred with no warning. Once she fell behind the washing machine and Jan had to call a neighbour to help get her out. Once the grocer, making house deliveries, discovered her unconscious in her front yard. Once she fell beside the open fireplace, the heat bringing her out of it just enough to get up and stagger to the toilet, where she fell again.

Slowly, over two years and with a lot of argument with doctors, it became clear. Nel's permanent legacy, courtesy of Cooke, was chronic post-traumatic temporal lobe epilepsy, which meant a lifetime of blackouts, seizures and dependence on medication.

Violent Nightmare

25 November 1958

Two-and-a-half months after running down Nel Schneider, Cooke was back on the prowl, taking risks again and succeeding. He'd quite recovered from the fear of a possible jail term which had overtaken him after he'd been nearly caught four weeks earlier. They'd found him unconscious at a bus stop in the city on 28 October. He was wearing bike clips on his trousers but no bicycle was found nearby. He regained consciousness in RPH, where he was asked what he had been doing and what had happened. He said he couldn't remember.

The next day he recovered from his amnesia enough to tell doctors that he remembered leaving work and being in the gardens of Government House. He told them he was concerned he may have committed some act that may lead to a further jail sentence. He hadn't been questioned at all on the hit–run, but it was still being investigated and he couldn't be totally confident that he'd got away with this venture into real retaliation against the lucky ones. He was a little anxious about it – he certainly didn't want to return to jail for that or any other crime.

Three days later he was discharged, with a note on his file that a Rorschach test suggested a patient of good average intelligence without serious psycho-pathology.

He'd gotten away with whatever he'd been up to before his amnesia attack. Reassured, he was all confidence. On Tuesday, 25 November, he headed to Applecross, a regular hunting ground. Wandering down MacLeod Road, where a few houses were scattered in the bush, he noticed one house in particular. No. 55 was fairly average, a standard red brick-and-tile war service home, but it stood out because of the size of the block – a half-acre – and the well-kept garden in the front.

The left side of the house was overgrown with bushes that offered plenty of cover as he searched for the easiest entrance. But he chose to go down the much more open area at the right of the house. It was in darkness, as were the few others in MacLeod Road. Nobody was up and about in the middle of the night, and it was the quickest way around the back.

Sneaking down the side to the back, he came to a huge lawn, dominated by a big cape lilac and two flame trees. He put on his gloves and tested the doors and windows, managing to get in through the louvred sleepout arrangement. A girl was asleep there. He stopped at her bed and looked at the mop of curly fair hair covering the pillow. He guessed she was about sixteen. He gained a lot of pleasure from stealing, and from watching young women and couples in their bedrooms. He was here to steal, but she looked so pretty. His wife was seven months pregnant again after having twins just a year before. This girl was slim, and so vulnerable.

He made his way through the dining room to the kitchen. Finding a few bob for starters, he was about to go in further, when he felt the urge to relieve himself. So he backtracked outside, to the spacious lawn, and moments later started in again, back to the sleepout and the girl. The back door slipped out of his hand and made a noise. He was back at her bedside when she woke up. He grabbed something handy and hit her over the head. He ran out and escaped down the road.

Lucy and Ern MacLeod woke up in the small hours of Wednesday, startled to find their elder daughter staggering around their bedroom, mumbling, stumbling and retching. She was trying to talk, trying to tell her parents something, but the words just wouldn't come out, as if she was having a nightmare. Lucy rushed to hold her, trying to get some sense out of the situation and out of the girl. But the child just uttered gibberish to all attempts to get through to her, her parents desperately trying all her names – her name within the family, Mackie, her nickname, Mollie, her real name, Mary. What could have happened to this bright, eloquent fifteen-year-old who'd recently gained a perfect score in an Art of Speech competition? How ironical now that *Daily News* photo and article about her 100 per cent score, headed 'When Mollie Talks, She's a Winner'.

Having succeeded in the struggle to her parents' room, the teenager passed out. Distraught, Ern carried her back to bed, where Lucy knelt beside her and prayed, reciting the rosary. She often took advantage of the quiet of night to go through the rosary peacefully in the dining room. But tonight there was no peace. As the Hail Marys tumbled out, nine-year-old Gay woke up in the adjoining room to the sight of her mother praying over her sister's bed. Gay could hear her sister moaning and muttering nonsense and her father repeatedly begging her to wake up. When her parents noticed their younger daughter had been disturbed, they told her everything was OK and she should go back to sleep.

The household was still in turmoil when Lucy's sister Nancy arrived next morning, after a telephone call requesting her help. Nancy came every Monday to do the washing and ironing for this professional household and willingly responded to the emergency call. By now Mackie could put enough words together to talk of a knock on the head and complain that her head was sore. Nancy took Mackie down the road to the family doctor. Her black eye and headache were as confusing to Dr Charles Greenacre as to the family, but it was clear she had been concussed and he ordered six weeks' bed rest. Still worried about the cause, he later called a colleague into the case and X-rays showed a small Y-shaped hairline fracture of her left temple.

Mackie missed her sub-leaving school exams and she missed collecting the school's Art of Speech prize. Gay collected it for her on Our Lady's College speech night, proud of her sister's achievement but not knowing how to answer questions about what had happened to her. The family didn't know what to say to two nuns, either, when they brought Mackie Lourdes water in a bottle shaped as the Virgin Mary. Nothing had been out of place in the home. There was nothing to explain it other than a sudden illness or accident. Had she had a fit of some sort? Had she had a bad nightmare? Or had she hit her head on the bookshelves just above her bed, with their unprotected edges and corners, or on the bed's headboard? The MacLeod family continued to wonder and speculate, finally deciding she must have had a violent nightmare and fallen out of bed.

The Season of Goodwill

27 December 1958

His first Christmas in Australia was a depressing shock to John Button. It just wasn't Christmas in the middle of summer. His father made every effort to make it special for the youngsters, taking John and Margaret to a city cafe for Christmas dinner. There were the traditional turkey and plum pudding, paper hats and crackers, but there wasn't any snow and there wasn't Mum.

John missed his mother even more than before. He was very homesick as he remembered those special Christmases of his childhood – the warm brightness they brought to dark winter days, jumping out of a snuggly bed to attack the pillow case filled with toys, the family seated around the holly-decorated table for the biggest and best Christmas dinner that only Mum could make, the thrill of finding threepenny pieces in the plum pudding. He tried his best to be part of the jollity in the Barrack Street cafe and to enjoy the drive to the beach afterwards, but he yearned for home, Mum and a real Christmas.

Mothers were missing from two other families in Perth at Christmas.

Nel Schneider was still weak and bedridden. Church people did their best for the family, including them in the Dutch-style celebrations held on Christmas Eve. But the attack had left Nel unable to join in as much as she wanted or to provide that special Christmas atmosphere.

In another outer Perth suburb, Belmont, 29-year-old Kathlene Mavis Bellis quietly suffered a deep longing for her mother, just as she had the previous three Christmases since coming west. Despite the joys her own children brought her on this day, it was always a time when she most keenly felt the distance from her home in Victoria. Kathlene missed the familiar Christmas of her childhood, the warm nurture of the big family of eight and, most of all, she missed her mother.

It had been twelve years since the petite brunette with large green eyes had married her handsome airman after he returned from the war. Phil Bellis was a West Australian, but he'd stayed in Melbourne with his eighteen-year-old bride Kathlene, known as Kathy, and had settled into married life there. He became part of Kathy's big family circle and readily agreed to their first baby, born a year later, being named Janet after Kathy's mother. Three years later they had a son, naming him Philip after his father and deciding to avoid confusion by always using the full name for their son and the shortened version for Philip senior. Then came the surprise – Phil's firm, motor spare parts dealer Joseph Lucas Australia, wanted him to transfer to Perth. Phil was pleased to go back to his home state, with his mother, brother and sister there, and Kathy was happy to experience something new.

Phil left at the end of 1954, preparing the way for the family and giving Kathy one more Christmas at home. On 3 January 1955 Kathy joined him with seven-year-old Janet and four-year-old Philip. They all moved in with Phil's mother in the big old family home at 174 Newcastle Street, North Perth, spending six months there while their house was built on a block carved out of the bush in Belmont.

The new outer Perth suburb was a shock for the Melburnian used to the old established streets. She'd come from a big cosmopolitan city gearing up for an Olympic Games to a capital city that was more like a big country town. The Belmont Road Board district was only four miles from the centre of Perth, but it was a sparsely inhabited area consisting mostly of paddocks, dairy and poultry farms and bush. There were just a few homes starting to spring up in streets with no footpaths and no street lights. The Bellis's new home at 9 Belinda Avenue was the last of five houses in a short street leading east from a dairy farm. On this outer edge of built-up Perth the land was reasonably cheap, so Phil and his younger brother John had taken the opportunity to buy adjoining blocks not far from their mother's brother, Uncle Albert, who had a poultry farm on the next corner.

Kathy was kept busy caring for Janet and Philip, along with baby Peter, who completed their family in 1956. She easily fitted in with Phil's close-knit family, becoming good friends with his sister and sister-in-law. In 1958 John and his wife Coral started building their home next door to Kathy and Phil, at 11 Belinda Avenue, in preparation for the arrival of their first baby the following July. During the building, they lived in a caravan at the back of No. 9, and the two sisters-in-law were company for each other while their husbands were at work.

Kathy got on so well with Phil's sister, Audrey, that she started doing some part-time work with her. Audrey had moved back to her mother's Newcastle Street house with her two young children after a road accident had seriously and permanently injured her husband. Audrey worked at E. G. Patman's, the tearooms on the corner of Newcastle and William streets, a few blocks from her mother's place, and Kathy joined her there as a casual counterhand and waitress, mainly working Sunday mornings.

Four years after their arrival in the West, the Christmas of 1958 was a homely and happy one for Kathy and Phil Bellis, who enjoyed a traditional family dinner at his mother's home. The children's excitement was infectious, eight-year-old Philip and two-year-old Peter joining Audrey's two in quickly tearing apart their presents.

But underlying the joy was Kathy's usual tinge of loneliness on this day as her thoughts wandered to her mother on the other side of the country. This year, there was another emptiness within her – her daughter Janet was missing from the Christmas table for the first time. The eleven-year-old had gone with Coral and John to Albany, thrilled at a holiday with her aunt and uncle, her first major adventure away from home in the south of the State. Her parents were happy for her to go, but her absence on this special day emphasised the absence of the other Janet so close to Kathy's heart.

Cooke spent Christmas at home in Rivervale with his family, being a good father and Father Christmas to his three sons and daughter. There was no sign that he was capable of those two vicious attacks on women. This was the other side of him.

On Boxing Day, Kathy and Phil relaxed quietly while the boys played with their new treasures. The day seemed a little strange without John and Coral nearby – no swish of the driver as John lobbed golf balls into the bush over the road, no chat over a beer and a smoke before dinner. But, sandwiched between Christmas and a big day at the beach, they enjoyed their lazy time at home – the odd household chore, a bit of reading, a few drinks, just keeping as cool as possible while the temperature soared past 90 degrees again.

The magpies heralded Saturday 27 December, a day only slightly cooler than the rest of the holiday break. Phil, an avid newspaper reader who always missed *The West Australian* when it wasn't published on Boxing Day, pored over the big Saturday paper, reading to Kathy the news that a nine-year-old boy had drowned in the river on Christmas Day.

Once ready, they made for Leighton. The old green dented van, which Phil had bought from his firm when it updated its vehicles, had been used for transporting car parts around Perth. With no seats in the back, it was ideal for transporting a young boisterous family. As Phil and Kathy settled on their towels at the beach, Philip headed straight for a surf mat. He was in and out of the waves on the black rubber blow-up board, dreading the hoisting of the coloured flag on the beach to announce his hire time was over. Toddler Peter stayed close to Mum and Dad at the water's edge, splashing and giggling in wonder at the ripples chasing him. An hour or so later, lunch brought a fast gathering of seagulls screeching for attention and squabbling for the titbits thrown their way. Choo Choo bars, toffee umbrellas and Peter's favourite chocolate frogs all added to the children's special outing.

A slightly sunburnt, happy troupe bounced back to Belmont mid-afternoon, still full of the joys of summer and planning another day at the beach during Phil's New Year break. They hadn't been home long, and Kathy was still out at the Hills Hoist near the chook pen, hanging up bathers and towels, when there was a knock at the front door. Phil was surprised to see the tearooms' owner, Eric Patman. Eric came by each Sunday to give Kathy a lift for her 7 a.m. start, there being no bus early enough on the restricted Sunday timetable. This was Saturday and Kathy wasn't due to work, but Eric had come to ask if she could help out. They were one hand down and he expected a busy night.

His tearooms were popular with taxi drivers, and Eric knew there'd be a lot of them about on a holiday Saturday night. Kathy didn't have a telephone and, realising she'd need a lift to the shop anyway, he'd driven out on the chance she could fill in. Kathy, always ready to help anyone in need, quickly cleaned up, changed into a simple skirt and blouse and arranged for Phil to take the boys to the drive-in to continue their Christmas treat with the 7.45 session of the Walt Disney film at the Metro.

Cooke was doing his Saturday night rounds again. Three-and-a-half months had passed since he'd run down Nel Schneider. There had been some publicity in the paper and an intensive hunt for that night's two hit–run drivers, but no police at his door. He'd gotten away with it, and with the attack on Mollie MacLeod – that didn't even rate a mention in the paper, and no questions had been asked. He was known only as a 'tea and sugar thief', as the petty crims were called. They'd never guess that he'd gone beyond that, that his hatred and thirst for revenge had become a madness that engulfed him. They'd never link him with murderous attacks on women.

Thank God for those gloves. What a lesson he'd been taught by being caught because of fingerprints. He'd never do that again. The police would never again see his fingerprints at the crime scene.

At the shop, Kathy quickly set to work in her usual quiet, efficient manner – milk shakes, sandwiches, ice creams, cigarettes, coffee. She worked quickly between the counter and the tables, a popular, attractive waitress with a friendly smile for everyone and a special hello for the regulars. It was as busy as Eric had predicted, taxis lined up along the street as the drivers came in for their breaks, and many people out and about enjoying the warm night and the city's holiday atmosphere.

There was no chance of Kathy leaving early when Phil came in on his way home from the drive-in. He'd dropped by on the chance he could collect her, but it was only about 9.30 and she knew she'd be needed until closing time. Reassuring him that she'd be all right on the bus, Kathy took a five-minute break to hear young Philip excitedly tell her about Old Yeller, omitting that he'd cried when the faithful dog died. She double-checked the holiday bus timetable so that Phil could pick her up from the stop as usual, saving her the walk home on the dark streets late at night, and kissed the sleeping Peter before getting back to work.

Young Philip was also starting to nod off by the time father and sons got home. Phil carried the two boys to bed, tucked them in and settled into the lounge to do the crosswords over a beer and a smoke while he waited for Kathy's bus.

Cooke walked along Coode Street in Como, on the lookout for a house to burgle or car to steal. He found the latter in the driveway of a house opposite the Como Primary School – a utility. It had a Geraldton number plate – nice of someone from the country to lend him a ute. He put on his gloves and helped himself. About 11 p.m. he was nearer home, driving slowly through Carlisle and Belmont.

Just before Kathy's bus was due, Phil looked in on the boys and, seeing they were asleep, he drove to the bus stop with a few minutes to spare. Turning off the motor, he wound down the windows to get a bit of breeze and sat and waited.

The bus wasn't on time – nor was it within the normal limits of running late. Obviously something had happened and, on a holiday Saturday night, it would be a while before the next bus. Concerned about the young children alone in the house, Phil returned and resumed his crosswords while he waited for Kathy, puzzled at what could have gone wrong.

The last customers left just after closing time at 11 and Kathy and Audrey cleaned up and emptied the till. Kathy gathered up some scraps and leftovers as she always did, putting them in a bag to take home for the chooks, and the two closed shop, parting cheerily. Audrey started to walk home along Newcastle Street and Kathy headed for the bus stop in William Street. It wasn't long before a bus came to take her into the city, but then she had a long wait in the Terrace for her bus to Belmont. Although she was wondering whether she'd misread the timetable and worried about Phil waiting at the other end, she didn't mind sitting there in the balmy evening air having a smoke and taking the weight off her feet after her busy night. When a bus finally arrived, the driver explained something about an earlier problem with a flat tyre involving a passenger transfer. She didn't take much notice; she was just happy to be on the way home, by an open window for fresh air, sitting high watching the traffic and the people along the Terrace, past the trolley-bus terminal and over the Causeway.

Out of the city, the streets became quieter and darker as the bus headed towards Belmont. When she reached her stop in Fulham Street the road was deserted – she wasn't greeted by the cheery sound of the old van starting up to whisk her home. Finding the torch she always carried in her handbag for walking in this unlit bushy suburb, she set off into the darkness.

Cooke was driving along Fulham Street in Belmont, heading back in the direction of the city, when he passed a bus travelling towards him. He drove on a little way, looking up and down the streets in case he was in luck and the bus coming from the city had just dropped someone. As he came to Homewood Street, he looked to his left to check the street. Yes, there was a woman walking away from the bus stop. She was alone.

It was just like before – a stolen car, a dark isolated street, a woman going home from a night out. That feeling started to rise in him again.

He'd driven past several Christmas trees during the evening, reminders of the Christmas spirit. But tonight he didn't feel peace on earth or goodwill towards men or women.

Kathy had to walk two blocks to get home, across Gabriel Street and into Belinda Avenue. Her light footsteps hardly disturbed the stillness as she walked just to the left of the centre of the road following the torch's small beam. It was quite isolated – there were no houses in Homewood Street and no street lights, the bitumen road just newly laid through the bush and paddocks.

Cooke did a U-turn at the next cross-street and drove back the way he'd come along Fulham Street to Homewood Street. He turned into it, quickly spotting the woman further up the road as she headed towards the intersection of Homewood and Gabriel streets.

The sound of a car a little way behind her was a relief to Kathy as she hurried home through the darkness. Phil had come to collect her after all. She turned and waved the torch to show him where she was. But then she realised it wasn't Phil's van. She'd have to keep walking. It wasn't far, anyway. She was nearly at Gabriel Street, across which was her street, Belinda Avenue. She moved to the edge of the road to let the car pass. As it came nearer, something in the sound of the speed and the revving told her to give it more room. She hurried off the road into the paddock alongside. She walked faster.

Cooke sped up and adjusted his aim at the small figure ahead in the darkness. He was too determined to let her get away.

Suddenly Kathy felt the menace of the car behind her. She didn't understand the knowing that came to her, but she knew the driver was out to get her. She knew that she wasn't safe in the paddock, that this speeding, revving car would leave the road to hit her. She turned around to look.

Who will look after the littlies? That was the final thought that raced through her mind as she put her hands up to protect her face from the inevitable, as the car reached its target, slewing in the soft sand of the paddock before the driver regained control.

Kathy was hit with such force that she was thrown and carried 60 feet across the intersection at the beginning of Belinda Avenue.

The young mother slipped in and out of consciousness as she lay badly injured in the sand. Her dead brother Milton appeared to her again, just as he did in her dreams – the recurring dream in which he was still alive, not taken prisoner in Singapore and killed in the bombing of the Japanese POW ship. In her dream, it was all a mistake, that awful moment when she, the only one home at the time, opened the telegram with the dreadful news.

Then the driver of the car came to her. Was it really him she saw leaning over her? The searing pain in her leg and pelvis told her she was alive – and she wanted to live. The driver was her only hope. Who else would find her in the lonely darkness? She begged him, 'Don't leave me, or I'll die.' The man or mirage laughed in her face, returned to the car and sped off.

Fourteen weeks after his first successful hit–run, Cooke had a second. Leaving Kathy, he continued along Gabriel Street, going left into Abernethy Road and left back into Fulham Street again. He continued on past the road leading home to Carlisle and turned into the Neptune Garage in Oats Street. He knew the garage, having friends he visited just across the road. It was run by well-known racing car driver Ray Clarke, who lived in the next house and tested his latest racers in the quiet back streets behind the 16 acres of swamp called Tomato Lake.

Cooke saw a post at the back of Ray's garage and nudged the ute up against it, just enough to hide the damage to the front. Leaving it there, he walked the one-and-a-half miles home.

It had been a busy night at the City Hotel in King Street as revellers made the most of the hot holiday night. Barmaid Lee Roberts was pleased to get home to Belmont to a relaxing cup of tea with her new husband, Dave. They were sitting in the kitchen at the back of their house in Robinson Avenue, one street away from Belinda Avenue, when Lee's chat about the evening's patrons was interrupted by a horrible noise.

'There's something wrong with the cat,' Lee said, thinking their pet was screeching and getting up quickly to see. Dave was right behind her, but it was too dark to see anything out the front.

'That's not a cat, it's a woman!' he exclaimed, listening intently. They walked along the road to investigate, thinking a woman was being beaten somewhere. After following the strange sound to the street corner, they were shocked to find a woman lying in the paddock by a banksia tree. As they peered closer through the darkness, their neighbour Taffy Lund joined them and recognised the broken, bleeding woman as Kathy Bellis from up the road. It was a gruesome sight, her right leg splayed at an impossible angle, her pelvis obviously broken, blood oozing from her mouth, her face blackened. She was lying there silent now, seemingly lifeless. Despite believing it was too late for an ambulance, Taffy immediately ran home to call one and to give the terrible news to her husband.

Phil was still wavering between concentration on the last clues and concern for Kathy when there was a loud, urgent banging on the front door. He opened it to face the big Welshman who lived near the corner at 4 Belinda Avenue. Taffy Lund was obviously agitated and before Phil could say anything or reach for the fly wire door to let him in, he burst out: 'Your wife's been killed, down the road.'

Lee cradled Kathy's head in her arms in an effort to comfort her in case she was still alive. Kathy momentarily regained consciousness, enough to feel excruciating pain and to panic about further injury.

'Don't move me, my legs,' she groaned to her rescuers before lapsing into unconsciousness again.

When the ambulance had gone, there was nothing more for Dave and Lee to do but to go back home. Living in the next street, they didn't really know Kathy, but they knew one of her sons, the little boy who used to come and play with their nephew. They talked about it over a fresh cup of tea, recalling the other strange occurrences in their quiet neighbourhood recently. One morning a few weeks previously, Dave, rising very early for his shift work at the State Engineering Works, had turned on the bedroom light to find a man standing outside the window gazing in. Just married and moved into the new home, they hadn't yet put up curtains. Nor, until this experience and that of the man over the road with a peeping Tom, had they thought it was a priority in this quiet, sparsely populated neighbourhood.

Phil was stunned by Taffy's outburst. He couldn't believe what he heard, but the look on his neighbour's face told him he had to. When Taffy went on to say he'd called the ambulance, Phil found a bit of hope to hang on to – maybe she was alive. He had to get to her immediately. He woke up his elder son. With no alternative but to put a mature load on his young shoulders, Phil told the eight-year-old that he had to go to hospital and he was to look after his little brother.

The old battered van had never moved faster as Phil flattened the pedal and headed for RPH. In Casualty, he was relieved to hear the news he'd been desperate for. Kathy was alive. She was in theatre and he could see her in the morning. Still in shock, Phil immediately drove to his mother's house. His mind was awhirl as he left the hospital, driving the wrong way down the central city's one-way Murray Street.

Early the next day Dave and Lee Roberts went back to the corner to look at the scene in the light. It seemed impossible, but tyre marks and the messy trail of food scraps spread along the street indicated Kathy had been hit in Homewood Street and thrown all the way across the intersection to Belinda Avenue. Phil saw it, too, as he drove home at daybreak, numb and weary. The street was strewn with Kathy's bits for the chooks. He stopped at the beginning of the trail, and saw the car's tyre marks in the sand, way off the road. It was clearly a deliberate effort to run Kathy down – a calculated, well-aimed hit–run that could easily have killed his wife.

Where were the police? Phil couldn't believe that the area hadn't been cordoned off, that police weren't poring over it for clues. He picked up Kathy's handbag and the things spilt out of it and put them in the van, going home bewildered.

The police were soon on the job, going over Dave and Lee's car and taking down their explanation of how they came to find the victim. It was Phil's turn next. The police went over his car, closely examining it inside and out, and questioning him. His car had been spotted at the scene earlier that night, there were lots of dents on it and her handbag was on the passenger seat. Phil was astonished and alarmed as it sank in that he was under suspicion. Finally they seemed satisfied, but he still could not convince them that someone had deliberately run Kathy down. Phil took them to the corner and showed them the tyre marks, definite tracks leaving the road and veering back on to it. The evidence was there, but it was too unbelievable.

It wasn't until the stolen car was found at the Neptune Garage next day that it was finally accepted. Kathy had been the victim of an unknown hit–run driver in a stolen vehicle.

Kathy woke up in hospital, blue-metal embedded in her lacerated face, a badly broken pelvis, two breaks in her leg, a shattered knee, a fracture in the base of her spine and a fracture at the top of her skull. Through the pain she remained haunted by the man's callous face peering at her and laughing as she begged him to help her. This vision permeated her sleep and semiconsciousness. Over and over, the car racing towards her, the man laughing.

It was a long slow road to recovery for Kathy. She really liked her doctor, orthopaedic surgeon Alec Dawkins, whose jovial manner helped her through the agony of her many operations.

'Come on, let's run away now,' he'd joke to the beautiful patient who wouldn't be able to run again as he explained the next operation on her permanently maimed leg.

Four weeks later, she was discharged after a decision to delay the next operation. Kathy was thrilled when told she could go home, even as debilitated as she was. The family was managing quite well without her: Janet playing little mother, Coral helping and Phil's mother looking after Peter while the others were at school and work. But she wanted to be home with them, even with her leg in plaster.

Over the next year she was constantly in and out of hospital for operations and manipulation. But she carried on as best she could. She didn't dwell on what had happened to her, believing it wouldn't do any good. She kept telling herself it was just one of those things – she'd been in the wrong place at the wrong time.

A Fight to the Death

29 January 1959

Cooke had gone about his usual life over the past month. He'd worked as a sheet metal worker at Belmont, prowled at weekends and waited for the birth of the baby that would add to the family of two boys and twin boy and girl.

His fifth child had arrived four days earlier when on Thursday 29 January, the proud father again went to King Edward Memorial Hospital in Subiaco to visit his wife and new son. Afterwards, he walked from the hospital to Wembley, crossing to the other side of Cambridge Street to the Wembley Hotel to celebrate with a few beers.

His wife's stepfather and half-sister had been living with them since Sally's mother died, so the children were cared for during his wife's confinement. He was free to pursue his usual nocturnal activity. After leaving the hotel, he put on his gloves and set about casing the Wembley area. Slowly making his way along Cambridge Street towards the city, he came to a two-storey block of redbrick flats on the corner of Daglish Street. At the back of No. 3, he found a bike leaning against the wall of the small back porch. Hanging over it was a skindiver's weight belt with a knife attached to it. The diver's knife had an eight-inch blade. He took it, slipping it behind his belt.

He walked further towards the city, until he reached West Perth. This was a lucrative area for him, with a mixture of flats and big expensive houses. It was good for his peeping Tom activities too. Lots of the young singles didn't bother pulling down their blinds, giving him the excitement of seeing them naked, or even making love. That really stimulated him – and made him angry. Although married, Cooke was quite successful with other women. But he still thought the unmarried women he perved on were dirty.

Sneaking along the back lanes from house to house, he eventually came to the flats at 44 Kings Park Road. At the back of the flats, he found a Volkswagen. No more walking. He pushed it into a lane before starting it and driving it along Stirling Highway to Fremantle and back towards the city along Canning Highway. He was just roaming, enjoying his freedom and the power to stop anywhere he liked and take whatever he liked.

He chose to stop in South Perth, another area of flats and singles where he often had luck stealing and watching. He was very familiar with it from his youth and from many nights sneaking around. He turned left into Brandon Street and parked the car.

He wandered along Mill Point Road a little way, into the forecourt of City View Flats, 322–324 Mill Point Road, a two-storey group of twelve flats on the corner of Hurlingham Road where several women lived alone. After having a look around, he found one with the window open, an easy entry. It was No. 1, on the ground floor facing Mill Point Road, nearest the driveway. It was easy to climb through the window from the small front porch. Inside, he could see the outline of a woman asleep in a bed with the foot-end against the window. Another single bed was empty. He could see only her outline, but it was a very shapely one.

Pnena Berkman was second in charge of perfumery in the cosmetics section of David Jones department store. The 33-year-old had come to Western Australia from Victoria with her eight-year-old son Mark on the break-up of her marriage four years earlier. Pnena was a glamorous woman and was seeing popular radio personality, Fotis Hountas.

Hountas picked her up from work this Thursday and they had dinner at her place, No. 1 City View Flats. At 8 p.m. he went home to where he lived with his brother-in-law not far away in Mill Point Road. He returned to his girlfriend's flat at 10 p.m., and shared a bottle of beer with her before going to bed and making love. Hountas left for home at midnight, leaving her sleeping naked and closing the front door on his way out.

Without disturbing the sleeping woman, the experienced burglar moved through the bedroom to search the rest of the flat. He carefully scoured the kitchen and lounge room, noticing an empty beer bottle. Then he headed back into the bedroom, to that shapely woman.

Pnena woke up. It was dark and he couldn't see her face, so she wouldn't be able to see him either, but Cooke panicked. He'd hit that young one over the head a couple of months back and silenced her. This time he could do better – this time he happened to have a diver's knife on him. Excitement at his extra power mingled with his panic as he quickly took the knife from his belt and stabbed Pnena.

She fought back – valiantly; screaming, kicking, scratching and struggling. She clawed at his mouth, dragging down hard and ripping it. She got him with her long nails three or four times down the side of his face – tearing his skin and flesh in long deep ridges from underneath his eye to his mouth. He hadn't expected this. Hand-to-hand battle was so different from hitting someone with a car or knocking a young woman over the head. He fought harder. It was difficult against the flailing arms and legs, but he was stronger and he managed to plunge the knife into her. He knew it was a bit high. It didn't stop her. He had to get it into her again. There was more of a fight before he managed his second strike. This one was better. He struck viciously, getting her lower down, on the left side of her body, just about where her heart would be. Success. She screamed and fell back limp. He'd won.

He immediately got to his feet, leaving her lying on her back across the bed. He ran out, not bothering to close the door, and drove away. He went quite a way, into Victoria Park, to make sure he was safe before getting rid of the knife. He stabbed it into the ground a couple of times to clean it before dropping it through the grille of a drain on the corner of Gresham Street and Shepperton Road. Free of the evidence, he drove another block along Gresham Street and left the

Volkswagen near the corner of Lichfield Street. He walked home from there.

Fotis Hountas noticed his girlfriend's window open and the door partly ajar when he passed by next morning. She always locked up before going to work, so he went in to investigate.

He found her naked body lying in a pool of blood in the lounge room by the sliding glass doors. She had a deep stab wound through her nose and she'd been stabbed in the heart. She had obviously fought to survive despite the mortal injury, managing to make it as far as the doors in an effort to get help. She'd probably been trying to open the doors when she'd slumped to the floor and died about 3 a.m.

The population of Perth was not only shocked by the murder, but scandalised that a divorced woman entertained a gentleman late at night and slept in the nude. The rumour quickly circulated that she was a prostitute – after all, ladies didn't do that sort of thing.

Cooke was worried. He'd wanted to hurt and maim those two women he'd run down, and he could easily have killed them. But they had survived. This time, it had been a fight to the death. This was murder.

When he brought his wife home from hospital three days later, he wasn't himself. Normally immaculately dressed, he was untidy, unshaven, slopping around in scuffs. For a week he sat on the front doorstep of the house, worried and moody.

He was suffering physically, too. The deep scratches became infected and took a long time to heal, as did his mouth. It was a couple of weeks before he could put in his false teeth. He made up a good story about his injuries, using as the excuse their eldest child, Michael, who was mentally retarded. He told his wife that he'd been playing with the four-year-old in the backyard and the boy had become over-boisterous and had scratched him. He explained his sore mouth as ulcers, but he wouldn't let her see them and he ignored her suggestions that he go to the doctor.

Cooke's first murder victim had been born Patricia Vinico Griggs in Melbourne in July 1925. She served in the Australian

Women's Army and married Polish Jew Gerszon Garry Berkman in the Melbourne Synagogue in June 1949, taking on his Jewish religion. She also took on a Jewish version of her name, becoming Pnena Berkman, but was also known as Penny. Separated in 1953 and divorced in 1955, her move west left behind memories of a childhood marred by the death of her parents in a traffic accident when she was at primary school.

She had been seeing the popular 6PR and 6PM radio announcer for about six months. People hearing his footsteps that night were able to confirm his statements about when he'd left her flat and when he'd returned, and young Mark gave a statement that he'd never seen Hountas with a dagger. However, to much of the general public, he remained the most likely person responsible for her death. He went home to Greece.

One person who wondered about Hountas was Ron Stone, the president of the Jewish Ex-Service Association. He felt awkward when Hountas came into his jewellery shop to contribute to the funeral costs. Since Pnena had no immediate family to make funeral arrangements, Stone took responsibility, wanting her to have a decent Jewish funeral. Pnena had just become involved with the association, acting as its secretary. On the suggestion of his wife Abigail, Ron collected the required £42 from donations, arranged for Rabbi Louis Rubin-Zacks to take the service and organised an honour guard and an army flag to drape the coffin. Despite being alone and being murdered in scandalous circumstances, Pnena Berkman had the full ritual of a religious burial in the Jewish section of Karrakatta Cemetery.

The Stones, with three young children of their own, also took in Mark, looking after him until his father could get to Perth to take him.

There was a huge police investigation. Their best evidence was a little blood found under the victim's fingernails and noises heard by neighbours. A couple in a neighbouring flat had been woken by gasping sounds and a sharp scream, a few minutes later hearing a car door slam and a car drive away. They estimated it to be 3 a.m. Another flat dweller heard screams and a car drive away, estimating it to be 2.45 a.m. The milkman had seen someone sitting in a blue Zephyr parked outside the flats early in the morning on a couple of occasions and there were many reports of prowlers in the area.

The previous night a prowler had been disturbed trying to get into a house a street away towards the river. At 1.50 a.m. someone trying to get in through the back door ran away towards Mill Point Road when the man of the house went outside. A neighbour saw the man, describing him as between 5 foot 8 inches and 5 foot 10 inches, with thick dark hair. She thought he might have been watching the flats from a phone box.

There had been a more serious incident in the same street six weeks earlier. A 21-year-old schoolteacher, Veronica Donovan, was attacked in bed in flat No. 2 at 338 Mill Point Road. Veronica and her flatmate Daphne Priddis had gone to bed late on 16 December 1958 after babysitting for Daphne's sister. Veronica woke up screaming at 3 a.m. She heard a noise like someone jumping out the bedroom window. Someone had lifted the venetian blind, moved the dressing table which was by the window, and grabbed Veronica by the neck, leaving deep scratch marks down her face and neck. Before attacking Veronica, the intruder had stolen a table from Rudolph Fellinger at 334 Mill Point Road and had placed it across the front door of the flat to slow anyone trying to give chase.

This attack and Pnena Berkman's murder remained unsolved. A coronial inquiry into the stabbing was adjourned for the police to make further investigations.

The Australian Way of Life

1959

John Button had been looking forward to his first hot summer and life on sun-drenched beaches. Instead he spent his days at the tiresome task of sweeping floors and polishing tables. Bored with his first job, the fourteen-year-old started to look for another, hoping there'd be a break between jobs for days at the beach. From Innaloo he could easily catch a bus to Scarborough Beach, cover himself with baby oil and get his first suntan.

He wasn't so lucky. His father used his contacts in the building trade to help John get a job with a ceiling fixer whose business was based nearby in Mt Hawthorn. John was immediately employed as boy to plasterboard fixer Ron Collins; his task was to carry buckets of plaster from the front of the worksite and climb into the roof with them. What a shock for the pale, slight English youth who'd dreamed of the glorious warmth of the Australian summer! The heat inside the roofs was unbearably searing and stifling. The job was tough physical labour, extremely hot and rough.

The casual way of life on a building site also came as a shock for innocent and gullible John. He was constantly teased by Collins, who couldn't resist it when the youngster easily fell for such jokes as being sent to the deli 'for a bottle of milk and a jock strap' and when he couldn't understand how everyone's girlfriend was named Sheila. He was also the butt of jokes for being so skinny and for having difficulty with the heavy loads of plaster.

'Come on, get yourself in overdrive,' Collins would keep urging. But he really did think John was too small for the job and he'd take pity on him, helping him when he could see John losing his struggle with the weight. 'You're only a little skinny bugger, so when I say lift, you lift.' John still couldn't manage it and it cost Collins a back injury when he was trying to help John lift large sheets of plasterboard at the Kwinana Refinery mess room.

Despite the teasing, Collins liked John. He lived in Innaloo, too, and gave him lifts home, and decided to take the kid under his wing – toughen him up, teach him the Australian way of life. He included him in his weekend and holiday activities, taking him fishing with his wife, June, and his parents, and teaching the English city boy what to do. Collins also took John out to teach him the best Australian pastime, roo shooting. Roo shooting was a serious hobby for Collins. It wasn't just the fun of the chase through the bush, but it provided meat for the family. He had butcher's equipment at home and took the hindquarters for roasts and the tail and off-cut for his mother's special brawn. At weekends, Collins would collect John and head for the bush north of the city. Three miles past Yanchep Inn there was a white limestone track leading to Lancelin. They'd get into the open country along that track.

John was upset when he saw the first kangaroo die from Collins' shot. The big proud creature slowly sank, trying to keep its head up as its blood seeped into the sand. Eventually it gave in to the inevitable, laying its head down and half-closing its eyes. John would never forget the terrible sight. But he still went along each weekend. At fifteen, he felt grown up and Australian, heading out into the bush like that. He was too soft-hearted to shoot, however, and couldn't bear to see little joeys orphaned by his friend's handiwork. He'd jump off the ute and collect them, holding them close and trying to keep them alive. Collins couldn't believe it. He'd have just cut their throats, but John wouldn't let him, taking them home and feeding them with an eye-dropper – even the ones with no hair, which Collins knew had absolutely no chance. John often stayed for dinner at the Collins' place, joining in the roo meals – pretending to like it. After all, you had to, that was what Australians ate.

With Margaret gone and father and son batching, there wasn't the need for the expense of renting a whole house. Charlie Button was trying to save enough to build a house for his wife's arrival, so he gave up the lease and went back to boarding. He and John moved into a boarding house in South Perth. They lived in a dormitory room of eight beds with an open wardrobe at the foot of each. It was hardly home but they were both working hard, and they only needed somewhere to sleep and have meals provided.

It also put them in mixed company, and John was growing up. He took a fancy to one of the girls staying there. He hadn't had anything to do with girls since Tessie on the ship. He'd had a letter from her in January, from an address in South Melbourne. He'd been thrilled to receive it in response to his, and he read it over and over: 'I will never forget you. I am always talking about you to my friends.' She signed it 'all my love' and added five kisses. He treasured the letter and kept it, but South Melbourne was a long way away.

Gillian was at the boarding house with her mother and brother after coming from England. John adored her and Gillian welcomed the attention, but her mother didn't. John's little adventures with Gillian got him into trouble. He was very unpopular with her mother when they cycled to the weir at the top of Kent Street, staying far too long. To make things worse, she fell off her bike on the way home, forcing them to walk much of the way back to Bowman Street with Gillian pushing the damaged bike. Gillian's mother didn't like John hanging around her daughter and complained to the landlady.

John was blissfully unaware of the complaint. He happily went on working and daydreaming of Gillian, looking forward to seeing her after work. One evening when she wasn't allowed out, he wandered along the foreshore alone. He was disappointed and lonely, his father away working in the country for a week. On the beach, among some rocks, he found a charity collection tin full of pennies. He'd never stolen anything before, but this was too tempting. And anyway, finders keepers. He emptied the tin, taking the pennies back to the boarding house and hiding them in his father's coat pocket. Wow, he'd be able to entice Gillian with some ice creams and lollies bought with this booty. He didn't have any spare cash to treat her, because he'd recently lent all his savings, £10, to the landlady to help her pay her account at the Mends Street grocer's shop. But before John could splash around his new wealth, the landlady's daughter complained about hitting her head on the heavy pocket while she cleaned under the clothes rail. Next thing he knew, the pennies had gone. John's theft got him nowhere – he couldn't complain to his father about his money disappearing because he'd have to own up to taking it first.

Gillian's mother's complaints resulted in the landlady threatening his father that she'd call the police. Charlie solved the problem by leaving the boarding house. John was certain the landlady's reaction was an excuse to get rid of them to avoid repaying the £10. Margaret, still playing mother and feeling for John's gullibility, argued with the landlady over the money, but unsuccessfully. John lost his savings.

On the advice of his doctor, Margaret took John to see a psychiatrist at Havelock Outpatient Clinic to have the matter sorted out. She didn't tell him where or why he was going there, and John did as he was told. He went in and looked at ink blobs. After a while the psychiatrist asked him if he had any idea of why he was there. He didn't, but when pushed, said he guessed it must be because of his homesickness and because he missed his mother.

John and Charlie moved in with Charlie's partner in an old house in Loftus Street, Nedlands.

John was suffering more and more on the job as summer wore on with its hundred-degree heat. The final decision that this wasn't going to be his career came when he was working on Belmont High School in Alexander Road. The floor joists were down but not the floorboards, involving a balancing act along the joists with his heavy load. Every day he'd fall and skin his knees. He was tired of the heat and tired of getting hurt. He was cycling home from that job one night, pushing across Garratt Road bridge, then rolling very fast downhill along Garratt Road towards the railway line. The light generator on the front wheel loosened and swung into the spokes. John flew over the handlebars. His knees, already skinned from work, lost more skin. It was a long walk home for John, bruised, grazed and sore all over. When he finally got home, he talked to his father about getting a new job.

Charlie Button decided then that if ceiling fixing wasn't going to be his trade, John had better work with him and get into bricklaying. He was a solid man who wanted to help his son, despite the two not being close. The age gap was too big and the strong, nutty bricklayer didn't really understand his slight, timid son. He was very busy with his hobby, too, the 60-year-old small-time gambler spending his spare time following the race forms for his TAB bets. However, his father's effort to get John into his own trade didn't work. The union wouldn't allow an informal arrangement between father and son – either he was a labourer, requiring full union wages, or he was an apprentice bricklayer and should be signed up. Charlie couldn't afford a full-pay labourer and his partner didn't want a formal apprentice, so John went to the Government's employment agency to look for work.

John's third job was at S. Boulden & Sons, a lawn-mowing contractor based in Stirling Road, Claremont. He loved the outdoor work, spending the days out and about the nearby suburbs on the lawn-mowing rounds and other odd jobs.

Knowing John's background, Len Boulden gave him a bricklaying job – John's first experience of his father's trade. Len, one of the two Boulden sons, was having a front path made at his home in Grange Street, Claremont. He sent John to his home to labour for the tradesman. John was proud of helping create the neat herringbone path up to the frangipanis by the front veranda, and wondered if one day he might follow in his father's footsteps after all.

Meanwhile, John thrived in the freedom of his work for Bouldens, particularly when it came to mowing big areas like the hockey fields near the Perth Chest Hospital. He loved spending all day on the back of the lawn mower and having a bit of a snooze at lunchtime. It was varied, too, his duties as junior including cleaning the offices and sharpening the mowers' blades in the workshop.

The firm also won the contract to plant lawn on the new land reclaimed from the river for the interchange roads around the new Narrows Bridge and Freeway. Its opening in November 1959 gave Perth people another city river crossing, enabling them to cross to South Perth at Narrows Point west of the city, in addition to the original Causeway crossing to the east. John was one of the small team collecting couch runners from Swanbourne, planting them and driving a tractor over acres and acres of land to push them in.

He wanted nothing more than to work outside for the rest of his life. But, having matured a bit, he realised he needed some more schooling. After six months, he went to night school and studied English and maths in an effort to improve himself.

Like Father, Like Son

8 August 1959

Alix Doncon was also studying hard. The seventeen-year-old was in her first year of nursing at RPH, after finishing school at Perth College. Life was busy for a student nurse – days were spent making beds, emptying bed pans and learning nursing skills; nights were spent studying the theory for exams.

Alix was taking some time off from her study this weekend. Two friends from home in Beverley were coming to Perth and she was looking forward to spending some time with them. She was also having a break from the RPH nurses' quarters, staying at her elder sister Jan's flat in Nedlands for the weekend while her elder sister went to Beverley. It gave her more freedom to spend the afternoon with her younger sister Kerry, who had a boarder's day leave from Perth College, and to enjoy the company of her friends in the evening.

Hedley Giles's utility went through the gate of Blackburn Farm early Saturday afternoon. The twenty-year-old farmer from Balkuling, twelve miles east, was stopping to pick up his mate George Draper for their weekend in the city. The Draper family's farm was twelve miles out of Beverley in the Wheatbelt, and the two had just over a one-and-a-half-hour drive to Perth. They wanted to arrive in good time to settle in at Hedley's sister's place in Mundaring before going to Nedlands to see Alix.

The two young farmers enjoyed the social life of the city whenever possible, but seventeen-year-old George was especially keen to see Alix. George and Alix had known each other a long time through Junior Farmers and other local associations and were close friends, although Alix had gone to the city for her schooling.

They arrived at the Nedlands flat at 5.15 p.m., chatting to Alix and Kerry for about half an hour before Kerry went back to boarding school. Then the trio set off for the Metro Drive-in, buying tea at the snack bar before watching *The Naked and the Dead* from the front seat of the ute. After the movie, they went to a coffee lounge in the city, then back to Alix's sister's flat. They had more coffee and listened to records until the boys left at 12.45 a.m., Alix waving goodbye from the top of the front stairs as it started to sprinkle with rain.

Cooke was prowling in Nedlands, the area he knew his way around from his earlier association with the Nedlands Methodist Church and its youth group. If only they could see him six years later – the deprived youth was now a successful family man, married with five children and another on the way. On top of that, he wasn't just a petty thief any more, he was far more powerful. He had the ultimate power over life and death. He could kill.

Nedlands was a wealthy suburb, with fine houses for good pickings and flats, especially around the university, with young single women to watch through windows. He regularly had luck as a peeping Tom in nearby Kings Park, too. Another place popular with local couples was the dark dead-end Government Road at the back of Karrakatta Cemetery.

Alix Ellyn Doncon was on her own in the flat. The upstairs flat, No. 3, was at the front of the eight-unit redbrick block called Bellaranga Flats at 93 Stirling Highway. It was a convenient location, near the university where Jan studied, on a main highway between Perth and Fremantle and diagonally opposite the popular Windsor Picture Theatre and Captain Stirling Hotel. Alix was pleased to have some space to herself after the cramped nurses' quarters. She silently thanked Jan – Jo to her – for the luxury while she prepared for bed.

She made sure all the doors were locked, securing everything except a long narrow window at the back. This window, in the corner of the wall leading from the back landing into the kitchen, was four-foot high and just fourteen inches wide, so narrow and awkward in the corner that she didn't think anything of leaving it very slightly ajar. She went to bed, sitting up for a while to start a letter, before pulling the blankets to her chin and falling asleep.

The climb up the stairs at the back of the block was worth it. After checking around the ground floor units of Bellaranga Flats, testing for an unlocked door or window, Cooke stealthily climbed the stairs leading to the back of two of the upstairs units. At the top, the door and windows to No. 4 were all locked. But he found an easy entry into No. 3 – easy for a lithe cat burglar, anyway. Gloves on, handkerchief over his face to hide his mouth, he got inside. He turned on his torch and looked around, finding his way to a bedroom. There was nobody in the room, so he relaxed a little as he searched for money. Finding none, he turned to the next bedroom. There was a woman asleep. He shone his torch around carefully and spotted a handbag on the floor next to the dressing table. Carefully picking it up, he took it into the kitchen and looked through it. He found £6.

Pocketing that money, he wondered if there might be some valuables on a table by the bed. He returned to the bedroom where the woman was sleeping, all alone; he could take what he wanted. The woman half-awoke and started to sit up. He hit her over the head. One blow was enough, this one didn't fight back.

He easily made his escape out the back.

When Alix opened the door to the boys next morning, they were shocked to see the state she was in. She wasn't dressed and her face and hair were covered with blood. There was a deep gash above her left eye. She had obviously been wandering around in a daze all morning, not knowing anything was wrong until they told her to look in a mirror.

They were horrified. George and Hedley quickly checked the

flat and found her pillow covered with blood. All she remembered was waking up about 3.30 a.m. and falling asleep again. Alix joined the search and discovered her purse was missing, but was confused when asked where she left it. But despite a terrible headache, she could remember exactly that there was £6 in it – a £5 note and two ten-shilling notes.

They checked the flat to see how someone could have got in, but couldn't find any sign of a forced entry. That made them wonder if Alix's assailant had been hiding in the roof of the building while they had been there. Alix rang Kerry at Perth College to ask whether she'd taken her purse. When she explained what had happened, Kerry immediately arranged leave to help her sister.

By time she got there, Alix had already gone, admitted to St John of God Hospital in Subiaco by her GP, Dr Illingworth. As well as the eye injury, she had a fractured skull. The small crack at the back of her head and the cut forehead indicated she had been hit at least twice. The doctor notified the CIB.

Police scoured the unit. The victim's uncle was a Special Inspector in the CIB, Cec Lamb, and the detectives worked hard, but found no trace of any weapon that could have inflicted the wound and no fingerprints. Detective Sergeant John O'Halloran noted there was no obvious point of entry other than through the very small back window, found ajar. They interviewed Hedley Giles and Alfred George Draper and before ruling them out as suspects, checked with Hedley's sister that they had arrived back at Mundaring at the time they said.

Headline news next day of the Queen's third pregnancy was lost on Alix. She was semiconscious and confused, and was to remain in hospital for six weeks. The only knowledge she had of the trauma was what the police told her, that a fire poker was missing and that it was most likely to have been used to inflict her injury.

The blow to her head caused a severe form of epilepsy. Medication would control it to some extent but it was incurable and she would be affected for the rest of her life. Study was out of the question; her ambition to be a nurse unachievable.

When she was able to leave hospital on 14 September, Alix

returned to her parents in Beverley to start the slow road to recovery and try to make some sense of it all.

While Alix Doncon was recovering from Cooke's attack, Cooke's mother was also recovering from a brutal attack. Her husband had tried to kill her.

Vivian Cooke's violence erupted on 30 May. One of the many ribs he smashed pierced her lung, nearly killing her. She was on the danger list in hospital for a while and a detective stayed with her for protection.

Detectives Jack Deering and Peter Johnson charged her husband with causing grievous bodily harm and assault. But the terrified woman was too much in fear of his retribution and refused to press charges. Without her evidence, the police had to withdraw the charge of grievous bodily harm. On 19 June 1959 Vivian Thomas Cooke was given a two-year suspended sentence on a £50 bond.

The Marker Boy

1959–60

John found another advantage of working for Bouldens – the opportunity of going to the northern wheatbelt on a crop-dusting team. Len Boulden helped his brother Bill twice a year by lending two of his young employees and a truck driver to his business, Air Culture.

John first went for seeding, thrilled at the chance to get out into the country for the first time, living in a caravan and feeling a part of an important team of men. This was the real Australia, and he loved it. His official role was to fill the hopper with the superphosphate and help load it into the plane. In practice, it also involved pitching in wherever he was needed.

That was a short taste of the life he'd lead later in the year when he joined Captain Bill for three months as a marker boy. He readily agreed when Len Boulden asked him to go. John didn't know the hazards of standing in a paddock to mark the line of flight for the low-flying crop-dusting plane, nor the possibility of long-term effect from the pesticides, but it wouldn't have put him off even if he had – here was three months of something different in the country. But best of all was the halfpenny bonus per acre. With 30,000 acres to be covered, he would double his normal wages.

So John jumped on Bert Messenger's truck for Northampton, becoming the temporary employee of Air Culture in one of Captain Bill's two teams, each consisting of a pilot, truck driver and two marker boys.

John spent the days walking across paddocks opposite another youth, marking out 27 paces between each of the plane's passes and holding a post with a flag for the pilot to see his line of flight. It took the rule-abiding John quite a while to discover that generally marker boys didn't bother counting out the paces, merely walking as far as they could before the plane passed again.

The lower the pass, the better the spread of pesticide over the crop, since less would be blown away. So the pilot would aim at flying so low that the wheels would just skim the ground, then lifting slightly to rise over the boys showing him the way. The boys were easy to see over the six-inch crops, but some paddocks had crops three feet high – in those, only the red flag indicated where the boys were. Even while lying flat on the ground to avoid the plane's wheels, the marker boys risked being hit.

John's day started well before sunrise. The marker boys' first duty was to boil two kettles – the first for the pilot's wash, the second for cups of tea. Then they made breakfast for the four-man team, each morning opening two tins of braised steak and onions to heat and put on toast. After breakfast, the boys washed up and packed the caravan, ready to move on overnight. Then it was out to the paddocks in the dark so that the pilot, already waiting in the plane, could start at first light. They took only a short break for their lunch sandwiches. Time was money for the team; the boys were eager to earn their halfpenny an acre bonus, the truck driver his penny an acre and the pilot his sixpence an acre. After working till last light and moving on to the next farm, the marker boys made dinner with farmer-supplied meat, listened to the New Zealand pilot's odes about crop-dusting and turned in early.

Once the truck driver and pilot had to return to Perth for a few days, leaving the marker boys alone. They treated themselves to the first proper meal they'd had in the time away – a sumptuous roast with all the trimmings. They were just about to sit at the table they had set up outside the caravan when the farmer arrived at the nearby shed to butcher some sheep. John couldn't touch the roast lamb he'd so looked forward to. After three months in the bush, he liked to think of himself as a tough Australian bloke. But he still wasn't tough enough for shooting roos or knifing sheep.

John went north on the crop-dusting team for a second time in 1960. While he tired of working such long hours and being confined with three other men in a small caravan, the wages were an incentive. So he was back on Captain Bill's team, even though he wasn't quite as keen as he had been the previous year. He was a little wiser about the danger and the other disadvantages.

He was looking forward to the arrival of his mother and Jimmy. It was two years since he'd seen his mother and being on the team meant he missed his long-awaited reunion with her when she disembarked at Fremantle with his thirteen-year-old brother, Jimmy. His elder brother, nineteen-year-old Peter, had decided against emigrating. He was already becoming quite established as a quantity surveyor in London.

When John returned from crop-dusting that year, it was to a new address. His father had bought 8 Redfern Street, Subiaco, as a family home. Too busy building other people's homes, he'd never fulfilled his intention of buying a block and building his own. But this three-bedroom brick home close to the city and not far from the beach was quite suitable.

Margaret moved into the home in Subiaco, too. Having been without his father from the ages of ten to fourteen and without his mother from fourteen to sixteen, John now had a real home and family again.

The Brookwood Flats Prowler

19 December 1959

Cooke left home, all dressed up again for his time out on the town. After his socialising, he donned hat and gloves as usual, and started to prowl, perve and steal, looking in on the world that didn't want him, watching them when they thought they were alone, taking their money and possessions. He thrilled to it all: the excitement of the things he saw as a peeping Tom; the satisfaction of invading their fancy homes and leading the good life on their money. The night side of Cooke had much more fun than the day one, the hard-working, polite and responsible family man with five small children and another on the way.

He had to be more careful in the wealthier suburbs now, since the arrival of television in October. While crowds of less well-off people were taking deckchairs and thermos flasks to the city to watch the sets in Boans shop windows, those who could afford their own televisions were staying at home at night. It was riskier sneaking through houses while the occupants were watching television, but that made his success all the more rewarding. They thought they were clever, but he had it all over them.

He cased houses in lots of suburbs, but the wealthier areas were his favourites. Peppermint Grove, the wealthiest of them all, was one of his haunts. And the area around Brookwood Flats on Stirling Highway, Cottesloe, just up from Peppermint Grove, had recently become a regular target.

Jillian McPherson Brewer lived in Brookwood Flats, at 396 Stirling Highway, Cottesloe. The glamorous socialite and heiress to the MacRobertson confectionery fortune had been in Perth for fifteen months. After leaving St Margaret's College (the Anglican private school) in Berwick, she studied interior design, then had moved west from Melbourne. She moved into No. 18, the most northern ground-floor flat in the back row of the block, next door to her mother, Mrs Betty Johnston. Jillian's arrival in Perth attracted an article in the social pages of *The West Australian* headed 'Interior Designer Will Settle Here'. It continued:

> Miss Brewer, who worked with a leading firm of Melbourne architects, has designed interior furnishing for a bank, insurance building and offices and supervised renovations of many Melbourne homes. Always interested in art, Miss Brewer originally intended to be an architect, but thought that interior design was a more suitable occupation for a woman.

Accompanying the article was a head-and-shoulders portrait of the sophisticated 21-year-old. The item appeared in the morning newspaper on the day that Cooke first gave vent to his rage and bitterness by running Nel Schneider down, on 12 September 1958.

In December 1959 Jillian Brewer was 22, happily settled in Perth and engaged to be married in February. She had a good social life and the company of a silver-grey French poodle, Dior, which her fiance had bought her from the Nedlands kennels of actor Neville Teede and Keir Matheson.

Cooke had been prowling around Brookwood Flats on a number of consecutive weekends in the latter part of 1959.

Earlier in the year, too. On 27 June he'd stolen a car from the garage at the back of the flats and driven it towards home until it ran out of petrol on the border of Maylands and Bayswater. Holden UEY 743 was found by police parked outside 10 Goldmead Street.

In October he had some success at the white house opposite Brookwood Flats, on the corner of Stirling Highway and Wilson

Street. He got in through the pantry window, and sneaked through the house, finding a handbag in the bedroom. He took a couple of pounds and the house key, but didn't bother with the pass to the trots. He left the house at 398 Stirling Highway undisturbed, and Mr and Mrs Reginald Summerhayes did not know anyone had been inside their home.

He moved around nearby houses. He went to a corner house, one with a Jaguar and golf clubs in the garage. It was 4 Renown Avenue, where he checked the windows as he had a few times before. Maybe one day he'd get a more exciting look at the young woman who slept in a bedroom on the southwest corner.

He crossed the road to Brookwood Flats, his gloved hands testing doors and windows. It was dark, about midnight, and there was nobody about. At No. 16 he was in luck. Inside Jillian Brewer's mother's flat, he turned on his torch and rummaged through the bedroom and the second bedroom, which was used as a dressing room. There he found a handbag, and he took its contents of a £1 note and some change, and a key with a leather tag on which the owner's name and address was written – B. Johnston, 396 Stirling Highway, Cottesloe. In the lounge room, he tested the key to find it opened the front door, at the same time noticing a brass coal scuttle, tongs and poker.

He sneaked around to the back of the flats, where there was an air-conditioner behind No. 14. He hid Mrs Johnston's key and another behind the air-conditioner. He hadn't found much money this time, but it would be easy to get in again and he might do better next time. He could get into that flat once or twice more over the next few days before she changed the locks. It didn't bother the bold burglar if she was home asleep.

He knew the flat next door. He noticed lights on once, and when he slammed the door shut behind him after one burglary, upset at finding nothing worthwhile, a dog started barking there.

One night, when he was casing Brookwood Flats, Cooke wandered up the side street a short way. He crept around the back at 12 Wilson Street, looking for an entry. It was easy. He got in through French windows. He didn't know the house belonged to Miss Flora Bunning, but he did know that the occupant belonged to a music society and had a Morris Minor car. He found 10 shillings, and moved on.

He went back to that house about a fortnight later, after prowling around Cliff Way, the small, exclusive street on the cliff next to Methodist Ladies' College. This time he couldn't get into the music lady's house, so he climbed over the side fence into the backyard of the two-storey house next door, adjacent to Brookwood Flats. As he climbed over, he could see lights on in the end flat, No. 18. He went over to the adjoining fence and stood on the lower beam, watching. He could see into the flat through the kitchen window at the back. But it was the people inside he was most interested in. He stood there watching Jillian Brewer's party, a group of beautiful people, enjoying themselves. He recognised one of the partygoers from his hockey days when he played for Old Wesley. It was John Doscos, the goalie for Old Scotch. While Cooke was watching, he saw the lady he'd stolen from next door. Mrs Johnston moved between the back doors of both flats several times.

After watching for a while longer, he left to steal cars and gradually made his way towards the city and home.

Jillian Brewer spent Saturday, 19 December 1959, with her fiance, returning to her flat at 9 p.m. They spent the rest of the evening there, apart from five minutes when they went next door to her mother's. At 11.30 p.m. the couple made love. Her fiance went home about midnight, leaving Jillian in bed, sleeping naked.

The lovers hadn't been alone. A peeping Tom was watching from a gap in the curtains.

Cooke had gone out for the night, looking dapper in his best light green slacks and jacket. He went to the Mayfair Theatrette in central Perth and then headed out to prowl around Peppermint Grove and Cottesloe, the area that included Brookwood Flats. He spent three hours doing what he liked. Then he caught a bus on Stirling Highway to move nearer the city. He recognised the driver as Bob, who used to live next door to his friend Ronald Johnston in Fourth Avenue, Kensington.

Alan Robert Balmer, who had previously lived at 34 Fourth Avenue, had driven the Perth–Fremantle route for fourteen years, and that night his shift was from 5.04 p.m. to 8.39 p.m. and from 10 p.m. to 1.35 a.m.

Cooke left the bus in Nedlands to walk along Louise Street into Adelma Road, another favourite area. He had a particular interest in a house on the corner of Adelma and Beatrice roads. The lights were on in the bedroom. He crept to the front veranda to watch, excited by what he hoped to see. But a young man walking along Adelma Road saw him and shouted. He jumped off the veranda and ran to the side of No. 94 Adelma Road, where four pickets were missing from the fence. He prowled there successfully, this time without being seen and reported to the police.

Checking around the houses along Adelma Road towards Stirling Highway, he turned into Gallop Road and then into Sutcliffe Street. There was a cream Holden at No. 30. He pushed it on to the road, down a slight hill, and started it. He had his transport to move around the suburbs and get home.

After using the car for the rest of the night, he drove it close to home and abandoned it in Alexander Road, Rivervale. Wilfred John Leader's Holden UDC 177 was found there by the police the next day.

Cooke walked the last quarter-mile, arriving home about 5.15 a.m.

In the middle of the night, while Jillian Brewer was asleep, the peeping Tom silently crept into the flat. He was after the sexy lady. But it wasn't just sex on his mind. It was murder.

Before breaking in through the back door, he'd gone to a garage a few houses away at 4 Renown Avenue, Simon Watson's open garage, containing a hatchet, Jag and golf clubs. The peeping Tom took the hatchet.

The intruder made sure he left no fingerprints as he stealthily moved into Brewer's bedroom. He didn't want to be identified. She was asleep. He raised the hatchet and brought it down with all his strength. The dog woke up and started barking. He managed to quieten it. He raised the hatchet again and chopped into Brewer ferociously, twelve to thirteen times. He hacked into her breasts, her genitals and her head, fracturing her skull and her pubic bone. He hit her with the flat side of the hatchet on the stomach, her thighs, her breasts, her face and across the throat, hard enough to sever her windpipe. The force of his frenzied blows split the wooden handle of the hatchet near the axe head. He took a bit of a break then, confident he hadn't been seen or heard, came back with another weapon, her own scissors. He stabbed her five more times, twice in the breast area and twice in the abdomen, driving the scissors right through her stomach and another time into her liver. And once more, very hard and deep, in the left buttock.

He was exhausted. She was on her back. He pulled a sheet up to her chin, hiding most of the wounds but not the blood on her face or that spattered on the wall at the head of the bed. He put a pillow across her chest and folded the sheet back over it. He placed her left arm on the pillow. Yes, he was happy with the scene. He wiped the outside of the scissors and put them back where he got them from. He left the flat, throwing the hatchet over the back fence.

Jillian Brewer's fiance returned at 9 a.m. the next day to spend Sunday playing golf with her. The front door, normally open, was locked, and Dior was jumping up and down at the bedroom window. A knock on the window and call brought no response, so he got his key from the car and went in.

The bedroom door was shut, the first time he had seen it closed. He opened it to the horrific scene and ran to her mother's flat and called the local doctor. Dr Rockett took a quick look and called the police.

The police found the hatchet on the other side of the flats' northern fence. A thorough search of the flat and the area provided no clues to the identity of the killer or the means of entry to the flat. Both the front and the back doors were locked and there were no fingerprints.

None of the neighbours could help, except for one, who heard a dog bark a few times about 1 a.m. before suddenly stopping mid-bark. There was little to go on. Everyone seen around the flats was questioned, but inquiries went nowhere.

Police started to question anyone picked up for other crimes, such as prowling and loitering. A man had been picked up for loitering outside Miss Brewer's flat about four months previously, but his alibi was watertight – he had been in Melbourne the night Brewer was killed. They questioned the young man who mowed the lawns around the flats, but quickly crossed John Button off the list of possibles.

They had no leads. How did the killer get in? How were there no fingerprints?

Two brutal murders of sleeping women in eleven months – the headline news shocked the people of Perth. Two women stabbed in their beds. It also titillated them. Women sleeping naked! And beautiful unmarried women entertaining gentlemen!

When Jillian Brewer's body arrived in the mortuary for the postmortem examination, the similarities to the January murder were noticed by mortuary staff. Colin Raven was a mortuary orderly who'd attended the autopsy on Pnena Berkman's body with the stab wound to the nose and the punctured aorta. He believed both murders had been committed by the same person. One murder in South Perth, the other in Cottesloe, eleven months later.

Sally Cooke was as horrified as anyone. She was reading about the murder in Monday morning's newspaper. Her husband snatched the paper from her hands, telling her she shouldn't read about it. He then asked his pregnant wife to provide an alibi for him, saying that with his record, the police might try to pin it on him. He asked her to say he was home early if anyone came checking.

Five weeks later, on 25 January, Cooke was arrested for loitering. He was discovered by Senior Detective Maurice O'Halloran and Detective Brian Bull in Lathlain Park. He'd cleverly worked out a long time before, that by quickly getting rid of anything incriminating if caught, he could avoid a breaking and entering charge – the worst they could get him for was loitering with the intent to commit a crime. The loitering charge brought a month's prison sentence.

In Fremantle Prison he was questioned about Jillian Brewer. Cookie, as everyone, including the police, nicknamed him, was an obvious one to question. He was known to the police as a sexo, and particularly as a snowdropper – someone who stole women's panties and often masturbated over them.

Cooke denied having anything to do with Brewer's murder and Sally was not questioned. He was released a week before his daughter was born.

Despite thorough inquiries by the police, the murders of Pnena Berkman and Jillian Brewer remained unsolved. More than a year later, a prowler and petty thief was questioned over the Brewer murder when he was taken in for other crimes.

On 7 April 1961 Darryl Raymond Beamish was charged with crimes of a minor sexual nature against young girls. Over a period of six months, he had taken four and five-year-old girls to a secluded spot and felt them up. He was sentenced to seven months' jail.

The nineteen-year-old metal worker from Swanbourne was a deaf-mute, the result of cerebral meningitis as a baby. Stone deaf, he communicated through sign language. Beamish had been in minor trouble before for defacing a large sheet of plate glass with a glass cutter with another juvenile, and for stealing money from a car. At nineteen, he had been before the Police Court for stealing from shops, houses and offices in the Perth area after breaking in through insecure doors and windows, removing fly screens and, once, by using a key, as well as for stealing money from gas meters with another youth.

Beamish was questioned on 7 April while awaiting sentence for his convictions on the charges involving the young girls. Detective Sergeant Owen Leitch and Detective Jack Deering questioned him through a sign-language interpreter who taught at the Deaf School. Without his parents or a lawyer present, he confessed to killing Jillian Brewer through the interpreter that day. He also confessed in a written form the next day and again through the interpreter in prison on 12 June. Words scratched with a piece of plaster on the bitumen floor of the Perth lock-up's exercise yard on 8 April were also taken as a confession, though not photographed until three days later when some of it was obliterated and though Beamish claimed it was in answer to another prisoner asking him why he was there.

Two months later, on 16 June 1961, Beamish was charged with the wilful murder of Jillian Brewer. Beamish pleaded not guilty and was tried before the 62-year-old Chief Justice, Sir Albert Wolff, who had risen through the prosecution ranks. The trial started on 7 August 1961 and lasted six days.

Beamish's defence was that the confessions were untrue and obtained by the police under threats and intimidation; many of the answers given as a result of suggestions either by the interpreter or by the police officers. The jury found Beamish guilty, but strongly recommended mercy. On being told of the verdict, he wept and said 'not guilty'. On 15 August Sir Albert Wolff put the black cloth on his head and sentenced Darryl Beamish to death.

An appeal against his conviction was rejected by the Court of Criminal Appeal, presided over by Justices Jackson, Virtue and D'Arcy. An application for leave to appeal to the High Court was refused. The young deaf-mute was transported to Fremantle Prison, where he lived an isolated existence in the condemned cell on Death Row. He didn't understand why he was there or why he couldn't go to work and to exercise with the other prisoners. Forty minutes after being placed in the condemned cell, he asked what work he would be doing the next day.

Waking early next day, he wrote 'I worried my Mum and Dad' and 'what for here'. Not realising what the condemned cell meant, an hour later he asked 'how many weeks I stay here?' A little later he asked what the observing warder was writing and told the warder he was not guilty and that Mr Leitch had teased him and fought with him. Still not realising he was to die, he told the observing officer: 'I will have marry with Kay five months – nice girl – she is 22'.

Beamish's conviction and sentence was very controversial. Despite general readiness to carry out capital punishment and the brutality of Brewer's murder, Beamish's death sentence was commuted to life imprisonment with hard labour four months later. At 3 p.m. on 13 December 1961, he was transferred from the condemned cell to live the rest of his life incarcerated in Main Division.

Cooke showed much interest in Beamish's trial.

Sally's stepfather, Thomas Dalziel Moffatt, was still living with them. When he was discussing the case one day, Moffatt said he didn't believe Beamish had done it. Sally told her stepfather that the police didn't make mistakes. Cooke said that he didn't believe Beamish had done it, either. Cooke again commented on the case when the death sentence was announced, telling his wife that he didn't think Beamish would hang.

The Other Side of Mr Nice Guy

9 April 1960

Glenys Peak started to run, worried that she'd miss the train. The twenty-year-old needed to catch the 8.15 from Bayswater to meet her workmates at Perth station for their night of dancing at Canterbury Court Ballroom. The station was a mile from her home and she knew there was no chance of a lift this time.

She was sometimes lucky of a morning, getting a ride from the nice truck driver who worked around the corner at Krasnostein's. Each weekday, Glenys met two other girls who lived nearby and the three walked to the station together, where she caught the train into the city to work in the advertising department of Sandovers. If it was raining or they were running when the friendly truckie passed them, he would stop and give them a lift. Glenys liked him. Such a kind man, driving two of his workmates to the job every day and helping her and her friends whenever he saw the need. He would even take them on to the next station, Meltham, if it looked like they'd still miss the train at Bayswater. He was very polite and friendly, and Glenys liked the way he talked so often of his family, showing particular concern for the future of his mentally retarded son. She could understand him perfectly, even though he mumbled a bit because of a hare lip.

Krasnostein's truckie did work on a Saturday night, but not for the metal and hardware merchants. He did happen to drive to the yard this Saturday night. It wasn't in time to give Glenys a lift to the train, but much later, around midnight, when he had that urge to hurt and maim.

Glenys lived at 2 John Street, 100 yards from the entrance to J. Krasnostein & Co. Pty Ltd. She lived with her aunt and uncle, Jenny and Joe McGhie, in a clutch of houses nestled between an industrial area and a dairy farm. It consisted of just a couple of roads, including John Street, which was a short dead-end gravel road with four houses on one side and the dairy farm on the other. Krasnostein's was around the corner, covering the whole block between Clavering Road and Munt Street, with a separate hardware department a little way up the next road, Irvine Street. A big timber yard took up most of Munt Street between John and Irvine streets. Around the few houses, warehouses and dairy farm was scrubby vacant land.

Houses were cheap enough in this backwater to enable Glenys's aunt and uncle to buy a place of their own after years of renting in Maylands. After emigrating from Scotland, Joe McGhie made a living as a tram driver while the couple raised six children – five of their own and their niece Glenys Peak.

Glenys, the youngest of the Peaks, had gone to St Joseph's orphanage when she was six. Her mother, once an astute businesswoman, had turned to drink, unable to cope with the tragic deaths of two of her children. John was one of the 645 who went down with the HMAS *Sydney* and Isabelle was killed in a car crash at the age of fourteen. Deep depression turned into alcoholism, making the marriage untenable for Glenys's father, Frank, who divorced Elizabeth. Elizabeth Peak ended up in Heathcote, the mental hospital being the only suitable accommodation for inveterate alcoholics, and young Glenys ended up in St Joseph's. Joe McGhie had insisted on taking in the eight-year-old Glenys despite his own large family, saying no niece of his was going to live in an orphanage.

Glenys thought of her foster parents as her real parents, easily calling them mum and dad, as well as aunt and uncle. Although she occasionally visited her real father until his death, she adored Joe McGhie and relied on the security of his wisdom and affection. She'd been easy to care for as a child, and had become independent as soon as possible, leaving school at fourteen to work in a shoe factory. Although grown-up and independent, she continued to be a part of the McGhie family. She shared a bedroom off the kitchen with one of the McGhies' married daughters, Janet, who still lived at home with her two small sons, her truck-driver husband being away most of the time.

The McGhies' eldest son, Joe, was still at home, and a boarder, Doug Wilson, shared the sleepout with Joe. Just around the corner in Munt Street was another of the McGhie daughters, Betty, who lived in a railway house with her husband Keith and three children. Glenys helped care for the grandchildren, as well as baby-sitting the neighbour's son. The close-knit group living opposite the dairy included an Italian family on one side of the McGhies and a Polish family on the other side, the corner with Munt Street. A huge storm-water drain ran along the opposite side of John Street, separating the houses from the cows that clinked their bells as they came in for milking.

Glenys managed to run fast enough, reaching Bayswater station in time to catch the train. At Perth station she found Margaret and Beryl, who had come in on the Armadale line, and the three walked to the ballroom two blocks up Beaufort Street. The round-faced, hazel-eyed beauty, wearing her favourite black-and-white spotted dress, was asked for lots of dances. She loved dancing and used to go regularly, but hadn't gone out much over the past eight months, since the McGhies bought a television set. She was enjoying her rare outing, too busy dancing to worry about one of her earrings breaking. She just put it in her handbag and left the other one on, guessing that no-one would notice under her shoulder-length hair.

The evening was marred later, however, by an old boyfriend who had stood her up after they had been going out for a few months. Brian just hadn't turned up for the date they had arranged. Glenys was still annoyed with him, and became angry when she heard him bragging to his mates about it. She was so mad that she took the out-of-character step of slapping him across the face.

'I'll get you for that,' he retaliated.

Cooke's job with J. Krasnostein & Co. was delivering metal products around Perth and collecting scrap metal for the yard.

There were lots of times he didn't work because of injury or imprisonment. He had been home from his one month's imprisonment for loitering only a few weeks when on 15 March, he had a bad accident at work. He fell twelve feet, knocking himself unconscious and injuring his back, putting him off work again on workers' compensation.

Three weeks later Cooke was prowling again, stealthily going through houses in the South Perth–Como area, getting in through unlocked doors and windows, creeping around looking for money, transistor radios, jewellery and so on.

Glenys sat on the train home, pulling the fingers of her gloves and thinking about Brian. She was shaken by her spontaneous action at the dance, surprised at herself and belatedly aware that even though Brian wasn't tall, she being only five-foot two-inches and seven-and-a-half stone meant she would have been the loser if he'd hit her back.

She had left Canterbury Court at 11.20 p.m. in time to catch the 11.40 train, declining the offer of a lift home and walking to the station with her friends who then left her to go to their platform. She would have kept mulling over Brian as she walked home from Bayswater station if it hadn't been for meeting two people she knew as they left other carriages. She set out along Beechboro Road with seventeen-year-old Betty Palmer and nineteen-year-old Barry Power, forgetting Brian's insolence as the trio talked about their nights out.

About 11 p.m. Cooke found his transport for the rest of the night. He was at the intersection of Gardner and McDonald streets, Como, and there it was in the open garage of the corner house – an early model fawn-and-cream Holden sedan, unlocked, the keys in the ignition. The house was in darkness and nobody was about. Cooke pushed the Holden down the driveway and into the street, where he started it and drove around the suburbs, heading in the direction of Bayswater.

The trio walking home along Beechboro Road split up as the two young women reached their turn-offs. Betty turned left into

Foyle Road and the others turned right into Raleigh Road, walking up the hill. After they turned left and walked a little way along Clavering Road, they came to Glenys's turn-off into Irvine Street. Barry offered to accompany her the rest of the way but she declined – it wasn't far and it was a moonlit night. So Barry continued along Clavering Road and Glenys turned right into Irvine Street.

Cooke was in Bayswater, driving towards his workplace, when he saw a man and woman walking along Raleigh Road. Then the man and woman took off in different directions. This could be his chance. It was dark and isolated around these parts and he was anonymous in a stolen car. He turned into Irvine Street and went a little way, then did a U-turn and turned into Munt Street. There he did another U-turn to face Irvine Street. He stopped, turned off the engine and the headlights, and waited.

Glenys set off along dark Irvine Street, walking on the right-hand side of the road to face oncoming traffic as she'd been taught, even though there was unlikely to be any traffic in such an isolated area at this hour. She had only just left Barry when she saw the lights of a car come up behind her in Irvine Street. As it passed her, she noticed that it was an early model light-coloured Holden sedan and that the driver was a short man wearing something on his head, maybe a beanie. She wondered who would be in the area so late. She saw the car again further up, turning into Munt Street in the opposite direction to the way she would go. It disappeared into Munt Street and she continued walking up dark Irvine Street, crossing the storm-water drain.

When she reached Munt Street, she looked to the right and saw the car parked there, facing her, the driver at the wheel. She idly wondered why anyone would make a U-turn and stop there like that. She turned left off the bitumen of Irvine Street into the gravel of Munt Street, just one block from home. She heard the car start up again and the gears grate. It edged up to the intersection and turned left into Irvine Street again, returning the way it had come and away from her. The headlights shone straight at her before the car turned.

The short block of Munt Street up to John Street was quite dark, despite the moonlight, so she moved to the centre of the road and carefully avoided the potholes. It was absolutely quiet – apart from the Holden that had now gone, there were no cars or people about. She had walked about 100 yards when she heard a car further back. It came up and turned left into Munt Street behind her. She moved over to the right side of the road to let it pass, wondering who could be coming up her way where there were so few houses. The wondering turned to worry when she heard the car accelerating behind her. But she still thought she was safe walking on the opposite side of the road to that of the accelerating vehicle. Then worry turned to alarm as the engine started to roar. She turned around to look at the revving car, recognising it as the one that had passed previously – it must have done another U-turn further down in Irvine Street. As she looked, it started to veer to the wrong side of the road.

It was heading straight for her, the engine roaring. Glenys made a desperate attempt to leap out of its way, trying to get off the road, but she didn't have a chance. The car struck her from behind, hitting her left hip. She was thrown over the bonnet. The force of the impact ripped her coat, tore off her watch and a shoe and scattered the contents of her handbag. She was hurled into a pile of broken glass in the gravel on the edge of the road by the builder's yard.

Cooke noticed the stacked timber as he swerved to miss a tree after he'd hit his target. He drove on a little way and turned around to where he'd hit the girl to have a look. But when he got back to the scene, she wasn't there.

Blood pouring down her face, her eyes, nose and ears full of gravel and glass and in total shock, Glenys tried to gather her senses as she lay at the edge of the road. That man had deliberately run her down! He hadn't hit her full on only because of having to avoid that tree. She saw the car turn up John Street, and knowing her street was a short dead-end and he would be coming back again, she was gripped by fear. He would be back to finish her off. She was in such agony that she was certain her back was broken, but she had to escape. She was just opposite her sister Betty's house. There was refuge close at hand. She called to Betty for help, but her cries were too weak. She couldn't believe Betty and Keith didn't hear the thud when she was hit, but the house remained dark and quiet. She called again, as loudly as she could. Nothing. If she tried to crawl across the road to them, she would be an open target for that killer car.

There was only one alternative. Home was further away, but she could get to it through the timber yard, where she would be safe from the car. Her survival instincts and determination overcame the agony and she dragged herself up, scrambling over the gravel and sand to the yard. She stumbled over piles of timber and rubble, glad that it formed some sort of barrier if the man tried to chase her. On the other side, somehow, she found the missing couple of pickets in the fence leading to her backyard. How glad she was to know about it, the narrow hole in the fence that she used as a short-cut from the back of the house through to Munt Street. She crawled through them, her grazed skin stinging more as she brushed against the pickets. But it was worth it. She was in her own backyard. She was home! She dragged herself across the lawn to the back door. She pushed it open. She was on the doorstep to the kitchen, and there were her parents, playing cards with their friends. Safe.

'Dad, Dad,' she called, before collapsing in the doorway.

Cooke stopped at the corner of Munt and Irvine streets and walked back to the scene. He had lost his victim, but he was curious. It was dark and quiet – no-one in the houses around had been roused by the thud. He had time to look around and he found Glenys's purse and one of her shoes. He took the purse and went back to the car to make his escape. But the car wouldn't start, as if it had run out of petrol. So he left it where it was and ran off.

Clutching the purse, he ran along Irvine Street into Clavering Road, turning right and running over a footbridge and up a sand hill. Then he continued along Beechboro Road to a culvert. There, a safe distance from the scene and well hidden, he checked the handbag for money before throwing the evidence into the culvert. Theft hadn't been on his mind at all as he ran down the girl – what he'd wanted was to hurt and maim her. But he wasn't sure how he'd succeeded at that – not too well, if she'd walked away. The bit of money he gained instead was something, at least.

He walked home, heading to Rivervale over Garratt Road bridge. Just over the bridge, as he walked along Grandstand Road, the street lights went out.

Jenny and Joe McGhie were in the kitchen playing their regular Saturday night poker game with Jenny and Jack Brymer. They were astonished when Glenys collapsed in the doorway, bleeding and dirty, her lovely coat ripped, blood and gravel over her best dress. It was lucky they were home – it could have been their turn to play at the Brymers' place around the corner.

Jenny knew to insist no-one should touch Glenys, so her aunt took a blanket from the bed to cover her. She wanted to give Glenys some brandy to resuscitate her but again was warned by her friend. Glenys momentarily regained consciousness to hear Jenny Brymer's Scottish brogue: 'Nae, you cannae give her brandy.'

She was just able to say, 'I've been hit by a car and he's broken my back' before blacking out again.

Glenys was rushed to hospital in shock, cut and bruised and rambling about her broken back. A quick assessment showed her back wasn't broken and she wasn't critical, so she had a long painful wait before it was her turn for further attention. Along with the pain of the cuts and bruises, she was freezing. It was a cool night, and she was lying there under the sheet with only her underwear on. Her aunt was with her, the robust Scot pale with concern as she waited. Finally Glenys was seen and her wounds stitched, the gash in her face requiring twelve stitches and the deep cut on her leg taking four.

Sergeant Bob Kenward, who had taken the call, arrived at Casualty and tried to find out what had happened. But Glenys was dazed and shocked and not clear on the accident. She was particularly confused about whether she had been thrown over the bonnet or been spun around and fallen into the glass heap.

Constable Jackson from the Perth Traffic Office attended the scene, finding tracks where the vehicle had left the road. About twelve feet from the tracks he found a woman's wrist watch – silver, with a band of little hearts, matching Glenys's description. There was no sign of the white clutch bag she said she had lost.

One hundred yards away he saw an abandoned car, Holden UFN 592. The keys were in the ignition and a quick examination showed a dent on the bonnet on the right side and the right side mudguard forced back, with scratch markings on the side of the right front mudguard and damage to the rear vision mirror. It was taken for fingerprinting and photographing.

After her wounds were stitched and she had been sedated, Glenys was allowed home.

When Constables Jackson and Smith visited the next afternoon, Glenys told them that it was a deliberate hit–run. She insisted that the driver had deliberately veered to the wrong side of the road to hit her. She would not accept any other explanation nor any suggestion that it had been a case of mistaken identity. She was certain it must have been Brian, making good his threat after she'd slapped him at the dance.

Brian was quickly cleared. He had a watertight alibi and the damaged car found close to the scene was not his. Nor had it been reported stolen. It belonged to William Kevin Annandale, of 23 Narrung Way, Nollamara.

A check with Mr Annandale led police in another direction – he had sold the car six months earlier. It was now owned by Adelaide Car Sales in Adelaide Terrace. They advised that the £285 car was being used over the weekend by one of their car salesmen, Ian Olden Thatcher, of 109 Gardner Street, Como.

Thatcher had not realised that the car was missing when the police visited him on Sunday morning. He told them he'd returned from Gosnells at 6.30 p.m. on Saturday and put it in the garage, leaving the keys in the ignition and the garage door open. He had gone to bed at 9.30 and knew nothing more about it. The traffic police were not satisfied with the explanation and called for further assistance.

They were convinced the 37-year-old was telling the truth

only after further questioning, corroboration by his de facto wife and the discovery of erratic tyre markings on the driveway indicating that the car had been pushed and not driven from the garage to the road. Strange, though, no-one else's fingerprints were in the car.

The next day, police found a part of Glenys's broken earring that had been in her handbag. It was on the road near where the car had been left. But there was no sign of the white clutch bag – until a few days later. Some children found it in a storm-water drain in Beechboro Road and handed it to the Bayswater police.

Glenys's adamant insistence that she had been deliberately run down led to headlines in the press after journalists interviewed her. One paper ran the headline: 'Maniac Car Thief Sought – Hit Girl Claims Attack by Car'. Another: 'Hit–run Girl Victim's Story – Deliberate, She Insists'.

The family GP, Dr Scott from Maylands, continued to care for Glenys, sending her to St Anne's Hospital to clean gravel and glass out of her eye. But mostly she needed bed rest and reassurance that Brian wasn't going to try to get her again. She was terrified, needing the light left on all night and was afraid to go outside alone. Eventually, when the wounds had healed and she had regained a bit of confidence, she went back to work. But she was left with a lifelong indentation and scars on her face, and the continuing nightmare of a man coming to get her, sending her flying in the air and hitting a windscreen, cutting her face open on the windscreen wiper and thumping into the ground.

It was a long time before Glenys went dancing again.

Life's a Ball

1960–61

John Button went dancing a lot – three nights a week and on Saturday afternoons.

His life was turned around when he discovered the joys of the ballroom. Forget trying to cope with the aggressive toughies at Brixton schools and roughing it out in the bush with men in a caravan. This was the life – friendly and orderly, girls in pretty, crisp, full-skirted dresses in your arms, close enough to smell their perfume and touch their gossamered hair. The shy youth was entranced by their freshness and loveliness. As he learnt to dance and gained confidence in the steps, he became popular and gained confidence in himself.

It started when Margaret came home one evening with a girl-friend from the Young Women's Christian Association and a young man. Margaret decided John should come along. He couldn't bear the thought of that sissy stuff, but he obeyed anyway – John was always obliging and could never say no to anyone. They drove to the Alan Butcher Dance Studio in Hay Street and the girls went in. They didn't make him go in with them. John was relieved; he and Brian Green would be doing something else. But the relief was short-lived. Brian took him across the railway line to Canterbury Court Ballroom. John followed him in and sat there all night. He could do nothing but watch Brian dance with every girl. John was mesmerised. He had to learn to dance.

Margaret took his hand to guide him through the next stage of her plan for her shy little brother. She took him to the studio for one private lesson to get him started. John had rhythm and took to it easily, and didn't need any more encouragement to continue with the lessons. It wasn't long before he had passed the first exam and had a bronze medal.

Alan Butcher was impressed with John's manner and readily promoted him to amateur teacher. He regarded John as a thorough gentleman, a serious, respectful youth who easily fitted in with the standard of behaviour expected at the studio and the social graces of ballroom dance. Butcher's students had to dress well, speak politely and observe strict rules. Alcohol and swearing were banned. The boys had to ask the girls to dance in the correct manner, hold them in the proper ballroom hold and return them to their seat with a thank you. Boys who met the requirements in dance skill and were able to set an example in manners were given the role of amateur teachers. These chosen students had training Saturday afternoons and free entry to the social dances, in exchange for ensuring all girls had dances and helping the beginners.

John had found dancing and the social life that he enjoyed. Not for him the rock'n'roll of the bodiges and widgies at the Snakepit in Scarborough, but the graceful ballroom dancing with demure girls who dressed nicely and smelt lovely. He was soon appointed an amateur teacher, and the girls looked up to him. He gained another advantage, too, when he turned seventeen in February 1961. He got his driver's licence and a car, a Fiat tourer he bought for £50 from Ron Collins' brother-in-law. He could give the girls lifts home. He became popular – a polite, good dancer with a car.

John always went dancing with his friend, John Saunders, who was even more popular, being tall and good looking. The two often succeeded in taking girls home, sometimes gaining a quick goodnight kiss after they'd walked them to the door. They had a pact that if one of them talked a girl into accepting a lift in John's car, the other would have to take her friend. The girls flocked to the other John, often leaving John Button to take home the friend. But he always stuck to the deal. It was even to his advantage once, when his friend started going with Gwen Andrews. John was very happy with the arrangement because he was keen on Gwen's girlfriend Rhonda. They made a foursome and started expanding their social life beyond dancing to drive-ins and having a good time.

It was John's first experience of a girlfriend – and his first experience of breaking up. When Rhonda finished the relationship, the newly confident John took a bit of a battering. But another girl from dancing helped him get over it. Diane started out as his dance partner, but they ended up on kissing terms.

The ballroom soon gained another Button recruit. With Jimmy's school ball approaching, John took him along to learn a few steps. Jimmy was as captivated as John.

Jimmy had a natural talent and was selected for competition. He went on to become Junior State Champion.

The Button household was filled with the strains of waltzes, foxtrots and quicksteps as Jimmy and John practised their steps, arms in the air, smiles on their faces. They danced through the kitchen, the lounge room and over the back lawn, perfecting their steps – spin turns, stutter locks, feathersteps, promenade runs, fishtails, open telemarks, double reverse spins, curved threesteps. They truly loved it – the music, the grace, the social aspect. Life was a ball.

Black Friday

13 May 1960

David Priest wasn't much of a dancer, but he loved going to the Canterbury Court and Embassy ballrooms. He had discovered they were the best places to meet girls.

That's how he'd met Frances Ruane a few months previously. She was slim and dark, a ballet dancer with a ballerina-like beauty, and David was really taken with her. And tonight he had a rare opportunity – he had the flat to himself. His parents had gone out for the evening, as had his two older brothers, and there was still some time after their dinner date before his girlfriend had to be back at the nurses' quarters. She had agreed to come in for coffee.

He drew the curtains right back to make the most of the river view from the flat high on a hill in Como, and they settled on the lounge overlooking the twinkling lights of the Raffles Hotel and the South of Perth Yacht Club. He was anxious to make something of this relationship and get a little further than a kiss and cuddle. His family had approved of Frances so much that she sometimes stayed over in the spare room on her nights off. But tonight the family wasn't around, so the coast was clear.

It was a cold night and Frances moved in towards him as he put his arm around her shoulders and chatted over coffee – but when he turned away from the view to manoeuvre into a full embrace, making his intentions clear, he met an early rebuff. Just 45 minutes after walking up the stairs to the first-floor flat, Frances was thanking him for the evening and reaching for her coat.

It was a rueful nineteen-year-old who put the cups in the sink and prepared to drive Frances back to Mt Henry Women's Home. Opportunities like this didn't happen very often. David couldn't get out as much as other young men – working, studying for his Leaving at night school and training to make the State tennis team didn't give him much time for girls. Frances worked odd shifts and often had to be back by 11 p.m. Owning a motorbike and scooter didn't allow him the back-seat adventures most of his mates were enjoying and it was rare for his parents and brothers all to be out.

However, as he led Frances down the back stairs he started to plan their next date, wondering how soon he could borrow the car again. At least he was lucky there – with a mother running her own business, both his parents had cars, providing far more chance of a loan. Much as he dreamed of being able to borrow his father's brand-new FB Holden, he was grateful for the occasional use of his mother's little Morris Minor.

In the dark at the bottom of the back stairs he succeeded with a quick kiss before taking Frances's hand to walk her across the backyard to the double carport. But as he started towards the car, David couldn't believe it. The Morris Minor wasn't where he'd left it. His was the only car in the four carports when he came in, now there was only the one belonging to the Judsons, who lived downstairs. His mother's car had just vanished.

Jill Connell didn't have a date this Friday night. She was working behind the counter of the London Court Milk Bar in the centre of Perth, as she had done most weekends for nearly five years.

The tall, slim eighteen-year-old with the beautifully permed short brown hair passed over the milkshakes and ice-creams with friendly efficiency, working fast when the audience spilled out of the nearby cinemas at interval, and chatting sociably to customers during the quieter times. The boss was pleased with her work. She was so capable and diligent and displayed such confidence and maturity that a month previously he had promoted her to senior, in charge of the shop and the shift's junior. In giving her the added responsibility, the only new instruction necessary for this hard-working girl was that she mustn't do everything herself, but make sure the juniors did their bit.

Tonight's junior was sixteen-year-old Yvonne Loaring, who had become friends with Jill during their working time together. Yvonne was the only person to whom Jill confided her fears about taking the bus home this night after her strange experience the previous Friday.

Alf and Jess Connell of 242 Daly Street, Belmont, were concerned for their daughter's safety every night she worked late. They waited up for Jill to arrive home from the 11.10 or 11.20 bus, one of which she caught without fail. When she had worked much nearer home in Victoria Park, Alf would pick her up after work. But he was too ill to make the late-night trip now that she worked five miles away and the job involved late shifts. Instead he and his wife would wait to know she was in safely from the bus before going to sleep. Jill's little border collie Sherry would generally answer her whistle and run up the road to meet her and often Alf would stand at the gate to bring her in after her half-mile walk from the bus stop in Alexander Road.

Jill adored her quiet, stoic father who never complained despite being racked by bovine tuberculosis, living by his often-repeated saying about self-pity for having no shoes until meeting a man who had no feet. But neither her hero nor her teachers were able to convince her of the advantages of further education over earning her own living. She left school at fourteen, despite her parents' opposition, exchanging Girdlestone High's navy uniform for a green pinafore and going to work at a cake shop in Lord Street on the outer edge of the central business district.

Life at home with her parents and younger sister Kerry hadn't been easy. Her parents weren't getting on well and her father was still very ill, convalescing after spending six months in the new Perth Chest Hospital at Hollywood. Revelling in the novel independence of a pay packet, she had stayed in the city after work on the first Friday, window-shopping and trying to decide how she would spend it. Her parents were worried when she didn't arrive home for tea. At 9 p.m. they went to the Belmont Police Station and reported her missing. When she finally came home they made her accompany them to the police station to clear the report. They were all surprised to be warned by the officer about the dangers to a girl working in Lord Street – Jess and Alf hadn't realised that it was considered to be the seamy part of the city. So her first job was short-lived. She soon found work at Arthur Litis's fruit and vegetable shop in Victoria Park, in easy distance for her father to collect her.

Her recent promotion reminded Jill again that she had made the right decision to leave the safety of the Victoria Park job for the more interesting milkbar work in the city. Seeing the advertisement for a fifteen-year-old, the fourteen-year-old put up her age and went to work for Dudley Case's milkbar in Forrest Place. It wasn't long before she was transferred to the busier London Court branch.

Cooke was in his old local area, Como and South Perth, getting the usual pickings. He could have stayed in the area – he knew it so well – but as he passed an open carport of a corner block of flats, he found a parked Morris Minor. It had keys in the ignition, beckoning him to another part of town. There was no-one around the empty street and there was a nice hill to roll it away from the units before starting it.

The London Court Milk Bar was on the corner of Hay Street and London Court, opening on to Hay Street, with a separate tobacconist section facing London Court. Working right next to the famous clock, Jill could hear the chimes every quarter-hour and the longer carillon on the hour as St George chased the dragon for groups of tourists clustered in Hay Street. Tourists made up a percentage of the milkbar's customers during the day as they wandered through and photographed the architecture of the arcade, built as a replica of a Tudor London street. At night the trade was mainly from the city cinemas, movie-goers stocking up on milkshakes, ice-creams and lollies before they went in and during the interval. Policemen were regular customers, too, as they took a break during their city beat. Often they would take their caps off, sit behind the counter and have a chat, partly to relax and partly to check the young counterhands were OK. The officers' protection was welcome, for as well as serving the busy passing trade, Jill and the other attendants processed orders for the milkbars at the Windsor Theatre in Nedlands and others as far away as Beaconsfield, Kalamunda and Scarborough. One would put these together in the upstairs storeroom, leaving the other alone in the shop during the quiet times.

At 11 p.m. this Friday, Jill started to deal with the takings in preparation for locking up and catching the bus home to Belmont. She was nervous, remembering the previous Friday when, as she had bent down to the put the final lock on the door, she noticed two men standing under the clock watching her. She had felt uneasy about it as she took note of a tall, heavy-set man and a shorter one wearing a brown and cream Fair Isle jumper.

She'd caught her usual 11.20 bus, reaching her stop in Alexander Road at about 11.45. Setting out for the fifteen-minute walk home, she was unnerved by seeing a blue FJ Holden ute slowly following her all the way home. Reaching home, she was disappointed to see that her father wasn't at the gate to greet her, as the ute caught up with her. She tackled the driver, asking him who he was and what he wanted. He told her his name was Arthur and he wanted to talk, starting by asking her about the milkbar. Not knowing how to handle the situation and always polite, she chatted a little. But at the first chance without seeming rude, she told him she'd better be getting in or her father would be coming out, whereupon Arthur took off. She took the ute's registration number. She'd had no problems since, but now it was Friday night again, and she was frightened of Arthur following her home again. She had asked her mother for a lift, but that hadn't proved possible, so Jill had no alternative but to risk Arthur's attentions again. She would have to face up to this Friday night, the last before she had a three-week holiday.

As she nervously started out down London Court to the bus stop in St George's Terrace, she had a feeling that this Friday the thirteenth was going to be unlucky.

Unable to believe his mother's car had just disappeared, David Priest ran down Henley Street to Leonora Street at the front of the flats, in case it had rolled down the hill. But there was no sign of it. As he walked back up the hill, thoughts of the next date with Frances were replaced by fear of the tongue-lashing his parents would give him.

What an end to a night full of hopes. David took Frances back upstairs and rang the police. She sat there equally nonplussed as he gave the details: a 1951 Morris Minor sedan, registration number 57 371, green, value £300; owner Catherine Hilda Priest, housewife, 46 Leonora Street, Como. Yes, the keys were left in the vehicle. Yes, it was probably driven away, but probably rolled down the Henley Street hill first. The police typed out the routine 'Unauthorised Use of MV' form, misspelling Catherine's name with a K, and mistaking the house number as 42 instead of 46. Time: 11.35 p.m., date: 13/5/60.

David made Frances another coffee as they waited for Bob and Kit Priest to come home, David's concern at their reaction overtaking any romantic notions. He had always felt his parents believed that he did everything wrong, and this was going to prove it. As it turned out, expressions of their mixed disbelief, anger and concern were muted in Frances's presence and his father gave David his car to drive her back to Mt Henry.

Knowing that Jill was worried about being followed home again, Yvonne waited until she was ready to leave the shop and they walked to the Terrace together. Yvonne wasn't surprised by Jill's tale of the previous Friday. There were often guys hanging around the milkbar trying to chat them up. Once a bikie had followed her home to Como, so a policeman had escorted her home the following night and, since then, Yvonne's father always made sure someone accompanied her home on the bus. If her brother was working late on the ferries, he would make sure he caught Yvonne's bus; otherwise her father, a tramways driver, would come in on the bus from Como to see her home.

After checking that no-one was following them, Yvonne waved goodbye to Jill at her Terrace bus-stop before crossing the road to the Como bus-stop outside Government House Gardens. Though Yvonne knew how worried Jill was and felt sorry that her friend's father was too sick to help, she had no premonition that this was the last night the two would work together.

Cooke was an incognito driver in a stolen car again, just over a month after running down the girl in Bayswater. He had got away with it once more, despite her public claims that she'd been deliberately hit and the headlines and photos in the newspapers. They hadn't connected it with those other two he'd done a year or so ago and they hadn't connected any of them with him. The police knew only one side of him, the quiet truck driver who had a bit of a problem with petty theft. He was in the clear, despite all that fingerprinting of the cars. Good old Maxy, finding those fingerprints way back – he would have been well and truly done for without that lesson. He was free, and that urge started to come over him again.

There were only two or three other passengers on the Belmont route this night. Jill recognised one of them, a regular, as she walked up the bus to take a double seat, putting her two parcels beside her. With a bumper pay packet including three weeks' holiday pay, Jill had gone shopping in the city before starting work. She'd picked up five yards of pale green material that she had on lay-by and a packet of light blue wool, in preparation for sewing and knitting during her time off. As well as those large brown paper parcels, Jill was taking a coat home for her workmate, Dot, whose little boy had left it in the shop.

Sitting on the bus, she nervously watched out the window for a blue ute. There was no sign of it.

She left the bus at the crest of the rise in Alexander Road near her street, anxiously checking the dark deserted street for signs of the ute. Relieved to see that the road was clear, she clutched her handbag, coat and parcels closer to her as she set off for home. She had worn one of her best dresses to work, a brown-flecked woollen frock with three-quarter sleeves, and a little velvet overlay jacket. For extra warmth she'd worn the jumper part of an Orlon twinset under the dress, but now she wished she had taken a coat as well. The crisp May night was colder than she'd expected.

She turned off Alexander Road into Daly Street to walk the half-mile home, straining to hear Sherry's welcoming bark through the darkness.

About an hour after stealing the Morris Minor from Como, Cooke was in Belmont, driving mostly past bush and paddocks. The suburb sported both of Perth's racecourses, by the river at the far end of Daly Street. Most of the few houses in the area were like the Connells' – more like small farms in this semi-rural suburb. Alf Connell, a carpenter, had built the house on three-and-a-half acres of bush and paddocks he'd bought for £10. He had made a comfortable home for Jess, Jill and Kerry, their daughter six years younger than Jill, and their horses. But recently, they'd sold some of the twelve blocks they owned and there were now houses under construction around them. They were about to get some more neighbours, but so far only one house had been finished and inhabited.

Jill hated walking down Daly Street late at night like this – it was so dark and eerie. There were no street lights and never any lights on at this hour in the couple of houses at the Alexander Road end of the street. She always walked close to the left edge of the road, as far as possible from the other side which bordered a paddock full of banksia trees. Jill feared that stretch of bush – it was frightening to hear footsteps crunching on dry, crisp leaves when it was too dark to see who or what was there. So she generally took off her high heels and ran home, ruining her stockings but reducing her journey and fear from fifteen minutes to less than ten. Most nights her whistling to summon Sherry was successful, and her little pet would come scurrying up to greet and accompany her.

Tonight, laden with parcels, she couldn't run, despite her nervousness about the blue ute. She kept to the left edge of the road and listened for any car sounds.

Suddenly, out of nowhere, a car roared past her, really close. Despite being right over on the edge, she felt the warmth of the engine. Jill was startled and angry. 'You bastard,' she muttered to no-one as the car disappeared and she wondered who the idiot could be. There was never much traffic in this street at night. The most activity was in the early hours of the morning, as horses cantered in the soft sand alongside the road on what was a popular training track. Clutching her bag and parcels tighter, she started to run, checking behind her and straining her ears for warning of anything else. Really frightened now, how she wished she had been able to get a lift home so that she didn't have to face this dark street alone.

Cooke was driving down Alexander Road towards his house when he saw a woman get off a bus and walk in the opposite direction. It was Black Friday and he was in his black mood, out to hurt someone, and there she was. Perfect! Clear of suspicion on his other three hit–runs, another stolen car, a woman alone, a dark deserted area. He drove on to the next intersection and did a U-turn, doubling back to the bus stop, where he slowed to see where she'd gone. Cruising gently, he spotted her again as he came to Daly Street. He turned into it and she was on his left, walking in Daly Street on his side of the road. No-one else was in sight.

He sped up and drove towards her. But he didn't hit her; he drove past her and continued on to the next intersection, Esther Street, turning there and doing another U-turn in Esther Street out of sight. He'd seen that she was tall and attractive, the sort who scorned him. He was flush with excitement and rage. He drove back along Daly Street towards her.

Suddenly Jill heard it, a car roaring. Looking up from her concentrated run, she saw it. That same car, coming at her, veering to the wrong side of the road. It didn't look as if it was going to miss this time. The intention she had wondered about when it passed her so closely a few moments before, she was certain of this time, yet could not believe. She leapt off the road in a panicked effort to get across the sandy strip and over to the safety of the fence.

She didn't make it. The car drove off the road and into the sand, straight at her. She put the parcel up in front of her face for protection as the dazzling lights came upon her. With a loud thump, Cooke's target came up over the bonnet, crashing into the windscreen before rolling off. Her bag and parcels flew high into the air, scattering their contents in the sand.

Maybe he could do more to hurt her. But the car was bogged in the soft, churned-up sand. He jumped out to make his escape.

He heard the young woman crying as he ran away. He was laughing as he ran a safe distance before dropping back to a walk, footing it the mile or so home. He left Jill lying there in the cold night air, bleeding into the sand from severe head and leg injuries and floating in and out of consciousness.

Jess Connell knew there was someone in the backyard. Sherry was a good watch dog and she was barking furiously at the back door. Jess let her out and she scurried to the back fence and kept barking. Realising the dog must have cornered whoever it was, Jess wondered what to do next. She was alone in the house, Alf was standing out in the cold at the front gate waiting for Jill. Jess was still deciding between two options, going out with a bottle of lemonade to hit the intruder over the head, or getting into their Vauxhall Velox and backing down the yard, when the barking stopped. Whoever it was had gone and Jess went back to bed.

Farrier Claude Walsh and his wife Glenis lived at 52 Williamson Avenue, the next street up from Daly Street. That night they had been to their friends, the Turveys, in Manning. The four of them had had an enjoyable evening, talking horses for most of it, as Walsh and Des Turvey were both in the trotting game. The Walshes were late home, despite Claude needing to be up early to train his horse before going to work.

Claude was in the bathroom at the back of the house when he thought he heard a strange moaning coming from way off. Calling his wife to listen, they opened the back door to try to make out what the sound was and where it was coming from. They peered into the dark, looking out past Bluey Dennison's place on the Daly Street corner across the vacant land at the back. They could just make out the outline of a car in the dull moonlight, a long way over in the next street. The car in the uninhabited section of street and the unidentifiable sound didn't make sense, so they put on their coats again and set off to investigate, following the direction of the low groans.

Jill had been there an hour when Claude and Glenis Walsh finally tracked down the source of the moaning. Claude, a boxer with the nickname 'Squasher Walsh', was used to seeing blood and injuries. But he was shocked at what they found, estimating that if they had been another 45 minutes it would have been too late for Jill.

She was lying unconscious in a huge pool of blood in the sand at the back of the car, which was almost on top of her. A bone was sticking out of her right leg, creamy white in the moonlight. Claude's first reaction was that she must have been drunk and she'd stumbled after her boyfriend had run off the road and then run away. He quickly went closer to check her breath for alcohol. Smelling none, he looked around the car as Glenis ran back home to get help. Glenis felt sick from the sight of that leg bone as she rushed to her mother-in-law next door to use her phone to call the police and ambulance. She then ran home to collect a blanket while Edna Walsh, roused from sleep, quickly pulled on some clothes and accompanied her daughter-in-law to the injured girl. A group of people had gathered at the scene and they had moved the girl into the car, out of the freezing cold. Glenis was surprised to find she'd momentarily regained consciousness enough to mumble something about being run down. People from the few houses around had gathered up her scattered belongings and the girl gave her handbag to Edna Walsh, asking her to give it to her mother. Then she became semiconscious, mumbling 'it hurts' over and over.

Detective Sergeant Bruce Brennan was on night motor patrol. At 1.30 a.m. his radio crackled and he listened to the message: 'A woman was found lying alongside a car in Daly Street, Belmont. There are signs of a struggle but there is no sign of the car driver. The ambulance has conveyed the woman to RPH. People are standing by the car until the police arrive.'

Brennan swung around to set off to the hospital, giving instructions for Detective Alan Atkinson to go to the scene. Atkinson arrived to find the Walshes waiting for him. He scribbled notes as they told him they had heard her calling and found her lying close to the rear of the vehicle. They said they didn't see any other person near the car, nor could they gather from the girl what had happened to her.

A headlight examination of the car revealed blood on the right front bumper, a dent on the right side of the bonnet, the right side of the windscreen depressed and the rear vision mirror appeared to be broken. Searching the scene, he noted tyre marks in the sand for about 50 feet, indicating that the vehicle had swerved from the road then back on to the road. The girl and the vehicle were in the centre of this 50-foot arc.

Checking the night's stolen car reports, detectives found that the Morris Minor Sedan No. 57 371 had been reported stolen about two hours earlier.

The Walshes went back home, mystified on two counts – how the girl and the car could have ended up in the centre of the wheel tracks and how they could have managed to hear her low moans from so far away, across vacant land and bush, probably just in time to save her life.

Alf Connell was standing at his front gate when he saw an ambulance rush past, followed by a police car. Not long afterwards, the ambulance sped back down the road, towards the highway. He went inside for a moment to tell Jess, that there must have been a fight up the street. Then he went back to his post to wait for his daughter. He was worried now, because she should have been home at least an hour before and she was very reliable. Sherry hadn't run off up the street as usual, but instead had started barking frantically at the back about the time her mistress usually arrived. That had started Alf's disquiet, somewhere around midnight, and now he was getting really anxious.

He was resting his tall, slim, TB-racked body on the front gate, his eyes scanning the long dark street, when a car appeared out of the darkness, cruising slowly towards him with a spotlight on him. He was surprised and dazzled by the light, and even more surprised when a voice demanded to know what he was doing there at that time of night.

'I pay my rates and taxes, so what I am doing at my gate is my business,' he replied curtly, displaying the affront he felt at the tone of the inquiry. But he capitulated when asked a second time.

'My daughter hasn't come home from work.'

The officer gave him the news that his daughter wouldn't be coming home, because she had been mixed up with a stolen car incident. It was fortunate that Alf was hanging on to the gate when he realised through the policeman's further information that he had unknowingly watched his injured daughter being taken off to hospital. He staggered in to rouse his wife, followed by the police.

Startled, Jess at first thought the officer was a taxi driver who had brought Jill home.

'Get up, Mum, Jill's been injured,' Alf said, collecting the keys to drive to the hospital. Jess thought Jill must have caught a taxi that had been in an accident, but then she saw the bigger man, who introduced himself as a police officer, telling her that Jill had been involved with a stolen car and wanting to know who her friends were. She was speechless; Jill didn't have any friends who would bring her home – she was always on the bus. But they understood from the police questions that the officers believed Jill had stolen the car with a boyfriend, they'd had an argument and he had run her down.

Assuring the police that their daughter would have been on the bus, they locked up as fast as they could and headed towards RPH. His little girl, the independent one who never asked him for anything, just two weeks off her nineteenth birthday – what could have happened? Alf was a man of few words, but he made many silent pleas that she be all right as he sped towards the hospital.

Suddenly Jess called him to stop. She had seen a car parked oddly on the corner of Great Eastern Highway, past the butcher's shop, its headlights blazing. It fitted the police description of the car that had hit Jill. They turned around and went back, and as they drove up to it, they could see it had to be the one. Jess saw blood all over it, some of it still dripping. She got out and spoke to the policeman standing behind it. She asked if it was the car that had hit the girl in Belmont and he told her that it was, he'd been driving it into central when it had run out of petrol. Further numbed, they continued their journey, arriving in Casualty ten minutes later.

Jill had arrived half an hour before them and was being treated by the resident, Dr John Hill, who wanted their authorisation for surgery. Brennan arrived soon afterwards, taking a brief report from Dr Hill. The victim had a compound fracture of the right tibia and fibula, a deep laceration on the right side of the forehead and a bruised right shoulder. She was semiconscious and confused, able to say coherently nothing more than her name and address.

Jill was wheeled into theatre at 4.45 a.m. After a long operation in which orthopaedic surgeon Bill Rowe realigned the leg bones, screwed and plated them and stitched her head wound, Jill was taken to Ward 3 at 7.30 a.m. Saturday. Though her skull was not fractured, she was not in a fit condition for interview and Brennan, though anxious to talk to her, had to wait.

The police checked the medical report and evidence at the scene, deciding that Jill had probably been struck by the car when it was being driven towards her on the wrong side of the road. The blood on the bumper was from her leg, the dent in the bonnet from her hips and the depression in the windscreen caused by her head. They worked out that maybe the driver, on seeing Jill, swerved to the right at the same time as she left the road in order to avoid the car.

But there was no explanation of why the wheel marks continued past the girl and the bogged car, back on to the road again, unless the car was reversing towards her when it got bogged. Was the driver trying to run over her again as she lay injured from the first hit?

Gordon Moorman, now a detective sergeant, went to see Jill on Sunday. She was still unable to help, remembering only that she'd been making up the pay sheet. The sister in charge offered to provide any help she could, saying she would contact the police if Jill remembered anything during her visits. Jill was still only semiconscious, rambling meaninglessly. The phone call she was expecting from an American sailor she had met in Perth a month before was on her mind. She was mumbling that she had met him in America and that he had telephoned her from America a few days ago and that she was fourteen years old. Her mother, who had rung the bus depot and confirmed with the driver that Jill had been on the bus, was bewildered about what could have happened, getting no clues from what Jill was saying. Her daughter kept talking about a chicken farm.

Jill regained full consciousness on Sunday afternoon. She opened her eyes to see a nurse watching intently. 'Do you know where you are, Jill?'

Jill looked out the window and when the blur turned into salmon-coloured bricks, she was able to connect it with visits to her grandmother. 'I'm in RPH.'

'Do you know how you got here?'

'No.' The nurse filled her in on the weekend she had lost.

At first Jill couldn't think past the pain – it wasn't just her plastered and tractioned leg and her head – it was everywhere. But the worst was the pain in her eyes, they ached and ached, and she couldn't look at anything for more than a few seconds. All she could remember was being at work on Thursday or Friday and making up the pay sheet. When she had finally recovered enough to talk to the police, she couldn't remember the registration number of the previous Friday's ute and so they couldn't connect the two incidents. She was horrified at how close she'd come to death if the driver had really been reversing to run over her again. It made sense that he had enough speed to get over the soft sand and back on to the road when he was driving at her, but not when reversing. What luck, that he should have bogged just before reaching her again. By churning up the soft sand, the horses had possibly saved her life.

Late on Saturday morning, David Priest and his 24-year-old brother Jeff were out at the carports, still puzzled at the previous night's events and looking for clues to the mystery. Cars just didn't get stolen. They searched all over the corner block, checked the sandy laneway at the back and spoke to the Judsons. The car had been there when the Judsons arrived home around 11 p.m. – so the thief had taken the car in the fifteen minutes between their arrival and David's discovery.

Suddenly their grandmother came running out of her downstairs flat next to the Judsons, calling to the boys. She'd just heard an item on the ABC's midday news. The car had been found. But the police hadn't notified them, and here it was on the ABC! They learnt from the ABC that a girl had been hit by a car belonging to Mrs Catherine Priest.

They immediately rang police headquarters and were given confirmation. The police had the car and David could come and pick it up. But he was advised not to bring his mother with him – the car was in a bit of a mess.

David and Jeff went to Perth in Jeff's car. When they saw the car, they appreciated the officer's warning. The bonnet was dented, the windscreen was pushed in and there was blood everywhere. There was black fingerprinting dust all over the door. But amazingly, the interior hadn't been disturbed – all of Catherine's valuable drapery merchandise was still there on the back seat. David couldn't believe his luck. He gingerly sat in the driver's seat. He felt strange about driving it, trying to picture what sort of brute could take this car and run someone down. He drove the Morris to the petrol station on the corner and washed it. Then he continued on to give Mum the good news, at least about her merchandise.

For Jill the questions went on and on. She gave the police the names of all the youths she knew. Their alibis all checked out. No-one was able to trace Arthur, and fingerprinting of the car, arranged by Detective John Dunne, revealed nothing. While her mother never thought she had been involved in the car theft, she couldn't believe that a stranger would do this to Jill. She insisted that it must have been someone she knew. The pain, the questioning, the horror, the uncertainty – they didn't make for much of a birthday when Jill turned nineteen two weeks later.

She was finally allowed to go home just after her birthday. Home, but not whole. That took a long time. Four months later, with the fracture still not healing, she was back in RPH for a bone graft: chips of bone were taken from her hip to replace dead bone in the tibia. Further treatment was needed in St John of God Hospital and she was in plaster for ten months, living on £2/7/6 a week sickness benefit, unable to work or go out.

A Powerful Car to Match a Powerful Urge

20 May 1960

Cooke scoured the newspapers during the week. There were only a couple of small items about Jill Connell's hit–run. Nothing pointing to him and nothing connecting this incident with the hit–run on the Peak girl five weeks earlier. He had done it again – he'd won another round against the world.

A grim smile of success crossed his lips as he sat outside Queens Park Railway Station the following Friday night. Train stations and bus stops were ideal starting points for finding women walking home in dark streets late at night, and he'd come by this one just as a train pulled in. It was a little after midnight and it was pouring with rain, which further darkened the long, sparsely inhabited streets. He immediately recognised the potential. He had a big six-cylinder car this time, no little Morris Minor that couldn't make it through a bit of soft sand.

He pulled up in the taxi rank alongside the Coronation Hotel opposite the station and watched as three female passengers crossed the road towards him and set off down the street.

Don and Glenda Williams had just retired for the night. It was about 10.30 when they got to bed after settling Don's father into the guest room. Saturday was a big day for Don, who had to be at his service station ready for opening at 7 a.m., before getting to the afternoon's important match against league leader South Fremantle.

Don was just drifting off, enjoying a warm feeling of family contentment. His one and two-year-old daughters were asleep and his father Clarrie was over from Melbourne again. The home at 210 Ewen Street, Doubleview, was now dark and quiet after the merriment of an evening reminiscing over old times. His thoughts went home to Prahran, which he'd left a year earlier, headhunted from the Melbourne Football Club to play for West Perth. He was happy in Perth, successful at football and business. At 24 he ran two big Ampol service stations, he was the assistant coach of West Perth Football Club, which was second on the ladder, and he had a huge 37-square, two-storey house. It was on a big corner block with garages and entrances in both Ewen Street and Huntriss Road and, being on the top of the hill, it had a panoramic view over the suburbs to the city five miles away. They had a lovely view at night, the lights of the growing suburbs spread out below like a glittering carpet.

He was pleased when his father took a couple of weeks off running the guest house to come west and see the family. He did worry about the 60-year-old driving over the Nullarbor, but at least he had a new car which was big and solid, less likely to break down than some making their way across the rough unsealed Eyre Highway, and now the old man had managed it twice without incident – last year and again this May. He'd arrived safely a few days previously, bringing Melbourne weather with him. It had been raining on and off all day and Don could hear it starting to rain harder. Thinking it would be a muddy game tomorrow, he pulled the blankets up tighter and fell asleep.

Just down the road in Grant Street, Innaloo, the gloved burglar was creeping through another house.

After finishing work at his temporary job in Victoria Park, he'd caught a train to Swanbourne to start his night work. He prowled around Swanbourne for a while, until he saw easy transport to another suburb. It was a Holden sedan in the driveway of a house in Rob Roy Street. Niftily procuring it, he headed north.

It started to rain heavily, but that didn't deter him from leaving the comfort of the car once he reached Doubleview. He parked the car outside the Innaloo Methodist Church on the corner of Grant and King George streets and walked along Grant Street, continuing across Scarborough Beach Road, on the lookout for a darkened house with a door or window unlocked. Soon he was inside one and adding £3 to the pay packet he'd received that day. Fossicking through the house, he saw a wedding photo and discovered he was in the home of a former workmate.

He walked further along Grant Street to Ewen Street where he turned right and went up the steep hill, remembering what good luck he'd had some time previously, when he'd found £70 in a car in the carport of 200 Ewen Street. This time, his eyes were drawn to the driveway of the house on the opposite corner – there was a beautiful big new American car. Crossing the road to No. 210, he found he was in luck again. The car was unlocked and the keys were in the ignition. He quietly opened the door and sat in the driver's seat, using the torch he always carried to study the automatic transmission. He had never driven an automatic before. He started it, backed out of the driveway and headed towards Perth, thrilled at this new experience and enjoying the thrust of the big powerful engine.

Don and Glenda woke with a jolt at the sound. Don rushed to the window, hardly able to believe what he saw – his father's new car leaving the driveway. He raced outside to his Holden ute in the second driveway, but it was too late, the other was out of sight. His father's £2000 car had just sped away.

They rang the police, woke Clarrie and sat waiting. The constables took the details as Clarrie described his Chrysler Royal, white with a red stripe, registration GXU 610. Don felt some comfort knowing that such an outstanding car with a Victorian registration couldn't go unnoticed for long, and he could fix any damage at his garage. But they were stunned and had difficulty getting back to sleep.

Cooke soon discovered an added bonus inside this beautiful car. On the passenger seat was a raincoat – just what he needed on a night like this. Luck was certainly on his side tonight. He drove to Victoria Park and checked a few suburbs for an hour or so. Just before midnight he ended up in Queens Park, driving along Railway Parade, when he saw the train. He pulled over and watched, looking past the big desert kurrajong tree to the platform, where the three Queens Park passengers were dashing to the shelter of the station's waiting room. A few minutes later, he saw three girls leave the station and walk across the road, huddled under two umbrellas.

The two teenagers and a girl were the only passengers leaving the train at Queens Park. One of the teenagers and the twelve-year-old girl were cousins. The other was a stranger they had spoken to in the waiting room. She was a petite blonde in a tight dress and perilously high heels, stranded with a long walk ahead of her and no umbrella. She briefly left the shelter to check the taxi rank outside the hotel, but there weren't any taxis, just a white car with a brick-coloured stripe, and a man at the steering wheel wearing a brimmed hat. They all decided to walk, the two cousins offering to share their umbrellas with the other when they found they were going in the same direction.

After crossing the road, the trio set off along George Street, with no alternative but to stay on the road in this isolated outer-suburban area with no footpaths.

The waiting, watching man in the brimmed hat started the engine and slowly turned the Chrysler into George Street.

With a half-mile walk ahead of them, they had time to get to know each other a little. Walking easily despite the high heels, Georgina Pitman did most of the talking. Far more chatty than the two cousins, she was soon telling the older one about her night out dancing. She drew in closer to Maureen Rogers, whose larger umbrella she shared and who was walking nearest the centre of the road, leaving the girl, Terese Zagami, leading them on the outside edge under her own umbrella, not so interested in hearing about dancing and boyfriends.

Georgina had been out dancing at the Young Australia League Hall, where she always went on a Friday night. The five-foot-one eighteen-year-old loved jiving and was so good at it that she had been chosen from the Canterbury Court regulars to be one of the club dancers on Channel 7's *Club Seventeen*. She danced at Canterbury Court Ballroom on Saturday afternoons, went home for a quick shower and then left again for more jiving on Saturday nights. She was fit and enthusiastic, with a neat, tiny body that she loved to show off as she did tonight, wearing, under her camel-coloured duffle coat, a tight blue Chinese dress with slits up the sides and, as always, the highest-heeled white shoes. It was her favourite dress, because it made the most of her figure – just like her other favourite outfit, her marching girls' uniform. She knew she looked stunning in the tiny white skirt with dark blue trim, topped by an aqua jacket with white buttons and enhanced by white gloves and boots. She worked at the Nevarda shirt factory in East Perth and was a diligent collar hand, but her life revolved around jiving and marching.

Georgina had migrated from Portsmouth with her parents and older sister Brenda four years previously. Anne and George Pitman wanted to give the girls a better life after enduring the shortages of war and the danger of living near a dockyard and ammunition supply. Georgina was three-and-a-half before her father returned from war and saw her for the first time.

Life had been tough for the Pitmans on arrival in Perth. George couldn't find a job, so their first house was in the cheapest area, Wanneroo, a dry dusty section of bush a long way north of the city centre, even more inaccessible without a car. The differences between Wanneroo and Portsmouth were depressing, straining an already tenuous marriage, and the Pitmans divorced.

Now, with Brenda married, Georgina lived with her mother and stepfather Wally in a comfortable State Housing Commission home on two-thirds of an acre much closer to the city, in Queens Park.

Georgina's new-found friend was sixteen-year-old Maureen Rogers from Narembeen. Maureen had come from the small country town at the beginning of the year to do a secretarial course at City Commercial College, after completing her Junior Certificate at Merredin High School. She moved in with her aunt's family, who had room to spare. Maureen missed the farm and mum and dad, but she was at home at 236 George Street, Queens Park, with her Aunty Jess and Uncle Vince, and felt part of the Zagami family with her two young cousins, twelve-year-old Terese and ten-year-old Patty.

Vince Zagami had worked on the railways all his life. Now assigned to the parcels section in central office, he was sometimes involved in the transport of sets and equipment for the occasional stage shows that made their way to Perth from the major Sydney and Melbourne venues. Sometimes he scored free tickets to shows. He'd been given two free tickets to 'The Bobby Limb Show' at His Majesty's Theatre for Friday, 20 May, and decided to give the tickets to the two older girls this time. They deserved a treat.

They were two excited cousins who dressed up in their best clothes for a rare outing. Terese had only one good dress and she loved any chance to wear it. Tonight was an occasion for that special white dress with the green polka dots. For Maureen it was the chance to wear her brand-new navy blue coat, the first she'd ever had. The blustery weather and the prospect of a long bus ride to the city and train ride home didn't dampen their high spirits. They were thrilled at the chance to see Bobby Limb live, having seen the popular entertainer on television. For this spectacular variety revue, he was accompanied by 25 world stars from London, New York and Paris. Terese and Maureen had never heard of Jimmy Wheeler, Lita Roza or Johnny O'Connor, but their star billing all added to the glamour of the gala event.

The show was as good as they had expected, and they were sorry when it was all over at about 11 p.m. The two finished off the night by buying ginger beer and chocolates before catching the 11.35 train.

Georgina, too, had stopped at a milk bar before catching the train. She had been given a lift from the YAL Hall in Irwin Street to Brownes milkbar in Barrack Street, where she'd met several girlfriends for soft drinks. She crossed Wellington Street to the station with her friend Irene Stevens and they caught the train together, Irene staying on board at Queens Park to go to Maddington.

Maureen pulled Georgina closer into the umbrella's protection, and was telling her about the Bobby Limb Rocketeers when a car zoomed up behind them, passing them at high speed.

Maureen said: 'Gee, this guy's an idiot' at the same time as Georgina, thinking it was a taxi at last, stepped into the road and tried to flag it down. Maureen and Terese were horrified to see her hailing a car like this – they'd been carefully brought up not to accept lifts from strangers, so they both saw Georgina's action as unladylike, as their mothers would say. They didn't know that Georgina had seen the same car at the taxi rank earlier and had now assumed it must have been a taxi after all.

The driver recognised Georgina's sign as a request for a lift and he wasn't surprised, given the heavy rain. But although he often helped women that way, he wasn't going to do so now. He was the other Cooke again, very different from the one who gave lifts. This one was bitter, angry and excited, even more so for seeing the opportunity to get two or three of them in one hit. He had a powerful car to match his powerful urge to attack and maim. He ignored the blonde's urgent signal and drove past to check out the next victims of his rage, observing that one was a girl of about ten.

He sped up the hill along George Street, which was a long, dark isolated road through big paddocks, apart from a few houses and a poultry farm. He crossed the Centre Street intersection and drove on to the next, Cross Street.

The trio, still startled by the driver who had come out of nowhere, saw the car do a U-turn at the top of the hill and come speeding down the road past them again in the opposite direction, then disappear down the street behind them. The street was quiet once more and they walked on, their chatter reduced by a little wariness.

Cooke turned off the motor for a few minutes and waited. Then he started it up. The powerful engine roared as he sped up the street to where the three would be walking in a deserted section past paddocks.

Almost upon them, and noticing that the little girl was walking next to the verge, he veered to the wrong side of the road and aimed the car at the two bigger girls.

Georgina heard it and turned to see the headlights a little distance away. Still hopeful of a lift, she said to Maureen that maybe a taxi was coming this time.

When Terese heard the car coming closer at such speed, she started to worry about the other two and turned around to look. She was aghast to see the car coming straight at them. She had just seconds in which to warn the others.

'Look out!' she yelled. But it was too late for the girls at the centre of Cooke's aim. Little Terese jumped further off the road as the car sped past so fast that it blew her dress up on the way through. It hit Maureen and Georgina with a bone-crunching thud, lifting Maureen up on to the bonnet and throwing Georgina into the ditch along the road.

Maureen copped the main impact. Catching her left side as she had turned around to look, the car's radiator grille broke off as it slammed into her leg, breaking both major bones before tossing her up on to the car and carrying her along.

Cooke didn't stop. With one of the girls pouring blood over the bonnet, he sped up the street until he came to the intersection again, 100 yards further on. He turned fast into Cross Street, getting rid of his unwanted passenger as she slid off.

He was away, escaping along Treasure Road to Railway Parade, where he turned right and drove on to the Oats Street railway crossing. On the other side of the railway line he turned into Beatty Avenue and parked the car. Another win. Putting on the raincoat and pulling his hat lower, he walked home from East Victoria Park to Rivervale.

Ernest Taylor at 222 George Street and Arthur Bale at 228 were in bed when they heard a car speed past and a bump – but they didn't go out in the rain to investigate. Maureen was left lying in the middle of the road, limp and bleeding profusely, blood soaking through her new coat and mingling with the rivulets of water trickling down the road.

A hundred yards down the road, Georgina was wandering dazed in the rain, her dress torn, deep bleeding gashes in her back and head. She was walking in circles, badly concussed, not knowing what had happened, her confused mind set on finding her shoes which had been thrown off her in the impact and lost in the dark.

Terese ran over to a hedge, not knowing what to do, petrified that the man was going to come past again for her. She was sure he knew he hadn't got her and would come back to finish her off. She could hear Georgina calling 'Mum, Mum' and that added to her terror, giving her the legs to run home, keeping close to the hedge so that he couldn't see her when he came back. She didn't know what had happened to Maureen, until she got to the top of the hill and saw her crumpled body lying in the middle of the intersection.

Risking the driver spotting her, she ran out on to the road, to touch her cousin: 'Maureen, are you all right?'

There was no answer and Terese realised she must be dead. Panic, horror and grief were all added to her terror, as the twelve-year-old stared at Maureen, begging her to come alive and tell her what to do.

Then through the shock and confusion, her legs started carrying her towards home again, only about 100 yards further up the road. She knew she had to get home. Or to Aunty's next door, anyway, somehow remembering that her parents were out at cards. Hammering on Josie Zagami's door, she woke her aunt, who was equally shocked to find her soaked, panicked niece at the door crying out that Maureen was dead, killed by a crazy man in a car.

'It was deliberate, it was deliberate,' the little girl kept screaming to Aunty Josie who, too alone and ill to do anything herself, took her to Mrs Bathgate over the road.

Mrs Bathgate immediately saw the need to deal with the drenched girl's shock before investigating further. She dried her and put her in her daughter's warm bed. The terrified girl wouldn't let her go to the scene to find Maureen.

'No, don't go up there,' Terese screamed at her. 'You'll get killed, he's coming back, I don't want him to get you too.' Mrs

Bathgate made a hot Milo for Terese and when she could finally leave to find out what had happened, she saw the red lights of an ambulance flashing down the road, and Vince and Jess Zagami arriving home to the same sight.

Detective Sergeants Charlie Loverock and Laurence Gibson had just started their midnight to 8 a.m. patrol duty and were driving along George Street checking Woodards Poultry Farm where there had been reports of chickens being stolen over the previous few weeks. Driving slowly, alert for signs of anything amiss, they encountered the scene just minutes after Terese had left it.

Constables Ivo Moscardini and Bob Kershaw in the Accident Inquiry Section received a message from the CIB night wireless motor patrol at 12.05 a.m.: a woman had been found lying in the middle of the roadway in George Street, Queens Park, approaching the intersection of Cross Street. There was a further message within a minute or two: a second young woman had been found about 110 yards away, wandering about in a dazed condition, suffering relatively minor injuries.

Constables Moscardini and Kershaw arrived at the scene one-and-a-half hours later. They searched the area and found a small piece of chrome-plated metal, thought to be a portion of the radiator grille from the car involved.

Dashing down the road to the ambulance, Terese's parents arrived at the scene to see Maureen sprawled on the road, the ambulance crew checking her.

There was a pulse. She was alive. That was a relief, but they were horrified and worried, all the more for the responsibility they felt for the niece in their care. Jess rode in the back of the ambulance with Maureen, anxiously watching the unconscious, bleeding girl during the emergency trip to RPH. Georgina sat in the front, babbling incessantly, telling the ambulance driver over and over in her confusion that she had to find her shoes and had to get home.

At home at 48 Donaldson Street, Anne lay awake waiting for Georgina's footsteps on the concrete path at the front. Georgina was reliable, always getting home in good time from her dancing, generally driven by her boyfriend. Knowing the boyfriend was out with other friends this time, she'd instructed Georgina to catch a taxi from Queens Park station. It was such a terrible wet, windy night that she and Wally had driven Georgina to the station before going over the road to their neighbours, Violet and Bill Short, to watch Richard Burton in *Last Days of Dolwyn*. With Anne now in charge of a C-class hospital in Mt Lawley, they could have afforded the 23/5d weekly television hire, but it hadn't been a priority because they enjoyed watching special shows in the company of their friends. When the Channel 2 screenplay finished, they stayed on to see the 10.30 p.m. repeat of *Newsreel* and have a cup of tea before bidding the Shorts goodnight.

Her husband tried to reassure Anne, telling her that Georgina had probably met someone and was getting a lift. The reassurance didn't work. Anne tossed and turned, unable to sleep until she heard the light clatter of Georgina's high heels. She finally heard footsteps at about 2 a.m., but they were heavy men's steps. Knowing that something had happened even before the urgent knock, her fears were confirmed by the police at the door.

Hurriedly throwing on the clothes they had taken off earlier, they drove to the hospital in a state of shock and bewilderment at what could have happened to Georgina. Road safety had been instilled in her by Anne, who had seen the results of too many accidents through years of nursing.

The ambulance roared into Casualty at 1.10 a.m. and Maureen was wheeled straight into an emergency cubicle. Her aunt spent anxious hours in the waiting room as the badly injured teenager was taken to theatre for an emergency operation on her leg. She had a double fracture of the left lower leg, a fractured left cheekbone and abrasions and bruises all over. Her prized coat had been hacked off her.

There was a quick assessment of Georgina's scalp injury and the two-inch by one-and-a-half-inch gash in her back. They gave her painkillers and had the adrenalin standing by. Anne and Wally made it to the hospital just in time to see her being wheeled away to have her wounds stitched up. It was 5.40 a.m. when Nurse Webster brought her out, and they accompanied the nurse and Georgina to the ward, where they sat with her until she fell asleep.

They arrived home in the early morning, and it was not long before a reporter and photographer from the *Weekend News* arrived, pressing them for details and a photo of Georgina. Anne refused to give a photo, knowing her picture in the paper would further worry her highly strung daughter who had told them someone was out to get her.

The police found the car abandoned in East Victoria Park just before 7 a.m. on Saturday. They were able to match it with the stolen car report, despite the report having the colours the wrong way round, describing the 1959 model Chrysler Royal Sedan as red with white stripes. Detective Sergeant Philip White, Detective Tony Branche and Traffic Constable Ron Wilson examined it and found a piece of metal missing from the radiator grille. The damage corresponded with the broken piece found at the scene. The car was fingerprinted and photographed, and Constable Derek Woolmer's vehicle examination report noted damage to the top portion of the bonnet, the left front of the bonnet and the radiator grille and a broken mascot.

Dawn was just starting to break as George Rogers headed out to start the long day's work of a farmer. The sun's rays brought a beautiful golden tinge to the clouds and misty haze across the top paddock, but George was too intent on his work to notice the beauty of daybreak. It was seeding time and he was busy. Nor did he notice a car appear on the horizon and head towards him one-and-a-half hours later, while he was standing on the back bumper of the combine filling the seed and super boxes. It was nearly on him when he heard the neighbouring farmer's truck, close enough for him to see the worried expression on his wife's face and know that something was wrong. Seconds later, Colin told him about the item that had just been broadcast over the early ABC news. George couldn't believe that Colin had heard correctly until his wife confirmed it. His stepsister,

Yvonne Hunter, had rung after hearing the 6 a.m. bulletin and Beryl had phoned through to Perth, getting her sister-in-law Jess only minutes after she had arrived home from hospital by taxi. George Rogers had to believe it. The tall, hardy wheat-and-sheep farmer paled at the thought of his youngest child being hurt and just dropped the super in his urgency to get to Perth.

George and Beryl were away in no time, heading the sixteen miles northwest into Narembeen and pushing the Holden up the 175 miles to Perth. They went straight to RPH, reaching ward 52 at about 1 p.m. Maureen was unrecognisable, bruised black all over, her face swollen, her leg and hip in plaster.

'What are you doing down here?' she mumbled through her swollen lips, amazed to see her parents walk into the room, her father still in his work clothes. Maureen didn't get an answer – her mother couldn't talk through her tears and her six-foot-three-and-a-half-inch-tall father crumpled to the floor, fainting for the first time in his life. He had seen many wounded mates in the Solomon Islands during the war, but this was his little girl.

Anne and Wally were back at the hospital on Saturday, anxious to see Georgina and to find out what had happened. So were the police. Georgina had slept only fitfully and was feeling nauseated and sore, but mostly, she was distressed, begging her mother to take her home. After giving statement to Detective Sergeant White, she asked the nurse if she could go to see Maureen before she left the hospital. When she got to Maureen's ward, she wished she hadn't made that slow, stiff, painful walk with nurses by her side. She collapsed at the sight of the puffed-up, blue face that looked nothing like the girl she'd met the night before. Going home that day was out of the question for Georgina.

Georgina was discharged the next day, to the continuing care of her mother, a professional nurse who could give her painkilling and antibiotic injections between visits to her local doctor as well as to Mr Bedford and Mr Dawkins in the orthopaedic outpatient clinic. At home Georgina was a bundle of nerves. She was permanently anxious and couldn't sleep, even with the light on all night and the wardrobe pulled across the window. Nothing could abate her insistence that someone was out to kill her and her fear that he would come back to get her.

Her mother was glad she hadn't provided a photo of Georgina when she saw the page-one lead stories in the *Weekend News* and *Sunday Times*, with photos of the other girls. 'Is a Hit–run Maniac on the Loose?' ran Saturday's headline, over a story by police roundsman Jack Coulter: 'Have we a hit–run maniac on a rampage in the suburbs?' Anne read on:

> Three apparently-deliberate run-downs in stolen cars in lonely roads late at night indicate this. Three girls were apparently deliberately run down by a powerful stolen car in George-st, Queens Park, early today. This climaxed what may be a series of cold-blooded attempts to kill or maim pedestrians. Three times in the past six weeks – each time in the weekend – girls have been injured by a stolen hit–run car (later abandoned) in different suburbs. From early today, a big squad of detectives and traffic police has been working on the possibility that a crazy car thief has committed all three crimes ...

The next day the *Sunday Times* ran much the same information, under the heading 'Grim warning on hit–run thief. Police hunt "maniac" driver':

> Every available police car and a 12-man C.I.B. and traffic patrol squad last night scoured Perth and suburbs for a man police believe could be a hit–run maniac. The hunt follows the apparent deliberate running-down of three girls in George street, Queens Park, early yesterday. It is the third hit–run incident in six weeks ... Each time the victims were girls, hit near their homes late at night. Each time a stolen car was used. And each time the girls were struck late on a Friday or Saturday night ...

They had a photo of Maureen in hospital and Terese out at the scene, with a map pointing to the three hit–run locations.

Anne made sure Georgina didn't see the articles or the small one in Monday's *West*. Georgina was still affected far beyond her physical injuries. In an effort to help her regain her confidence, Anne took her to Wally's sister, far away in the small town of Kojonup, where she could relax and heal body and mind.

Terese's nerves were in an even worse state. The girl suffered terribly from visions of the man in the hat out to kill her. It was worst at night, with the same nightmare occurring over and over. It was only in the security of her parents' bed that she could get to sleep. She left the front bedroom she shared with her sister and slept with her parents in their bed at the back for six months before they could coax her into a single bed alongside theirs. It was a year before she would go back to her own room.

Maureen was in hospital for three weeks. Her parents made the two-and-a-half-hour trip to Perth to see her as often as they could in busy seeding time, trips that cost them more time and money than they could afford. George arranged with the Red and White Taxi Service for Jess to go to see their daughter regularly and later for Maureen to make the trips to Perth for more operations and follow-up physiotherapy. Discharged from hospital but still quite disabled, Maureen had to give up her course and go home for the rest of the year.

Despite the terrible injuries and pain and the effect they would have on the rest of her life, Maureen was glad for the others' sake that she had borne the brunt of the attack. She was a solid country girl, five-foot seven-inches tall and weighed about ten stone. She firmly believed that if Terese or Georgina had been hit as she had, they would have been killed. They were both such slight girls.

Cooke saw the newspaper articles. It was the first time his hit–runs had been connected. But they still hadn't linked them with his first two from one-and-a-half years ago, nor with him. The police continued their investigations into the three latest hit–runs. Known car thieves were closely questioned and special patrols were started on Fridays and Saturdays between 5 p.m. and 1 a.m.

Two-and-a-half months later, on 9 August, Detective Brian Bull interviewed Georgina again and took a statement. Two days later, Detective Sergeant Ron White concluded his written report: 'I am of the opinion that all three hit–runs were committed by the one offender, but have no evidence to prove this.'

A notice was issued, informing other officers of the special patrols on the watchout for an offender who steals a car, drives around looking for a deserted section of road near or a little distance from bus stops and deliberately runs down selected victims if the time is opportune.

Seven months later, after an unsuccessful investigation into Jill Connell's hit–run, the officer-in-charge sent a memo to Inspector Lamb. Dated 15 December, Detective Sergeant John Wiley informed his chief that after inquiries by the motor squad, no trace of the offender had been found, nor any information leading to his identity received – despite special motor patrols, questioning of suspects and extensive inquiries. He noted that the hit–run was similar to those committed on Glenys Peak and Maureen Rogers, in company with two other girls.

The police were getting nowhere, frustrated by the lack of fingerprints in the cars.

The City of Light

3 March 1962

Perth had grown in the two years since Cooke's last hit–run. Its population had increased to 500,000, and there were now 49 sets of traffic lights sprinkled through the expanding road system as new suburbs spread further into the outlying bushland. Tall buildings were starting to change the shape of the city; the construction of the thirteen-storey T & G building led to calls for skyline controls. Perth was gaining an international reputation, too, despite Western Australia still being the Cinderella State with just 750,000 people, 7 per cent of the country's total.

Perth had been selected to hold the Seventh British Empire and Commonwealth Games, only the second time an Australian city had been so honoured. There had been a building spree to update the city and to prepare for the influx of athletes and spectators from all over the Commonwealth in November. The airport terminal was modernised, Perry Lakes Stadium and Beatty Park pool had been built to provide competition facilities and a big housing estate, the Commonwealth Games Village, was under construction at Wembley Downs for the teams. The people of Perth were anxiously awaiting this big event, sorry only that they would miss out on witnessing an under-four-minute mile from their home-town hero, Herb Elliott, who had retired after the Rome Olympics two years earlier.

In February, Perth had gained international renown when it turned on its lights for America's first space flight. Thousands of residents responded to the idea of *The West Australian* journalist,

Bill King, and left their lights on all night for the momentous step into the space age. The city was aglow with the lights of houses, city buildings and airport runways when astronaut John Glenn went over. He radioed the world from space that he could see the 'City of Light'.

A few weeks later, on the Labour Day long weekend, Perth was back to its normal lights-out and Cooke was on the prowl. He had nothing to do with the City of Light; he liked it when it was dark, when he was free to give reign to his dark side.

He'd been caught only once over the past two years, on 11 September 1960, four months after he ran down the three girls in Queens Park. He had been arrested in West Perth by Detective Sergeant Bill Nielson and Detective Bud Martin. As usual, he had thrown the evidence away, so he could only be charged with loitering. It had landed him in jail for another month, leaving his wife at home with six children under seven years of age, including a six-month-old baby girl.

In prison for a month from 12 September, he wasn't questioned any more about Jillian Brewer's murder, or about the other two unsolved murders of the time: Barbara May Williams, killed on 7 November 1958 and found in a shallow grave at Sorrento Beach on 16 December, or Patricia Vinico Berkman, murdered on 30 January 1959.

After Cooke's release from prison, he left his wife and children alone again, while he went out in the country as a subcontractor to Reg Woodings for about three months. He didn't know, when building a sheep shower on Hope Farm, Kulin, that it was Rosemary Anderson's grandparents' farm.

Cooke had been extra careful and a little bit lucky. He only just got away when Fred Schruth took after him with a waddy in Cottesloe. Cooke had been watching through the front window of the house at 84 Broome Street, where a group of teenagers were having a party. He didn't think he'd be noticed – there were only four houses in the street and opposite was the dark expanse of the Sea View Golf Club leading down to the ocean.

The Schruths' elder daughter Lorraine, who was leaving St

Hilda's Church of England School for Girls to go to business college, didn't know about the unwanted guest at her party. But her mother Norma spied him when she was clearing up at about midnight. She calmly told her husband, Fred, about the man wearing a large-brimmed hat hiding behind the apple blossom hibiscus bordering the porch. Fred kept a waddy under his bed – a part of a banister he had souvenired on the demolition of his first dental surgery in Corot House. He retrieved it and went to deal with the peeping Tom.

Cooke took off, dashing across the lawn, jumping over the end of the driveway's limestone retaining wall, through the oleanders dividing the Schruths' property from their neighbours, along Broome Street. Schruth chased him past a half-built house and across a vacant block, the short, slight dentist noticing that he and his quarry were about the same height. Then the man in the army great coat and hat sprinted through a building site on the corner into another behind it in Forrest Street, where his pursuer lost him.

By now the Perth police had four patrol cars fitted with cameras and two-way radios. And still Cooke succeeded in avoiding arrest.

His close shaves didn't affect his bravado. While he generally watched women in the dark, hiding behind walls, hedges and trees to spy on them in their bedrooms, he also sometimes watched them openly during the day. He was brazen, not caring if he was seen. At the Joy Beauty Salon in Newcastle Street, he even went in and asked for a shampoo and set after standing outside for a few days. That hairdresser thought she was so smart, saying she didn't do men's hair to try to get rid of him, her dog barking at him all the time. But he had the last laugh, she realised, when she found her new transistor radio missing. When Joy Maynard reported the missing transistor and the man hanging around outside the salon, the police told her it fitted the description of a peeping Tom other people had complained of on many occasions.

Now there was a seventh child in the Cooke family, another little girl who was sixteen days off her first birthday.

Cooke dressed smartly in his suit and favourite pink-grey tie on the hot night of 3 March and left home for the city at 7 p.m. After enjoying the evening as the dapper single man there, he caught a bus to the Mosman Park area for more fun stealing and watching. Working his way back towards the city, he ended up in the Crawley and Nedlands areas, where there were expensive houses and young women living in flats.

He snuck around the back of Aloha flats on the corner of Fairway and Clark Street, looking for a window. On the clothesline he saw some lengths of towelling, the off-cuts of a white beach robe a young woman had been making. He usually took women's panties on clotheslines, but he pocketed one of the off-cuts. It didn't matter that it was still damp. It would be useful for the urge that was starting to come over him – the added excitement of doing more than watching and stealing.

He continued along Fairway, his secret weapon tucked away. At one house he noticed a push-bike, but he didn't need it right now. He was happy sneaking around on foot. He continued walking, eventually turning into Broadway.

Anne Melvin left her flat at 2/124 Broadway at the same time Cooke had left home. The leggy, beautiful 23-year-old was the manager of a city coffee lounge and worked most nights. But on this Labour Day weekend she had a rare Saturday night off and was accompanying her friend Nicholas Treleaven to a school swimming carnival at Guildford Grammar School. Nicholas, a former Guildford student, wanted to see how the swimming team was going in its preparation for the interschool swimming sports the following Saturday. While Nicholas cheered loudly for Guildford, Anne silently barracked for the only Catholic school included in the carnival, Aquinas College. Anne was a devout Catholic who had gone to Loreto Convent and had also taught kindergarten there. But it was Guildford's night, the Anglican college winning twelve of the 26 events in the school's new swimming pool and becoming the favourite for the inters.

After the swimming, Nicholas took Anne for a coffee at his place, where she politely chatted with his parents. He still lived at home, but Anne had moved out from hers a few weeks earlier to set up flat with her eighteen-year-old sister, Pauline. The girls believed it was time to reduce the load on their parents, who had seven children.

Tonight was a new experience for Anne. She was sleeping on her own for the first time, Pauline having gone to Rockingham for the long weekend. She was anxious at the thought of it, especially because she and Pauline hadn't yet put up curtains, making do with sheets hung across the windows. She was extra nervous after noticing a small man standing watching from under a street light by the flats as Nicholas dropped her home. She didn't say anything, but when he walked her to the door, she asked him to wait while she checked inside. She looked everywhere, under the beds and in the wardrobes, then bade her friend goodnight and closed the front door, locking it behind her.

Alone in the middle downstairs flat, Anne sat in bed for a while. She finished her sandwich and coffee and was filing her nails when she heard a noise on the porch. She stopped filing and listened, keeping very still. It sounded like a cat pouncing on to the porch. Convincing herself that it really was a big cat and hearing nothing more, she settled down again. It made her realise, though, that she hadn't locked the back door and she thought about getting up to lock it, but again chided herself for her nervousness, turned off the light and slipped under the sheet, falling asleep quickly despite the hot night.

The cat burglar pounced on to the porch from the low brick wall he'd been creeping along. He tried the fly wire and the door of the middle downstairs flat. He was in luck. Both were unlocked and he easily made his way into the lounge room, shining his torch around. He unlocked the other door, always careful to prepare a getaway. It was about 4.45 a.m. when he went into the bedroom, where a young woman was asleep in a single chrome bed. It was just light enough to see her. She was very beautiful. And she was all alone. She was sound asleep.

He put the length of towelling to use, wrapping it around her neck and pulling it tight – very tight, enough to almost strangle her. He was careful to stop before that one last twist, though. He wanted her unconscious, but alive.

He pulled back the sheet, right down to the end of the bed. Then he removed the pyjama pants from his unconscious victim whose lungs were struggling to get enough oxygen. He was the one with the power now. Anne lay there helpless, the innocent young woman thankfully unaware of the terrible violation he was preparing for.

There was a noise outside, just when he didn't want any interruption. He went to check. It was a stray cat trying to get at some milk bottles on the porch. He went back to the bedroom. But Anne was starting to regain consciousness! He was amazed, but he wasn't going to be thwarted now. He'd make sure this one couldn't fight back. With no diver's knife on him this time, he went into the bathroom, where her stockings were drying over the towel rail. He took one. This would stop her fighting or escaping. He tied it to the bedhead and then tied a loop around her left arm, pulling it tight. He was fast and nimble with the knots, despite the gloves.

Lady Winifred Seddon in the flat across the way was up early, preparing her granddaughter's next feed. Her daughter Jean had just lost her husband, and so Jean and her baby were staying with her. Lady Winifred went outside to collect the milk, quickly going back inside to prepare it for the baby.

Hearing another noise outside he again left his prey to go to the door to see what it was. It was safe to leave her this time; even if she started to regain consciousness again, she wasn't going anywhere. Checking outside he saw no-one, and he went back again, undoing his belt, ready.

But in his short absence, Anne had somehow managed to get enough oxygen through the tight stricture to come to again – enough to sit up, wrenching at her throat with her free hand and starting to scream. He hadn't counted on that. The noise could wake up the neighbours. He took off, running through the lounge and out the front door, slamming it shut behind him and running as fast as he could.

Anne was having a terrible nightmare that she was suffocating. She started to wake out of it, but waking didn't change it. She found to her horror that it was no nightmare – she was in fact suffocating and there was a man by her bed, removing his belt. The sheer terror of it made her scream as loudly as she could. She tried to struggle, unable to work out why she was so ineffective. But the noise was enough. The man ran from her room.

She kept struggling, managing to free her arm tied to the bedhead. Tearing at her throat, desperate to get air, she succeeded at loosening the strip of towelling. Gulping for air, she could make out that Pauline's bed was empty and, in her shock, forgot her sister was away. She was certain that he'd kidnapped her. Forgetting herself and determined to save her sister, she ran outside after him, screaming that she would get him and kill him.

Cooke ran fast, retracing his earlier steps along the path to Broadway, along Princess Road and into Kingsway to the house where he'd seen the push-bike. He ran up the path and took it, making a fast getaway as far as Subiaco, where he left the bike against the fence of a house in Bagot Road. He walked through Subiaco to Leederville. There was a taxi at the rank in Oxford Street. He hailed the driver for a ride home, noticing how light it had become by the time he reached Rivervale and his unsuspecting wife.

Schoolteacher Terence Merchant and his wife Geraldine were woken by screams from the neighbouring block of flats on the other side of the courtyard. Terry said it was a couple having a row and they shouldn't interfere. The 30-year-old started to settle back to sleep again, but Geraldine insisted there was something terribly wrong and someone was in trouble. So Terry got up, hurriedly pulled on his trousers and shirt, and went outside to investigate, his wife close behind in her dressing gown. The noise was coming from the flat exactly opposite, but they were unable to see anything. They hurried across the courtyard.

When they got closer they could see the woman on the front balcony. A young woman, naked below the waist, with something around her neck and blood dribbling from her mouth, screaming hysterically and trying to run, but staggering and seeming to be in a half faint. They couldn't work out the cause of it, wondering if she was drunk, until she focused well enough through the shock to see them and shout that there was a prowler and he was still in there.

Terry went in to investigate, his practical wife Geraldine, an RPH nurse, following him to find something to cover the young woman. Geraldine found a blanket and tried to reassure her as Terry searched the flat. There was no prowler inside, but he saw a stocking tied to the bed. Geraldine stayed with Anne, while Terry ran back to their flat and called the police and her parents, who lived nearby.

Detective Graham Lee was soon on the scene, and amazed at the sight of the young woman, who was 'almost dead'. Anne's father arrived soon after. But Harold Melvin didn't recognise the young woman who was bleeding from the mouth, her eyes bloodshot, strangulation marks across her neck and severe red marks on her left wrist. He ran past his daughter, calling for her.

Anne was too terrified to go back into the flat. Her father took her home, where he called the family GP, Dr Claude Anderson. Dr Anderson sedated her while they waited for the police photographer and the District Medical Officer, who came at 7.30 a.m. and recorded the signs of near strangulation – bloodshot eyes and slightly cyanosed face.

Detective Sergeant Bruce Brennan and Detective Peter Johnson investigated the assault over the following months in an unsuccessful effort to find the man Anne had described.

For Nicholas Treleaven, the phone call from Anne's mother next day was a bolt out of the blue. Shocked and bewildered, he visited Anne at her parents' home and was interviewed by the detectives.

The Merchants withdrew and tried to forget about their strange Sunday morning, apart from going to see Anne and having to answer questions from the suspicious police who wanted to know why Terry was there fully dressed so early in the morning. Geraldine's brother also had to face some heavy questioning

– he'd visited a few days earlier and his car had been reported as having been parked at the flats.

A few days later, Terry and Geraldine Merchant went out to find their car covered in women's panties. The FC Holden parked in the courtyard had panties tucked under the windscreen wipers, through the door handles and jammed into the door edges. They called the police, who found footprints in the gardens past the windows on their side of the courtyard and some broken plants. It seemed the prowler had spent a long time looking through the windows. The Merchants were worried. Besides teaching, Terry ran a gymnasium in the evenings, leaving Geraldine home alone until about 9 p.m. They decided to go somewhere safer, quickly moving out of the flat to live with Geraldine's mother in Shenton Park.

It took Anne more than a year to recover from the trauma. During that time the 23-year-old slept between her parents and only ventured out of the house to go to Mass. Adding to her terror was a long series of phone calls in which the caller just hung up. Anne was certain her attacker had somehow found her parents' number. Two years later she left Perth to get away from the memory and the fear, settling in New Zealand.

Love in the Air

SPRING 1962

Occasionally John Button would find the time to catch up with Frank Garrett for an evening – not often, because Frank wasn't involved in dancing, but the two kept in touch. John had become mates with Frank at work. The two met when John first joined Bouldens, where Frank did mechanical work, but they didn't get to know each other for quite a while. Frank was on the other crop-dusting team and then he went into the Army. They became mates on his return. Frank was six months older than John and quite different, but the two opposites got on well. Frank was a character; nicknamed Buster Garrett – he was the handsome, popular Fonz type with personality plus, slicked-back hair and a Norton motorbike. He lived in Swanbourne and raced at the Claremont Speedway.

John answered the phone one day to hear Frank's typical cheeky forthrightness, 'Hi. What are we doing Saturday night?'

John had arranged to take Diane out. He knew Frank was about to use him for his car and he wasn't available to help him that night, but he always found it difficult to say no and he didn't like to disappoint his friend.

He hesitated till Frank prompted him. 'Surely it's not that hard a question.'

'I'm going out with Diane – or I thought I was. Why?' John still couldn't just say he was busy.

Frank was suggesting a blind date. He was hoping John would help him out of two difficulties – the disadvantage of the motorbike for a night at the drive-in with his girlfriend Laraine, and the problem of Laraine promising to spend the evening with her girlfriend, Rosemary. So he needed to find someone for Rosemary, and someone with a car. John felt pressured. He would have to say yes and somehow get out of his previous arrangement. He agreed to be at Laraine's house in Alfred Road, Mt Claremont, at 7 p.m.

John spent Saturday cleaning the Mark II Zephyr 6 he now owned, his feelings fluctuating between curiosity, excitement and fear. He really couldn't understand why he'd agreed to it. He'd never been on a blind date before and didn't need to – he had a kissing and cuddling relationship with Diane and there were plenty of other lovely girls at the dance studio. But this was different – going to a drive-in, with someone he'd never met.

He swung off Alfred Road into Strickland Street and saw Frank, Laraine and another girl standing by the driveway of the corner house. Frank had dressed up for the occasion – replacing his leather jacket with a red jumper over his white T-shirt and jeans. John knew he'd done well for a blind date at first sight. There was a tall girl with lovely shoulder-length hair teased high, determinedly pulling a little cardigan around her. She was Rosemary Anderson, Laraine's neighbour across the road. Laraine lived on one corner of Alfred Road and Strickland Street with her parents and brother Joey. Rosemary lived on the other corner with her parents and younger siblings, Helen and Jim. Laraine and Rosemary were both sixteen and had gone through Graylands Primary School and Hollywood High School together. They were best friends, with two other local girls, Pam Pringle and Leslie Matthews.

Frank and Laraine had met at the Lakeway Drive-in when they were watching a movie from the outdoor seating. Laraine's slight, doll-like beauty captured Frank's heart during the advertising slides, and he wasn't going to be put off this night by her commitment to her girlfriend. Rosemary was taller and bigger-framed. She was also more confident and strong-willed, having been given a lot of responsibility for helping look after her brother and sister. But tonight Rosemary was quiet and diffident. It was a new experience for her, too.

Rosemary sat in the front seat, saying a shy thank you when John opened the door. John, already entranced, was reeling from the exquisite smell of her hair spray as he walked around to the driver's side. They covered the short distance to the Lakeway Drive-in without a word. Frank and Laraine had quickly snuggled together on the back seat but John, without dancing as his prop, was tongue-tied. The other two were too interested in each other to make conversation, and John couldn't think of a thing to say apart from asking for four tickets. He set the speaker in the back window and sat against the door on his side of the front bench seat, aware of the distance between himself and Rosemary, but awkwardly not knowing what to do about it. They sat silently, until Frank broke the ice, 'Hell, John, if you're not going to talk to her, at least kiss her.'

As usual, John couldn't say no – nor did he want to. He was thrilled to get closer to the smell of her hair spray. It was even nicer than the perfumes he loved at ballroom dancing. They cuddled in the front seat all night, taking no notice when Frank piped up, 'Hell, don't suffocate her.'

John couldn't wait to see Rosemary again when the night was over. He arranged for the four of them to go for a drive the next day.

The foursome that had started that evening continued for the next few months. John saw Rosemary every weekend, missing out only when the group from Alan Butcher's Studio went to Bunbury for the October long weekend. Rosemary wasn't part of his dancing world and with his new romance still just starting, he left her waving him goodbye as he set out for Bunbury with Diane and the rest of the group. The Alan Butcher team had some success in Bunbury and exuberantly celebrated their competition win – too exuberantly for John, who fell asleep in a drunken haze, and for one of the girls, who snuggled in with him. He'd slept too heavily to notice, but despite the innocence of it, they were in trouble the next day. They'd broken Alan Butcher's strict rules.

John got into trouble another time he left Rosemary to go dancing.

On 24 October the group from Alan Butcher's went to the

Windmill, their regular post-dance coffee shop in West Perth. John left at the same time as Fritz, one of the professional teachers. The two happy young men decided to race. Revving up Beaufort Street, John had hit 50 miles-per-hour when he sped past police in the petrol station on the corner of Walcott Street. He was fined for speeding and lost his licence for a fortnight.

John was a little shaken – he had never come to the attention of the police before. He stuttered nervously when face-to-face with the authorities, horrified at the thought of having a police record. He promised himself that he'd never do anything to come before the law again.

John was in awe of the police. He didn't know that two sisters he danced with at the studio were the daughters of a police officer. Nor did he know that Constable Ralph Featherstone and his wife Peg had heard about him over the dinner table. He didn't know that sixteen-year-old Margaret Featherstone was a little keen on him and that her sister liked him because he danced with her. Helen, at thirteen, was younger than most at the studio, so wasn't asked to dance as often as the others. As an amateur teacher, it was John's duty to ensure all girls had some dances, so he regularly asked Helen.

One-and-a-half weeks before John's brush with the law, the Featherstone family unknowingly had a brush with Cooke. He had been up to his usual cunning trick of raiding brides' houses on their wedding day, knowing there'd be no-one home. On 13 October, he chose the home of a friend of the Featherstones.

The bride was Vicki McPhail, whom Peg Featherstone knew from the time they'd worked together at Boans. The two families had become friends over time, Peg and Ralph's daughters Margaret and Helen befriending Vicki and her sister Rae. Margaret, an apprentice hairdresser, had spent the morning giving the bride and bridesmaids their special hairdos.

The Featherstones went back to the McPhails' house in Joondanna after the wedding to collect Margaret's hairdressing gear and to relax with their friends after the excitement of the day. But as soon as they arrived at 10 Waterloo Street, Ralph

Featherstone went into work mode. A piece of leadlight had been neatly removed from the front door. Immediately recognising a cleverly executed break-in, Constable Featherstone did a search of the house with his friend Bert McPhail. Margaret was worried about her expensive hairdressing equipment which, as a poorly paid apprentice, she would have difficulty replacing. That was safe. But £4/15 was missing from the bedroom, as well as the bridegroom's special bottle of Scotch.

The Featherstone girls gradually lost the amateur teacher they admired, as John's dancing gave way to spending more time with Rosemary. John was in love, seeing a lot of Rosemary and a lot more of his mate Frank, now they had the additional connection through their girlfriends.

Sometimes John and Frank would go out on their own, generally roo-shooting around Yanchep towards Lancelin. John enjoyed the mateship and the drives into the freedom of the bush, and now owned a .22 rifle. It was the Australian thing to do, and he enjoyed shooting at inanimate objects. But he kept up the pretence, shooting at kangaroos and making sure he missed. Frank used to tease him for being such a bad shot, while secretly knowing his soft-hearted friend missed on purpose.

Occasionally John and Frank would take two other mates and have a boys' night out, seeing the girls on Sunday instead. Those youthful fun nights were generally spent at Yanchep, the parents of one of Frank's friends owning the Yanchep Inn. One night, the four drove out in the Zephyr, arriving about 10 p.m. with their bottles of Barossa Pearl and beer, talking their mate into opening the gates of the guests-only swimming pool. It was very dark, so they stripped off and enjoyed the horseplay in the cool water on the hot summer night. They were all lined up along the edge of the pool when one decided to play a joke and flicked on the floodlights – unaware that four elderly lady guests were walking past. They screamed and the youths grabbed their clothes and ran to the car – taking off and leaving the owner's son to the explanations.

As much as John loved such mischievous adventures, he soon wanted to spend more and more time with Rosemary. He started going to her place for tea during the week, spending the evenings with her and her parents, Joan and Jack. More often than not, his car was parked on the big back lawn of the double block.

He had a new car again. He'd recently sold the Zephyr and bought a Vauxhall Velox – but now he really wanted to impress Rosemary with a fancy new car and his boss at Bouldens agreed to give him a loan. He'd looked around several car yards before going to Wentworth Motors on Stirling Highway. Not knowing exactly what he wanted, he was diffident when approached by a salesman. But Danny Varney was experienced and sensed the likelihood of a sale if he put some work into a follow-up.

Having taken John's address, Danny arrived at 8 Redfern Street with a new Simca. He invited the eighteen-year-old on a test drive, using his sales technique to dissuade John's mother and brother from coming along. Experience had taught him how easily potential buyers could be put off by mothers, fathers and friends, so now he insisted on a one-to-one demonstration. Varney clinched the deal, taking the Vauxhall Velox as a trade-in and selling the latest Simca, registration UKA 547.

John was very proud of his brand-new car with all the latest gadgets – heater/demister, windscreen washers, radio and, best of all, reclining front seats.

Margaret was gone from the Button household again. After six months at home, she'd moved into a flat with a girlfriend, and had since married Jim. Jim was in the Air Force and had been posted to Wagga. Only fifteen-year-old Jimmy was left at home in Redfern Street. John started to become part of the Anderson family and it was becoming clear that the two young lovers would be spending their future together.

Happy New Year

29 December 1962

Cooke went out in his car at 7.30 p.m. He drove to Fairlanes Bowling Centre in Adelaide Terrace, at the eastern end of the city. He had become a keen ten-pin bowler, spending some time there most nights and being an active player and official at many of the tournaments. It provided a good social life, where he could forget the responsibility of home and seven children and pretend to be single and free again. At Fairlanes he was the cavalier nice-guy, making up stories about his life, giving the players lifts home and going to their parties. He was always well dressed and was very sociable. None of them suspected he was married.

Friday and Saturday nights were always his nights out on the town, with never an explanation to his wife of where he was or what he was doing. Tonight he was especially ready for some social life, after the family focus of Christmas. He had enjoyed his children on Christmas Day, but now it was coming up to New Year, when the happy singles got out and had fun.

Finishing at Fairlanes about 9.45 p.m., he drove around the corner to the Grosvenor Hotel for a few drinks before moving into the Cottesloe area to start snooping. In case any police were about, he parked his car at some flats in Eric Street, so that they would assume it belonged to someone in the flats. Putting on the gloves and hat as always, he skulked around the back lanes.

About 3.30 a.m. he walked along Hawkstone Street, a long street from the railway line to an area of sand dunes leading to the beach. He reached the beach end, where a house had a good hedge for hiding behind, and watched the young woman living opposite. He knew not to cross the road and go into No. 8. They had an Alsatian that had chased and bitten him eighteen months earlier as he ran from the backyard up the side path. But there was no dog at No. 6, and there was an exotic-looking young woman in the front sleepout, where he'd found some money previously. The asbestos cottage was a family home; she wasn't alone – but the sleepout, leading off the front porch, was separated from people in the main part of the house. He was excited – money and a young beauty.

He tied his handkerchief around his face. Although it was dark, he felt safer with the extra precaution; his mouth was too recognisable. He was worried he might have been seen that time a couple of months ago when the young woman in the Nedlands flat made such a noise, surely waking the neighbours. He had run for it when she started screaming and throwing things at him, but any of the other tenants could have seen him leave.

He crept along the porch and tried opening the door to the bedroom. There was a chair pushed up behind it. She must have been nervous – maybe she'd noticed the missing money, or seen him hanging around previously. But this small impediment wasn't going to put him off. His urge was too strong. He reached around the door to see if he could move the chair. Yes. He gently and quietly pushed it forward, opened the door enough to squeeze inside and tiptoe in. Silently shining his torch around, he saw the woman asleep in the bed opposite the door. She was beautiful – but first he looked for her purse. On the previous visit, he had found money on a chair by the head of her bed.

After checking the dresser and the room's empty second bed, he went to her bed. There might be some money along the bedhead – but anyway, the exotic woman was certainly there. He started to remove the bedclothes. She suddenly sat up and started to scream.

He flashed his torch in her eyes to stop her getting a good look at him. Even with the mask, you couldn't be too sure. He had to stop that scream too. He hit her in the face with his fist. Was it once, or more? He didn't notice, he just had to make sure she was silenced. He'd hit her solidly, but she didn't stop screaming – so loudly that he decided he had better run for it. He ran all the way back to his car two blocks away and started for home, carefully leaving the headlights off until he was out of the Cottesloe area.

Margaret Esther Terese Fleury, known as Peggy, was a 25-year-old bookbinder and the only one of the French–Indian family's three children still living at home.

She awoke with the feeling that someone was removing the bedclothes and taking hold of her. She opened her eyes to the most frightening sight. A man with a mask or handkerchief covering his face and with gloves on and something like a knuckle-duster over them. He was wearing a hat, looking just like a bandit from the westerns. She screamed in shock and terror. He hit her over the head with the torch and then over the eye with his fist. The attack made her scream louder. The attack stopped, but the terror didn't.

The screams woke her parents and some of the neighbours. Running to the sleepout, her parents found Peggy screaming in bed with an eye looking like it was half gouged out. Blood was pouring from it. Ron Fleury screamed at his wife Phil to get the carving knife. He pounded up and down the front pathway with it until the police arrived.

Peggy was so hysterical that at Fremantle Hospital Dr Cohen had to give her a sedative even to be able to examine her beyond seeing the injured eye, bruises on her forehead and scratches over her face. He reported cuts and bruising of the left eyelid and bruising to the eyeball.

The Fremantle police were called to the hospital at 4.45 a.m., but when Constable Brian Illingworth tried to interview her to find out what happened, she started screaming again. The doctor suggested they leave the interview until the next day.

Detective Peter McGrath, on night motor patrol of the area, arranged for a day-shift officer to interview Peggy next day, but she was still too traumatised. They tried again later that night and managed to get one piece of information out of her – that she'd had £10 or £11 in notes in her handbag under the bed – but she was still incapable of saying anything more. Checking with her father, they learnt the money was missing. Sergeant Gillies' search for fingerprints brought no results.

The McKenzies, next door to the Fleurys at 8 Hawkstone Street, were alarmed at the attack. There were rumours about their neighbour's activities in the sleepout, but an attack like this was just dreadful. It made the McKenzies more worried about the safety of their teenage daughter, especially when they had also had an incident with a prowler.

Eighteen months previously, seventeen-year-old Janet McKenzie had seen the outline of a man walk down the path in the narrow gap between them and the Fleurys. Not long after she and her father had arrived home at night from visiting her mother in hospital, Janet was in her bedroom and her father was cleaning his teeth. Realising that the man must have been hiding in the backyard when she drove into the garage, Janet called out to her father, who sooled Roddy on to the intruder. At the call of 'get him', their Alsatian-kelpie cross was off, followed by Bruce McKenzie, the head of the State Housing Commission. An active, fit member of the North Cottesloe Surf Life Saving Club and part of its sprint team, Bruce believed he could catch him, until he ran into the prickles at the edge of the sand dunes. Stopped by double-gees, he gave up and called Roddy, who was barking furiously a bit further away. In the light of what had happened to Peggy, they now wondered what could have happened to Janet if it hadn't been for Roddy.

Inspector Athol Wedd wrote in his report on the Fleury assault that the police should concentrate on this inquiry because there had been a number of such offences in the area. Detective Cyril Wilcox at Claremont CIB had similar concerns about these recurring incidents. On New Year's Eve he wrote to Chief Inspector Lamb:

> For the past 6 months reports have been received at the Subiaco and Claremont CIB offices of a person committing thefts of money from flats in these police districts.
>
> Of late these reports have become more frequent and some concern is being felt for the safety of women who are being disturbed by the offender after he has entered the premises and stolen what money he can find. It would appear from the

reports that the offender is active from dusk until midnight and again about dawn.

Many of the complainants, single women sharing a flat, leave keys in doors, leave windows open and unscreened or leave their doors open altogether.

The offender is in the habit of using these means of entry rather than forcible entry to the premises . . . In checking through the MOs showing these similarities, it would appear that the offender always steals money . . . He does not ransack the premises and invariably no signs of entry can be found.

No fingerprints have ever been found at the premises.

There has been the odd occasion where the offender has disturbed the female occupants of the flats which he raids . . . Photographs have been shown without result as no person has actually seen his face enough to be able to identify him again.

In view of a more recent complaint wherein the description of the offender is almost identical with that of previous reports and the fact that the woman in this instance was assaulted, a more serious view of these offences is being taken ...

A Mrs Pittaway and her husband occupying the flat immediately above the complainant's [Miss King's] saw the offender leaving and described him as being 30–40, tan complexion, 5'9" to 5'10", thin to medium build, particularly well dressed in a blue/grey suit, light coloured tie and maybe a black felt hat. One quite indelible feature was that he wore close fitting white gloves which came an inch or 2 up his wrist.

The fingerprint bureau have found numerous glove prints on this type of offences ...

Perhaps the contents of this report could also be brought to the attention of the night and afternoon patrols and afternoon shift and read for general information.

The response from Inspector Lamb was immediate. A memo was sent to night motor patrols ordering special attention to be paid to Detective Wilcox's report whenever possible. He further suggested that if no work was at hand, patrols be maintained in the area, and that the matter was to be regarded as urgent, because it was necessary to apprehend this offender before offences of a more serious nature were committed. Another paragraph was added to the bottom in handwriting: 'When checking on persons in street, look for torch, gloves (possibly white) and mask.'

Peggy Fleury's eye was so badly damaged that it required an operation. She missed her big night out on New Year's Eve and lay in hospital for the first four days of 1963.

John Button had a wonderful New Year's Eve. Jack Anderson had set up a bar in the backyard and invited John and the Button family to join them.

It was a warm feeling of acceptance for John to see his and Rosemary's parents together, relaxing on the back lawn where he spent so much time horsing around with Rosemary. These games usually involved the sprinkler and were often under the guise of washing the car – washing Rosemary, too, as she sat on the bonnet. Helen and Jim often joined in the fun, and Frank and Laraine were sometimes over, too, now they were living with Laraine's parents over the road. John and Rosemary had been shocked just before Christmas to see Laraine dressed in white, whisked off in a car. Her pregnancy at sixteen had led to a quick, quiet wedding that even her best friend Rosemary hadn't known about.

It had made John think seriously about his future and settling down with Rosemary. With marriage and children in mind, he'd decided he needed a solid trade. He had resigned from Bouldens with the intention of following his father into bricklaying. He told Rosemary about it on New Year's Eve.

The new year was full of promise for their future. At midnight, they walked up and down the street, calling Happy New Year to everyone else partying outside in the cool of the summer's night, and thinking that for them, at least, it would be the best year yet.

Judy Craig and her friends had a happy New Year, all full of excitement for the imminent wedding of one of them.

The kitchen tea was held in the bride-to-be's home in East Fremantle a few weeks later. Judy drove home from the party, quite relaxed about being on her own late at night. Like the rest of Perth's young women, the twenty-year-old was not aware of police concerns about the burglar. Even if she had known, she would not have worried. Her home was in Floreat Park, outside the area involved, and her father was the Honourable Jim Craig, Minister for Police.

The bride's family were friends of Judy's family, and her father was to be master of ceremonies at the wedding reception at the Como Hotel on 26 January. Judy had borrowed her mother's Hillman to get to the party, so she was driving carefully as she made her way home along Canning Highway and on to Kwinana Freeway. It was then that she noticed a car following her. She was still on the freeway, with this cream FE Holden on her tail, when the street lights went out at 1.15 a.m.

There wasn't much traffic about, and her first thought was that this was pleasant company. But as the car stayed behind her, she wondered why she was being followed and for how long he'd been there. As she drove west along Wellington Street and Roberts Road, it was still with her, she started to get edgy. She crossed the railway line at the Axon Street bridge, turning left to head west along Railway Parade.

On Railway Parade, the car behind came up really close – then closer, till it rammed the back of her car. It fell back and came close again, almost level with the back door, then veered and hit the back door. It came up again, this time hitting the front door. Judy didn't panic, but started to say Hail Marys while looking for a way out of the situation.

She decided to stop. She got out and ducked behind the car. The Holden pulled up about 100 yards in front. The driver started running back towards her, waving what looked like a stick. As the petite five-foot bookkeeper crouched behind the damaged car, she could see he wasn't tall, had rather a wiry physique, looked Greek and had a funny mouth.

Just as she wondered what this man was going to do to her, she was rescued. A man and a woman were walking on the other side of the road. The man pushed his girlfriend into the bushes and ran across the road towards Judy. That was enough to send the driver running back to his car. He sped away. Her rescuer asked if she was all right. Stunned, she said yes and gathered her thoughts enough to ask him if he could ring home for her. He knocked on a nearby door, waking up the residents, who rang her parents. She stayed by the car until her father arrived and took her to Subiaco Police Station to report the incident.

About two weeks later, Judy's father came home and told her a cream Holden, stolen from a car yard, had been pulled out of the river. Its damage matched the damage to her mother's car.

A week into the new year, John Button again had dealings with the police over a minor accident.

On Monday 7 January, he was driving along St Georges Terrace in the city, heading west towards home in Subiaco at 7.45 p.m. He was three to four yards behind a Ford Prefect and was travelling slowly, at 15 mph. It was far below the 30 mph speed limit, but not slow enough to stop in time when the Ford braked suddenly at a pedestrian crossing. A couple had stepped on to the cross-walk. John's Simca slid into the Ford, damaging the left of his car as he tried to steer around to avoid it.

Both drivers got out and looked at the consequences. John was lucky. He had hardly done anything to the Prefect, virtually just a scratch. That driver didn't have to worry. On his car, though, the parking light was broken and the grille was bent in. He quickly estimated it to be about £25 worth. They exchanged addresses. Then Clarence Beckerdyke Wilson of 43 Kidman Avenue, South Guildford, continued on his journey. John went straight to the Subiaco Traffic Office and reported the accident, giving the details to Officer 2881, L.J. Bracks.

The formalities over, he went home, disappointed that his brand-new car was no longer pristine, but not letting it affect the happiness of the new year and the promise it held.

Australia Day Bloodletting

26 January 1963

The birth of Australia as a British colony 175 years back was of no interest to the young couple. Basking in the joys of summer and love, Australia Day meant a long weekend – three glorious days to be with each other. They had no particular plans, it didn't matter what they did – the beach, drives along the coast, hamburgers, romance. The highlight would be tonight's special night out at The Hideaway with the Andersons. Rosemary had turned seventeen the previous Monday and John saw the invitation to join them at the party as a sign of their acceptance of him as part of the family. He was thrilled. He couldn't imagine his future without her and he believed that Rosemary and her parents were also including him in her future.

Impatient to see her, he was at her place early. It was already hot, so the decision to clean the car happily combined the fun of a cooling water fight with the work needed to have it spick and span for its special passengers that night. John wanted to impress the people he expected to become his parents-in-law.

He looked ruefully at the damaged front of the car, commenting to Rosemary that he really should do something about it, especially the broken parking light and indicator. The left headlight rim was buckled and the light was out of alignment, giving him less than perfect vision to the left at night. He had asked his friend from Bouldens, workshop foreman Leonard Robinson, to look at it. He wanted to save his no-claim bonus by having Leonard fix it instead of claiming against his insurance, but he'd done nothing more about it. He pondered over his delay. Why hadn't he had it fixed during the past three weeks? It wasn't really time or money that had stopped him, he just hadn't got around to it. He was sorry that his new car was less than perfect for taking the Andersons on the long trip along Wanneroo Road to the northern edge of suburban Perth – especially as he'd been embarrassed about it before. He'd offered to take the Andersons to visit Jack's sister in Mt Hawthorn and had said then that he would have to get the blinker lights fixed. Thinking about it now and reaching for a cigarette, he chided himself for having been too preoccupied to get around to it.

The cigarette pack was empty. He told Rosemary he was off to the shops for a new packet, her disapproving look reminding him of her many pleas for him to give it up. But he'd been smoking for nearly five years. He was addicted. And not only to smoking, but also to the pinball machine in Pete's deli under the old picture theatre in Swanbourne. It was further away than the shops down the road, but John figured that with the whole weekend ahead of them, he wouldn't be missed for ten minutes or so while he had a quick game. But he wouldn't tell her where he was going, either. He would rather avoid a repeat of the conflict they'd had previously. She didn't like this addiction any more than the other and the last time he'd been to Pete's with her, she'd become angry when he couldn't drag himself away from the game at her bidding. That's when he had discovered how stubborn she could be. She'd picked up her bag and announced she was walking home – and no amount of begging could make her change her mind. Only when she'd walked some distance and had time to cool off did she relent and let him drive her the rest of the way.

Despite the memory of her anger, he drove to Pete's. He loved that noisy competition with the machine, and he had quite a few sixpences in his wallet, having mowed Pete's lawn in Claremont recently. Greek Pete knew how to get his lawn-mowing money back through the pinball machine by paying John in coins. Figuring he could have a few games before Rosemary noticed, he put the first sixpence in the slot and started flipping the controls. He wasn't as long as he expected, however, quickly losing the games and all his money. Now keen to get back to Mt Claremont before he was missed, he sped, not noticing much else as he concentrated on the road. When he pulled on to the Andersons' back lawn, he was relieved that Rosemary didn't comment on the time he'd been gone. The young couple resumed their playful car-cleaning. They were still horsing around when Laraine arrived, feigning anger and thanking him for the lift. But where had he passed her and missed her?

He shouldn't have asked.

'On the way back from Pete's,' came the reply. Rosemary gave him a stern look and pointed her finger at the car radio which happened to be blaring out the latest hit the 'Night has a Thousand Eyes'. Recognising the warning that this was her theme song and she would always find out what he was up to, he wondered when he would manage to get back to Pete's for the next bout against the machine.

Lunch broke the tension and, while finishing the drying up, Rosemary suggested a drive. John readily agreed, happy to get away on their own for a while. He was sure Joan Anderson always kept an eye on them on the back lawn from the kitchen window. It was a real scorcher of a day, the temperature well over the century and no hint of a sea breeze. Rosemary chose Luna Park, the amusement park at Scarborough, where they could have fun on the rides as well as go to the beach and have ice-creams. John didn't know that it would also give Rosemary the opportunity to get her own back.

She headed straight for the Gee Whizz, a ride with spinning chairs on a platform that also spun around while rising and falling in a wave-like motion. John tried desperately not to show his fear as Rosemary stepped into a chair and held up the bar for him. He tried to rationalise that if Rosemary could handle it without worrying, then surely a man could. But he tried to will the operator into keeping it turning slowly, terrified of the build-up of speed that Rosemary was obviously eagerly anticipating. Neither his efforts at thought transference nor his prayers were successful. The pitch of the motor changed as the seats and

Left: Pnena Berkman, Cooke's first murder victim, January 1959.

Above: Nel Schneider with her second child Judy, a few months before becoming the victim of Cooke's first hit-and-run.

Jillian Brewer, and (inset) the man convicted of her murder, Darryl Beamish.

Above: Glenys Peak at the time of the hit-and-run.

Left: Kathy and Phil Bellis just before the mother of three became Cooke's second hit-and-run victim.

Above: Lucy Madrill.

Right: Jill Connell at the time of the hit-and-run.

Terese Zagami, aged 12.

Georgina Pitman at the time of the multiple hit-and-run.

Above: Maureen Rogers, who took the main force of the impact in Cooke's multiple hit-and-run.

Right: University student Shirley McLeod, whose ambition was to become a social worker because she believed so many people needed help.

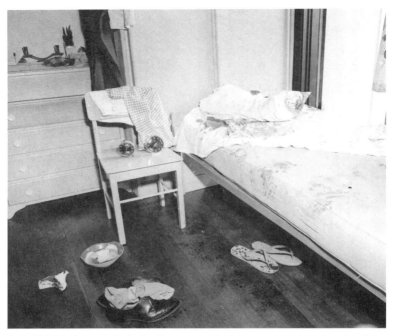

Brian Weir's bedroom in Cottesloe, the scene of Cooke's second Australia Day shooting.

Brian Weir (front right).

John Sturkey.

George Walmsley.

Back verandah bedroom, the scene of Cooke's shooting of John Sturkey.

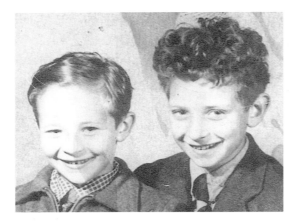

Jimmy (left) and John Button, aged 6 and 9, in the UK.

John Button at the time he was courting Rosemary Anderson.

John Button's parents, Charles and Lillian Button.

Rosemary Anderson in John Button's Simca.

John Button's Simca in the police yard. There was no skin, hair, flesh or fibre on or under the car.

Detectives examine the Chrysler Royal V8 used in the multiple hit-and-run. Note the extensive damage to the front of the car. Compare this with John Button's Simca (above) that supposedly hit Rosemary Anderson at 35 mph. Rosemary and Maureen Rogers both weighed 10 stone at the time, and both landed between 60 and 100 yards from the place they were hit.

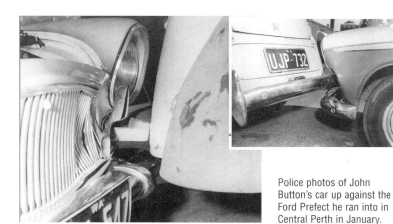

Police photos of John Button's car up against the Ford Prefect he ran into in Central Perth in January.

The grim bare exercise yard for Death Row prisoners.

John Button's cell in Main Division (centre of centre row).

Detective Sergeant John Wiley in 1963.

platform spun faster and John's stomach reached for his throat. Managing to hold lunch down until the torture was over, he tried to look casual as he stepped off the platform, but his legs buckled under him. His refusal to answer Rosemary's laughing enquiry about how he'd enjoyed it encouraged her to rub it in, and she imitated his shaky exit. John good-humouredly admitted defeat and put his arms around her, pulling her close and suggesting something that didn't move. Rosemary laughed again and led him over to the shooting gallery. There he could regain his supremacy. He was a good shot when it came to aiming at wooden ducks rather than live animals.

Cooke fingered the gun, his mind drifting back to his time in the CMF's 16-28 Battalion, when he was such an expert shot. He had found the .22 calibre rifle and a packet of 50 cartridges in the dark back bedroom of a house in South Perth.

Australia Day meant nothing to him, either. There wasn't anything to celebrate about the beginnings of a nation that had kept him an outcast. It was just another weekend, when he could take what he wanted from the happy-go-lucky people who gave him nothing.

Earlier he'd taken some of the children with him to do the regular weekly shopping at the deli in Kooyong Road and had his normal friendly chat with Gladys Holly as she put together the vegetable order. He worked a few hours a week in the shop for Gladys and Percival Holly, emptying the cartons and packing the shelves. He was such a good, hard worker that they kept employing him, despite being aware that he was a petty thief.

'Poor Eric, but he's harmless,' Gladys would say, finding him to be quiet and polite, though she was a little concerned at the temper she sometimes saw him display towards his children.

After the shopping, he played with the children for a while, then left home at 1.30 p.m. with no word of where he was going, as usual. He walked to the bus stop. His own car was in the repair shop after he'd had an accident on 11 January, while taking a girl home from Fairlanes. There was £300 damage to the car, which ended up through a front fence.

He caught a bus from Rivervale into the city, leaving it in

Adelaide Terrace at Fairlanes, where he played his favourite game for most of the afternoon. Finishing at 5 o'clock, he went to another favourite haunt, the Mayfair Theatrette, a small downstairs cinema in Hay Street showing continuous features. He sat there for an hour-and-a-half watching *Wild Life Paradise*, *Blue Angels* and *Aces in the Air*.

At 6.45 p.m. he caught a bus to South Perth to his parents' home, staying with his mother for about half an hour. From there he followed his father's well-worn route to the Hurlingham Hotel on Canning Highway, stopping for a middy of shandy. Then he walked along the highway to the other local, the Como Hotel, where he had another couple of middies. Little did he know the Minister for Police was there, as master of ceremonies at a wedding reception, as was his daughter, whose car he had rammed a few nights previously.

He left the Como at about 8.30. It was time to stop drinking and start prowling, now that it was dark enough. He walked around the corner along Norton Street towards the oval and past several unlit homes before picking on No. 5, a solid grey house. Pulling on his gloves, he crept down the right of the house, checking the windows. On the back veranda, he found one open. He carefully removed the fly wire from the kitchen window and climbed through. He wasn't worried when he saw someone in the lounge room – he knew he was deft enough to creep around undetected. He searched the house for valuables, finding £4 in an envelope in a bedroom. Looking for more money in a back bedroom, he opened a wardrobe to find a shotgun and .22 rifle, which he thought was a Lithgow. Searching further for money, he came across a gladstone bag which had a number of packets of .22 calibre bullets and some shotgun cartridges. He put a packet of bullets in his coat pocket and took the rifle without disturbing anything, so that owner Donald Cornish didn't notice them missing. He silently opened the front door and walked out, carrying the rifle at his right side.

He crossed to the footpath on the other side of Norton Street, turning into Sandgate Street and noticing a woman sitting on a chair at the front of her house, the veranda being well lit. He continued on towards the Royal Perth Golf Club and the river, prowling around houses in several streets. Getting through a bathroom window into the home of Senator Shane Paltridge at 122 Forrest Street, he managed to find quite a lot of money, taking £36 from a handbag in the main room and a further £1 from a child's money box. There was no-one home, just like the last time he'd been in this house.

Continuing along Forrest Street he came to the T-junction with Karoo Street and that huge impressive Anglican church, St Mary's. Opposite the church iwas a two-storey house on the top of the hill. A light was on in the top storey, but there was no movement anywhere. There were two cars at the end of the driveway – a Morris Minor inside the garage, and a cream-and-yellow FE Holden on the driveway behind it. He walked along the two parallel sets of concrete slabs and looked inside the Holden, finding the keys in the ignition. He noticed the engine was warm as he carefully removed the globe from the interior light to help prevent recognition when the door was open. He'd devised many ways to camouflage his identifiable hare lip, but was careful to take this extra precaution. He released the handbrake and pushed UHK 268 out of the driveway of 30 Karoo Street on to the road, before sitting at the wheel and easily coasting down the steep hill. He started it at the bottom, well away from the house. Turning into Onslow Street he saw a black police car parked nearby and so turned right into Labouchere Road and to the Narrows Bridge, crossing into the city and heading west.

The OBH on the North Cottesloe beachfront was filled with thirsty drinkers as usual on summer weekends. Officially called the Ocean Beach Hotel, it was known only by its initials to the hundreds who frequented its bars and dining room. Popular barmaid Rowena Reeves had a busy night, so the attractive blonde was pleased to socialise with friends after closing time. She and three others went a couple of hundred yards south along Marine Parade for a meal at Mario's Restaurant at Cottesloe Beach.

Rowena was with a married man – Nicholas August, the proprietor of a poultry business in West Perth. Last to leave the restaurant at 2 a.m., they and their friends Beryl and Vic drove to Vic's unit nearby in John Street, the men sitting in the front of the car and the women in the back. They decided to have a few more drinks from Nick's well-supplied Esky in the boot before ending their night out, but thought better of doing so at Vic's unit because of complaints about party noise the night before. So they drove to a quiet place around the corner in Napier Street and parked on a gravel section on the verge at the base of the wall surrounding the Cottesloe Civic Centre. They parked with the car facing west towards the ocean so that they had a view out to sea. But they weren't there long when Vic and Beryl started arguing over the attention Beryl had received from the swarthy, romantic guitarist at Mario's. Vic left the car and started walking home. Beryl followed him, leaving Rowena drinking alone with Nick, who remained in front at the wheel while she was still in the back.

Just around the corner from them, in an upstairs flat at 124 Broome Street, an accountant was asleep. Brian Weir had moved his bed across the doorway leading to the front patio which was also the roof of the garage underneath. After a scorching day without any sign of the afternoon sea breeze known as the Fremantle Doctor that normally brought some relief from Perth's searing summer heat, he was hoping to take advantage of any breeze during the night. He left the door wide open and slept with his head at the foot of the bed.

The 29-year-old had gone to bed after doing some study for his next accountancy exam. He had earlier driven to City Beach to go over the guest list with his brother, who was to be best man at his April wedding. But Colin was out. Surprised, because a night out was rare for Colin and Judy since the arrival of their second child, Brian stayed and chatted to their boarder for a while before going back to his books. Later, he set two alarm clocks to make sure he was up in time for training in the morning and went to bed. When his flatmate came home, he sat up in bed and smoked while they chatted for a while, then went to sleep. He would go over the guest list later in the morning, when his fiancee rang from Adelaide.

Two students living in a boarding house in Nedlands had gone out this evening. Twenty-year-old Scott MacWilliam went to the OBH, but first he gave a lift to his eighteen-year-old room-mate John Sturkey. He took John on his scooter to see his girlfriend who lived with her parents in Malcolm Street in the city. Julie Hogg was down with chicken pox, requiring a quiet home visit rather than the outing she and John would have preferred on such a hot, still summer's night. John didn't want to miss seeing her, despite her spots, because in just a week he would leave for Brisbane to continue his studies as a second-year veterinary science student at Queensland University. They had an agreement to get engaged after his first year there and married the following year, when eighteen-year-old Julie finished teachers' college and could move to Brisbane.

John arrived at the Hoggs' house, giving Julie's mother a big hug and a leg of beef he'd brought from his holiday job at the abattoir. He stayed for tea and had a pleasant family evening before it was time for Julie to get back to bed. Her father suggested he stay the night in the spare bed in the attic, rather than hitchhike from the city to Nedlands, as he generally did. Hitchhiking was popular and considered safe by most people, but not by Julie's father, Magistrate K. H. Hogg, who faced the dark side of human nature every working day. Julie, though, didn't want John to stay. The pretty teenager was self-conscious about her face ravaged by chicken pox, and didn't want him seeing her first thing in the morning. So, easy-going John walked the short distance to Kings Park Road and quickly hitched a ride to Nedlands and the house where he boarded at 54 Vincent Street. Wearing just shorts, he went to sleep in his bed on the back veranda at 11 p.m.

Scott had arrived home around 7.30 p.m. and gone to bed early. Waking again at about 1 a.m. he took a bottle of milk from the fridge and went out to the cooler veranda for relief from the stifling house. John was sleeping, but awoke and they had a brief chat as Scott sat on the edge of the bed and drank his milk.

In the next street from Scott and John, George Walmsley arrived home just before 11.30 after his night's work. He pulled his

Ford Consul into one half of the double garage at 51 Louise Street, knowing from the empty side that his wife and daughter weren't in yet.

The 55-year-old former grocer was a talented musician. He had played piano and organ for pleasure in his small home town of Waroona, southwest of Perth, and since retiring to the city, had regularly played professionally. He often played at home, his fingers caressing the keyboard of his grand piano to fill the house with such favourites as 'Tigo Tigo'. His talents were in demand for weddings and parties and so he was regularly out working on a Saturday night. He often played at the OBH, but this night he'd played for a dinner at the Palace Hotel in the city, while his wife Margaret and 22-year-old daughter Sandra went to a movie in Dalkeith. They arrived home at midnight, after he'd gone to bed, and they too retired. Sandra went to her elder brother's bedroom at the front, opposite her parents' room, which she was using while 26-year-old Neil was working in Sydney. They would all be up in the morning in time for the 10 a.m. service at the Nedlands Methodist Church, as usual.

John Button arrived back at the Andersons at 7 p.m. sharp to pick up Rosemary and her parents. Almost an hour later they were on the dark northern outskirts of the city and turning off Wanneroo Road to The Hideaway, the Spanish-style party venue. Walking towards the coloured lights strung above the swimming pool behind the building, the young lovers dropped back behind the Andersons to cuddle a little.

'Black Rose,' John whispered in her ear. He adored her hair and the way she teased it high and secured it with the perfumed hair spray. Months of nuzzling into the scent had established it as her essence, the scent that roused his love.

John was proud to hear Jack Anderson introduce him around as his future son-in-law. It was a satisfying start to a romantic night of cavorting in the swimming pool and dancing on the portable dance floor on the back lawn. Another indication to John of Rosemary's parents' understanding of their future marriage was their ready acceptance of the two going back to the car to change into their bathers, unchaperoned.

In their bathers and carrying their towels, they raced back to the pool, Rosemary winning and trying to splash the runner-up. John was in two minds – to dive in to impress her or to lower himself in slowly as he usually did. Then he compromised, joining her in an easy flat dive from the second step six inches under water. The relief from the heat, the romance of the reflections of the coloured lights dancing in the breeze overhead and the chance to hold each other close, weightless, kept them in a long time until Joan Anderson called them to the barbecue.

'I love you,' he told her again as he reluctantly let her go so that they could emerge and race each other to the table.

It was a long night and it was well past 3 a.m. when John drove the Andersons home, contentedly feeling part of a happy family. As they were nearing Mt Claremont, a news flash came over the car wireless. A couple had been shot in a car in Cottesloe. The startling news had no impact on the young couple in the Simca. They were in high spirits from their special night out, and nothing existed beyond each other and their plans for the future.

Another young man was driving back from The Hideaway with the three girls he had taken there for the evening. The 21-year-old arrived home late to find the woman who had been shot was his mother.

Reaching Cottesloe, Cooke stopped in Grant Street. He pulled up on the nature strip and parked between two pine trees. Leaving the rifle on the back seat while he prowled, he ensured its safety by taking the car keys and hiding them on top of a nearby PMG telephone junction box. He was back in the vicinity of the house where he'd hit that screaming woman three weeks earlier, around Hawkstone and Hamersley streets. After wandering for a while, he returned to the car and drove to Marine Parade, along the ocean front a short way, before turning into Napier Street. As he passed the Cottesloe Civic Centre he saw a Holden sedan on the verge by the Civic Centre's large limestone wall. He could see a couple in the car, parked facing the water. Dirty people. But he was aroused, and there was scrubland opposite to watch from. He would park and go back for a thrill.

He turned around the next corner into Broome Street, parking about 30 yards south of the corner of Geraldine Street. This time he took the rifle from the back seat. He walked back , not down the street but by a hidden route around the tennis courts. He then snuck across the scrubby vacant land until he was opposite the car, on the other side of the road. He moved forward, out of the scrub into the open to get a closer look. The couple in the car would be too distracted to notice him and the area was deserted. A little earlier, there would have been quite a few people at that part of the beach because of the proximity of the late-night hamburger spot, Van Eileens. Some would have driven especially to this popular caravan perched on the cliff above the beach, others would have been beachgoers enticed by the aroma of fried onions on the breeze. They would have been milling around the front waiting for their orders or looking over the ocean at the back as they ate. But now it was late, Van Eileens was closed and shuttered, and there was no-one at all.

The interior light came on, giving him a better look at them. But he was noticed. Rowena Reeves was sitting in the back seat drinking pink champagne when she spotted their observer. She mentioned it to Nick August, who thought that his wife had arranged someone to spy on him. He threw the bottle at the stranger, yelling at him to piss off.

Another one treating him like that. Another insult, to add to those years of cruelty, disdain and rejection. The rage burst in Cooke. He would get his own back this time. He had a gun. He could just blast this one away.

'Look out, he's got a gun!' Rowena gasped, seeing their observer raise it as the beer bottle rolled a little way down the street. She instinctively leaned forward and pushed his head down to safety below the level of the window as Cooke took aim at the man and squeezed the trigger from 25 feet away. August felt a stinging pain in his back as the bullet went through the skin of his neck and shattered her wrist.

'He's got me,' he said in shock as he started the engine and took off down Napier Street at such speed that pebbles flew and hit Cooke. Ejecting the shell and reloading, Cooke ran to where the car had been parked and fired after it, missing and watching it disappear around the corner into Marine Parade.

August wanted to get as far away as possible, but in confusion, shock and terror and with blood spurting all over the back seat from Rowena's wounds, he started up John Street to his friend's place before Rowena convinced him it would be best to get straight to hospital in Fremantle. Arriving in the port city ten minutes later, August was still not able to think straight enough to find Fremantle Hospital and Rowena kept passing out. He didn't get any help from the person he stopped to ask – on seeing the couple covered in blood, the startled pedestrian ran off without giving any directions.

Ian McGlew was junior surgical registrar on one of his first nights as a second-year resident at Fremantle Hospital. It was a quiet night, which gave him the opportunity to catch a bit of sleep.

It felt as if he had just nodded off when a nurse woke him to tell him he was needed in emergency for a shooting. Surprised at such an incident in Perth and interested at the thought of a medical condition he'd not dealt with before, he hurried to the department to be confronted by a man shouting for his solicitor and a woman whose clothes were covered in blood.

Ignoring the man's panic about his legal position, Dr McGlew organised for the police to be notified and quickly set about examining his patient's neck, recalling his forensic medicine lessons. The man had a laceration in the right side of his neck and another in the left side. X-rays showed there was nothing lodged in his neck. Dr McGlew concluded the bullet had gone through the skin only and lodged in his companion's wrist, and he decided it must have been a shotgun. He dressed the man's wounds and discharged him, unable to believe anyone could have been so lucky. If it had hit his spinal cord he would have been killed or left a quadriplegic. The woman had a small laceration in the left wrist and he could feel a hard object beneath the skin on the other side. X-rays revealed a fractured radius and a foreign body. Dr McGlew extracted the bullet fragments under a local anaesthetic in the operating theatre, stitched the lacerations and applied a plaster before having her admitted.

Detective Sergeant Bert Burrows, based at Fremantle, was in Car 14 on night patrol. At 3.30 a.m. he received a VKI message to attend Fremantle Hospital where a man and a woman had been admitted with what appeared to be gunshot wounds. He sent Detective Frederick Clarke, who took statements from the couple and examined August's Holden, which had a lot of blood on the back seat and floor. Later, with Sergeant Burrows and Constable Litterick, he escorted August back to the scene to point out the bottle and the positions of the car and the gunman.

Rowena gave the police a description of the marksman as tall and slim. August described him as about 20 to 25 years old, slim build, about five-foot nine-inches tall and wearing dark clothing. August said he noticed something odd about the man's lower face – he could have been wearing something over his mouth.

Having failed to stop his prey escaping, Cooke ejected the second spent shell where he stood. He was enraged. He was an expert shot, but the target had moved. He had to take it out on someone else; anyone. He walked along Napier Street past the tennis club to Broome Street, where he turned north and headed towards the stolen car.

He stopped opposite a block of four flats at 124 Broome Street. There was a door open above the garage. Climbing up the concrete steps at the front of the block, he held the rifle in his left hand and jumped over the railing at the top on to the large front patio of the flat on the right. The open door led to a bedroom, where a young man was asleep in a bed which had been pulled up to the doorway. His head was at the foot of the bed, nearest the door. This was an easy, immobile target. This one wouldn't duck for cover or escape down the road. He eyed the sleeping man, full of revenge.

Cooke walked to within three or four feet of him, pointed the rifle at his head and shot him.

Brian Weir was thrown into the air by the impact. He fell back across the bed, his head hanging down the side, his blood dripping on to the floor.

Brian Vincent Weir was the middle child of Harry and Trudy Weir, born in Three Springs in 1934 when his parents were farming wheat and sheep. In 1937 consecutive crop failures forced them to walk off the farm and go to the city, moving to North Cottesloe with their two sons and baby girl. Three years later Harry Weir marched off to war. Sent to work with army transport in Singapore, he joined thousands of other diggers who slaved on the infamous Burma Railway after Singapore fell to the Japanese.

Like thousands of other wives, Trudy spent three-and-a-half years not knowing where her husband was and struggled to raise the children on her own. To make things easier, she sent the two boys to a boarding school attached to the monastery at New Norcia, a Catholic mission in the middle of the bush 80 miles north of Perth. They stayed on at the school when their father finally returned, one of the small percentage of POWs who survived the starvation, disease, torture and back-breaking work in the tropical heat. But it had taken its toll. Harry and Trudy separated and he became a long-distance bus driver. The boys saw him regularly as he passed by on his 300-mile route from Perth to Geraldton, stopping to catch up with their progress at school while passengers joined or left the bus. Brian completed his secondary schooling at New Norcia, where he did well in all his subjects, including passing the Alliance Française exams and joining the Air Training Corps in his final year.

From school he joined the Rural and Industries Bank, studying accountancy at the same time. Avoiding a country posting by resigning at 21, he found work in other firms, ending up at the big international, British Petroleum, at the beginning of 1962. At BP he was the accountant in charge of service stations.

He was in excellent condition. In winter he kept fit by playing squash; in summer, by running on the beach, swimming and actively participating in the Swanbourne–Nedlands Surf Life Saving Club – a lifestyle that led him to choose the flat a few hundred yards from nearby Cottesloe beach. Life couldn't have been better for him. He'd celebrated his twenty-ninth birthday the previous weekend and would celebrate his wedding in three months.

The 31-year-old married man with the seven children waited until the noise from the shot died down, then left the flat and walked to the car. Guessing it was between 2 and 3 a.m., he drove towards Perth.

He stopped in another of his favourite suburbs, Nedlands. Driving along Kingsway, he thought of his recent good haul at No. 70 – £30 from a handbag on the bed after getting in through an open window. He passed another place where he'd done even better five months back – £100 from No. 2 of Coorinda Flats in Princess Road. He was after something different tonight, though; he was still enraged and mad with power, and he had a gun. No screams and spattering of blood like those close-up times, and no ripped, bloodied bodies rolling up on to the bonnet. This was quick, neat and clean. He wanted more.

He parked three blocks away from the highway, on Princess Road, a few yards from the corner of Louise Street. Taking the rifle with him, he wandered down Louise Street, crossing to Vincent Street and on to the memorial rose garden on Stirling Highway.

The sound of breaking glass shattered the silence of the still, hot night. He looked across the highway to Shirleys Frock Salon and saw the hole in the window, made by the handle bars of a bicycle. Cooke raised the rifle and got a bead on the youth who'd entered the shop. Then he saw the youth remove one of the mannequins from the window, take its blouse off, lay it on the shop floor and start having sex with it. Cooke lowered the rifle and walked away, turning back up Vincent Street. He wanted revenge against the happy, beautiful people, not this poor fellow.

Prowling in and out of houses on the way, he ended up at 54 Vincent Street, a big house with a concrete front porch and bevelled glass windows and door. He tried them all, unsuccessfully. This house was solidly locked. Not to be so easily defeated, he wandered around the back, through the easy access of an open carport. There was a clothesline strung between two of the veranda poles and a sheet hanging over it. He pulled the sheet back over his shoulders and ducked under it, to find a youth in a bed on the veranda. He was asleep, facing the wall. An easy target. Cooke looked around first. He went to the back door and, finding it unlocked, entered the kitchen and checked the fridge. On the way out, he noticed the youth had turned over in his sleep and was now facing the garden. That made it easier.

About two feet from the bed, he held the rifle at his hip and shot the teenager in the forehead.

John Lindsay Sturkey was living in the private boarding house for the summer, between finishing first-year science at the University of Western Australia and starting the new university year in Brisbane. He and three other Department of Agriculture cadets had just collected their train tickets and the four were due to travel within the week to Brisbane and Sydney, to the only two veterinary science schools in Australia.

A bright boy, he'd been a very successful student at the private Methodist boys' school, Wesley College, gaining a good Leaving at the age of sixteen, a year younger than the average school graduate, and a cadetship with the Department of Agriculture, which paid his way through university. He was also a good sportsman, rowing in the school's Head of the River fours, and an excellent all-rounder, gaining the coveted Queen's Scout Award for endeavour.

His parents adored the warm, personable child, the youngest of their three, and had hated having to send him away to boarding school. But with his father working with Katu Kim Dredging Limited in western Thailand, there was little choice. John left his parents and amah at the age of ten to come to Perth for a good schooling. When Bob and Jess Sturkey returned to WA, it was not to Perth but the southwest town of Capel, so for the sake of his education, John continued boarding in Perth. On Bob's retirement as manager of Westralian Oil Ltd eighteen months previously, the Sturkeys stayed in the country, and John taking a room at the university residence, Currie Hall.

The five-foot nine-inch teenager had a good social life. Girls were drawn to his sunny personality, warm smile and ready laugh. His many interests had hampered his studies in his first year of university, and like many others trying to establish their social and professional lives at the same time, he failed his exams. Repeating first year and settling down to the work, his natural intelligence and intensity of purpose brought good results. Now he was enjoying the department's summer duties, ranging from animal health to abattoir work, and the company of his new girlfriend and future fiancee, Julie Hogg. John Sturkey was happy and full of optimism, on the way to achieving personal and professional fulfilment.

Having to vacate Currie Hall for the university holidays but needing to stay in Perth to work for the department, John had found board in a Nedlands house for the past two summers. He slept on the back veranda of the boarding house, through a deal struck the previous year with his friend and fellow boarder. Scott MacWilliam, a country boy from Kellerberrin, had been a boarder at the Presbyterian boys' school, Scotch College, before going to university and taking up residence at Currie Hall with John. He too wanted to stay in the city for the holidays, so the friends had moved into Mrs Allen's house at 54 Vincent Street. It was a large red brick house on a huge block, too big for a widow to live in alone. Her children had grown up, so Connie Allen took in boarders.

The two Currie Hall residents decided to board there for the summer of 1961–62, after their first year of university, despite Mrs Allen not having sufficient bedrooms to accommodate them both. The young men solved that problem easily – while they would share a bedroom, one would actually sleep on the back veranda. They pulled a single wooden bed out to the back and tossed a coin to see who would be the one lucky enough to enjoy the warm summer nights in the fresh air. John Sturkey won the toss.

It was a narrow concrete veranda leading to the laundry and toilet. John set up his bed against the outside kitchen wall, his head not far from the laundry door. At the foot of the bed he had a cane chair and a small wooden table placed under the milk hatch. Wet clothes could be hung on a line strung the length of his bed from a veranda post to the end of the asbestos partition which screened the laundry and toilet. A sheet draped across the line partitioned off his makeshift bedroom from the big back garden with an almond tree and a cape lilac, as well as a tea-tree hedge sectioning off part of the garden and concealing a gate through to the Drys' house at the back in Louise Street.

John was quite satisfied with this simple sleeping arrangement – happy enough to take it up again in November 1962, after he'd repeated his university year and needed accommodation for the summer. Scott had stayed on at the house through the year, having changed his university studies to part-time accountancy and taken up a cadetship with Commonwealth Industrial Gases. The other spare bedroom was taken by 22-year-old Keith Martin, a customs officer, and there was also a temporary guest, Mrs Allen's niece. Pauline Fenton, also 22, had just returned from England and was staying for a while, working at Custom Credit, before returning home to Canberra. Aunty Connie had rigged up a temporary bedroom for her by partitioning off part of the dining room with a sheet. The house was full of young people this hot January night. John felt so lucky to be sleeping outside where it was a little cooler.

He'd got another one. But he still wanted more. It was so easy, so satisfying. He planned to leave the house by the other side, but he found it blocked so he headed for the back fence. There was a gate leading into the backyard of the house in the next street. He ejected the empty shell on the concrete driveway as he walked through to Louise Street across the back lawn and along the driveway of No. 55.

Turning left in Louise Street, he walked past one house and stopped at the next, No. 51. He was virtually opposite the home of his special young friend from the Nedlands Methodist Church, but he'd lost touch with her since his marriage. He walked all the way around this single-storey brick house. At the front again, he propped the rifle against the downpipe at the outer edge of the double garage and walked to the front door. He rang the doorbell twice, hearing the double chime sound inside. He hurried back to the gun and picked it up. Resting his left arm against the downpipe, he drew a bead on the doorway with the rifle. It was about 4 a.m. when he saw a light go on in the front room and through the open venetian blinds, watched a man walk quickly to the front door as he threw on a red dressing gown. The man turned on the porch light and opened the front door, peering to see beyond the pool of light.

Cooke aimed and fired. George Ormond Walmsley sagged at the knees and folded over, slumping across the doorway – a bullet hole in the centre of his forehead.

Engineering student John Biggins was riding his scooter along Princess Road at 3.45 a.m. and was nearing home at 72 Louise Street when he noticed a near-white Holden parked on the northern side of Princess Road, a few feet from the driveway of his neighbour at No. 70. Arriving home he heard a sharp sound, then someone in the car, driving off quietly.

Woken in the middle of the night by the chimes of the doorbell, Sandra Walmsley heard her father walk to the front door. Then she heard a shot.

'Dad,' she shouted as she and her mother ran to the front door to find their loved one lying in the doorway, his blue eyes glazed, blood starting to mat his wavy hair. Sandra ran back into the kitchen and rang central police station and their neighbour over the road, Allan Sharp. She returned to the doorway and gently tried to pull her distraught mother away from her father. The three of them were close, and it was unbelievable that this warm, talented man could have been coldly gunned down like that. They went back to the kitchen, sitting there in shock with Allan Sharp and his son Ian trying to help, until Detective Sergeant Ray Jeffery arrived and took over.

It was over. He'd had his fill of revenge. That feeling left him – that feeling of power that made him light, coming over him like a mantle or cloud, telling him he must use the gun. He didn't know where it came from – his heart or his head – but it was stronger than an impulse or an urge. He felt a power as if he were God, with power over life and death. Now it was gone.

With the vision of the sagging man still before his eyes and the yell 'Dad' ringing in his ears, Cooke jogged back to where he'd parked the car at the corner of Princess Road. He drove into

Kings Park, the huge area of dark bushland where he could safely get rid of the ammunition. With an overarm motion through the driver's window, he threw all of it into the bush to the left. He emerged from the park at the city end and drove towards Narrows Bridge, just as it was getting light.

On the bridge, he stopped for a moment, got out and threw the gun into the river. Neither his concentration on getting rid of the evidence nor the sharp pain of the foresight cutting his finger as he threw stopped him noticing and remembering the number of the light pole he was beside. With the rifle safely where it wouldn't be found, he drove to 30 Karoo Street. He put the car back in the driveway exactly as he'd found it except for the interior light globe – just for a laugh. Then he walked home to Rivervale and went to bed, not disturbing his sleeping wife, and slept until midday.

It was about 4.15 a.m. when Scott MacWilliam was roused from a deep sleep by Pauline calling out frantically that something was wrong with John out on the veranda. She'd been woken by gurgling sounds. Keith was woken by the commotion, too, and the two boys went out the back to see what was causing it. Keith had arrived home one-and-a-half hours earlier, going out the back for a brief moment before going to bed. He saw John asleep but hadn't disturbed him.

Scott switched on the back veranda light and to his horror found masses of blood on the concrete beside John's bed and on the bed around his head. John was making a choking sound. The two young men tried to lift his head to help him breathe. The gurgling youth's head fell back to reveal a gunshot wound at the top of his forehead, surrounded by bruising and powder burns – a wound immediately recognisable to Scott, who'd shot many rabbits as a youth in Kellerberrin. He couldn't believe anyone could shoot his friend at point-blank range.

Shocked, terrified and shaking, Pauline called the ambulance and the police. She passed their instructions on to the rest of the household – they were to stay inside, below the level of the windows, because there was someone in the neighbourhood shooting people. All in the house readily obeyed, hiding frightened and numb while they waited for the police, unable to comprehend what had happened to their friend.

Detectives Ray Jeffery and Bruce Brennan arrived about ten minutes later. The experienced policemen took over, examining the scene while Scott and Keith helped carry John into the back of the ambulance for an emergency trip to RPH. Scott and Mrs Allen followed it into Casualty, too shocked to talk.

Ambulance driver Arthur Griffin applied first-aid to George Walmsley and lifted him into the ambulance. He drove as quickly as he could, arriving at RPH Casualty at 4.30 a.m. Dr Max Sloss and all available staff immediately started emergency procedures.

Exactly five minutes later another man with a gunshot wound in the forehead was rushed into Casualty. Nothing could be done for John Sturkey – he died three minutes after arrival.

Neurosurgeon Ross Robinson was called in to deal with the emergency. Only while scrubbing up did he hear it was the result of shootings near his home. He asked a nurse to ring his wife and warn her to stay indoors.

Despite an hour's frantic efforts, George Walmsley died at 5.35 a.m.

Detective Sergeant Bill Nielson was called from his Mt Pleasant home. It was an inhospitable hour to be required at the scene of a shooting, but that didn't worry the 50-year-old bachelor, who was married to his job. The six-foot one-and-a-half-inch former farm labourer had joined the force just before turning 25 and had steadily made his way through the ranks, joining the CIB after a three-and-a-half-year posting to the desert town of Wiluna. Now a first-class Detective Sergeant, he answered the call at any time of the night or day – the social life of the racetrack and his other interests of painting, growing orchids and squiring beautiful women taking second place to the job.

He arrived at 51 Louise Street at 5 a.m., to be met by Sergeant Bruce Brennan, in charge of the night wireless patrol, and his crew, as well as Acting Inspector Athol Wedd. From that grim murder scene, he was directed to another in Vincent Street.

Nielson was then directed to RPH. After getting the facts on the deaths there, he left in the patrol car to go to the office. Before he could go the short distance up the road, he was directed to 124 Broome Street, Cottesloe. Another man had been shot in the head.

Oarsman Brian Weir didn't turn up for the 7 a.m. surf-rescue boat training. Even though he was a fit and enthusiastic member of the Surf Life Saving Club, Brian led a full life and was often late for the training sessions, especially on the three days a week they started at 5.30 a.m. Sunday-morning practice didn't start until 7, but the crew wasn't surprised when Brian was still late. With a championship coming up, they were keen to get going, so after waiting a while, Len Bath volunteered to drive the short distance from Swanbourne Beach to Brian's flat to wake him up.

It was just after 8 a.m. when Bath pulled on to the verge in Broome Street and ran up the steps. Seeing Brian's bedroom door open on to the balcony, he straddled the railing at the top of the steps, crossed the balcony and went into his room, expecting to shake him awake. He found his mate lying across the bed, his head hanging over one side. There was blood everywhere. Brian was stiff and greyish, his breathing slow and heavy. Bath could only think he must have been in a fight and been terribly beaten up. Horrified and not quite knowing what to do, he raced back to the clubrooms to tell the others. One of them knew about the overnight shootings from the radio reports. All of them – three oarsmen and the sweep – went back to the flat to see what was wrong with Brian, worried at what they would find.

Their worst fears were realised instantly on taking a good look at Brian. The top left side of his head had been blown away. They woke the people next door, rang for an ambulance and the police, and roused flatmate Robert Swindells. Sleeping in the second bedroom just 50 feet away, he had heard nothing.

Sergeant Nielson arrived in time to see the night's third victim being carried out of the flat to the ambulance by Sergeant Owen Leitch and four men in bathers. He accompanied the victim on the emergency ambulance ride to the hospital.

Colin and Judy Weir were about to leave for Mass when the doorbell rang. The two huge detectives wouldn't tell Judy why they wanted her husband. Colin came to the door to be told that his younger brother by two years had been in a shooting accident and was at RPH in a serious condition. The policemen couldn't answer any of Colin's questions except to say that they didn't know what was going on, only that there had been various shootings in several suburbs. They asked Colin to go to see his father and break the news to him gently. Colin could see Bob Swindells sitting in the back of the police car. He wanted to talk to Brian's flatmate and good friend of many years, but Bob wasn't allowed out of the car. Colin couldn't understand anything – but he did know Bob wouldn't harm Brian, even though it appeared the police weren't so certain.

It was impossible to comprehend. Everyone liked Brian, or Lou as he was generally known. He was tall with broad shoulders – well-built, athletic and fun-loving. The brothers were very close.

The two-year-old boy and baby girl they had just dressed for church were handed over to the boarder and Colin and Judy drove as fast as they could to Mt Hawthorn to see 58-year-old Harry Weir and his second wife, Stella. Bearing in mind the detective's suggestion, Colin prepared his words as he drove, working out how to break the news gently to his father who'd already suffered enough during the war. When Harry Weir answered the doorbell, Colin's carefully prepared words gave way to his shock.

'Brian's been shot,' he blurted out from the doorstep.

The third shooting victim arrived at RPH just after 9 a.m. and the medical team again went into full emergency surgery on this patient with a part of his head blown away and bullet fragments scattered through his brain. Neurosurgical resident Dr Terence McCarter helped neurosurgeon John Lekias in an eight-hour operation. Colin, Judy and Harry Weir waited in a nearby room, unable to think of anything but the doctors' warning that it would be a miracle if he survived. And if he did, at what cost?

At one stage when they were taking a break, Colin understood them to be discussing what sort of a 'social problem' they would be causing by keeping him alive. They had removed a bullet lodged in the left temporal region, but it was so fragmented that a lot of irreparably damaged brain had to be removed. If Brian lived, it would be without much of his brain. The doctors worked on into the afternoon, and the family waited. Reporters were everywhere, trying to get through the police protection to interview them. They couldn't have told them anything, anyway. They were as nonplussed about the shootings as the rest of Perth.

The surgeons were working to stop the bleeding in the shattered part of the brain while avoiding cutting the blood supply to the undamaged area. While they were carefully removing bullet fragments and splintered bone, 23-year-old Mary Headland in Adelaide was putting aside the wedding dress she was making to connect her weekly trunk call to her fiance. She'd met the husky six-foot surf lifesaver eighteen months previously when she was in Perth on a working holiday, staying with her cousin who was a friend of his. With their engagement turning her temporary WA address into a permanent one and Brian busy at night studying for more qualifications, she went back home to South Australia to spend six months with her family before the wedding.

The call connected and Mary expected to go through the guest list. Instead she received the shattering news from the detectives busy at the scene of the crime. She was on the first plane she could get to Perth to join the family in their bedside vigil. So was Brian's younger sister Kay, who was working in Melbourne.

Scott MacWilliam left 54 Vincent Street early to break the terrible news to Julie. He rode back to the Hoggs' place along the route he'd taken just a few hours earlier with John on the back of his scooter. Julie heard the doorbell at 5.45 a.m. When she heard her parents whispering, she knew something was wrong. When they approached her door, she knew something had happened to John.

Her mother started, 'Darling, I have some bad news about John . . .' but Julie cut in with a desperate cry, 'I don't want to hear it'. How she wanted time to stop, wanted her mother never to finish what she was saying. John's shooting sentenced Julie to years of life with no direction, unable to find a point to it. She went numbly on, feeling lost.

Julie had met John at a nearby party a few months previously. He already knew the name of the petite pixie-faced girl in the elegant white dress when he sat down beside her and started chatting. She accused him of being forward, but was instantly attracted to his fine skin and beautiful blue eyes, his open face and cheerful manner. They spent the rest of the party together and not long afterwards made their long-range marriage plans. His parents were happy with his choice, Bob Sturkey immediately putting his arm around his future daughter-in-law on their first meeting. The two fathers already knew each other professionally and Julie's parents took to John instantly.

'John loved his fellow beings,' she continued. 'Loyalty and truthfulness were his character and joyousness and cheerfulness were his personality.'

Scott MacWilliam, too, was in shock, finding it impossible to believe that John was dead. Just a month earlier, the two of them had joked lightheartedly about the vicious attack on Peggy Fleury. A few days after returning from a stay on Rottnest Island with Julie's family, they had visited Scott's friend from school days, Janet McKenzie. Scott and John were talking to Janet in the lounge room of her Cottesloe home, when she described the astonishing attack on their next-door neighbour and the police search for the culprit.

'Well, we can't be blamed for it,' Scott had joked, 'we were at Rotto.'

His mind awhirl at John now being the victim of another strange attack, Scott was unable to face returning to a house teeming with police and stained with his friend's blood. So he went straight on to the city's Barrack Street jetty, catching a ferry for Rottnest in the impossible hope that the island's lazy, happy holiday atmosphere would erase the horror. He hadn't heard the shot that killed John, but he now heard over and over again the sounds of the Northam rifle range that had so filled him with terror as a Scotch College army cadet, provoking delayed reaction to the terror and violence of his early childhood spent in a

POW camp in Manila. At school he had the understanding and help of a teacher who was a Burma Railway survivor. Now there were no such soothing words to help him through the trauma of the prison camp or last night.

For the next six months Brian Weir was in a coma in Ward 74 of RPH. He had survived the operation. The police were there around the clock in case his unknown attacker tried to finish him off, and ready to catch anything he said should he regain consciousness. His fiancee was constantly by his side, planning how she would change careers and take up nursing to care for him. Colin and the others were also devoted, joining the vigil whenever possible, willing him to come back to them and thankful that their mother, who had died two years earlier, wasn't suffering this heartbreak.

Colin was very angry and bitter about whoever had done this to his beloved brother, vowing to volunteer to pull the lever if ever he was caught. Just at New Year, he'd been shocked by the news of an attack on Peggy Fleury, the sister of his former girlfriend Joan. Where would this craziness end? He was worried for the safety of the rest of his family. Not knowing if it was some unknown vendetta against them, he slept with a knife under the pillow and the police regularly patrolled past the house, coming in most Saturday afternoons to update them on their inquiries.

When Brian finally emerged from his coma, his disabilities became clear. He was paralysed down one side, he couldn't move his arms, he couldn't walk and he couldn't speak. He was blind in one eye and deaf in one ear. The brain damage caused epileptic-type fits. He would need full-time care for the rest of his life. Brian Weir was not officially the third murder victim of that horrific Australia Day night, but in practical terms, he was. The close-range shot had ended a healthy, independent life.

He was moved to the former tuberculosis hospital at Wooroloo, where he was kept for a long time before being moved to the Royal Perth Rehabilitation Hospital at Shenton Park. Dental experts were called in to fit a dental plate type of structure to his forehead to build up the part that had been blown away. He gradually improved to the point of regaining some control over his left hand. At one stage he managed to stand with splints and a frame, but constant pain in his legs and spasms required an operation to cut the tendons, stopping the problems but also any hope of his walking again. His progress was remarkable considering the brain damage, and his family never gave up hope.

Colin visited him every evening after work, remaining unrealistically hopeful of his brother getting back to normal. He kept all the newspaper accounts of the shooting in the belief that he'd be able to show them to Brian one day, and encouraged the surf-life saving club to raise funds to send him for specialist treatment in America.

There was the occasional sign of the old cheeky Brian inside the useless body – enjoying frightening his family by teetering his wheelchair on the edge of a drop, and grinning and pointing to Judy's stomach and to Colin when they told him about her third pregnancy. Colin and his father took turns to collect Brian each weekend for an outing, taking delight when he indicated an understanding that Claremont Football Club had scored a goal, and dreading the sad moment when they would have to prise his fingers from the car roof guttering, defeating his effort to avoid returning to the old-age nursing home he'd been put into.

Brian suffered many setbacks, including infections and serious fits. Such a fit led to his death in the Home of Peace a month before his thirty-second birthday. The brother who loved him so much said 'thank God' when he took the call.

The life robbed of its rich potential on 27 January 1963 finally ended nearly three years later, on 19 December 1965.

Fear City

PERTH 1963

Terror struck at the heart of Perth. There was uproar at such incomprehensible random violence and panic at the realisation that he could strike again at any time. The character of the city changed overnight.

People turned their homes into fortresses, hiding behind locked doors and windows, sweltering through the long hot summer nights without the benefit of air-conditioning or any breeze. They kept weapons by their beds, whatever they could get: rifles, batons, knives, dogs, cans of fly spray. They didn't go out at night, they didn't answer their doors, they rang the police at any noise they heard outside.

The government responded to people's panic by leaving the street lights on all night between Nedlands and Fremantle. There was an eerie silence on the streets at night, broken only by patrolling police cars.

The Police force had a huge task before it. The Chief of the CIB, Detective Inspector Cec Lamb was away. 'The Boss', as he was called by his men, was taking overdue leave. Commissioner O'Brien, the 61-year-old former chemist who had been head of the force for five years, appointed Detective Inspector Pat Hagan as acting chief. Inspector Hagan and all his men were under immense pressure to put an end to the terror. All CIB officers were called in to duty and they worked day and night.

First-class Detective Sergeant William Henry John Nielson, known as 'the Swede', was put in charge. Other senior detectives were assigned to each shooting. A special operational room was set up to receive the hundreds of phone calls that sometimes jammed the switchboard. All detectives worked with very little rest for the first 24 hours. Then a coordinated system of round-the-clock investigation was set up, putting 40 extra police officers on duty each night, cruising the suburbs in fourteen patrol cars.

They combed Kings Park on foot and horseback, about 50 officers armed with carbines. There was a general feeling that the culprit may have hidden there, or committed suicide. But the thorough search came to nothing.

They had two immediate suspects, both having committed crimes at Shirleys Frock Salon. Someone else besides Cooke had seen the young man who broke in that night. He was in the area of the murders at the right time. He was a suspect. His fingerprints were known to police from similar acts he'd committed in dress shops in Subiaco and Nedlands over the previous two years. Now they had a description of him as well.

The other suspect had passed a false cheque when paying for a dress he said he was buying for his mother. When it was revealed that he had previously been at a party with Rowena Reeves, the police really thought they had their man. He was questioned about the killings, and confessed to them. In his confession, he said he'd thrown the gun over the Garratt Road bridge. No gun was found and the man was released.

It was imperative that they find the murder weapon. While police divers checked the river by Garratt Road bridge, the army was called in to minesweep North Cottesloe beach.

They had a breakthrough when they found a spent cartridge on the driveway of the Drys' house in Louise Street behind Mrs Allen's place. Lindsay Dry couldn't believe how lucky he was that night. The eighteen-year-old had come in at 1 a.m. and gone to bed in the sleepout at the back of the house. The cartridge meant that the murderer had walked right past him on his way from shooting John Sturkey to shooting George Walmsley two houses away. But Dry heard nothing, not knowing of the double horror so close to him until the police knocked on the back door at 6 a.m.

Detective Sergeant Leo Murphy in ballistics carefully examined the bullets taken from George Walmsley, John Sturkey and Brian Weir in an effort to narrow down the type of gun they were looking for. The bullets were badly damaged by impact and bore no identifiable rifling striations. But microscopic examination revealed a mark on the front of the rim, a straight cut mark and an imprint of the breech face marking which were consistent with their being from either a Lithgow or Winchester single-shot rifle. Murphy concluded that the three bullets were all from the same gun, confirming that one gunman had moved between the suburbs that night.

The police set about checking all .22 single-shot rifles licensed in WA, calling for the 75,000 rifles registered in the state and test-firing them. In all, 60,000 guns were tested.

There was a public appeal for information. WA Newspapers Ltd offered a reward of £1000 and TVW Ltd offered an additional £500 for information leading to the capture so that Perth could have some peace again. Calls came in about a light-coloured sedan seen near the scene in Nedlands and a similar car was seen being driven without headlights in Cottesloe.

The police started checking the owners of all FB and EK 215 standard Holden sedans.

Another call led the police halfway to Kalgoorlie, when it was reported that shots had been fired at the Carrambine pumping station. A 400-mile round trip and search proved fruitless.

The detectives could not believe that Nick August and Rowena Reeves did not know their assailant. They were convinced that the couple were holding back information to protect themselves or their reputations. The police agreed not to release their names to the media, but were suspicious about August's reason for the request, not believing it was because of the scandal. When they asked again if that was the only reason, August answered with a high-pitched note of alarm: 'Isn't that enough?'

The detectives accused August of not having any idea of the magnitude of the shooting and decided to test the truth of the pair's statements by re-enacting it a month later, when the moon was next in the same position. In the early hours of 22 February a group of detectives took August back to the scene, going to the northwest corner of the Civic Centre wall, eight to ten feet back from two white-painted guide posts. Inspector Athol Wedd, Inspector Fred Douglas, Detective Sergeant Nielson, and Detectives John Dunne, Jim Patterson and Brian Bull waited there until exactly the same time, 2.40 a.m. Nielson brought a mop with a long handle and Bull was given the task of standing in the spot pointed out by August – 30 to 40 feet away, directly opposite the driver, on the other side of Napier Street – and raising it in place of the offender's gun. The detective couldn't even see the outline of the parked car, let alone anything of its two occupants.

August suggested that maybe he had accidentally had his foot on the brake, its red light adding to the visibility. This was rejected by the police as a further lie and reported to Inspector Hagan as 'fairly obvious that this submission was made by August in an unconvincing effort to bolster up his story'. August was told that the police could not accept his or Reeves' statements since the facts didn't measure up.

The lecture from Inspector Wedd went on: 'The feelings of persons who may be concerned are a secondary consideration – in other words, the gloves come off and I am telling you now that as a result of what we have observed, both you and Reeves are lying. It is glaringly apparent that the marksman was right up against the car when he discharged the firearm.'

August was nonplussed. 'Why would we lie in the matter?'

The detectives suggested that they were not revealing everything because they were protecting someone close to them who was responsible for the shooting. Or alternatively, they didn't like whoever it was, and didn't want some intrigue between them revealed to the police.

August said, 'There is nothing like that about it at all.'

Then the detectives tackled him about his ban on publication of their names. Still insisting that August must know the identity of the attacker, they suggested that he was afraid that by publicising their names, someone else would be able to put two and two together and identify the marksman. August denied it.

Wedd didn't let up. 'In my opinion, even with the marksman right up close to the car, you or Reeves would not be able to see the rifle in his hand. You've claimed to have seen the rifle because you've heard the report.'

August insisted, 'We both saw the rifle raised by the man before the shots were fired.'

Wedd wrote in his report: 'August could see no logic in any of all the well-considered points which I had made. It was obvious that he was determined not to consider a point for fear of it being the beginning of the breakdown of the impossible story put up by him and Reeves. In my considered opinion, August's main concern in respect to no publicity for his and Reeves' names is not so much the fear of the assailant looking him up but hinges more on the fear that the publication of the names may lead to a disclosure by some third party which would tend to reveal that which they appear to be hiding.'

August and Reeves had to wait seven-and-a-half months for the police to discover the truth of their statements.

Unable to work for nearly four months, Rowena Reeves lay on Leighton Beach, her left arm plastered from wrist to elbow. She was hounded by the press and by vicious rumours. Though they had succeeded in suppressing publication of their names, word got around quickly. Everyone was sniggering about her relationship with Nick August and many OBH customers were boosting their egos by laying claim to similar relationships.

Reeves was worried about her reputation and frightened that, because she was the only person to get a good look at the marksman and survive, he might be back to get her and her two young sons. She was put under police protection, officers constantly watching her parents' home where she was staying and escorting her to and from work. It was also frightening for the other staff at the OBH, which was under the spotlight from the police and the curious public – the hotel seemingly the only connection between the shooting victims.

The receptionist, Tania Masel, was just seventeen and had to continue at her first job under the pressure of wondering which customer could be a murderer. She lived nearby and was escorted home each night after work by an armed security guard. As well as her fear at work, she was frightened at home. She lived at 20 Hamersley Street, which ran into Hawkstone Street where Peggy Fleury had been attacked three weeks earlier. Some lovers parked in the vacant block at the back of the house had recently reported a prowler. One night, when she was asleep in the closed in veranda at the back of the house, she awoke to hear someone trying to get in the back gate from the lane. She was woken by her part-Labrador's loud barking, over which she could hear a male voice telling it to shut up. Tania froze, clutching a mirror for protection, expecting someone to come in through the window and attack her. Nothing happened, and she thanked her watchful pet for her safety.

The rest of Perth was just as edgy. The man with the rifle could be anywhere out there in the dark. Anyone could be the next target.

One of the many mysteries for the police was the time lapse between the Cottesloe and Nedlands murders. They wondered if the killer had cycled between suburbs. The *Daily News* put the theory to the test, timing a cyclist over the presumed route. They chose a fit one-time farmer to cycle from one murder scene to the next. He was one of WA Newspapers' drivers, Cyril Head, whose parents lived next door to Jennifer Cleak in Mackie Street, Victoria Park, where there'd been trouble with a prowler, peeping Tom and car stolen for a hit–run five years back.

Cyril Head rode the distance, and the time he took gave weight to the theory. The exercise added to his keen interest in the police hunt, which he heard all about each night from *The West Australian*'s police roundsman, Ralph Wheatley, as he drove him home after Head's 2 to 11 p.m. shift in the car pool. It was the 6 p.m. to 2.30 a.m. shift worked on a five-week rotation that most worried Head because his wife Marlene was home with the children.

The current panic reminded him of the night two years earlier when Marlene had been so frightened by a strange visitor to their new house in Darnell Avenue, Mt Pleasant, an isolated area with no street lights or neighbours. After deciding not to answer a late knock at the door, she opened one slat of the venetian blinds in the bedroom on hearing footsteps move away. She looked straight into the eyes of a man peering in. Shocked and frightened, she put the children under the bed in the back room, barricaded the door with the dressing table and wardrobe and crawled under the bed until Cyril arrived home. The footsteps continued around the house, stopping at every door and window.

Now they had just moved to another new, isolated house in Rossmoyne. There were only four houses in the street, and again there were no fences. There hadn't been any murders in Rossmoyne, which was a long way from the western suburbs, but who knew where he would turn up next? Cyril Head felt a little comfort that a policeman, Peter Skeehan, lived just three doors up , but was aware that his neighbour was also working late at night a lot, as part of the huge manhunt.

On Tuesday 29 January the Perth Coroner's Court completed its inquest into the 1959 murder of Pnena Berkman. The inquest, opened on 27 May 1959, had been adjourned for nearly four years.

Coroner R. P. Rodriguez found that 33-year-old Mrs Berkman died at her flat in Mill Point Road, South Perth, at 3 a.m. on 30 January when she was wilfully stabbed in the nose and chest by an unknown person. Detective Sergeant Bert Burrows had told the court that he was satisfied that Mrs Berkman's murder had no connection with the weekend shootings. He said that no evidence had been obtained that would have enabled the police to charge anyone. However, the public had no need to fear the person who committed the crime. They could forget about the existence of that person forever.

This bold statement was reported in the next morning's newspaper, giving the Perth population the relief that at least one murderer must have either left the country or have died. They didn't have to worry about the stabber. But the other one, the one who randomly shot people, was still on the loose. They were still in a panic, demanding the police catch him, quick.

Lover Come Back (II)

9 FEBRUARY 1963

Exactly two weeks since his shootings, Cooke was on his way to where the well-off people lived. The manhunt and panic hadn't worried him. He loved it: what power he had over all those people, and what fools he made of the police. He was in his glory, and he was ready to do more. Tonight was his opportunity. The police and all of Perth were out at the Gnangara Pine Plantation chasing the kid who'd shot a policeman and a Goggomobil passenger and escaped by taking a taxi driver hostage. All of Perth was steamed up about someone else. The heat was off him.

He'd started out in South Perth and Como. After breaking into a house in Leonora Street, he'd wandered further along and planned to break into No. 1 after seeing people leave in a car. But they had suddenly returned just a few minutes later while he was looking for a way in, so he'd stolen their car instead. Peeking through a window first, he'd seen them watching the manhunt in the pine plantation. Good, the police were still right up the north end of town.

After quietly reversing the Holden out of the driveway, he guessed it was somewhere between 9 and 10 p.m. when he drove across the Narrows Bridge. He headed for the western suburbs, just like he had a fortnight earlier.

The lights might be on all night there, but there were no police around. He could hurt or maim or kill – the opportunity was there; he would just have to find the right target. He didn't have a gun, and he couldn't get hold of that one again after throwing it in the river. Maybe he should've hidden it somewhere so he could retrieve it next time he was in a killing mood, as he was tonight.

But cars had proved good weapons before. He hadn't actually killed any of those women he'd driven into, but he'd sure succeeded in hurting them a lot. This FB Holden was brand new, and it had a bit of power. He was in the mood to run someone down. He would drive around and watch for an opportunity.

Doug Wilkie could see the light-coloured Holden in the rear-vision mirror as he set out from his Graylands home on his motor scooter with a girl on the back. The car had appeared out of nowhere in Stubbs Terrace and was coming up behind them much too quickly. He twisted the accelerator of his little Vespa as he turned into Alfred Road and sped up. He'd been so proud of doing a deal with Malvern Star in Fremantle, trading in his push-bike for this new Vespa, but he'd had trouble with it ever since. Maybe he should have bought a Lambretta after all, but they didn't have the same status as Vespas with the Graylands boys. He was praying the Vespa wouldn't let him down now as the Holden bore down on them.

The Vespa did speed up, but this didn't distance them from the vehicle behind. It was getting closer, roaring, and Wilkie knew that it was going to go right over the top of them. On purpose. He couldn't understand why, and he was scared as he made the bike go at top speed, keeping his eye on the mirror, watching in horror. He couldn't see the driver to know who was acting so crazily, and he wasn't sure what sort of Holden it was, just that it was a late model one with a shiny chrome grille and mudguards and hoods over the headlights.

His pillion passenger saw the danger, too. She squeezed his waist tighter and screamed. She turned to see the car almost on them and screamed louder. It was obvious the driver had no intention of braking or swerving, but was purposely going to run them down. The little grey Vespa was going full speed. Wilkie knew he couldn't go any faster to get away from this unbelievable attack. They were so vulnerable – no metal around them for protection, not even helmets. He owned two helmets and his father was always on at him about wearing them. Now the twenty-year-old apprentice bootmaker wished he'd listened, but all he could do was hope for a miracle.

Cooke saw the scooter in Stubbs Terrace as he drove towards the Nicholson Road subway. The scooter, with a man at the front and a woman on the pillion seat, was travelling towards him. He noted they weren't wearing helmets. Good – they were more prone to injury. This was the opportunity he'd been waiting for. He didn't need a gun after all. His lips tightened and his eyes narrowed as he decided to run them down. He did a U-turn to follow them.

They were quite a fair way in front of him. He accelerated and caught up with them on the hill in Alfred Road. He was almost on them, ready to hit them, when a car appeared, travelling towards them. He dropped back. There were to be no witnesses to his attacks. He waited a little then sped up for another try.

Doug Wilkie couldn't believe his good luck. Just as he thought their number was up, a car appeared in front and the Holden behind them dropped back. He took advantage of his lucky break and turned quickly into a side street. He shot up Mimosa Avenue between the Graylands Migrant Hostel and houses backing on to a huge paddock. He sped around the back of the migrant hostel.

The car didn't follow. What luck. Just to be sure, he pulled over near Jacaranda Avenue and waited for a while at the back of the migrant hostel. The Pommie Camp, as he called it, was a good place for meeting girls. He spent a lot of time there and generally succeeded in getting a girl on to the back of his Vespa, which helped to make him popular as only a few boys in the area had one. Now the Pommie Camp was a good escape route. When he felt safe, he went back into Alfred Road and, seeing the coast was clear, he kept going. He arrived home at 45 Mengler Avenue, Graylands, shaken by the incomprehensible experience.

Cooke saw the scooter turn towards the Claremont Mental Hospital. He thought they disappeared up Davies Road, two streets beyond Mimosa Avenue. Whichever it was, he'd lost them. He felt cheated. He'd already given up on a target a bit earlier, when he noticed a little girl walking between a couple he planned to run down. As he looked at the girl in the white dress, he thought of his children at home. He loved his kids, and wouldn't want anything to happen to them. He was good to the other children in the street, too, sometimes taking them to the shops and buying them ice-creams.

He drove on towards Swanbourne. He saw a woman walking on the footpath in Narla Road. Yes. He drove around the block to come up behind her and get a good hit, but when he got back, she was just walking into the Lakeway Drive-in. He drove closer and saw her talking to the ticket collector. He'd missed that one. He drove back towards Mt Claremont, looking for someone else he could run down.

John was distraught. Rosemary was striding away from him, down Redfern Street and across the road, insisting on walking home. John couldn't believe his birthday could end this way over a silly mistake. And it was all his fault. To have snapped like that without looking, thinking it was his brother who was taking his piece of fish. To have so badly hurt Rosemary of all people, and over such a silly thing. If only she had given him the chance to explain that he'd thought it was Jimmy being cheeky. He felt guilty and remorseful, as well as desperate at the thought that he could lose her. His stomach was in a knot as he watched her go, about to disappear out of his sight, turning past the corner butcher's shop and away along Hensman Road.

Or maybe, just maybe, he could still manage to convince her to make up. He had to try. His heart was torn apart by the thought of losing Rosemary and he wouldn't be able to sleep till he was sure this silly mistake wasn't going to cost him the only thing that really mattered to him.

He ran inside, grabbed his car keys, told Jimmy not to wait for him, started the Simca and drove after her. Turning into Hensman Road, he saw her walking on the footpath a few houses past the corner. He pulled alongside her, wound down the passenger's window and called to her, begging her to forgive him and pleading with her to get in. She looked as miserable as he was, crying as she walked, but walking purposefully. He had to crawl along the road beside her to finish his plea. There was no response. It wasn't working. John stopped, desperate about what else he could do. He just sat there, dismal, his head slumped on to his hands clutching the steering wheel. How could such a silly little mistake ruin such a beautiful day? He had to try again; he couldn't let it end like this.

He drove on slowly, peering down the dark street to keep her in sight. Towards Nicholson Road he caught up with her again, and begged her to get into the car so they could talk about it. No. Driving slowly alongside her he kept pleading, explaining again that he'd thought it was Jimmy. But no, the damage was done – she kept walking.

He gave up, slumping over the wheel again. What more could he say or do? He couldn't do anything but keep trying to talk her around, hanging on to the hope elicited by her mention of his returning her stockings the next day.

He started up again, turning into Nicholson Road and cruising slowly along till he came to her. 'Come on, Rosemary, I'm sorry, just let me drive you home.' She was still crying and ignoring him. He continued alongside her.

'Please, Rosemary, please.' She strode on, tears streaming down her face, trying to sniff them away. This time he wouldn't give up and he kept alongside her, matching her pace. But nothing would work, his words didn't seem to be making any impact at all.

John stopped the car. He wasn't going to give up, but he'd decided that his only hope was to let her walk a little way to cool down. They were nearly at the end of Nicholson Road close to the subway under the railway line. John turned off the engine just before the small road by the petrol station on the corner of Nicholson and Railway roads, 150 to 200 yards from the subway. He would have a cigarette while he waited there for a few minutes. It was dark and isolated on the other side, so hopefully she'd relent. John took a cigarette from the packet on the dashboard and lit up. He watched Rosemary continue under the subway and turn left, disappearing up Stubbs Terrace towards Mt Claremont.

As they drove along Nicholson Road after a night at the trots, the three men were still recounting their wins. They weren't big punters, in it for the entertainment rather than the money, but that made it no less a thrill when their chosen horse was first to get its spider and driver over the line. It was a great atmosphere at Gloucester Park on a hot night and the three single young men, long-time mates from the Graylands/Mt Claremont area, went often to enjoy the colour, the action, the beer and the thrill of an occasional win. They'd had a good night and they were still enjoying themselves as they made their way home after the final race at 10.30 p.m.

Twenty-one-year-old storeman Barry Hansen had enjoyed a few wins on the tote. Twice his selections had managed to pull out of seemingly impossible positions to come home. His friends Wilson White and Nigel Phillips had seen it for themselves and had relived the wins through Barry's descriptions, but it had been exciting, and as passengers in Barry's car, they had no choice but to hear it again.

There was much merriment among them, Phillips loudly reminding Hansen from the back seat of the Volkswagen that he'd still made more on his 12/1 Brandy Lad coming in second than on the 5/4 Mighty Service, despite the win Hansen was crowing about. Once they were through the Nicholson Road subway, they turned left and entered the home stretch, the three mates starting to think about the final beer they would have at White's place when they dropped him off in Alfred Road.

John stared straight ahead at the darkness while he smoked. He noticed three cars pass across the subway on the other side along Stubbs Terrace. Drawing in deeply and exhaling slowly, he reflected on that time before, when Rosemary had set off to walk home from Pete's because he wouldn't stop playing the pinball machine. No amount of persuasion could change her mind as she set off down the road.

John felt terrible; he had let her down a bit, but it didn't really call for her marching off like that. That time, too, he'd offered to take her home and she had refused. But after waiting five minutes, he'd driven up alongside her and she was OK; she'd got in and they had made up. Why did she react so strongly to little upsets like this? He knew she was stubborn and headstrong, and she always made it very clear when he'd done something she didn't like. But there must be more to her taking it so badly. Had something else gone wrong that he hadn't realised? Had he really misunderstood her needs? Was she so upset about not getting a friendship ring for her birthday? Did she feel insecure about his love and his plans for their future?

He remembered how a few weeks previously they'd been driving past Karrakatta Cemetery and she'd said she would die if he ever left her. What a strange thing for her to say out of the blue like that, when the last thing he'd want in the world was to leave her. He had to get to her and explain again the mistake and how much he loved her and needed her. Maybe he would have the chance now.

Hopefully, like last time, she'd have cooled down a little and would listen to reason, especially since Stubbs Terrace was dark and deserted. It was a sudden change from Subiaco's built-up streets, which would now be hidden from her view by the steep railway embankment. On the northern side of the railway line there were no houses in the direction she was walking. There were a few industrial premises on the left alongside the railway line, and just bush on her right. And then further up past the Shenton Park Railway Station there was nothing at all on the left, only the long entrance driveway to Lemnos Hospital on the right. John knew it wouldn't be pleasant walking along that long dark road alone at night, with no sign of human life except for those occasional passing cars.

The Volkswagen with the three young men from the trots was moving along Stubbs Terrace. Then out of the corner of his eye Hansen saw something odd on the left, over in the sand at the edge of his headlight range. His first thought was that it was a bundle of clothes, about three yards off the side of the road. Then he started to realise that it was maybe something more worrying.

'Did you see that?' he asked them.

'No.' Neither of them had seen anything.

'It looks like a body.' He wasn't sure. He decided to go back for a better look and drove on more slowly, looking for an easy spot to turn around.

Three or four minutes after he'd stopped near the petrol station, John finished his cigarette and started the car. Moving slowly over the intersection to the subway, he was filled with anxiety and anticipation. As he drove under the railway line, he focused on the image of Rosemary walking along the road on the other side. He tried to imagine her making her way up the slight hill towards the railway station, walking a little slower, her shoulders a little more relaxed, her face softer as she thought about what she was giving up. Turning left into Stubbs Terrace, nervously wondering how far she had walked and how she would react to his next plea, he peered up the road ahead. There was no sign of her. Surprised that she'd made it all the way up the hill past the railway station and out of sight, he sped up, now in a hurry to catch up with her. Straining his eyes, he searched the darkness ahead, wishing he'd had the front of his car fixed. The left headlight was skewed, limiting his vision – he could see only seven-and-a-half feet ahead with the left light, compared with the right light's correct low beam range of 80 feet. His eyes were straining to the left, but there was no footpath along this stretch, so he swept both sides of the road in case she'd crossed over. He leaned forward over the steering wheel and peered ahead as he raced along, anxious for the first glimpse of her.

He sped up past Floreat Iron Works, Smit's Splicing Service and Howe and Cruikshank Builders. Still further, she wasn't to be seen as he passed the building yard and Kando Engineering Service. He drove on towards Shenton Park station. Nothing. He was amazed at how far she'd managed to walk in those delicate high-heeled Italian sandals.

As he drove by the station something caught his eye, in the sand over to the left. He had driven past by the time it sunk in. He slammed on the brakes and reversed till he was level, stopping with his left wheels just off the road. Looking directly over, his sudden fear was confirmed – it was Rosemary, lying in the sand near a tree stump, about three yards off the road towards the station. He sat there stunned for a second or two, trying to believe that in her misery she had hurled herself sobbing on to the sand. He knew she wouldn't do a thing like that, but his brain would not accept anything but the easy solution to why Rosemary was lying eerily still.

He lurched into action to get to her so he could fling his arms around her, pick her up and tell her everything was all right. He slid across the seat to the door nearer to her, leaving it open as he ran across the sand, desperate to hear her call his name, or even to speak angrily to him. But there was no sound. He found her lying on her left side, her legs sprawled, her left arm raised, half her face in the sand, her eyes open but unseeing. Not a flicker of recognition as he cried her name.

And there was the blood. Blood on her face, her legs, her clothes. Blood on her forehead, a big wound had bled into the sand under her head, where there was a patch of blood. It was just oozing now, as was the wound on her big toe.

John's head and stomach were awhirl. He felt sick and confused.

'Rosemary, Rosemary,' he shrieked in desperation. He couldn't tell whether she was alive, but refused to allow the alternative to enter his mind. He was desperate and couldn't think of anything but getting her away from there, away to safety.

None of his knowledge of first-aid and never moving injured people could get past the deep shock, panic and fear of losing Rosemary forever. There was only one thought. Get her to her doctor. He knew Dr Quinlivan, whose house was on his lawn-mowing round. He knew the surgery was next to the house, just two miles away, almost opposite the Andersons' home in Alfred Road. John had to get her to Dr Quinlivan.

He bent to pick her up. There was no reaction as he struggled to get her limp, blood-covered body out of the sand. Straining, he got to his feet, Rosemary in his arms. Cradling her head on his right elbow, he staggered as fast as he could back to the car. She didn't carry any excess fat, but she was a big girl, weighing ten stone. John was slight, five-feet nine-inches and nine-and-a-half stone, and it wasn't easy for him to carry her the distance across the sand to the car. But his desperation gave him strength and he made it – just. As he reached it his strength gave out and he dropped her a bit, her head falling on to his leg, the blood from her wound smudging his trousers before he could hoist her up again. He didn't care about the blood on his trousers. It was on his hands and body, anyway. Lucky he had left the door open. Still struggling, he managed to get her on to the front seat, her head lolling as he reclined the seat a little to keep her in place. He had trouble getting her left leg in, unsuccessfully trying to shut the door several times before it fell out. He opened the back door and tried to lean over and hold her leg in place, again unsuccessfully. Finally he opened the front window and held her leg with his right hand while he closed the door with his left.

John rushed around the car to the driver's side, pulling himself around the front of the car by his right hand as he wheeled around the two headlights. Slamming the door shut, he started up and sped away on his horror mercy dash, holding Rosemary's hand and listening to the terrible sound of her laboured breathing.

Barry Hansen and his two mates found a place to turn at Lemnos Hospital, 50 or 60 yards further on. Turning into the driveway and back into Stubbs Terrace, they drove slowly back to have a closer look at what Hansen had first thought was a bundle of clothes and then maybe a body. When they got back, Hansen saw someone at the wheel of a car stopped on the road in line with whatever it was.

They passed the car and drove on a little way further towards the subway before doing another U-turn and pulling up behind it. The three occupants of the Volkswagen were subdued. It was exactly a fortnight since five people were shot in this area, two killed outright and another one in a coma fighting for his life. They were fearful and curious as Hansen pulled up about ten yards behind the car that had stopped. Hansen told them not to get out, because this might be the killer. He turned off the headlights to avoid being noticed and the three sat and watched. Hansen saw the driver leave the car and dash across the sand to the body, pick it up and struggle with it to the car. He saw in the headlights as the youth ran around the front of the car that he had a bare chest. He thought his rolled-up trousers were shorts.

The Volkswagen wasn't alone for long. Another car soon pulled up in front of the parked car and four people in that Morris sat and watched. Lynas Motors mechanic Stanley Rogers and his wife had also been at the trots with their friends Wilfred Rynn and his wife. Not long arrived in Australia, they were all living at the Graylands Migrant Hostel and were on their way back there when Wilfred Rynn, in the front passenger seat, saw up ahead a man about three yards away from a car, carrying a limp body.

'There's something funny going on here,' he said to the others, and as they slowly passed by, they saw the man putting the body into the car.

They stopped 20 or 30 yards ahead and turned back to watch, Stanley Rogers starting to get out of his Morris Major sedan but deciding better of it. When the car sped past them and down Alfred Road, they started up and went on home. Rogers rang police headquarters from the hostel to report the matter.

In the Volkswagen the young men watched the drama, hushed apart from some brief discussion about whether it was a body or an unconscious girl; but anyway, the victim was a girl and she was limp. They saw a shirtless young man carrying the girl in his arms, trying to run towards the parked car and partly dropping her as he struggled to get her inside. He was having a lot of trouble, but Hansen wasn't going to offer to help someone who could well be the Australia Day weekend killer. No, he would watch quietly and maybe what he was witnessing would help bring him in and return Perth to safety and peace.

The suspected killer put the girl in the car. It was enough for Hansen. He took off, continuing the way he was going towards Wilson White's house. He had travelled 300 or 400 yards when the Simca sped past, going about 70 mph. Looking as the car passed, he saw a girl lolling in the front passenger seat. He pushed the pedal hard to follow and managed to keep the red tail lights in sight. Just past Rochdale Road, almost opposite White's house, the Simca suddenly turned left and stopped outside a big house. White said it was Dr Quinlivan's surgery and the driver had parked in its small off-road parking area, next to the doctor's Morris 850.

They stopped in the little side street outside the surgery and watched as the young man ran from the car to the front door of the doctor's house. White then broke the silence with a gasp of astonishment, his eyes wide with the realisation from a closer look, 'That's John! Rosemary's boyfriend!'

The car was abuzz. White knew Rosemary Anderson, the girl from four doors away, quite well – they had gone to the same school and although she was two grades below him, all the kids of the area knew each other.

White had seen Rosemary with John over the past few months and it was generally known around the area that she had a boyfriend from Subiaco. Just a week or so back, White had been hitching at the side of the road in an effort to get to the beach on a hot night, and John had given him a lift. He'd been in that very Simca with John and Rosemary. They had stayed together at Cottesloe Beach, so he'd been lucky enough to get a ride home, too, and had got to know John a little – though only a little, because he was a quiet guy and totally engrossed in Rosemary.

Now safe in the knowledge that he wasn't going to be gunned down by a trigger-happy murderer, White felt able to help.

'Do you want a hand?' he called out to John as he returned to the car and opened the front passenger door.

'No, it's all right,' came the quick, breathless reply.

A light went on in the back of the surgery. It was a relieved but amazed trio who watched as John pulled the girl from the front passenger seat, losing his grip and having to heave her up. White had guessed it must have been Rosemary and now he could see for sure. John had to half put her down, still supporting her, as he closed the car door. He picked her up again and carried her down the path towards the surgery door. Just as he got to the door, Dr Joseph Quinlivan appeared. Dr Quinlivan examined Rosemary on the path outside his surgery for a few minutes then helped John carry her inside.

Hansen and his friends left the doctor's place for White's house across the street, at 153 Alfred Road. There they mulled over the night's weird events as they downed several beers. The horses were quite forgotten as they tried to come up with theories about what could have happened to Rosemary. Their night ended with the sound of an ambulance heading towards the city.

'I have a girl in the car with a bad cut over her eye, it's bleeding badly,' John blurted out as Dr Quinlivan answered the fast knocking on the glass door at the front of his house. He was used to being called out in the middle of the night for emergencies, but it was usually the shrill of the phone that woke him up. This knocking was so urgent that he acted instinctively, answering immediately without stopping to throw his dressing gown over his pyjamas.

'Who is it?'

'It's Rosemary Anderson.'

'Take her to the surgery, I'll turn the lights on.'

The doctor reached for his dressing gown on the way through to the other end of the house, where he turned on the surgery and entrance lights, getting to the door as John was struggling to carry Rosemary in, the unconscious, gagging girl slipping from his arms. He'd made a heroic effort carrying her as far as he had, but he wasn't able to make it all the way to the surgery, half dropping her and finally laying her down on the cement porch, where the doctor examined her briefly. He could see she was critically injured and thought she had obviously been hit by a car. He could immediately diagnose a head injury, from her unequal pupils and the laceration above her right eye which had bled heavily and was still oozing blood. He thought that she had internal injuries to the chest as well. Her pulse was very fast and was quickening, and examination of her chest showed him it was dull on the right side. Her breathing was made more difficult by the large amount of sand in her mouth. There were abrasions on her thighs, knees and hips, which were also oozing blood.

John stood anxiously over Rosemary as Dr Quinlivan went back into the surgery to call an ambulance, returning with a pillow for her and doing a quick spinal examination. Deciding it was safe to move her, he asked John to help him carry her into the surgery and place her on the examination couch, where he had a stronger light. There he cleaned out her mouth to help her breathing and put a pad over the cut above her eye. Her injuries fitted John's explanation to him that it must have been a hit–run, and because the injuries were critical, the police had to be advised. He asked John to hold her head up while he went to make a second phone call. John held her head, speaking desperately to her, trying to encourage her breathing and willing her to open her eyes.

Back from the phone and unable to do anything more for the girl, the doctor was able to tend to John, seeing that the quiet young man with blood smudged on his chest was looking a bit faint and rather upset. Dr Quinlivan gave him a glass of Dexsal. The ambulance arrived quickly, and as John watched Rosemary being carried out on a stretcher, Dr Quinlivan asked him to wait at the surgery until the police came. John desperately wanted to go with her, and couldn't bear the thought of being torn away from her as the back doors slammed shut, the light started flashing and Rosemary was speeding away from him, to the sickening, urgent sound of the siren.

But he was obedient, doing what the doctor asked. He had been so relieved to hand Rosemary over to his expert care.

Cooke drove into Kings Park. It was dark and isolated at night, a favourite place for lovers to park anywhere off the road or along the front overlooking the river. It was a favourite place for Cooke, too, to sneak up and watch them. But tonight he wasn't interested in watching lovers. He wanted to dump a stolen car. He just went in a little way, far enough to get away from any cars or people along the main roads.

He drove in on the western side, along Saw Avenue. There wasn't anyone around. Turning left into May Drive he selected a commemorative tree on the right, seven up from the intersection, and drove the stolen Holden straight into it. He drove at low speed, just enough to nudge the tree and hide damage caused by his activities of the night. Then he left it, opening both doors to make it look as if there had been two joyriders who'd crashed into a tree, damaging the front.

No-one could guess that Holden UKN 547 could have been used for anything more sinister.

John was sitting in the doctor's surgery, anxious about Rosemary and devastated by the night's events. He'd been told to wait for the police, so he did, even though he'd desperately wanted to go in the ambulance with Rosemary. He sat there meekly, waiting.

Constables Ron Wilson and Ivan Martinovich were on duty in the Accident Inquiry Section of the Perth Traffic Office when Dr Quinlivan's call was received at 11.05 p.m. There was a second call about the same time, from Central Police, passing on a report from someone seeing a girl being placed in a car, registration number UKA 547. Wilson called for a check on the owner of the vehicle, and was given the name John Button. The two constables left for the doctor's surgery, pulling out of Accident Inquiry on the corner of Adelaide Terrace and Plain Street, and manoeuvring their motorbikes beside John's car in Mt Claremont about 11.30.

John was so relieved to see them. Like the doctor, here at last were people of authority who could help. Even though he wanted to be with Rosemary in hospital, he wanted to help the police, too, to tell them everything he knew. He easily answered Wilson's questions, giving his name and address and confirming it was he who had brought his girlfriend to the surgery. But then his shock and misery accentuated his stutter as he told them what had happened.

He stumbled his way through the events of the night: 'Rosemary had tea at my house. We had an argument. She started to walk home along Nicholson Road. I got in my car and I followed her. I stopped a couple of times and spoke to her. The last time being in Nicholson Road, the Subiaco side of the subway. I then sat in my car and waited about four minutes. I saw Rosemary walk under the subway and turn left into Stubbs Terrace. I followed her. I then found her lying unconscious on the side of the road near the Shenton Park Railway Station. I put her in the car and took her to the doctor's surgery.'

Wilson assessed John with an experienced policeman's eye. The 34-year-old former carpenter had been a constable for nearly thirteen years and his initial period of service had been in Kalgoorlie, where brawls and domestics were common. His assessment of John wasn't good. The youth's story wasn't believable and he looked extremely nervous, as though he had something to hide. The officer knew he had to keep an open mind and not go jumping to conclusions, but in this case he just had a gut feeling that something was wrong.

He went out to John's car, parked next to the doctor's car in the small carpark just off the road. He walked around it, looking for any clues. He found them at the front. The front of the car was damaged, on the left-hand side. His suspicions deepened and he went back in to ask John how his car had been damaged. The youth stammered that he'd been involved in an accident in Perth a few weeks previously. Wilson was suspicious, even when John said he had reported the previous accident to the Subiaco Traffic Police.

'None of this jells, Marty,' he said to his colleague. 'It's not right.' It was time to bring the CIB in on this one.

Dr Quinlivan had to leave to deliver a baby, giving the police the use of the surgery. Wilson used the doctor's phone to call the Perth CIB, speaking to Detective Bob Crowe. While he waited for a detective to arrive, he called the Subiaco Traffic Office. It was confirmed that John Button had reported an accident in St Georges Terrace a month before, on 7 January, reporting running into the back of another vehicle and sustaining £25 damage to the grille and park light. But this information did not change Wilson's feelings. Nor did the fact that the damage was nothing like the broken grille and badly dented bonnet of the Chrysler Royal stolen and used in the Queens Park hit–run he'd investigated three years previously. He was still suspicious of this youth standing there bare-chested, stuttering and looking uneasy.

Detective Jack Deering was on wireless patrol in the manhunt for the Belmont murderer when he got the call to switch to Mt Claremont. He arrived in an unmarked police car at 12.30 a.m., looking at the Simca as he walked towards the surgery and noticing damage to the left front. Wilson was pleased that an ace detective had been sent on the job. He went briefly through the facts, mentioning that the damage to the front of John's Simca was consistent with the accident reported a few weeks previously.

The tall, lean 34-year-old detective with the dark wavy hair went through the same questions with John and got the same answers, stammered out anxiously. Deering was unconvinced. He had been in the police force for twelve years, half of those as a detective. He too, had served in Kalgoorlie, four-and-a-half years in the Gold Stealing Detection Squad. He'd handled some tough cases.

He asked again, and John noticed a different tone of voice. Realisation of the subtle change in attitude slowly came over him. He felt a distinct unfriendliness as the detective asked him if he was sure it wasn't his car that had hit Rosemary. He discerned a change in the expression on the detective's face and the way he stood, looking down on him. Realisation slowly dawned that these policemen weren't seeing him as someone who was helping them. John couldn't comprehend it. He'd grown up with the understanding that policemen were people you could turn to in times of trouble. They were the protectors, security, authority. He needed them now to help him make sense of the horror and confusion. His whole sense of reality was based on order and safety, a world in which you walked along a road and got to where you were going. Being run down while you walked just wasn't comprehensible – it didn't happen in the world he knew. He needed their help.

But he wasn't getting it. Instead, his world was being turned even more awry as he felt them making him a part of the disorder. He felt they weren't there for him, they were against him! He couldn't believe it – he was trying desperately to make sense of it all, that this couldn't be happening as he tried to fight against the feelings of hostility and oppression.

Wilson came back into the surgery from having another look at the Simca and noting that the damage was consistent with a tail-end collision. Deering asked John to take them to the scene.

John was pleased to get out of the surgery. He was happy to help, still trying hard not to believe they could take him as anything but also a victim of the madman who had run down Rosemary. But his mind's efforts to fight the obvious were shattered when his presumption of driving his car to the scene was met with a stern voice of authority that he would be accompanying them in the back of the police car. Deering took a .303

rifle off the back seat of the police Chrysler, needed during the manhunt for his colleague's killer. The way he picked it up and put it in the boot was seen by John as a menacing warning to him. He sat in the back seat with Wilson, his mind awhirl from this perceived threat and the shock of it all, as he was driven back the two miles he'd sped along a few hours earlier.

Charlie and Lilly Button arrived home from their friends' place between 10.30 and 11 p.m. They noticed John's car wasn't parked on the verge and presumed he must be dropping Rosemary back and would be home soon. Jimmy was asleep in his room at the back. Lilly turned on the front light for John and prepared for bed while Charlie watched a bit of wrestling on television.

Just after the Andersons arrived home from the surf club barbecue, a policeman knocked at their door. It was Constable Martinovich, who'd been standing by John's car at the surgery and had seen the Andersons' lights go on. The news that their daughter had been injured in an accident and was in hospital was hard to grasp. What could have happened, and where was John? They couldn't work it out. The only thing that was clear was that they had to get a taxi to the hospital to see Rosemary. Jack walked over the road and looked at John's car while he was waiting. He didn't notice any extra damage.

John was back beside Shenton Park Railway Station with Deering and Wilson. A strong easterly breeze was blowing as they stood in the sand by the road. He pointed to the blood-stained sand to show Deering and Wilson where he had found Rosemary. Wilson took his yellow chalk and made a mark on the road to indicate the position of the moist patch. He wrote blood and drew an arrow. He didn't mark the actual position in the sand where John said she'd been lying.

John told them that she hadn't been wearing any shoes when he took her to the doctor's, so they started a search, using Wilson's torch. They drove as far as the subway, searching the road and verge with the car's mobile spotlights.

John's heart sank even lower when a taxi stopped at the scene while they were standing around on the sand. Rosemary's father got out of the taxi and ignored him. Mr Anderson spoke only to the detective, totally disregarding John. John desperately wanted to talk to him, but Mr Anderson quickly got back into the taxi, which left immediately. John felt sick as he carried on searching around in the sand with the policemen.

He didn't know that Jack Anderson wasn't ignoring him at all. He hadn't seen him. On his way to RPH he was shocked to see the police outside Shenton Park Railway Station and stopped the taxi, hoping to have some of his many questions answered and find out what had happened. He saw only the detective near the edge of the road, not aware that John was further over in the dark with Wilson. He didn't get any answers. He was told he was needed at RPH. He obeyed and returned to the taxi to resume his mission, not realising that John, the person he so wanted to sort this out with, had been right there, wanting to talk to him.

They continued the search, finding some of Rosemary's belongings scattered over quite some distance – eerie reminders of an innocent girl's tragic walk home. They found one of her sandals lying on the road opposite the traffic island and the other one across the road twelve feet further up. Then there were things that had been thrown out of her handbag – her brush, comb, lipstick and bottle of perfume, scattered along the road over 50 feet. Wilson marked their positions on the road with his yellow chalk. Search as they did, they found no sign of her handbag. It was all a sickening blur to John, standing there seeing her walking, carrying her bag with those things in it. Then the horrific vision of someone hitting her and driving off leaving her there like that. His beautiful Rosemary, so full of life, left lying there, broken. How could somebody do that? Who?

The ambulance screeched to a halt on the tarmac outside Casualty at 11.35 p.m. The unconscious girl was wheeled straight past the triage nurse into a cubicle. Her bloodstained dress and pyjama panties were quickly hacked off and the registrar assessed her. She was deeply comatose, with fixed dilated pupils, one turned up and one down, and total absence of reflexes. She did not respond to painful stimuli in any way at all.

Needing help on that busy night in Casualty, the registrar called for the orthopaedic resident. Dr Alister Turner went down from Ward 62 and checked the Registrar's assessment. From her severe internal injuries, it was decided the patient was unlikely to survive. There was a laceration to the right forehead and generalised abrasions and lacerations to the front part of her body. Her left leg was externally rotated. There were no other signs of bone injury and there was no indication of brain damage. Dr Turner worked fast to put a tube down her throat, clearing her airway and helping her breathe more easily.

She was quickly X-rayed. The X-rays of her chest and hip showed no apparent fractures and a skull X-ray showed only a questionable small fracture in the occipital region.

Dr Turner was asked to attempt resuscitation. He started intravenous therapy, pumping two pints each of blood and serum into her within the hour. A nurse cleaned up her head wound and bandaged it while Dr Turner kept a constant check on all her vital signs.

John's sad images of Rosemary being hit were interrupted by the two policemen. Deering told him he wanted him to accompany him to CIB headquarters. The tone of the officer's voice led John to believe he had no choice. And at just nineteen and completely ignorant of his rights, he didn't know that he had a choice. He didn't know he was free to go at any time and he wasn't told.

There was no suggestion of the detective ringing his parents to let them know where he was; John didn't know he could ask. He did know he wanted to get dressed, though, before going somewhere as ominous as police headquarters. He felt awkward just wearing the trousers he was left with after the strip jack naked games. He sat in the back of the car again, remembering the gun that had been where he sat and now in the boot. They returned to the surgery for Wilson to collect his bike and go on to RPH.

The trip into the city was a numb haze for John. At least it was a break from the interrogation. Deering had another quick inspection of John's Simca at the surgery then drove it to police headquarters, reversing it into the police garage beside a Goggomobil and a Consul. There was a lot of activity in the police yard with these cars coming in from the Belmont murders. Deering's driver pulled into Roe Street and John was led up the jarrah staircase of the imposing stone court building, to the CIB offices. There was a lot of activity there, too, the officers relieved of the manhunt at 9 p.m. having been told to report back by 3 a.m. for its resumption at daybreak. They were now coming and going, reporting for duty and collecting guns, ready to get back out to the Gnangara Pine Plantation to get the man who had killed one of their own.

Deering took John into the muster room, a room with a table and some chairs, and a typewriter by the big window looking out on to the street. He sat him at the table. Through the numbness, John felt exhausted and cold, and his throat was dry. He badly wanted a cup of tea and needed a smoke, and how he wished he'd been able to collect his shirt and a jacket from home.

Deering asked John again about the damage to the front of his car. He told him again about the previous accident. The detective asked him to explain how the blood spots had got on the front of his car. Surprised at the question – which did not inform John that the spots were very small – and through his confusion, unable to think of the possibility of a spattering as he swung around the front of the car or flicking from her hair as he carried her to the surgery, John just said 'no'. The reply increased Deering's suspicion of him, even though all the usual signs on a car of a collision between a vehicle and a body at the front were missing – the glass wasn't smashed, the bumper wasn't bent, the number plate wasn't knocked off.

At 2.15 a.m. Deering asked if John wanted to make a statement, saying he was not obliged to do so. John agreed – after all, he had nothing to hide. Deering cautioned him, sat at the typewriter and typed out the answers to the same questions.

> I have been cautioned by Detective Deering that I am not obliged to make a statement unless I desire to do so and that anything I do say may be taken down and given in evidence. I

am 19 years of age, single, a bricklayer's labourer and I reside at 8 Redfern Street, Subiaco. I know a girl by the name of Rosemary Anderson who is 17 years of age and lives at 145 Alfred Road, Mount Claremont. I have known Rosemary for about six months. I met her on a blind date and I have been going with her ever since.

On 9/2/63 at about 12 noon I went to her home. Her sister and brother were home. I had my lunch with the three of them. I stayed there until six o'clock then I drove with Rosemary to my place at 8 Redfern Street, Subiaco. My mother and father were home with my brother. Rosemary and I had tea with my parents and my brother. My parents went out at about 8.30 p.m. Then Rosemary and I stayed home with my brother. At about 9.30 p.m. Rosemary and I went out in my Simca Sedan motor car to the fish shop in Shenton Park and we bought some fish and chips. We took the fish and chips home and ate them with my brother.

At about 10.30 p.m. Rosemary and I had an argument over the fish. The argument was over Rosemary wanting my piece of fish. She wanted it and I would not let her have it. She got up and said that she was going home. My brother was present. She went out to my car and got her make-up, which was in a bag together with her shoes. She then started to walk home. I asked her to stay. By this time I had come out of my home. We were standing by the side of my car. Rosemary picked up her things and started to walk home. She was wearing her shoes and carrying her small cloth bag.

I got in my car and followed her stopping occasionally to ask her if I could take her home. She refused. She was in a bad mood but I was not. She walked down Redfern Street to Hensman Street and walked down Hensman Street to Nicholson Road. I stopped her three times before she got to the subway at the Nicholson Road and Railway Street. On each occasion I would pull the car up and ask her but I did not get out. She refused on each occasion. I would ask her if I could take her home, she would say 'no' and keep walking on. I stopped my car and turned off the ignition at the Nicholson Road Subway. I sat there and watched her walk under the subway. I saw her turn left under the subway. I waited there for three or four minutes then went after her.

I drove my car under the subway, turned left and drove up Stubbs Terrace. I drove my car up to the Shenton Park Railway Station where I saw her lying on the side of the road. It was on the left hand side of the road. I stopped my car and got out and went around to where she was lying. I saw that she was bleeding rather heavily from the head. I picked her up and put her in my car. I put her on the front seat. I folded the front seat half way down and she was lying on the back seat. I then drove down to Doctor Quinlivan's Surgery and knocked on his front door and he came out. I helped him carry her into the surgery.

When I stopped my car where Rosemary was lying I did not see any other vehicles at the time. One passed me when I stopped. I got out of my car and put her in just as another car came towards me turned around and stopped in front of me. Just as he stopped I drove off. From the time that I picked Rosemary up to the last time I saw her at the Doctor's Surgery she was unconscious. When I put her into my car I put her in the front left hand door. I shut the door then walked around the front of the car and entered the driver's door. Rosemary did not move but lay perfectly still the whole time. She bled a lot and I got blood over myself, over the seat of my car.

I have read this statement. It is true and correct given on my own free will without threats, promises or inducements.

Surely it would be over now. He'd given the detective the statement he had asked for. It might not have been totally accurate – he was at Rosemary's place much earlier than noon and he hadn't thought it important to say he'd mistaken Rosemary for Jimmy with the fish, but he was too disturbed to worry about little things. The important parts were right.

Jack Anderson dug into his pocket for the £7 taxi fare and hurried into Casualty. He was led into Rosemary's cubicle straight away. He got a shock to see his daughter lying there unconscious with tubes in her mouth and a bandaged head. As he held her hand and talked to her he noticed how distended her stomach was. He decided she must have been hit front on. But she seemed to be breathing easily enough and the doctor was giving her his full attention. Her father tried to make sense of it all, but he couldn't understand what could possibly have happened to her. If only she would wake up and tell him all about it, or if he could talk to John.

Dr Turner checked her breathing and all her vital signs again. All OK. He walked up the aisle with her father, explaining what he had done and that he needn't worry, she was fine and he would soon be taking her up to the ward to recover. Jack had seen his baby and would be seeing her again in the morning on the ward, so he told the doctor he'd get out of his way. Asking Dr Turner to notify his mother-in-law and squeezing his daughter's hand, he left Casualty, found a taxi at the entrance and headed home.

Deering did not believe the statement he'd just typed out. He showed it to Detective Sergeant John Wiley, the head of the Fatal Accidents Squad, who came in as it was being completed. At 2.45 a.m. Deering told his superior about his suspicions, that he believed John was the driver of the car that hit her. He told the sergeant there were blood spots on the front of John's car, but he didn't think to tell the sergeant that the usual signs of a collision between a vehicle and a body were missing.

Wiley had joined the police force in 1946 and become a detective after five years, being promoted to sergeant in 1959. He'd been in charge of the Fatal Accidents Squad for the previous two-and-a-half years, and had investigated around 40 motor vehicle fatalities over that time. He was a big man of five-feet-eleven inches, nicknamed Whopper Wiley, born 37 years earlier in the mining town of Yalgoo, playing football in Norseman and serving the war years in the Navy. He'd seen three years' active service during the war, and regarded joining the police force as continuing his service to the community through faithful and diligent police work. He too had worked in Kalgoorlie, in the Gold Stealing Detection Squad.

Wiley had been in the office most of the night organising the Gnangara manhunt. He'd been home for a short break at 10 p.m., had something to eat and changed out of his suit into more appropriate clothes. He looked at John, read the statement and left.

He went out to look at the car, examining it for damage to the front. Looking at it with his torch, he found the left headlamp rim was bent and there was some damage to the grille. He'd been told there'd been damage caused some weeks earlier but not exactly what. From his check now, he thought the car could have hit a body. The bent headlight rim, particularly, could have been consistent with that. All in all, he believed this was the vehicle that had hit the girl. Certainly the story about having an argument over fish and chips was very strange and highly suspicious. Shining his torch through the car windows, he saw a girdle and stockings on the back seat.

About seven minutes later he was back, demanding to know what the stockings and suspender were doing there. Worried about the shame of the game and to protect Rosemary's honour, John lied, saying that Rosemary always took her stockings off in his car for fear of laddering them. John, unpractised at telling lies, didn't do very well. Wiley thought he was lying.

The interrogation continued. John wasn't told he had the right to contact his parents, or to get any advice, or about any other rights. Sitting in the chair by the table, he was faced with a big detective exuding authority. He felt at a terrible disadvantage, being small and slim, and sitting there half undressed. To John, the questions from Wiley seemed more like accusations than questions. He couldn't understand. He'd waited for the police, he'd helped them, he'd answered the questions truthfully, he'd given a statement. Why did he feel such menace from the way this detective was questioning him?

He hated aggression. At school he left through the back gate rather than face bullies wanting to fight at the front gate. Now there was no back gate.

John cowered and stuttered out again his request for news of Rosemary. Wiley told him she was still unconscious. If only she'd come to, and could tell them who hit her. She would be able to explain everything and this interrogation would end.

The same questions continued; John stuttered and stumbled through the same responses. He was frightened, tired and miserable. It was 3.15 a.m. So many questions over so long – his mouth was dry, he felt sick, cold and exhausted. He asked after Rosemary, wishing he could be with her and not asking about her from worlds away. Wiley went out and asked Constable Martinovich to phone the hospital. John so badly wanted to get out of the room too, run out the door, away from this madness, to the hospital just a mile up the road. But he sat there dutifully, his head bowed, waiting for the next round of the same questions.

After a couple of hours working on Rosemary, Dr Turner was confident she was stable. She was breathing OK. The last pint of serum had gone in at 1.15 a.m. but her blood pressure, 80 systolic on admission with an unrecordable diastolic, had not responded. She would be transferred to a ward for continuation of treatment.

Five weeks into his working life as a doctor and the new medical graduate had discovered the truth of all those stories about interns' long hard shifts. But it was the start of his dream. He'd always wanted to be a doctor, following in the footsteps of his great grandfathers, grandfathers and his late father, who'd been killed at Dunkirk.

Neil Alister Turner had enrolled in the University of Western Australia's first medical school and done well, gaining a distinction in surgery in his final exams. He had chosen to do orthopaedics in his first intern term, and as one of two orthopaedic residents alternating night shifts, he was often called to help the casualty registrar. And what a time it had been – those three shooting victims a fortnight ago and the expectation of more coming in from the manhunt tonight. They were on alert for any number of casualties to come in from Gnangara, with so many armed police and curious onlookers out there.

It had been a long and busy night and the doctor was pleased to have another emergency resolved, with the patient going up to the ward for continuing treatment. He called a nurse to help him escort the unconscious girl to Ward 62. Making sure the bottles and tubes were secure, they pushed the bed into the lift.

The doors closed and there was a slight hum as they started ascending. Dr Turner kept his eyes on his charge while he slumped his shoulders a little, glad of a slight respite from the long, busy shift. He wondered how busy his girlfriend Diane had been on her nursing shift at the Perth Chest Hospital.

Dr Turner looked at Rosemary's face, noting again how pretty she was. Suddenly, to his horror, the girl's breathing stopped. No! Dr Turner immediately started pounding her chest in a desperate attempt to bring her around. Breathe!

He was stunned. How could this happen when all the indications were that everything was fine? How could she die now in the lift, with just the nurse and him? The lift arrived at the sixth floor, the nurse calling for help as the doors opened, Dr Turner still trying desperately to resuscitate her. A sister and nurse on the ward joined him in his efforts. It was in vain. Rosemary Anderson was dead on arrival at Ward 62.

'10.2.63. 2.30am. Respirations stopped. Heart beat absent. Life extinct.' The shattered 23-year-old doctor wrote the final entry on her case notes, signed it 'N. A. Turner', called the police and steeled himself for the terrible task of informing her family.

John looked up as the door opened, hoping to hear that Rosemary was awake and telling them who did it. Martinovich had been given the news by the casualty clerk.

Wiley said, 'I have to inform you that Rosemary is dead.'

John's stomach lurched into his throat. 'I'm going to be sick.'

He was led to the toilet. His stomach convulsed as he retched in his shock and emotional agony. Rosemary dead! He didn't care what he said or what happened to him. Life was worthless without her. He didn't care what they did to him now, he just wanted to be left alone. And he felt he wouldn't be left alone until he gave them what they wanted.

Rosemary gone! Never to feel her touch, to smell her hair, never to make up that stupid argument. He had snapped at her. How could he have spoken so harshly, breaking her heart, never to be able to mend it? He felt distraught and guilty. He believed he was responsible for her death. If he hadn't upset her she wouldn't have been walking home. He hadn't hit her, but he led her to her death. He killed her, and now she was gone forever. He didn't care what happened to him any more. Nothing mattered. If only he'd looked after her as he should have, as he wanted to. He wanted to be punished.

He came back from the toilet and made a confession.

Death and Defeat

3.40–4.30 A.M.

John Button states:

I have been cautioned by Detective Deering that I am not obliged to make a statement unless I desire to do so and that anything I do say may be taken down and given in evidence.

I now wish to say that the statement that I gave to Detective Deering earlier this date is not the truth and I now wish to state:

I have now been informed that Rosemary Anderson is now dead and I now wish to tell the truth about what happened.

On the 9/2/63 at about 12 noon I went to Rosemary's home at 145 Alfred Road, Mount Claremont. I stayed there until about 6 o'clock. During this time I watched television and had lunch with Rosemary and her brother and sister.

At 6 o'clock in the evening Rosemary and I drove to my home in my Simca sedan. We intended to have tea at my home. When we arrived at my home at 8 Redfern Street, Subiaco, my mother and father and brother were home. We all had tea together at about 7 p.m.

My parents went out at about 7.30 p.m. and left Rosemary, my brother and I, home. The three of us sat around and played cards. We played strip poker. This means that the loser of each game had to take off one article of clothing at a time.

We played quite a few games and my brother and I won most of the games. Rosemary took off her jumper, then both stockings and then her suspender belt. My brother walked out of the room and I tried to get fresh with Rosemary. I kissed her and I tried to play with her breasts. She would not be in it and said that she was going to walk home.

Before we started to play cards we had gone down to the Shenton Park fish shop and got some fish and chips. We were eating them while we were playing cards.

Rosemary got in a lousy mood because I tried to play with her breasts and said that she was going to walk home. She picked up her make-up from my car which was parked out the front of my home.

I followed her out of the house and when I saw her walk off down the street I went back into the house and got my car keys. I also picked up her suspender belt and stockings and put them in my car. I decided to follow Rosemary and see if I could make it up with her.

By the time I got into my car she was at the corner of Hensman and Redfern Streets. I got going and caught up with her when she got into Hensman Street. I pulled up alongside her and asked if I could make it up. I told her that I was sorry for what I did.

She told me that she did not want to make it up and kept on walking. I kept on driving slowly alongside her and followed her along Hensman Street into Nicholson Road. Twice along Nicholson Road I pulled up alongside her and asked her if I could take her home and make it up. She refused and kept on walking.

When we got near Railway Street and Nicholson Road I pulled up and Rosemary walked through the subway and turned left. I sat in my car for a few minutes; then started my car up and went after her.

I went through the subway and turned left into Stubbs Terrace and drove up Stubbs Terrace. I was then pretty wild because she would not get into my car with me and I caught up to her when she was nearly opposite the Shenton Park railway station.

I decided to scare her by driving the car at her and as close as possible. At the time I was doing about 35 miles per hour.

Rosemary was walking on the left hand side of the road close to the edge of the bitumen. Before I realised what had happened I had hit her with the left hand side of the front of my car. When I hit her I felt a loud crunch and I carried her a few yards on the front of my vehicle. I stopped my car and got out. I saw Rosemary lying on the left hand side of the road level with the front door. She had a cut over the right eye and was bleeding. She was unconscious and not moving. I opened the passenger's side front door and laid the back of the front seat back, and then picked up Rosemary and laid her in the car.

I then got in my car and drove to Dr Quinlivan's surgery in Alfred Road, Mount Claremont. I helped the Doctor carry Rosemary into the surgery and then waited for the arrival of the police.

I stayed at the surgery until the police arrived.

I have read this statement and it is true and correct given of my own free will without threats, promises or inducement.

Deering typed it out. John Button signed it, with Deering as witness.

John got what he wanted: the interrogation stopped.

Wiley informed him he would be charged with wilful murder. John could be hanged. He didn't care. Right then, nothing mattered.

Tears on My Pillow

10 February 1963

Jack Anderson sat in the taxi looking out into the blackness as he was driven home from the hospital. He was relieved. His girl was going to be all right. But his mind was still awhirl. He couldn't come to grips with his daughter being run down and how it could possibly have happened. And where was John? Why wasn't he with Rosemary?

The taxi passed the railway station and he looked out at the spot where his girl had been hurt. His thoughts were interrupted a few moments later as they passed Hobbs artillery park. The taxi's radio was sputtering out a message to the driver. He was deep in thought and it was just incoherent background noise until two words were suddenly distinguishable – his name. The driver was being asked if he had a passenger for Mt Claremont by that name. Mr Anderson should contact RPH. The driver stopped at a nearby phone booth while Jack Anderson phoned, to be told to return to the hospital. They turned around and drove back the way they'd come, Anderson's heart pounding with worry. It was obvious her condition must have deteriorated.

The news when he arrived was beyond even his worst imaginings.

The detectives were now being kind. The hot night had moved into cool morning long ago. Now Wiley noticed John was cold and gave him his coat to put over his shoulders. He gave him two cigarettes and a cup of tea. The tea was made by Detective Sergeant Colin Power, wearing a neck brace. Power was the only person on office duty after all the detectives had left on the manhunt – confined to light duties with a fishbone break in his neck from a jacknife into low tide while teaching his sons to dive. About ten minutes later, Power made a second cup for Wiley and John.

Jack Anderson was desperate to see John Button, to find out what had happened. He checked everywhere he thought the youth could be. His parents-in-law, Ellen and James Barker, had arrived at RPH and they drove him around in his search. Anderson went to the main police station in Roe Street, asking for John, but was told he wasn't there. Then he went to the Subiaco police station, but he wasn't there either. His next stop was John's home.

Charlie and Lilly Button were woken by the door bell. Charlie got out of bed to see who could be at the door in the middle of the night. It was Jack Anderson, ashen-faced, his shoulders slumped.

'Rosemary is dead,' he said simply.

Charlie was so shocked he hardly heard the next question about John's whereabouts. Charlie let him in and told Lilly the unbelievable news.

'Where's John?' Anderson asked again, 'Is he in?' It was nearly 4 a.m. and they'd been sound asleep, assuming John had come in quietly as he always did. Charlie went to his room to look, and saw the bed empty. They were all in shock, three distraught parents trying to find out what could have happened to their happy, besotted children.

They were all desperate to find John – only he could help them make any sense of what was too difficult to believe. He must be with the police – they couldn't imagine what could have happened, or how, but that was the only place he could be. Shaking, Lilly looked up the phone book and found the number for central police. She got through to the CIB but while waiting, felt too sick to talk to them and handed the phone to Anderson. He told the officer who'd taken the call that he wanted to speak to John Button. He announced himself: 'My name's Anderson, I'm Rosemary Anderson's father,' before quickly correcting himself to use the strange past tense for the first time: 'I mean I was Rosemary Anderson's father'.

Wiley left the muster room to take the call, just as John's confession was being completed. He told Anderson that he couldn't talk to John. Anderson offered to go in to see him, but was told no, the detectives would come and see him and his wife instead, later in the morning. Charlie got on the phone and was told that John was there and that they'd be bringing him home in five minutes. Charlie told them not to bother bringing him home, he'd come in and pick him up in the ute. It was about 4.20 a.m. and at last they had found John, but they still didn't have any answers.

Jack Anderson went home and the Buttons left to go to the CIB to collect their boy. They went upstairs to the first floor and were told to wait at reception. Wiley met them and sat down. He expressed his sympathy for them, and told them that he'd charged their son with Rosemary's murder.

They were speechless as they were taken to see John.

'Was it your fault?' Lilly asked, knowing it couldn't have been.

'Yes,' John said numbly. He felt that it was his fault – all his fault that she'd been walking home and had been alone in that deserted street. He felt so guilty, the cause of it all. He wanted to explain and let them know that he didn't actually kill her, tell them the whole awful story. But he was too scared to. Deering was there and John was too frightened to say anything.

But his mother asked the right question: 'Did you do it, John?'

'No.'

John was taken back to the scene with the two detectives and Wilson. Wiley asked if he could show them where he had hit Rosemary.

'No.' He felt it was pointless to expand on that and he was too exhausted to try. They hadn't believed him when he insisted he hadn't hit her, so they wouldn't believe him now. But how could he show them where he had hit her when he hadn't at all?

The two detectives were looking around the area again. John

was shuffling through the sand, trying to help look, but he was too dazed to see anything other than the vision of Rosemary lying there, alive, just a few hours earlier. He could see her, feel her warm body as he carried her. He just couldn't grasp the reality that he'd never see or feel her again, that she didn't exist any more. She was real, a part of her was still with him, her blood was on his trousers. John gazed at the sand, in a dull haze of incomprehension.

The detectives hunted for more clues, spreading farther afield. Yes, there was another item, so far away it had been missed in the dark. Sergeant Wiley found Rosemary's handbag, twenty yards away in Selby Street, the road branching off Stubbs Terrace. The little white plastic clutch bag lay on the road, empty, its contents scattered. Wiley picked it up to add to the collection of Rosemary's belongings found earlier.

Further scrutiny of the sand alongside the road also revealed a tyre track that hadn't been noticed before. There was no pattern on it, so they couldn't identify it or relate it to John's car. They didn't know whether it was significant, but they measured it anyway.

Then they took John home. How he wanted to fall into bed and wake up to find it was all a bad nightmare. Instead he just stood silently, not knowing what he could or could not do, anxiously looking at his parents but feeling he wasn't allowed to talk to them. He was allowed to collect his shirt and shoes. The detectives collected the pack of cards.

He was taken back to central and escorted to the charge room. At 7.10 a.m. he was charged with wilful murder, fingerprinted and ordered to sign for his belongings. Only then did the magnitude of it all suddenly hit him. He froze. It took a terse order 'hurry up, sign' from the sergeant to force him shakily to write his name. The prisoner was then led across the courtyard to a padded cell. It was bare except for a mattress and a blanket on a raised section of concrete.

Exhaustion from the trauma and the long night took over. About 9 a.m. Sunday, exactly 24 hours after he had so joyfully arrived at Rosemary's for his birthday, he collapsed in tears on the thin mattress and fell asleep. Rosemary's blood had dried on his trousers. His tears dried on the pillow. The accused murderer slept right through Sunday and Sunday night.

There was no sleep for John's distressed parents. Murder! He would be hanged! It was just too impossible. They knew their nervous, quiet son could never have killed anyone, let alone the girl he loved. They'd been able to sort out his little troubles in the past, but now they felt a desperate impotence.

Murder! It wasn't the unsettled mischievousness of running away from school – this was totally out of their control. The awesome authority of the State had taken their son away from them for the most impossible of reasons, could even execute him and they were powerless to protect him. Lilly, strong as she was, nearly fainted at the thought of losing her John to the hangman's noose.

All they could do for him was find the very best lawyer. It didn't matter that Charlie was a humble bricklayer and she just a househelp. She wanted her son cleared and she wanted him to have the very best chance, no matter what the cost. And she knew who could help her with that. Lilly ran over the road to Ninke Burns, her desperate need overcoming the manners normally preventing her from disturbing people so early in the morning.

It was 6.30 a.m. when her quick footsteps down the side of 1 Redfern Street woke Ninke. A baker's daughter, Ninke was used to early mornings, but this was Sunday. She only had a few seconds to wonder before the frantic knocking on the back door told her that something was amiss. She hurriedly pulled on her dressing gown as she rushed to the back. Opening the door, Ninke immediately saw the distress in her neighbour and househelp.

'Whatever's . . .'

The answer beat the end of the question. 'John's in trouble, he's been arrested and taken to the lockup. I've got to get a solicitor. Can you help me with Ken Hatfield?'

'Ken's not cheap,' Ninke said as she drew Lilly inside and along to her mother's bedroom so that they both could find out what the quiet lad over the road could have been arrested for.

Ninke wasn't sure how Lilly would afford Perth's most

renowned silk, but she could see her neighbour was determined. Lilly was their househelp, coming from 9.30 a.m. to 4 p.m. four days a week for the past couple of years. She cared for Ninke's widowed invalid mother Gertrude, as well as housekeeping and cooking for Gertrude and 42-year-old Ninke, who worked at the family bakery, Brown & Burns. It was a big old house on a big block and cleaning it kept Lilly busy. She also cooked dinner in readiness for Ninke's return from work each day and prepared their favourite pies for the weekends. Lilly was always willing to help at other times when needed. If Ninke went out on a Saturday night she only had to ask and Lilly would be there, keeping company with Gertrude, or Pet as she was known. Ninke knew Lilly as a hard-working, kind lady with a lovely nature.

The lawyer Lilly was asking for, Ken Hatfield QC, was a close friend of Ninke and Pet Burns. They'd met originally through Pet's husband, Thomas, whose brother Jack Burns and his wife were close friends of Ken Hatfield and his wife Gwennie. He was the trustee of the family business and a friend to all of them. For the past fifteen years since Thomas Burns' death, Hatfield had cared for his widow and single daughter. Despite being a busy barrister, Hatfield would make the time to drop in for a beer, a chat and a laugh. Having once found the beer too warm for his liking, he generally greeted them at the front door with a cheeky 'Got the hot beer on again?'

He was generous, too. One evening when he was having a drink with them and watching television, he rose and kicked the TV set, announcing they needed a new one. Next day a huge box was delivered to the door, the TV in it a gift from Ken Hatfield.

But Hatfield also had a huge reputation and was in demand. He was considered the best in Perth, a barrister who fought tenaciously for his clients. Ninke knew there was no-one better to represent John, if their friend would take the case. She suggested Lilly approach him via Uncle Jack – and Lilly was off, leaving Ninke with no doubt that Uncle Jack would be getting an early morning call.

Allan Drummond wasn't at all surprised when the phone rang early in his Scarborough home. The Public Health Laboratories' principal technologist was used to being called out at odd hours to collect specimens from crime scenes. This time it was another murder, just two weeks after the Cottesloe–Nedlands shootings and right on top of the Belmont two. It was a strange and busy time in Perth.

Because one victim had been a university student, Drummond was a little worried for his son, who also attended the University of Western Australia. But this latest crime didn't increase his concern. It was a hit–run and they already had the culprit. He left his wife and three teenagers to another Sunday morning without him and drove to this latest murder scene.

The bespectacled, tall angular scientist was a serious and dedicated professional in the forensic section of the laboratories. Forensics was in two parts – forensic autopsies carried out by the pathologists under the laboratories' director, Dr William Laurie, and forensic serology. As head of technical staff, Allan Drummond's concern was the identification and grouping of blood, tissue, hairs and body fluid, and to some extent fibre identification. He was generally the one called out to investigate blood stains and other signs at the site, and take samples back to the laboratories at the Perth Chest Hospital.

He was quite used to being phoned at something like 3 a.m. and asked to go to a body somewhere and check for blood and other stains and collect samples for analysis. The calls came from all over Western Australia's one million square miles. The police generally sent the samples to Perth from great distances, such as from Derby and Kununurra, but it was not unusual for him to go as far as Southern Cross to investigate a case. He was interested in his work and enjoyed the trips, except that the time away often put extra pressure on those back at base. The staff of the laboratories were busy, spilling out from their first-floor location at the hospital into the fourth and fifth floors and into demountable buildings between the hospital and the bush. The specimens had to be examined as quickly as possible. Some were quite unstable and the temperature generally affected them. In cool conditions, liquid blood would keep for only about

24 hours, and less if it was hot. Dried blood kept longer, for a week or so – as long as it was well looked after and protected from the cockroaches, flies and ants which it attracted.

Drummond arrived at Stubbs Terrace at 7.30 a.m., joining Sergeant Murphy from the Scientific Bureau and the other police officers, Wiley and Deering and Wilson, Martinovich and Borshoff. Constable Nicholas Borshoff was a draughtsman in the plan room of the Perth Traffic Office. He had been there since 6 a.m., measuring the scene and specifically the markings pointed out to him by Wilson. Wilson pointed out the main patch of blood where he said Rosemary had been lying. It was in the sand about 18 inches off the bitumen.

Drummond was briefed, then set to work examining the latest homicide scene. On the road on the west side of the Shenton Park Railway Station, an arrow and the word 'blood' marked in yellow crayon pointed to an irregular shaped reddish-brown patch about six inches in diameter in the coarse sand, between 12 and 18 inches from the edge of the bitumen. It appeared to be blood. Looking around a bit, he found another patch about three feet further on from the main patch and he pointed it out to the police. It was about two inches by one inch, and between this and the main patch of blood that the police had marked, there were five small spots, each about the size of a threepenny coin. Back towards the subway from the main patch of blood, about two yards back, there were more stains marked with yellow chalk on the edge of the bitumen. It was a group of eight small reddish-brown stains about half an inch in diameter. There were no other markings pointing to blood and he found no other blood, so he set about gathering samples from the sand and the bitumen.

After stopping to pose for the police cameraman, helping identify positions where evidence was found, Drummond left with the police officers for the yard of the central police station, arriving at James Street at 9 a.m.

Examining the Simca in the police garage, he saw small reddish-brown stains on the left headlight – four spots and two smears in the centre of the glass, so minuscule that they wouldn't show up in a photograph, and four small spots on the metal rim – two above the glass and two below. The spots were microscopic, less than one-sixteenth of an inch, and the smudge was faint, no thicker than a pencil smudge – but this experienced scientist had a good eye. The headlight glass wasn't broken and there was no other blood.

Bending to examine thoroughly the rest of the front of the car, Allan Drummond found a patch of reddish stains on the other side – on the top of the right front mudguard, about five inches in diameter, with one thick section about two inches long and half an inch wide. Moving around the car, he found two spots of what appeared to be blood on the left front door. On the inside of that door there were horizontal smears of what appeared to be bloodstained coarse sand, and marks resembling blood on the back of the front passenger seat. There were further reddish brown stains on a matchbox and some papers on the floor between the front seats.

The car was moved on to the hoist in the adjacent part of the garage for a close examination of the underneath parts for blood, hairs and fibres. He carefully looked at the underside of the front bumper and all the mechanical parts under the car, looking for blood, flesh or human hair, which was likely if the car had hit a human being. There was none.

The left headlight and bumper were not damaged, and there was no trace of blood, human flesh, human hair or clothing fibres on the bumper. Nor did he see any of these normal signs of collision with a body on the right side of the bumper, right headlight or mascot.

The car was moved outside into the open yard where the light was better, and there he noticed a broad shallow depression in the top of the bonnet, about eight to ten inches in diameter. But there were no bloodstains on the bonnet, nor particles of flesh, hair or fibres. The windscreen wasn't damaged and there was no evidence of blood, hair, flesh or fibres on the windscreen or the windscreen wipers. The blood inside the car was consistent with a bleeding person sitting or lying back in the passenger seat.

Taking the stain samples back to the laboratory, he found them to be human blood, group A. The smears and spots on the left headlight gave reactions for human blood, but they were too tiny for the tests to determine their group.

Deering went back to the house to question Jimmy. Jimmy was aware of the tiff, but he hadn't taken it seriously and had gone to bed. The sixteen-year-old thought all girls did things like that to get attention and then enjoy making up. Deering didn't take a formal statement, but reported that Jimmy had said John 'is very quiet and reserved when in the company of his parents, but in their absence, he often shows a change of temperament and is given to periods of bad temper'.

The information was later tendered in court as though Jimmy had spoken to Wiley. John's counsel told the court that Jimmy denied ever speaking to Wiley and denied saying he was given to periods of bad temper, but instead had told Deering that while sometimes John went off at him, he did not do so without proper cause.

The detectives took another look at the Simca. It had been pushed into the yard in front of the police garage. The bonnet was open and Drummond was examining it. Deering gave it a good look over, noticing some damage that he had not noticed the night before. There were some dents on the bonnet, on the driver's side. He hadn't seen them in his two other checks of the car or while he was driving it about six miles to the city.

After their further look at the car, Wiley and Deering went to see the Andersons. Sitting in their lounge room at 10.10 in the morning, the detectives told the grieving parents about the confession John had given. They told them of the strip poker game, John's attempt to get fresh, her rebuff and his anger at it. Jack Anderson listened to the detectives telling them that her liver had been torn by the mascot on the bonnet of John's car. Joan Anderson drew comfort from the words that she would always remember: her daughter had died saving her honour.

Jim James, who'd reported the theft of his car as soon as he arrived home, received a phone call from the Subiaco Police

Station early Sunday morning. He was told his stolen car had been found. It had been driven into a tree in May Drive, Kings Park. There was damage to the front radiator and bonnet and the front assembly. It had been towed to the CIB for examination and fingerprinting. No fingerprints were found.

He was told both front doors had been left open, indicating it had probably been taken by youngsters for a joyride. There was no reason for detailed forensic testing.

Mid-morning, James and his wife borrowed their son's Morris Minor and went for a drive in Kings Park to see where their car had ended up. Driving slowly along the row of memorial trees bordering the road, they found the one the police had referred to. Kathleen noticed some damage to the bark and nearby, she found a polishing cloth and another small item that she kept in the glove box. The joyriders obviously had rifled through it looking for money. She bent down and read the plaque to see which unfortunate soldier this tree was commemorating, and read the name Cpl W. J. Longmore. She'd gone to school with a Peggy Longmore and wondered if this corporal was any relation. She read on: 11 battalion – killed in action – Meteren – Apr 24 1918 aged 27 – planted by his mother.

They drove on to Police Headquarters to identify their car, Kathleen's thoughts as much on the life cut short in the fields of France during the Battle of the Lys as on the strange theft of their car. She was brought back by the sight of their Holden, the pale green car with the dark green flash no longer looking new and shiny. Jim checked the petrol gauge, to figure how far the thieves had gone in it, and calculated it had been between 30 and 40 miles. Sad at the sight of the car he'd been so proud of and annoyed at having to make do with his son's car, he arranged for the vehicle to be sent to City Motors for repair and repaint immediately the police were finished with it.

The damage was so great to the bonnet, grille and front bumper that they had to be completely replaced. The 'D' of HOLDEN on the front had broken off and the right headlight was broken. When the car was finally returned to them ten days later, Jim James checked the repair work. He noticed a small dent on the left hand side of the roof. It was approximately seven to eight inches from the drip mould and almost centre of the left-hand front door. He wondered how it had got there, as the only mark he'd seen on the tree was from the right-hand over-rider and it looked like the car had hit it at low speed. There was nothing to explain this dent on the top of the car.

While one of the night's accused murderers slept through Sunday in the police lockup, almost every on-duty and off-duty policeman in Perth was out trying to hunt down the other one. They were determined to get the killer who'd turned their mate, Noel Iles, into the fortieth name on the Roll of Honour of police killed on duty. The main search had been called off at 9 p.m. because of the difficulties of scouring a pine forest at night. Just a cordon of 50 men and searchlights were left there overnight to prevent any escape from the forest.

The search resumed at daybreak, police lining up along the five-mile front of the plantation ready to move in. But Aboriginal trackers discovered that the fugitive, now barefoot, had succeeded in slipping through the cordon under the cover of darkness and had crossed into scrubby bush country in the Camboon Road area of Morley. The police spread out and covered the vast smokebush, blackboy and banksia-covered terrain on foot and motorbikes and in jeeps. In the mid-summer heat, the men were exhausted, hungry and thirsty. Their nerves were strained as they moved through the bush, expecting a sighting or a shooting at any moment.

In a news flash telecast over Channel 7, Sergeant Fred Douglas called for help. The people of Perth responded in their thousands, a huge rabble of untrained civilians with guns joining the police. They combed the scrub, hunting through the occasional farm sheds and shacks in the area.

Finally, just after 5 p.m., there was the much-awaited sighting. Their man had been seen crossing Victoria Road. Cars immediately drove to the spot, two miles up from the hunt headquarters. It was early evening when the quarry was cornered near Widgee Road. Ted and Fay Brown, their three children and some visitors were outside their shack, where they'd been keeping a watch most of the day. Nearby caravan dweller George

Hammond was about 25 feet away from them, walking with two constables, when one of them spotted Robinson.

Detective Sergeant Jack Callaghan called on Robinson to surrender. Shooting broke out and George Hammond was injured when a bullet passed through his leg. Constable Bob Masters fired at Robinson. At about 6.30 p.m. Brian William Robinson's run for freedom was stopped by two bullets from a .243 rifle.

At RPH, Dr Alister Turner was still on the same long intern's shift. He hadn't been home since the night before, despite the trauma of losing his young patient in the lift. It was early Sunday night and he was called again to leave the ward to help in Casualty. Brian Robinson was brought in with bullet wounds to his elbow, diaphragm, spleen and a kidney.

Robinson went straight into theatre, where surgeon Denis Kermode worked on the stomach injuries and retrieved a bullet, handing it to the gowned and masked Detective Sergeant Max Baker. Then it was Dr Turner's turn to tend to the patient, turning to the shattered elbow.

John Button was woken on Monday morning by the cell door opening. He faced a policeman holding a breakfast tray and the sickening realisation that the nightmare hadn't ended. Grateful for the coffee and making an effort to get some porridge down, he talked to the policeman through the open door. The officer, who was pleasant to him, told him he had a newspaper, but didn't know whether he would want to read it or not.

John took *The West Australian* and read the main headline: 'Shot From Constable Ends Two-Day Manhunt'. To the right was a much smaller story. He read the article headed 'Murder Charge Follows Girl's Death By Car'.

'He's guilty,' John thought, not realising he'd been reading about himself.

Stunned, still unable to make sense of anything, John dutifully followed all instructions. He was led to a small room and given clean trousers. They were khaki, a prisoner's uniform. He was led down a passage on to a stage where he was dazzled by the bright light, through which he could hear people talking. He couldn't see, but heard instructions and answered the questions he was asked.

Every metropolitan detective was there for the read-out at 9 a.m. It was a requirement each morning, the only exemptions being the three or four on night motor patrol, afternoon motor patrol and afternoon shift. The sergeant-in-charge read out the latest incident reports, so that everyone was informed about what was happening and could comment or provide information that might help the officer handling the case.

The report on Robinson's crimes was hardly necessary – absolutely everyone had been involved and most had celebrated his capture in the canteen the previous night. But there were other incidents over the weekend that they needed to catch up on before they broke into general discussion. They'd all been too busy to flip through the arrest book to read the summaries of charges, so most were not aware of Saturday's other murder.

They learnt the details of John Button's confession and charge from the read-out and from sitting around talking afterwards: John had an argument with this girl, ran her down and was carrying her to the railway line, before being interrupted by oncoming cars. How cunning – a body mangled by train wheels had no way of revealing at autopsy that there'd been any prior injury. Detective Sergeant Max Baker thought it made sense: the old boyfriend/girlfriend thing, usual argument, 'Oh my god I've killed her, what'll I do? Well there's the railway line over there, I think I'll carry her over there'. He could just see it, that's what happened.

This killer had coughed, so at least that murder was closed, as no doubt Robinson's would be when he could talk. At least the weekend's three murders weren't going to cause any further diversion to the pressured investigation into the ones of a fortnight previously.

Then there was the line-up, the weekend's arrests on stage so that the detectives could see what they looked like from all sides and what they sounded like, to file away in their memories for any future reference.

John Button was on the board and they had a good look at

him, the first time they'd seen him. They heard him stutter out the answers to the regular questions like whether he was married and such, and took good note of his nervous speech mannerism and his defeated style of walk, his arms hanging motionless by his sides.

Robinson, whom they had seen before, was absent – in hospital under heavy police guard. The session over, the detectives headed in all directions about 9.30.

While the police were gazing at John on the stage, Jack Anderson was gazing at an alabaster face. He sadly identified the body with the bandage wrapped around the forehead as his daughter, Rosemary Margaret.

He drew some comfort from Dr Quinlivan, who'd told him that if she'd lived she would have been a vegetable. He couldn't bear the thought of his little darling being gone, but having her like that would have been worse. It looked like that would be the case with one of the surf club boys. Just two weeks back, Brian Weir had been shot and he was still in a coma. If he lived at all, it would most likely be as a vegetable, and Jack Anderson couldn't bear that for his baby.

An hour later, while John was facing the magistrate, the District Medical Officer started the postmortem examination. Dr Alvah Pearson was a rheumatologist with a practice in St Georges Terrace and also the part-time police doctor, seeing to police officers' and detectives' medical needs. The District Medical Officer position involved him performing forensic postmortems , even though he had no specialist training in pathology. The body had been taken out of the cabinet and photographed, and one of the two mortuary orderlies and Martinovich were waiting for the doctor's arrival.

Dr Pearson noted the cuts and bruising on her face: a large laceration of the whole of the right eyebrow, with ragged edges. A smaller one half an inch above this; an abrasion one-and-a-half inches long under the chin; small abrasions on the bridge of the nose. Moving to her arms and legs, he noted a large abrasion on the outside of the right forearm and small abrasions on the back of the left hand and five fingers. Large abrasions involving the whole of the fronts and sides of both thighs and knees, laceration of the right big toe and bruises on the outer side of both calves. The right leg bruise was four inches long and two inches wide, and the left was five inches long and three inches wide. Under the left bruise there was a fracture of the upper quarter of the shaft of the fibula. On her body there was a one-inch laceration on the front of her pelvis, but it was not fractured.

The external examination over, Dr Pearson examined the internal body parts. Starting with the head, he found an extensive sub-arachnoid haemorrhage over the whole surface of the brain and small bruising in the under-surface of the right temporal lobe. The skull was not fractured. There were areas of haemorrhage discolouration in the lungs and the abdominal cavity was full of dark fluid blood. The front edge of the liver was torn, there was extensive haemorrhage in the regions of both kidneys and a small haemorrhage in the region of the root of the spleen.

There was a small amount of blood in the vagina, and he noted on his report that the hymen was 'apparently intact', giving no further explanation.

Formally noting the cause of death as haemorrhage from the torn liver and the sub-arachnoid haemorrhage, he dictated his notes and handed blood samples and vaginal swabs to Martinovich, who took these and hair samples and the girl's clothing to the Public Health Laboratories.

On Monday, Martinovich handed the postmortem specimens to Drummond. His tests on the liquid blood showed it to be group A rhesus negative. The dried stains could only be identified as group A, matching 40 to 45 per cent of the population. The tests on the vaginal swabs showed epithelial cells and bacteria, but no spermatozoa. He gently removed the clothing from the parcel, spreading the bloodstained frock on the table and examined it closely, cutting out small pieces of stained sections for the examination which showed blood group A.

At 10 a.m. John Button was taken to the small fingerprint room, where his parents, Jimmy and Frank Garrett were waiting for him. They were too much in shock to speak. All Charlie and Lilly could mumble through their tight throats were words of hope – Don't worry, son' and 'Everything will be all right'.

All John could get out was the one important message to his young brother, 'Jimmy, whatever you do, just tell the truth.'

The Perth Police Court was a big formal building dating back to 1905. John hadn't noticed it the previous night when he'd been taken upstairs to the CIB rooms. Now it was daylight when he was led back into the two-storey French Renaissance-style courthouse on the northern side of the railway line. He walked two paces and three steps up into the jarrah dock. Inside, the huge courtroom was as overwhelming as the formal exterior. The magistrate sat behind polished jarrah panelling with a coat of arms above him. There were reporters and other people sitting at the back. But John didn't have time to take it all in, only getting the impression of a formal formidable world unknown to him. It was over in two minutes. Magistrate Alan Smith remanded him to appear again in eight days.

John Button was on his way to another foreign world. Sitting in the back of a police car, his heart sank as they drove past Karrakatta Cemetery, remembering the last time he'd been past with Rosemary.

At Fremantle Prison, they drove up to big solid gates under the broken-down clock permanently showing five past twelve. The massive gates swung open and he was inside the high limestone walls. It was grey, drab and forbidding. The car went slowly under a barbed-wire arch and pulled up at a door where the police handed him over to prison officials. He was made to sit on a bench while officers processed his few belongings, putting them in envelopes. He gazed at the bench opposite and a section at the end that was enclosed for dangerous prisoners. Then he was given a set of prison clothes. After showering in the nearby open cubicles, he was covered with a disinfectant powder and dressed in the special clothes done up with tapes. There were no buttons which could be used to commit suicide by choking. Khaki trousers, blue shirt, thick socks and shoes with no laces. No underpants. He handed his own clothes over and they were tagged and put on a hanger.

He was escorted out the back door across a courtyard to a huge building, then across the yard past main division. He was full of dread. Looking up to his right, he saw the huge main division with its row on row of tiny windows. Looking up to his left, he saw watch towers on the walls, and guards carrying rifles. It was very quiet, except for music from the radio, played from speakers in the cells. They arrived at the new division, when the quiet was broken with the clanging of seemingly endless gates unlocked in front of him and locked behind him, leading to a line of nine cells in a small segregated section of new division, caged in behind a wire enclosure covering all of them.

The end of the journey was Death Row.

Evil Valentine

15 February 1963

It was the Friday after the hit–run murder in Stubbs Terrace. Another week had gone by without Cooke being suspected of anything. There was no reason for him to be worried about any of the hit–runs – John Button had confessed to killing the girl six nights back, and no-one had connected it to the others a few years previously, or suspected him of any of them.

The night was hot, a good omen for cat burglars and peeping Toms, with a greater chance of people sleeping with their windows and doors open to catch any slight breeze. He might have some luck, although most people in the western suburbs were keeping their windows closed despite the terrible heat. They were stifled in their hot locked-up houses, just because of him. Ha, what power this insignificant misfit had. And there was panic everywhere. If only they knew, when they laughed at him or ignored him, that he was the one who held them in the grip of fear.

He dressed smartly in his shiny gaberdine pants and reefer jacket and left home at 7.30 p.m., catching a bus to the city. He would have taken his car this time, but it was at the panel-beater's. After enjoying the single life in the city, he went to Wembley for the other kind of fun. He prowled in Wembley until about 2 a.m., then headed back towards the city, walking to West Perth, the prowler's paradise with lots of hiding places – dark, leafy, overhung back laneways crisscrossed the area.

It was the day after Valentine's Day – maybe some of the young people in the flats there would be in a romantic mood, relaxing at the end of the week and making good their

Valentine's promises. There could be plenty of exciting action to watch.

He hadn't had much luck finding couples in cars during the past three weeks. The police were going around warning them because of those two by the Cottesloe Civic Centre.

Dr Alister Turner and his girlfriend were startled to see a torch shone into the car and a huge bulk behind it. Then a deep voice announced he was a police officer, advising the couple of the danger of parking like this.

It was just after that fraught night in Casualty and the new doctor and Diane had managed to coordinate their rosters and get an evening off together. It was good timing for Valentines. He had delivered her back to the nurses' quarters at the Perth Chest Hospital but they were both delaying the moment when she would leave him to disappear into the red brick building. The parking area off Verdun Street was a quiet spot, only a few cars around belonging to those on night duty and some nursing quarters residents, and the privacy suited them for a lingering goodnight. It was cut short by the frightening warning. A final peck and the officer escorted Diane into the safety of the quarters.

Two young women were spending the evening polishing the floors of the flat they'd rented for the past two-and-a-half months. Social worker Lucy Madrill and schoolteacher Jennifer Hurse had moved into the West Perth flat on 1 December after Maria Smeets and her boyfriend Joe Smit had ended their lease. The new tenants didn't know that twenty-year-old Maria had been nervous about a prowler around the flat. Maria, who three years previously had been anxious for her friend and colleague Jill Connell after she'd been run down, was now so nervous after her waitressing night shifts that she asked the taxi drivers to see her inside.

The two-bedroom flat was at the northern half of the house at 70 Thomas Street, the solid old house having been converted internally to two flats. The area was renowned for prowlers and break-ins, but the two single women who'd roomed together for several years weren't worried – it was on a busy road, and the

Duncans and their seventeen-year-old daughter were close by in the other half of the house. The solid front doors of the two flats were next to each other on the shared front veranda. There wasn't much of a door at the back of the flat, just a flywire door with a flimsy bolt. It was rarely bolted or even closed – Lucy generally keeping the door propped open with a broom for her pet Siamese cat, Mudguts.

The flat was two houses away from the corner of Richardson Street with its impressive houses, one being the home of the famous young television personality with the big smile, Carolyn Noble. The house the Channel 7 star lived in with her parents, brothers and sisters was behind Lucy and Jennifer's place. During their couple of months in the flat, they hadn't seen twenty-year-old Carolyn or her elder sister, but had met the younger Noble boys several times. The two teenagers often played cricket in the laneway which ran between the side of their house and the back of the flat. Many a ball which would have made a few runs on a different pitch ended up over the fence, the boys taking it in turns to ask Lucy or Jennifer if they could fetch it from their backyard.

At 45 Richardson Street the boys' father, real estate agent and well-known sportsman Max Noble, was enjoying Friday night at home with his family and some friends, having a few drinks around the kitchen table.

The visitors left about 10.30 p.m., all except one of the girls' friends who was staying overnight and joining them on a day trip to Rottnest the next morning. Max and Joy Noble enjoyed the balmy summer night a little longer. By midnight they'd finished the bottle of Scotch, and Max tossed the empty bottle out on to the back lawn.

The polishing chore finished, the two flatmates relaxed and read – Jennifer Hurse taking her book to bed and Lucy Madrill reading in the lounge room. Between 11 and 11.30 p.m., 24-year-old Lucy, now in her blue shortie nightie, walked to Jennifer's room to return a book and say goodnight, then went to bed in her room at the back of the flat. At 1.30 a.m. Jennifer went out the back to the toilet, looking into Lucy's room on her return and noticing that her friend was asleep on top of the bed, the blankets and sheet turned back. The bedroom blind was open, as usual. Lucy only pulled it down while she was undressing, opening it again to sleep. There didn't seem to be a problem with that. The window wasn't open to the public, facing instead the side fence of the house next door, across the driveway running down the side of the flat.

Cooke had made his way to West Perth along Churchill Avenue, which ended at Thomas Street just opposite Richardson Street. The small man feared by the whole of Perth crossed Thomas Street. He crossed diagonally, walked into the front garden of a house, jumped a flower bed and went over to a front open window. Shining his torch in, he saw a dressing table against the wall to the right of the window.

It was on a rather busy street. Maybe another window would be open around the back. He walked down the driveway to the back of the house, where he found such an easy entry – the back door was propped open with a broom. First he pulled the power out at the mains. Maybe he'd been noticed prowling around here before. He'd been there just three weeks before. No-one was home and he'd only taken a bottle of beer. He didn't want to be seen or recognised tonight. He had serious business to do.

Putting on his gloves and taking his torch from his pocket, he walked in, creeping up the twelve-foot passageway silently in his rubber-soled shoes. There was a bedroom. But there was no-one sleeping there and no money in it. Retracing his steps, he shone his torch in the bathroom and then in another room which was unoccupied. He saw a mattress on the floor under the window and an old-fashioned chair with padded arms. He noticed a lamp on the table. Then he turned around and walked towards another bedroom, where he saw a woman asleep. She didn't interest him. He turned away into the kitchen and found a plastic purse on a shelf and £1 in it.

Pocketing it, he walked through the lounge room to the last bedroom where there was another woman asleep. This bedroom was some distance from the other one, towards the back of the house. And the woman didn't have a sheet over her. She was sleeping on top of the bed, wearing just a flimsy nightie; virtually nothing to hide her nakedness. The feeling that had been stirring all night grew stronger. It was a balmy night, thoughts of young love had been on his mind since the previous day and she was alone, nearly naked. He could have her and avenge himself again. He had the power; he'd proved it over and over. The excitement and madness took hold.

He was at the dressing table by the woman's bed when in his eagerness he knocked a framed photo and it fell to the floor. She woke up, her eyes wide with terror at a man standing over her. She sat up, swung her legs off the side of the bed and desperately reached to grab something off the table. Something to defend herself with.

Oh no, not another one who was going to fight him. He had to get in first. He hit her with his fist, so hard that it thrust her head hard against the wall and hurt his hand. She opened her mouth to scream, but he grabbed her throat before the air reached her voice box. He had to stop any screams that would wake her flatmate. He was angry, too, at being thwarted again. He shifted his grip to a stranglehold around her neck with his right arm. That silenced her.

With his arm tight around her neck, he dragged her out of her bedroom into the spare room. He put her on the mattress, convinced she was almost dead. But he had to make sure she wouldn't regain consciousness like that other one did. He looked for something to strangle her with. The flex from the table lamp? Perfect. He twisted it around her neck, tightly. He'd have her while she was unconscious. But what if she managed to struggle out of it and scream like that other one did? And this one with a flatmate in the next room. He could twist it once more, and really make sure. What a feeling of power – whether she lived or died was entirely up to him and one twist of the flex. He was used to killing now, used to making the ultimate strike against society. It was easy. He twisted the flex again, holding it there for several minutes till he was sure she was dead. What a thrill. One of those lucky people who had everything. Now she had nothing.

But again he'd missed his chance to have that other thrill. She was dead, but only just dead, and her nightie was see-through as she lay there. He took it off and, already inflamed by his ultimate power, the sight of her vulnerable, naked body overwhelmed him. She was still warm and fleshy. It didn't matter that there was no response – he burst with excitement and power. A big word, necrophilia, and what an outrage. Even after death he could do more to violate her.

There hadn't been a sound, nor was there blood spattered around like before. If he got rid of the body somewhere else, nobody would know what had happened. If he could get her outside, he could steal a car and take it away. He dragged the well-built girl out through the back door, the coir mat sliding with the body. He struggled under the weight, one arm under the shoulders and one arm under the thighs. He put her down for a bit when she started to slip, then managed to get her out the back door, across the lawn and through the gate to the laneway. Slipping again, he tried to fix his grip, but she was too heavy and fell back on the laneway, striking her head on the bitumen surface. So he took her feet instead and dragged her across the lane on to the expansive lawn of a house at the back. He was oblivious to the risk of being seen or heard. As well as struggling with her dead weight, he had to fight off Mudguts, who attacked the stranger. Cooke had a way with dogs, he could quieten that corgi across the lane, but not with cats. His hand was badly scratched and bleeding as he dragged Mudguts' mistress almost 80 feet to the neighbour's lawn.

He dumped her under the rotary clothes hoist, near an empty whisky bottle. People in one of these big fancy houses had been having a party, enjoying themselves. He was still enraged, and drunk with his power. He picked up the bottle and thrust it into the lifeless body. One more abomination. He withdrew it and placed it in the crook of her right arm, just so. A pretty picture; a final insult.

Leaving her nightie on the lawn beside her, he walked down the lane to Ord Street, looking for a car to steal. In a garage at the back of a house in Kings Park Road there were two cars with keys in them. He chose the light-coloured sports car. He pushed it out of the garage into the backyard and was just getting it to the entrance of the lane when a light went on in the house. An airline pilot was up early to get to work. Thwarted again. Too bad about the body on the back lawn, he'd leave it – it would make a fine sight for those revellers in the morning, and could never be linked with him, there being no fingerprints.

He ran through the streets of West Perth, across the railway line towards his old workplace, Plaistowes, and into Carr Street. He found a bike on the veranda of a semi-detached house at 73 Carr Street and rode it home. He dumped it behind a shed in the yard of the Rivervale State School and walked the rest of the way. It was nearly daylight when he arrived.

The Noble family was up at 6 a.m. to prepare for the Rottnest trip. Joy Noble was the first to go to the toilet out the back. She saw what she thought was just a bundle on the lawn. She peered closer, seeing it was a young woman, lying naked face up with a bottle under her arm. There was a blue mark on her throat. Joy Noble screamed and ran through the house calling for her daughters. Relieved at finding them safe, she gathered all the children into the kitchen while her husband called the West Perth police.

Constance Lucy Madrill had been born on her parents' station near Katherine in the Northern Territory in December 1938. Her father had died when she was four. Her mother, Constance, worked the station in a partnership until Lucy was six, when she sold her share and moved to Adelaide, buying a small orchard. Mrs Madrill moved again when her only child was fifteen, leaving the Oldgate orchard for Western Australia. They lived in Carlisle for eight years before moving to an outer part of Perth behind the airport, Newburn. After attending the Victoria Park Seventh Day Adventist School, Lucy went on to tertiary study, obtaining her Bachelor of Arts degree with a major in psychology from the University of Western Australia. Initially she had thoughts of becoming a missionary, then settled on social work with the Native Welfare Department. She had been at the department for two years, working mainly with Aboriginal women and children in the metropolitan area and devising a scheme for non-language intelligence tests for Aboriginals.

Soon Richardson Street was filled with detectives in big black cars. The Noble family left for the day as planned, but it was a grim party that sat in Thomson Bay trying to forget that terrible sight. They returned from the day trip early, but not to their home. The Nobles allowed the police to take over their house as investigation headquarters, billeting the children out to relatives.

Another murder, when the police were already under huge pressure from a population in panic after the shootings three weeks back. Detective Sergeant Jerry Parker was put in charge of the investigation, assisted by Detective Sergeant Graham Lee.

They and their men scoured the back lawn and lane for clues, bringing in a Malay tracker from the north, Mervyn Hunter, who was on holiday in Perth. He could see that she had first been dragged with the heels trailing, before the murderer had reversed his grip, pulling her along by her legs for the last half. In the sandy laneway, any further clues were lost among the many footprints of the two young cricketers.

There was no sign of disturbance in Lucy's room. A dress and underwear were in a heap on the linoleum floor against one wall, where she would have tossed them before going to bed. A dressing gown was across the foot of the single bed, and the blankets and sheet were turned back. In another room a piece of flex had been broken from a reading lamp. The Duncans next door awoke to find they had no power – it had been pulled out at the mains, along with their neighbours'.

The possibility of an Aboriginal killer was canvassed, and police questioned Jennifer's estranged husband, a friend of Lucy's. Detective Sergeant Owen Leitch went to Williams to interview him. These inquiries leading nowhere, the police decided the main probability was that the murder had been committed by a prowler.

They were puzzled by several aspects, one being the quietness of the killer, who didn't disturb her flatmate or the corgi in an Ord Street house bordering the lane. Its owner, Jack McDaniell, said it was usually a good watchdog, barking at the slightest movement in the lane. They couldn't understand the killer's decision to drag the body so far, risking detection, nor his whisky bottle quirk.

They took the mattress and put it under a table in CIB headquarters and they started to investigate the hundreds of reports of prowlers in the area before and after the murder.

Inspector Lamb offered to return from leave a month early. Commissioner Jim O'Brien said he could see no reason for recalling him to work and Inspector Pat Hagan would continue to act as head of the CIB.

The people of Perth were further horrified; another shocking murder so soon after the Australia Day horror and the amazing night of the Gnangara manhunt and the running down at Shenton Park. And this time, the killer had subjected the poor girl to indecencies. The titillated gossips got busy again, with talk spreading about the flatmates and their relationship.

It was a busy time, too, for Allan Drummond, with two murder scenes on 27 January, two on 10 February and now another. At this, there was the forensic evidence of semen around the top of the bottle. Scotland Yard had tests that could get a more specific blood grouping from semen than from blood.

Drummond flew to London, carrying the empty Dewars whisky bottle in a sealed envelope in a leather briefcase he borrowed from the director, Dr Laurie. He sat with it on his lap for the whole journey and went directly from Heathrow to Scotland Yard. He stayed in Harrington Hall in South Kensington waiting for the tests to be carried out. But they didn't come up with anything.

The police were no closer to finding the killer. They were convinced of one thing, though – this murder was not linked to the earlier shootings. Commissioner O'Brien announced that the methods of the crimes differed too much for them to have been committed by the same person.

Death Row

FEBRUARY–MAY 1963

John Button, isolated in Death Row, was totally unaware that another young woman had been murdered, six days after Rosemary's murder.

His entire world was a stark, concrete cell measuring six yards by three yards, with a mattress on the floor and a sanitary bucket in the corner. He knew nothing but the deepest despair.

At 1.15 p.m. on Tuesday, 12 February, a solemn group gathered behind the black hearse at the entrance to Karrakatta Cemetery. Rosemary's cortege had set out from Horace L. Green Funeral Parlour in Cottesloe and slowly made its way along Stirling Highway and Railway Road, leading a line of cars with their headlights on. More mourners joined in a long grim walk through the length of the cemetery, past rows of white headstones shimmering in the midday heat, through the patches of shade from the occasional box trees and peppermint gums, to almost the eastern perimeter.

Jack Anderson led the group to the freshly dug-up mound of sand in the far Anglican allocation. Joan Anderson was at home, heavily sedated. The family and friends who were at the graveside were also struggling to come to terms with the death as they heard the Graylands/Mt Claremont Rector Edward Stanley go through the ritual burial service for a girl so vibrant and in love just three days previously.

How John wanted to be with them, to share their loss and to be comforted. He longed to be there, saying goodbye to his love and having them all understand how great his loss was, too. He so wanted them to understand that he hadn't done it, and that he wasn't their enemy but their companion in grief. He was frustrated that he couldn't tell them the truth. The isolation of the tiny empty cell in Death Row was unbearable. He felt so terribly alone.

When his mother brought him the death notices from the back page of *The West Australian*, he read them over and over. 'Our angel, God's angel now' from Mum, Dad, Helen and Jim. 'Sadly missed' from Frank and Laraine. 'The President and Committee Members of the Swanbourne-Nedlands Surf Life Saving Club extend their deepest sympathy to Jack and Joan.' And more, from aunties and uncles, neighbours and friends. But none from him. How he wanted to pour out his grief and his love in this public expression of his loss.

As Rosemary's family and friends gathered to bid her farewell, the police and the forensic serologist were just across the railway line, again inspecting the area where she'd been hit. Wilson had been given instructions to go back and look further and he'd called Drummond, who arrived at midday and examined more small bloodstained stones at the side of Stubbs Terrace. They had been found 50 yards nearer the subway than the other blood stains, indicating the girl had been hit earlier than previously indicated. There were seventeen pieces of loose road metal spread along almost three feet of road. In the laboratory the stains on them proved to be human blood, group A. Near them, Wilson found a three-foot white metal scrape mark on the edge of the road and some white metal shavings. There were two or three small flakes as if pared off with a rasp, like the filing left from a file. The blood was spread over a large distance – there were 74 yards from the blood nearest the subway to the last patch. There were no signs of brake or skid marks on the bitumen.

The new finds didn't fit John Button's confession. It said he'd hit her nearly opposite the Shenton Park railway station – but it was clear now that she'd been hit 50 yards nearer the subway.

The three mates who'd happened upon the scene that night were fascinated by the news that buzzed around Graylands and

Mt Claremont the next day and Monday, as the radio and newspapers spread the news. So it wasn't the big murderer they'd come upon, but a murderer nonetheless!

An open-and-shut case, solved through John's confession. They didn't think of making a report to the police until Barry Hansen noticed something wrong in a newspaper item. Only then did he realise that they, as first on the scene, should give statements to the police. In his lunch-hour on Thursday he walked over to the CIB, only a block away from his work at Beaurepaires in Stirling Street. Hansen still wasn't really sure of the point of it, and felt the police officer wasn't all that interested, but the officer was polite and efficient, asking Hansen questions and typing out the answers in formal paraphrases.

John Barry Hansen states:

> I am a single man aged 21 years and reside at 36 Mengler Avenue, Graylands. I am employed at Beaurepaires, Perth.
>
> On Saturday night 9 February 1963 I was returning home from the trots, I was driving my VW car, I had two friends Wilson White and Nigel Phillips as my passengers.
>
> I came down Nicholson Road and went under the subway and turned left into Stubbs Terrace, the time would have been approximately 10.30 p.m. to 10.40 p.m. I had driven along Stubbs Terrace from the subway I would say about 100 yards I had travelled when I noticed a cream Simca which appeared to be stopped on the left hand side of the road about 30 yards in front of me. As I passed this car I looked over to my left and saw what I thought was a bundle of clothes in the sand about 3 yards off the side of the road, and then said 'that looks like a body'. One of my friends made a remark.
>
> I travelled for another 50 or 60 yards further on and turned my car around and came back and pulled up opposite the car which was parked on the side of the road. I saw a young man, who I thought was dressed in shorts and did not have a shirt on.
>
> I could see that this man had a figure in his arms. I saw him put the figure into the left hand front side of his car. Wilson White called out something to this man. He looked up when Wilson called out to him, but he did not say anything.

I then went further down the road and turned around and came back and passed him again. I pulled my car up about 10 yards in front of this car which was still parked on the side of the road.

About this time I saw a Morris car I think a few yards ahead of my car. I then drove off going south in Stubbs Terrace. I had travelled 300 to 400 yards when I saw the Simca I mentioned before go past my car. He was travelling at a high speed I estimated to be about 70.

As he went past I saw what I thought to be a girl in the front passenger seat. She had her head lying backwards. I decided to follow this car, which turned right into Alfred Road, still travelling at high speed. I kept following it and I saw him pull up at Dr Quinlivan's surgery.

I pulled up on the side street near the surgery, I saw this young man get out of his car and run up to the front door of Dr Quinlivan's house. He then came back to the car and I saw a light go on in the back of the surgery.

I then saw this man pull a girl from the front passenger seat. When he pulled her out he did not seem to have a very good grip on her and he heaved her up, he then put her down and closed the door of his car. He was still supporting her. He then picked her up and carried her down the path towards the surgery door. As he was near the door I saw Dr Quinlivan come outside and I saw the man put her down on the path. I saw Dr Quinlivan examining her a few minutes later I saw the doctor and this man carry the girl into the surgery.

I then went to Wilson White's place which is nearby.
B. Hansen
14/2/63

Hansen scanned the statement so quickly that he didn't notice the errors. It was just a formality, seeing as they had the murderer already. He didn't take much notice of the order of events, like when he saw the car, or that he hadn't stated that the driver was still in the car when he first saw him and that he saw him go over to the body. He didn't notice that he was wrong about when Wilson had called out – it was at the doctor's surgery, not on their first pass of the car. Nor that he said he pulled up in front of the car, when he'd pulled up behind it. A quick glance, all seemed OK and he signed and dated it. Then he returned to work for the afternoon.

He urged the others to give statements, too. Wilson White told Hansen he didn't want to, and Nigel Phillips said there was no point, but on Hansen's persuasion they gave statements, as did the two men in the front seat of the Morris.

For John Button, the outside world had disappeared on Monday when the officer had unlocked the door to the wire cage and escorted him to the door to one of the cells.

He'd ordered the remand prisoner to take off his shoes and leave them outside the door. Then he'd unlocked the heavy door of the third cell from the end and ordered John inside, clanging it shut behind him and leaving John alone in a hot concrete cage. It was bare and dismal, containing only a thin horsehair mattress and a bucket, and smelling strongly of phenol.

There was a window high up, in the right-hand corner, casting a shadow of bars on the opposite wall and showing him small slivers of blue. He just stood there, gazing at those glimpses of the real world, his mind screaming his innocence and his disbelief. He was all alone, no-one was listening to the truth, no-one to save him from this crazy injustice. No-one? What about the God of Justice he'd learnt about in Sunday School many years before?

'God, if you are who you claim to be, then free me,' he beseeched. 'If you are indeed a God of Justice then make the wall fall down or the window fall out.' He stood there, fists clenched, putting all his prayers and mental strength into helping God's justified intervention. Opening his eyes, he was desperately disappointed, standing there behind the uncompromising wall, feeling deserted and alone. The prison grew bigger and bigger, swallowing up an insignificant creature who could not compete with its size and might. It was even bigger than a supposedly all-powerful God.

At 3.30 p.m. an officer came and told him to strip. This was his day cell. Each afternoon about this time he had to strip and, completely naked, move to the neighbouring cell. The day cell and his clothes were thoroughly searched. The routine was repeated in the opposite direction in the morning. John was embarrassed and humiliated. Twice a day he ran between his day and night cells, rushing to cover himself as quickly as he could.

It was solitary confinement – there was no company, no work, no mixing with the other prisoners. He was not part of the normal prison routine where they worked during the week and spent weekends out in the yards together. Work would have given him company, distraction and some sense of worth. There was nothing for him to do but pace the cell – two paces across, three paces down. The only relief from the solitude in the small space was an hour's exercise each day – if there was a warder available to escort him. The exercise gave him a break from the confinement, but not from the loneliness or bleakness. Death Row had its own narrow exercise yard quite separate from the general yard. Walking up and down outside didn't give him any colour, company or much contrast to the constant view of bare floor, walls and bars. It didn't give him anything to take his mind off his grief and misery, and the threat of the noose.

He didn't need the exercise. He walked all day and night – up and down his cell. He couldn't sit still, he needed movement. The days seemed endless, but the nights were even worse. It was stifling in the small cell during this hot February. The small, high window allowed no breeze to bring relief. With the heat, grief, confusion and isolation, he had a constant headache and found sleep impossible as he went over and over what had happened.

There was no privacy, either. As well as the indignity of the naked run between his two cells, the door of the bathroom opposite was left open when he was allowed to use the toilet during his exercise hour. A bath was allowed once a week, again with the door open and a guard outside.

His cell was only three away from the condemned cell. He could see it every time he was led to the bathroom across the corridor and he constantly felt its proximity and its grim reality.

His only contact with the outside world was a radio speaker outside the cell, its three stations controlled by another prisoner, Tex. It was on all day – but John was too lost in his own miserable world to listen to the news. He hardly heard what was broadcast at all, just aware of some noise out there beyond the repetitive questions and screams running through his head.

He only took notice of the radio at 4 p.m. That was an hour of the latest hits, with half an hour of special requests at 4.30. John took the opportunity of reaching up and turning the switch to 6KY as he ran naked to his night cell. He waited for this time of day when the songs transported him from his few square feet of grey concrete to his carefree life and happy love: from a 'Jack to a King', 'Wolverton Mountain', 'Great Pretender'. Some, though, only deepened his grief, loss and loneliness: 'Tears on My Pillow', 'Lonely is a Man Without Love', 'There Goes My Reason for Living', 'Teen Angel'.

Lilly Button cried the whole way down in the car. Just quietly, turning towards the window to dab at the trickle of tears escaping under her glasses and down her cheeks. Her head felt thick from the mixture of anguish and bewilderment that was overwhelming her, allowing her no relief from the tight knot in her stomach and the heavy rock on her chest. It was unrelenting, denying her any experience of life other than this pain and dull patience.

She'd always loved trips to Fremantle. It had meant a drive along the beaches and fish and chips on the beach beside the Roundhouse. She'd loved the earthy, hearty atmosphere of the port city, full of dockside workers, sailors and seamy pubs and cafés to cater for them. She loved the salty air, the screaming of the seagulls and the smells of the sea which reminded her of the docks at home in Liverpool.

Today she did not enjoy the first view of the glittering Indian Ocean as they passed Buckland Hill. She had turned the other way to hide her tears from Charlie, looking out instead at the scrubby limestone hill scarred by Harley Scramble tracks, but seeing nothing. She didn't see the river as they crossed the Fremantle Traffic Bridge straddling the Swan close to its mouth, nor did she notice the limestone grandeur of the old asylum or the Victorian houses on Nob Hill on the outskirts of Fremantle.

It was the first sight of the overpowering walls that took her out of her unseeing haze and plunged her into an even deeper despair. She felt totally impotent as she looked at the huge thick walls that appeared to have entombed her son.

Grateful for Charlie's mostly successful efforts at portraying the Englishman's stiff upper lip, she pulled herself together for John's sake and walked steadfastly to the small breach in the wall, an unwelcoming door marked Visitors' Entrance. Filling in the form, passing through the narrow entrance room, seeing for the first time what lay inside, being led past the mammoth Main Division, through the iron gates, through another wire cage into the small bare cell next to his, set up for visiting with a table and three chairs – it was all like a dream in which she watched herself and Charlie acting brave and proud.

Her act fell apart when she saw her John. There was her son, in prison khaki. He looked so small, so lost, so defeated. She clasped him, her tears sinking into his shirt, his tears spilling on to her head. They had so much to say, but nothing was said. No voice could get through Lilly's and John's tears nor the lump in Charlie's throat. They hugged and cried, the only way they could express the grief, anger, disbelief and incomprehension that they all felt.

Charlie gently took Lilly's shoulders and drew her away when the warder announced they should prepare to leave. She gazed into her son's eyes and squeezed his hand in farewell, knowing it conveyed all she couldn't say. Charlie clasped John's hand in both of his, rasping 'Take care, son', and the warder led them out. They stumbled through all the gates and past the towering cell block into the visitors' reception and through to the sunshine beyond the walls.

Out of that oppressive place, relieved of the effort of trying to hold it together as much as possible in front of John, Lilly let go, her small body shaking with her sobs as she gave in to the physical and emotional pain. She sobbed all the way home. Charlie kept begging her to stop crying, and he tried to talk about other things to take her mind off it. She knew he was trying to help, but she needed to cry and nothing could stop it. At home she went straight to bed, relieved to be alone to cry into the night and think of nothing but John's misery, just as she had in private each night since the horror began.

John's desperate loneliness was relieved slightly after a few days by an awareness of someone else on Death Row. He heard movement in another cell. That gave him some feeling of togetherness, even though he couldn't see or speak to his faceless, nameless companion.

Two days after John's arrest, police who'd gone into the country on the hunt for the marksman had been directed to a small town to make another wilful murder arrest. Detectives, including Sergeant Wiley, headed east in response to a report of shots fired at the No. 5 pumping station on the 350-mile pipeline transporting water from Perth to Kalgoorlie. Full of hope of a breakthrough, they'd gone to the pumping station at Carrabin to investigate the reports. It was a red herring. They found nothing there, but returned to Perth with seventeen-year-old Richie Uziel, from the small pig iron foundry town of Wundowie.

Richard Jozef Uziel had shot his mother the previous year, but it was only when the gun was found hidden in the slag heaps that there was enough evidence to charge the youth. Helena Uziel had been walking home with several of her children at 6.30 p.m. on 16 August, after delivering tea to her husband at Wundowie Charcoal Iron Industry. Richie shot her in the back with a .22 calibre rifle as she walked under a street light. An illegitimate child, he had been left in Germany when his mother married there and the couple migrated to Australia. He was later sent out at the instigation of German authorities. His mother resented this and, with a deep hatred of the boy, she ridiculed him and mistreated him until he snapped.

With the arrival of young Richie on Death Row, John Button felt just a little less alone. Someone else shared the horror of his predicament, the noose awaiting both of them. About four weeks later they finally met. The two teenagers were allowed out into the caged area at the front of their cells. They were allowed to walk and talk together for a couple of hours morning and afternoon, as long as they didn't discuss their trials. The nineteen-year-old from England and Perth had little in common with the seventeen-year-old from Germany and Wundowie, except for their loneliness and misery; but at least they had some human contact.

A third person arrived on Death Row nineteen days later. On 2 March Brian William Robinson was brought to Fremantle Prison after three weeks in a carefully guarded bed at RPH. His shattered elbow was still in plaster, but he'd recovered from his abdominal injuries enough to leave hospital and wait in prison for certain execution. The increase of the Death Row population reduced John's quarters to one cell. He was relieved of the dreaded naked runs.

It was a whole new world for John Button, who'd never had anything to do with police or criminals before. Now his only companions were a boy who'd killed his mother and a man who'd cold-bloodedly shot two strangers. Conversations between the isolated Death Row inmates were restricted by the ever-present warders, who banned any talk about their cases or trials. But Robinson did touch on it once. John was outside in the corridor preparing for his exercise when the warders left them alone for a moment. Robinson called John over to his open-barred cell and after quick introductions, he told John he didn't really feel sorry for what he did to Noel Iles; he just didn't feel anything about that. And he thought the policeman's wife would get over it and would get married again. But he really felt for the children, who had to live the rest of their lives without a father. John was amazed. He just couldn't comprehend how someone could kill someone so callously yet still have any feelings at all.

John managed to get a small view of the outside world every eight days when he was driven to the court in Perth for a further remand. The trips provided some light relief from the drab confinement of Death Row. The police escorting him in a police car gave him a little company, too. And he enjoyed their trust. Once, on the way to the Beaufort Street court, they stopped and left him alone in the car while they dashed into a shop for some cigarettes. They were that certain that their prisoner, an accused murderer, would not try to escape. It gave John confidence that they believed he was innocent and that soon it would be equally clear to a jury. This unbelievable mistake would be rectified. The nightmare would be over.

After the preliminary hearing on 8 March, the trial date was set for 29 April.

The defence team of Ken Hatfield QC and Bart Kakulas worked hard on this case. They firmly believed their client was innocent. Not at first – the confession sounded right, so they had a lot of reservations. It took a while for them to assess John and the situation. The turning point had come when Margaret arrived from Wagga and talked to them. Margaret, heavily pregnant with her first child due in June, had caught the train across Australia to help her brother and parents. She knew John better than anyone, having been with him throughout his youth – better than his father, who'd missed four years of John's growing up, and his mother, who'd missed two. Margaret was able to explain John's personality – his shyness, his problems at school, his inability to stand up for himself and his loathing of aggression. The lawyers were convinced.

Lilly Button's desperate early-morning run over the road to Ninke Burns had paid off. She'd managed to secure the top QC, giving John and the family confidence. Ken Hatfield had a reputation for defending the underdog and had succeeded in gaining a spectacular number of acquittals of clients charged with murder and other serious offences during his fifteen years at the bar.

The 56-year-old Kenneth Watts Hatfield had always been clever, doing his Leaving Certificate at just fifteen and filling in the two years until he could go to university by teaching at Hale School, when he was younger than some of the students. After doing an arts degree, in the absence of a law school in Western Australia at the time, he did five years of law articles with H. S. Keall, joining the firm Villeneuve, Smith & Keall as a partner in 1934 and spending the first several years concentrating on conveyancing work and coaching law students.

His powerful court ability began to emerge in the 1940s, when he defended clients against his former university colleague and team-mate in the varsity football club, Crown Solicitor

Gerald Ruse. The fast-speaking, dynamic barrister quickly revealed his knowledge of the law, thoroughness, tenacity and eloquence – with a distinctive showmanship that made his advocacy original and entertaining.

He rose at 4 a.m. each day and was driven to the office by his taxi driver brother-in-law by 5 a.m. at the latest. Clients given a 5 o'clock appointment were surprised to discover it didn't mean 5 p.m. But starting at that hour let him work uninterrupted and gave him time later in the day to chat with his old university friend and fellow lawyer Leo Wood in the Terrace and to have a few beers at the Tattersalls Club with his articled clerk, Bart Kakulas, before being picked up by his wife Gwen.

It also gave him time to coach football at Christ Church Grammar School. He was a football enthusiast, often seen practising drop kicks at the bus stop and kicking an invisible football down the Terrace, and a keen race-goer, finishing work on Saturdays in time to join Gwen at the racecourse in summer and to go to the football in winter.

On Sundays he went to the office a little later, around 8 a.m., coming home for lunch at midday. Christmas Day was the only day of the year that he didn't work and his wife and four daughters had him at home all day. He considered holidays a waste of time, only ever having a weekend in Singapore once and once a few days in Coral Bay. He practised law for the sake of law, not for financial gain.

Just as he supported clients wholeheartedly, regardless of personal embarrassment or concern to his friends, he was eclectic in his friendships, which embraced every walk of life. Sunday lunch always included his secretary, Joy Pell, and an Aboriginal Christ Church boarder he coached at football. At evening social gatherings at his home he had an alarm clock on the mantelpiece set for 9 p.m. That was his regular bedtime and the signal for the guests to leave.

A stroke in 1961 didn't change his working habits. He gradually recovered from slurred speech and a slight limp. The only long-term result was a life-long friendship with his neurologist, Dr Mercy Sadka, who was drawn into the family circle.

In early 1963 he was in fine form, ready to do his best for the son of Ninke Burns' neighbour, convinced the defence of John Button was a worthwhile cause.

Hatfield chose 29-year-old Bart Kakulas as his junior counsel for the case. Barthalamos Peter Kakulas was working for himself at the time, but had worked for Hatfield for many years. After finishing his law degree at the University of Western Australia, he was taken on to do his articles with Hatfield in 1955. Admitted to the bar in 1957, he worked one year with his role model before taking the big step of going out on his own. Hatfield said he'd support his protégé, who was almost like a son to him and he did, putting a lot of work his way.

Hatfield and Kakulas made several trips to Fremantle Prison to talk to John Button. It was a shy, reticent youth they met in the Death Row cell set aside for visits. Their client stuttered and stumbled and at first they weren't certain they were getting the truth. After all, the confession, with its argument and resultant anger, all fitted. In frustration, Hatfield jumped up and grabbed him by the collar, 'Look, you've got to tell me everything. You are going to hang, my boy.'

John went through the night minute by minute, telling them everything – except for one thing. He didn't mention his intimate relationship with Rosemary. He could never bring such dishonour to his beloved.

John never wavered from his insistence that the confession was false, not even when Hatfield told him he could talk to the prosecution about a deal. If John would plead guilty to manslaughter, Hatfield believed the Crown would accept the lesser charge and he'd probably get ten years' jail. John insisted he would not plead guilty to something he hadn't done. He'd rather risk execution.

Charlie agreed with this decision, even though he would have saved a lot of money if John had pleaded guilty to the lesser charge. Charlie sold his utility to pay the first legal fees – a sacrifice for the bricklayer who needed it for his trade. Charlie believed implicitly in his son and stood by him.

Hatfield went to see Lilly and Charlie Button on two or three occasions, his eldest daughter, 24-year-old Jill, accompanying him each time.

He lived in Dalkeith with Gwen, their three daughters and his sister's daughter, Libby, whom he had adopted when her mother died. The four girls – Jill and Libby, aged 24, Anne, 21, and Sally, 19 – were all living at home and were very fond of their father. But Jill, nicknamed Jillypots by her father, had a special relationship with him and loved being with him.

Already fascinated by what her father had told her about this unusual case, Jill immediately asked if she could come when he announced he was going to see John's parents. He didn't mind, but told her she'd have to bring a notebook. He didn't need notes taken – he had a photographic memory that he'd trained, insisting that a case be remembered totally without having to fossick for notes. So, pretending to be his secretary, Jill sat there listening to the interview while she wrote her name over and over in the notebook.

Presenting the case for the Crown was Ron Wilson, a top prosecutor renowned for his hard work and persistence. The 40-year-old had made a big name for himself.

Being orphaned at the age of fourteen had forced him to leave school and start work as a messenger with the Geraldton Local Court. He was transferred to the Crown Law Department in Perth at seventeen, but his progress was interrupted by the war, in which he piloted Spitfires and Tempests in the UK. After the war, having studied privately to pass the four subjects required for matriculation, he enrolled for an arts degree at the University of Western Australia, studying full-time and working for the Crown Law Department in the university vacations.

At the end of first year, he transferred to law – effecting a career change from the administration of law to its practice. He gained twelve distinctions and graduated with first-class honours in 1949. Articled in Crown Law, he was immediately appointed solicitor, Crown Law, when he was admitted as solicitor and barrister in 1951, a position that was retitled assistant prosecutor in 1954. Two years later he won a fellowship to do his Master of Law at the University of Pennsylvania. In 1959, at the age of 36, he was appointed WA's chief crown prosecutor, heading a team of six prosecutors. Just three years later he became crown counsel.

As chief crown prosecutor in the 1950s he'd worked very hard and was renowned for it. With a workload that had him prosecuting eight or nine trials in the one month, he organised a routine for each month's sittings. He prepared all the cases in the week before the sittings started, getting the outline of facts into the form of an opening address to the jury before going on to the next case. As the month progressed, he would finish a trial one day, then pick up the address he had prepared the previous month to bring the next case back to mind. After addressing the jury at the end of each case and listening to the judge's summing up, he would close his mind to that one and direct it to the next, spending no time or emotional energy on the jury's decision.

He was very active in the Presbyterian Church, having been taken there by the housekeeper on his mother's death when he was four, despite his Anglican baptism. He became a Commissioner of the Presbyterian Church in 1959 and had attended the third assembly of the World Council of Churches in New Delhi in 1961.

At the same time, his prosecution sent a few men to the gallows, starting with the controversial execution of Karol Tapci in 1952 for murder, when capital punishment had normally only been used for wilful murder, indicating intent. Ron Wilson assisted Gerald Ruse in prosecuting the unfortunate Czechoslovak migrant, whose execution was opposed by various church people, including the Archbishop of Perth. Because of his job, Wilson was not identified with that opposition.

With him for the Button prosecution was 39-year-old Alan Dodd, who personally believed the charge should have been a lesser one like dangerous driving causing death. Dodd had also been involved in capital punishment cases. One, four years back, had prompted him to bring his Hornet rifle down from the top of the wardrobe after threats following the death sentence. The tough father of three, who'd seen active service during the war, felt precautions were necessary when the multiple killer Robert Jeremiah Thomas made a number of threats against him. Thomas had been convicted of shooting a taxi driver and a married couple on 22 June 1959 and was in jail awaiting execution, but the prosecutor wasn't taking any chances. He'd taken the bolt from its hiding place and put the weapon together and placed it under the bed just in case Thomas should somehow try to make good his threats. The gun was back under the bed now.

Dodd had won a scholarship to attend Wesley College and then went on to gain an arts degree from the University of Western Australia. After war service, he was articled to Len Seaton and admitted to the bar in 1949. He joined the Crown Law Department in 1955, served as a Parliamentary draughtsman and was appointed chief crown prosecutor in 1963.

It was a top team arguing for and against John.

Wilson believed that justice was best served by both sides arguing their case vigorously – and he was known for being tenacious and dogged. Facing Hatfield in John's trial, he felt he would be dealing with the best counsel of the time and a determined fighter. Wilson and Dodd had clashed with Hatty on many occasions, but they all respected each other.

On 18 March Detective Sergeant John Wiley prepared the precis of evidence that was forwarded to the chief crown prosecutor by Inspector Lamb. After detailing the events of the night according to John's confession and mentioning that at no time had the accused requested the attendance of the police, Wiley concluded with a section headed general remarks:

> Stubbs Terrace runs parallel with the railway line which is about 30 yards from where the body of the deceased had lain on the side of the road, nearly opposite the railway station. Blood patches were found about 18 inches from the edge of the bitumen in the sand. The accused admitted that this was the spot where he had picked her up from. The deceased received a severe laceration over the right eye which was bleeding freely and it was quite evident that this was the position where her body had been lying. No other patches of blood were found in the vicinity.
>
> The significance of this point is that witnesses who came upon the scene soon after saw the accused with the body two to three yards over towards the railway line. It is considered

that there is a possibility the accused may have been in the act of taking her body to put it on the railway line, but desisted when he saw lights from vehicles of the witnesses coming towards him as they turned left after coming under the subway.

Witness Wilfred Rynn claimed that when he first saw the accused, he was three yards from the edge of the road towards the railway line and that he then had the deceased in his arms. She was very limp and appeared to be unconscious.

The precis showed that Wiley was aware that there was a discrepancy between the patch of blood found fifteen inches from the side of the road next morning and the descriptions by the witnesses of Rosemary lying several yards off the road. If John's confession was correct, there had to be some way to explain the witnesses' accounts of her being further away. The prosecution was given this hypothesis although there was no evidence at all to support it. The hypothesis was not given to the defence.

Circunstantial Evidence

29 April–6 May 1963

'John Button, you stand charged by that name that on the 10th of February 1963 in Perth you wilfully murdered one Rosemary Margaret Anderson. How say you, John Button? Guilty or not guilty?'

'Not guilty, Your Honour.' John's youthful high-pitched voice rang out firmly, despite his nerves and bewilderment at the unfamiliar, formidable environment he'd stepped into. Led up the stairs from the holding cells beneath the court, he'd reached the dock of Court No. 2 and a scene that overwhelmed him. No prior descriptions by his counsel could have prepared him for the grandiose, high-ceilinged, jarrah-panelled court and the imposing appearance of the judge in his robes and wig. The scene was totally alien to John, the intimidating size and formality adding to his feelings of helplessness. He anxiously looked around for something familiar and found Hatfield and Kakulas, seated in front of him, to his left. He recognised them, but in their strange attire, they, too, seemed to be from another world. John felt quite alone in this huge amphitheatre in which his life would be decided.

A small man seated at the same bench as Hatfield, to his right, rose to his feet. 'May it please your Honour, I appear with my learned friend, Mr Dodd, for the Crown.'

Hatfield rose, a large figure in comparison. 'May it please your Honour, I appear with my learned friend Mr Kakulas for the accused.'

His Honour was Mr Justice Oscar Joseph Negus, about to turn 61. He'd had a tough youth as the eldest child of parents struggling to raise a family of eleven in the goldfields town of Boulder. Winning a scholarship to Perth Modern School, he went on to study law and was admitted to the bar in 1926. He joined the law firm of Parker and Parker, concentrating on civil and commercial litigation. He'd been president of the WA Law Society and president of the Law Council of Australia and was called to the bench the previous year. Hard of hearing, he was known for interjecting when he'd missed something and was considered to be rather ponderous, but humane.

The empanelment of the jury began. John heard numbers and names being called and watched people peeling away from the group he'd seen earlier at the back of the court. They walked forward into the court – some reaching the two rows of seats to the right, others being stopped midway by objections he didn't understand. The chosen twelve took their places in the jury box, looking around as they adjusted to their new surroundings.

They didn't remain there for long. Hatfield was quickly on his feet, wanting to put something to the judge in the absence of the jury. Mr Justice Negus turned to the twelve and explained that they were to retire for a few minutes and be ready to come back when called on. They filed out.

Hatfield then embarked on his effort to save John's life by barring the use of his confession as evidence. He would detail his points later in a *voir dire*, but had to raise it now to request an order from the judge that no reference be made to it in the prosecution's opening address. The defence would be arguing that the confession was not a voluntary statement by the accused but was given under some persistent questioning by the detectives, and that further questioning had been improper, when he had given his statement a number of times. Hatfield told the judge that the Crown should not outline evidence if there was to be some question about its validity.

The prosecutor's response was that he would be giving a distorted picture of the Crown's case if he had to refer to the first statement as the first and last, when the Crown's position was that the first statement was not true.

'A man's life is at stake,' Hatfield said. 'The competing matters are the life of the accused and the inconvenience of the opening remarks.'

There was more argument on both sides before the judge ruled that the Crown must not refer to the second statement in the opening address. The defence had won a point. There was a chance for John – surely he couldn't possibly be convicted without the confession?

The jury was brought back in, taking their seats to hear an outline of the case. Their eyes moved between the man addressing them and the accused as they heard the prosecution's summary. They saw a youth sitting impassively in the dock. He had neat, short curly hair, a big nose and a nervous twitch.

Listening to the opening address, John was amazed to hear that he was accused of deliberately running Rosemary down, with the intent to kill. The confession he signed didn't say that. All it said was that he'd driven at her to scare her and had hit her before he realised it. Yet here was the Crown saying that he had followed Rosemary and deliberately run her down, intending to kill her. The prosecutor was explaining why the charge was wilful murder and not manslaughter:

> This is not an ordinary case of a pedestrian being unfortunately struck by a car as a result of which the driver of the car is charged with manslaughter. In such a case, the car driver is alleged to have been criminally negligent or reckless in the way he drove the vehicle, so that he has to be held responsible for the death that resulted from his carelessness. In a case such as that, there is never a suggestion that the driver of the car intended to cause death or grievous bodily harm. The question of intent does not arise in such a case.
>
> That is where the difference arises between such a case and the present case. In this case, the accused is charged not with manslaughter but with wilful murder because it is alleged that he, being the driver of a motor car, followed this girl as she was walking along Stubbs Terrace, she having gone under the

subway and walked down Stubbs Terrace, and followed her and deliberately ran her down, intending to kill her.

Later in his opening address, the prosecutor reached the point about the damage to John's car, referring to the damage sustained in the previous accident:

> In addition to this damage there was seen on Sunday 10th February when the car was examined, a number of indentations on the bonnet of the vehicle. They were on the bonnet to the right of the mascot as you are sitting in the car, and there was also observed a small indent in the front bumper bar to the right of the number plate.

John did not know anything about indentations on the bonnet or bumper and could not work out what Wilson was talking about or how any indentations could have got there. He was hanging on every word, wondering what it was about, when he had to wait – the prosecutor's voice was drowned out by an aircraft passing overhead, so he stopped. When the plane had passed, he continued:

> this damage has nothing to do with the impact with the Prefect and was caused when the car struck Rosemary and she was flung heavily on to the bonnet of the car, thereby causing the serious abdominal injuries described, which were not attended with any external injury, indicating that it was a very severe blow on a smooth flat object, with no projections to break the skin or lacerate the body. There will also be evidence from someone who knew the car fairly well and had seen it shortly prior to Rosemary's death and confirms that the indentations on the bonnet were not there shortly before 9 February.

John was amazed, and had no idea about the indentations on the bonnet.

The succession of witnesses began with Dr Quinlivan, Dr Turner from RPH and the District Medical Officer, Dr Pearson, who gave the results of the postmortem. He explained that subarachnoid haemorrhage was usually caused by a severe impact and her abdominal injuries were consistent with being flung with some force on the bonnet of a motor car. The ragged edges of her forehead injury were consistent with her head impacting on a rough surface such as the roadway. The abrasions on the lower part of her body were consistent with skidding along a rough surface, probably the road, at some speed, burning off the outer surface of the skin. He believed she had skidded along the roadway face down and feet first.

Wilson asked Dr Pearson about her chastity. 'The hymen was apparently intact. In other words, she was a virgin,' he replied, expanding on his curious postmortem report.

This was another surprise for John. He was so glad Rosemary's honour was being preserved – just as he had sought to maintain it by lying about her stockings and girdle and by not telling anyone of their intimacy. He knew the truth would be shameful, even though marriage was their long-range plan, but how could a doctor get it wrong?

The truth showed that the first part of his confession, about her rejecting his advances, was false. He was astonished, but pleased. He had done enough to hurt Rosemary by snapping at her and letting her walk to her death. He didn't want to hurt her more now by having her reputation tarnished.

Next Mr Anderson was called to the witness box. He referred to the damage to the front of John's car, but said he had not previously seen any damage to the bonnet. He'd last looked at the car a week before Rosemary's death, when it was being washed on the back lawn and Rosemary and her sister Helen had been having a water fight. When he was shown the car in the police yard again on 21 February, he said there were two dints in the right hand side of the bonnet, just by the mascot, which he had not seen before.

Indentations, dints. John couldn't understand them.

After Constable Martinovich gave evidence, Nigel Phillips was called. Phillips had been sitting in the back of Barry Hansen's Volkswagen. He told the court that as they drove along Stubbs Terrace, he could see a Simca car on the side of the road with two wheels off the bitumen. A person was bending over a body lying on the ground about two yards off the edge of the road. He admitted under cross-examination that he had a poor view of the scene.

The two sitting in the front of the Volkswagen were not called. Hansen, the driver and the one who saw most, and front-seat passenger Wilson White sat in the witness room throughout the trial, awaiting their turn to give evidence. They'd both given statements at the preliminary hearing in March: Hansen said then that he saw a cream Simca a couple of yards up from the subway and as he drove past it, he noticed something two or three yards off the side of the road. He turned around and saw a man wearing a pair of shorts pick up a girl and put her on the front seat. White said that when he first saw the man after passing the car and turning around, he was lifting the girl into the Simca. Now, prepared to give these statements again and to be cross-examined on them, they waited in vain. The monotony of the wait was broken only by lunch at Alhambra Bars in Barrack Street and looking at the Simca next to the courthouse each time they passed it. Hansen noted what little damage there was to it and commented to White that it didn't look like it would have killed a girl; but they didn't think more of it – with a confession, it was an open-and-shut case.

It was only on Hatfield's reminder and the judge's insistence that the prosecutor told the jury that in Hansen's car there were two others apart from Phillips whom the Crown would not intend to call. He offered Hansen and White for cross-examination by the defence, which declined the offer to call them. Without knowledge of Wiley's hypothesis about Button carrying her to the railway line, the eyewitness accounts of everyone first on the scene were not so relevant.

Wilfred Rynn, called next, was the front-seat passenger in the Morris Major Elite that arrived after the three in the Volkswagen. He said he first saw a man about three yards from the side of the road, carrying a limp girl. The driver of the Morris, Stanley Rogers, was not called.

Constable Ron Wilson was the next Crown witness, telling the Court that when he and Deering took John back to the scene that night he pointed to a dark stain on the side of the road and informed them that it was where Rosemary had been lying. He told the court it was about eighteen inches off the road.

After evidence by the police draughtsman came Allan Drummond with his forensic evidence. Then the jury, counsel and John went outside to examine the car.

Next, the prosecution produced Clarence Beckerdyke Wilson, who owned the car John had run into in January. The 57-year-old tallyman told the court that at the time of the accident he had looked at the front of the Simca and seen damage to the grille and radiator. He also said he'd examined the car and there was nothing to be seen on the bonnet, only the grille. He said Wiley and Deering had later gone to see him at his workplace and asked about the damage to his car. They had asked him to bring his car in to the police yards for photographing with the Simca, which he did. He said that when he saw John's car again during the photo session on 13 February, he saw more damage than he had seen on 7 January. There was damage to the lower part of the left front headlamp and there were indentations higher up on the bonnet. He said the car had hit something.

The police vehicle examiner, Constable Trevor Stephen Condren, gave evidence about the damage to the Simca. Under cross-examination he agreed there was no damage to the bumper, the headlight glass was not broken or scraped or scratched, nor were the windscreen or windscreen wipers damaged. He told the Court that the damage to the left-hand grille and headlight were consistent with the accident on 7 January and that it would appear that the damage was of some weeks' duration.

Detective Jack Michael Deering was called to the witness stand. He went through the events of the night. He reached the point of Wiley's arrival in the muster room. Now was the time to argue the defence's only hope – the barring of John's confession on the basis that it had come about as a result of pressure.

The jury was asked to leave – and they stayed out for more than a day while the judge heard the arguments for and against inclusion of the confession. It was like a trial within a trial, John Button being called to the witness stand for the *voir dire*. He nervously took the five steps up into the witness box, from where he could catch a glimpse of his mother and Margaret trying to give him encouraging smiles from the back of the court.

John Button said the more he denied having run down Rosemary, the more the detectives tried to question him. He said they were unfriendly and kept saying his statement was all lies. He said Deering was unfriendly at the surgery, asking him two or three times, 'Are you sure it wasn't your car that knocked her down?'

John said Deering had told him things like if it was his car that had knocked Rosemary down, it would be better if he told him then. They would find out the truth when they examined the car. He said that when Deering removed the rifle from the back of his car before taking him to the scene, he'd said something about not trusting him.

John said that when they got back to the surgery, he asked Deering if he could go home to get a shirt, some shoes and socks. His request was refused with a 'No, it will be quite warm enough down at the office for you.' John recalled that Deering was unfriendly in the CIB office, and didn't believe what John told him, asking if he was very sure he was telling the truth. John said he wasn't feeling the best at the time; he was cold and upset.

John said Wiley's attitude was the same as Deering's – unfriendly. Despite his replying 'no' each time, Wiley asked him the same question about a dozen times, and his manner was very unfriendly as he asked it. It was quite apparent to John that neither Wiley nor Deering believed him.

Wiley had told him there was a police officer with a tape recorder to take down anything Rosemary might say. If it was his car that knocked her down, she would most likely tell them. John repeated it was not his car that knocked her down. They asked him about his statement, picking out a paragraph and asking if he was sure that's what happened. The more he said yes, the more they tried to question him about whether it was his car. He said they were quite unfriendly and it appeared to John that they would not believe anything he told them, both referring to the statement as false.

John recalled that they said: 'This statement is all lies' and

'This is all a lie, isn't it – it was your car that knocked her down.' Wiley kept asking him if it was his car and every time he said it wasn't, he wouldn't believe him. It went on for about an hour.

He said Deering made suggestions about how it – the Crown's position was it wasn't an accident but deliberate – might have happened. Deering asked him if it could have happened in a way like him driving at her with the intent to scare her. John said he kept saying no, he hadn't knocked her down.

John told the court that when he was told that Rosemary was dead, he didn't really care what happened to him. He denied having said, 'What have I done, it was all my fault.'

He said Wiley asked him if he wanted to change his first statement. He thought about it and said 'yes', because it seemed that they weren't going to let him go until he had admitted doing it. He gave them the second statement to get away from the questions. He was never told he could leave or go home or contact his father.

According to John, Deering sat at the typewriter and typed out the confession. John took the suggestions Deering offered him, about driving at Rosemary with the intention of scaring her but knocked her down instead. When he had earlier told Deering they'd had a game of strip poker, Deering made the suggestion that maybe Rosemary had lost quite a few of her clothes and he'd got fresh with her. So when he made the second statement, John just adopted the detective's suggestion. He said the bit about trying to fondle her breast was Deering's idea as to how the argument developed. The detective suggested that it could have been how the argument originally started, and he took his idea. She didn't get wild when he got fresh with her because there was nothing for her to get wild at. It didn't happen. But it seemed to be the only explanation they would believe. They were all suggestions Deering made up after John gave his first statement.

John said they'd got the fish and chips after they'd finished playing cards, not before. He said in the statement that they'd been eating them while playing cards because he didn't want to argue with Deering any more. He said his confession about taking the suspender and stockings to the car before following her was also wrong – he took them after playing cards. He said he wasn't wild, but he had to have a reason for wanting to drive his car at Rosemary with the intention of scaring her and that was the only reason Deering would believe.

Deering had suggested it, saying, 'I suppose that after the argument you would have got quite wild with Rosemary, wouldn't you?' John said it wasn't true that it sounded like a loud bang when he hit her, and the confession wasn't given of his own free will. Neither did he put his head in his hands and say it was all his fault. 'They took advantage of me in getting me to make a statement, the continuing of the questioning and after I was told that Rosemary was dead, I was rather upset and they more or less took advantage of my state of mind.'

John said that after his confession, he was given the two statements to sign. Wiley gave him a cigarette and took his coat off and put it around John's shoulders. They were then quite friendly.

He said that in Deering's evidence about the night's events, what he had said was true, but there were quite a few questions he asked that weren't referred to.

At 10 a.m. on Thursday 2 May, Mr Justice Negus gave his decision to allow the confession, saying he could see no impropriety or unfairness in the manner in which any of the statements were obtained and that nothing that happened was likely to result in an untrue admission. He was impressed with the clarity of Deering and Wiley's evidence, who told consistent stories and were unshaken in a very determined cross-examination.

The decision was a blow to John. He felt devastated and had visions of the noose Hatfield had warned him about.

Deering returned to the stand and continued his evidence. He read John's confession to the court. He said the first statement had been completed and signed when the questioning continued. He said when he examined the car again the next day in the police yard he noticed dents on the bonnet that he'd not seen the night before.

He faced a tough cross-examination. He admitted that until

being told Rosemary had died, John had not been told he needn't answer any questions. Nor had he been given any warning or caution about his statements being used in evidence against him. No-one was there to advise John, and he was not told he had the right to communicate with his parents. He was not told anything about any rights. Deering admitted John had not been cautioned until he'd said 'Yes, it was my car'.

Deering denied saying 'I don't trust you' as he took the .303 rifle from the back seat and put it in the boot.

Wiley entered the witness box. He denied ever saying, 'I don't believe you' or 'You're telling lies' during his interrogation of John. He corroborated Deering's evidence, saying that when he told John that Rosemary was dead, John put his head in his hands and said: 'What have I done, it's all my fault'. He said that when John was asked if it was his car that had hit her, he said 'yes'. Wiley said he had asked all the questions during the interrogation, apart from a few from Deering at the end.

Most of the legal argument was beyond John. He gazed at the lion and horse in the coat of arms high up above the judge, trying to work out what the foreign words meant. He watched his counsel, looking foreign, too, in their white wigs, the curls falling off Hatfield's.

By Thursday afternoon, the Crown had finished calling its witnesses. The hearing continued on Friday morning, with John's testimony leading the defence.

Back in the witness box, John went through much the same evidence as he had in the *voir dire*, again saying before the jury that Deering had said something about not trusting him as he moved the rifle from inside the police car and refusing his request to go home for some clothes. He also described Deering and Wiley as being hostile to him and persisting in asking him if it had been his car.

The jury heard his explanation of why he confessed. 'Well, up till the time before they told me that Rosemary was dead I had the impression that they weren't going to leave me alone, or believe me or anything until I'd admitted that I'd done it; then when they told me that Rosemary was dead, well, I just thought

– I didn't care what happened to me. I just gave in and gave them this story that had been suggested to me by them.'

Why did you tell that story if it was untrue?

John said that at that moment, he didn't value his freedom. He just wanted the questioning to stop.

Finally he realised what it was they'd been referring to as 'indentations' and dents – the ripple he'd seen on the bonnet the day before Rosemary's death. He'd seen it on the Friday at a garage when he was filling up with petrol, but had no clue as to the cause.

When asked if he knew how it got there, his reply sounded evasive: 'I don't know, but maybe it was caused by the accident a month ago, or maybe when we sit on the bonnet horsing around.'

Jimmy was outside in Supreme Court Gardens. He wasn't allowed inside, in case he was called. He'd spent hours thinking over what happened that night and feeling for his big brother, who'd once bought him a fishing rod and reel for his birthday, saving for it by doing newspaper rounds. It was a long wait. He'd finished counting the storeys in the new building next to the gardens. Council House, opened a fortnight earlier, looked just like a pack of cards. Now he was counting the seagulls picking at the scraps left by lunching office workers. He was wondering about them being so far inland, when Hatfield came rushing towards him. He asked Jimmy to confirm that he had seen the dent on the bonnet previously. John had told Hatfield that Jimmy was with him at the petrol station. Jimmy could not remember. The QC was exasperated.

'What a funny family you are. Your brother's life's at stake and you can't remember.'

He strode back into court, unable to call Jimmy to confirm his brother's story about the petrol station. Only after the trial did Jimmy remember John stopping for petrol at Manolas Motor Garage in Subiaco, when giving him a lift to work. At the station, he'd said to Jimmy that he couldn't understand how the accident had caused a ripple effect on the bonnet. Jimmy had suggested that it might have been from pushing hard on the bonnet to close it, which had been more difficult after the accident. But John hadn't thought so.

Next was Charlie Button. The tough bricklayer broke down several times, particularly when he was trying to say Mr Anderson had told him Rosemary was dead.

There were three other defence witnesses. A private investigator, former traffic police officer George Edward Gamble, testified that it was that possible to see cars passing across the other side of the subway from where Button was stopped in Nicholson Road, and Dr John Wakefield Dewitt Gray Thornton testified that the injuries to Rosemary disclosed in the post-mortem report were not consistent with her being thrown on to the bonnet of a car that had done about 10,000 miles. The workshop foreman at Bouldens, Leonard Russell Robinson, told the Court that he had inspected the Simca after the collision with the Prefect because he intended to help Button repair it. He had inspected it again after Rosemary's death, and could see no damage on the second inspection which wasn't there on the first.

The week-long trial continued into Saturday, the day spent on the closing addresses. Hatfield was the first to address the jury, telling them no evidence could be presented that could show John was guilty, emphasising the lack of damage to John's car consistent with hitting a ten-stone girl. He pointed out that there was no damage at all that anyone could say had been caused recently and there was no hair, fabric, threads or particle of Rosemary Anderson's clothing on the car. The tiny specks and smudge of blood were not consistent with impact with a body, but with coming from her blood on Button's body as he swung around the front of the car in his urgency to get her to the doctor. He also made the point that if the girl had been scooped up on to the bonnet from the left-hand side of the car with enough force to make a dent on the right side of the bonnet, indicating the course was from the left to the right, she would surely have fallen off to the right on to the bitumen road, not to the left on to the sand.

All the physical evidence, all the objective evidence, all the evidence of the police examiner prove conclusively that even though this lass may have been hit by a car, she certainly wasn't hit by this particular car. He told the jury that the District Medical Officer's theory about how she sustained her injuries were also not consistent with the damage to the car. The physical marks on the car, the physical marks on the dead body, prove beyond conscionable doubt at all this was not the car that struck Rosemary Anderson.

He spoke of the officers' interviewing techniques, describing the first traffic patrolman, Constable Wilsons, as a credit, but reminding the jury that nothing John said would convince Deering, and nothing would have satisfied him until he got a statement in conformity with the irresponsible suspicion that Deering had engendered towards the accused.

Hatfield told the jurors that Wiley was proved to be a plain liar, on the first word on his cross-examination. He said a premeditated lie, 'No, I haven't', when Dodd asked him if he'd previously seen the draughtsman's plan of the scene. On cross-examination he said he had seen it.

'He was geared to tell lies from the minute he got in the witness box.' Hatfield said Deering and Wiley had already tried Button and found him guilty:

> They believed that it was his car that did it; they didn't worry a tuppeny bit about the absence of damage – they couldn't prove that, and the only single remaining way that they could get any evidence that the accused was the person involved, the only way they could produce any evidence to satisfy a jury that he was the person involved, was by 'inducing' him to make a statement in accord with their views.
>
> They rejected out of hand his statement and when he had made a written statement explaining his part of the evening, that was only to bounce the ball again when Wiley took over – that was the second half. And the third and fourth quarters of this tragic battle with this boy against the detectives then commenced.

Hatfield said the detectives didn't warn John that anything he said would be used in evidence until after he had, according to them, said it was his fault. After John had returned from being sick, he should have immediately been told he was not obliged to make any further statement – he could correct the first if he wanted – and been warned then that anything he said would be used in evidence. Hatfield continued:

> No, no such thing because he was about to accomplish what he wanted to do: by some method get an admission from the boy... that it was his car that struck the girl, despite the manifest absence of damage to the vehicle...
>
> Once Deering got him in the trap and locked the door, he then warned him. It didn't matter a button what he said then. What good was the warning when the boy said yes, it was my car?
>
> That was the first time he had made a statement acceptable to them because nothing was acceptable to them unless it was in accord with their preconceived wrong decision of his complicity.
>
> Then the second statement goes on and do you think that during this intervening period, Wiley didn't suggest to him and coax him as to how it might have happened? 'Are you sure you didn't drive at her to frighten her?' 'Didn't you get fresh perhaps, that is why she walked out?'
>
> Button said in evidence he knew he would be kept there, whatever he said they wouldn't accept unless it was in accord with their views and suggestions. Then he saw the gateway start to open, he kicks it along by adopting their suggestions and he did.
>
> The structure has been given to him by the detectives – the framework. He had a built-in ready-made structure in order to incorporate it in his statement which he knew would be acceptable to these two detectives.

Hatfield said that Deering and Wiley were intent on pinning a major charge against his client from the moment they knew the girl was dead. They pestered John until he revoked his initial statement and made one that better suited the police theory of what had happened.

'When you were a child at school, in copy books you wrote: "water wears away stone". And so will two bullies wear away a youth of nineteen.'

The prosecution had the last say. Wilson referred to Hatfield's two hours of impassioned and vehement address and said his function as counsel for the Crown was to present the evidence and to see, as far as he could, that the evidence was presented fairly and truly to a jury, to cross-examine witnesses called for the defence and then at the conclusion of the evidence to comment on that evidence as it had been given in its entirety and to endeavour to see that when they left the box to consider their verdict, they had as fair and clear appreciation of all the evidence as it was possible for him to give them.

He said the evidence was that John's car hit the girl. The jury members had to decide John's intention.

Wilson pointed out John's strange reluctance to get help from the cars that stopped at the scene, suggesting he might have asked them to get an ambulance or the police quickly, the fact that he didn't complain about the detectives' attitude to his mother and father straight afterwards, and the colossal coincidences required if it wasn't his car that hit her.

What a tremendous coincidence that she should be struck when the accused was sitting in his car just 300 to 400 yards away. What a coincidence they should have had an argument. What a coincidence he doesn't seek help from cars that stop in the vicinity, that he doesn't volunteer anything to Dr Quinlivan about how it happens that his car should have blood spots, that there should be dents on the bonnet consistent with the girl's body having at some stage come up on the bonnet. Remember when the accused said in his statement that her body came up on the bonnet for a few yards, the police didn't know the dents were there.

Wilson recounted the Crown's case:

> The accused was angry when Rosemary flounced out of the house in anger at his overture. We know she was a virgin, you will remember. There was the game of strip poker which the accused suggested, and although he denied that they ganged up on Rosemary, it is there in the second statement. If you accept it and it might well accord with the facts and the accused told Wiley that Rosemary stopped the game . . . She goes out of the house in such a hurry that she only stops to get her shoes and leaves the girdle and stockings in the house and the accused then regretting or not wanting to see her go off, goes after her and three times she rebuffs his overture to make up. By this time he is near the subway and he was by this time wild. Now he spoke because she touched a bit of fish – whether there is anything to be gleaned from this I don't know, but you observed the kind of person he appeared to be in the box, his own admission in the statement is that he was then wild after three or four minutes of watching Rosemary walk under the subway and go up Stubbs Terrace, he started the car and then drove after her and if you followed through the precise words of the statement, 'I was pretty wild.' He drove at her in his temper.

Wilson suggested that events unfolded this way:

> She starts running. She is scooped up as she runs, her foot is dragged on the ground, her toe is cut, she loses her shoes and various articles and the car continues at speed for 50 yards or so. It slackens and the body leaves the car and comes skidding to a halt in the sand. The bumper hit her calves, her toe was hurt then or shortly afterwards, injuries to the liver caused by her contact with a smooth flat surface of the car, injury to the head when it hit the ground, and the scratches to the front of her thighs were caused by her skidding along the ground feet first.

It was apparent that the course of the vehicle striking the girl occupied at least 60 yards.

Wilson said the facts cohered and formed a pattern of the events of the night which pointed strongly, if not conclusively, to the fact that the accused's car did strike the girl.

'If the accused's car wasn't the car, the coincidences required would be colossal.' He said there were so many variables as to the damage to a car hitting a pedestrian – such as whether the pedestrian is stationary, walking or running, that it was impossible to look at the car's damage and say that car couldn't have killed a pedestrian.

Wilson told the jury that the evidence, apart from the statement, was circumstantial. He said circumstantial evidence could be better because it was relying on a whole variety of circumstances, whereas a witness might be mistaken in his apprehension of what had happened and subsequently made a mistake in his relating of it.

The jury had to decide whether to believe the police or the accused. He said the detectives acted with complete propriety throughout the night. It was their primary duty to investigate what appeared to be a serious accident. John said himself there were no threats.

Wilson ended his summary:

> If the detectives are the villains, you might wonder why there are any loose ends. In this case, there is a loose end, of course, as far as intention is concerned. The statement doesn't amount to a confession to wilful murder. It has never been suggested that it did, and this is worth bearing in mind.
>
> 'The question resolves itself into this: What does a person intend when he drives a car deliberately at a girl at 35 miles per hour . . . a man doesn't wear his intention on his sleeve, he doesn't announce before he does something the reason why he is doing it, and it is a matter entirely for you . . . to say with what intention he did this.
>
> . . . He is charged with wilful murder because his conduct, it is suggested to you, is consistent only with an intention to kill, or if not to kill, to cause grievous bodily harm.

The judge started speaking at five past four, carefully summing up the Crown's and defence's cases for the jury to consider and explaining that they could find him not guilty or guilty of wilful murder, murder or manslaughter.

> The evidence, apart from the accused's own statement, is circumstantial.
>
> The Crown case depends on the oral statements made by the accused to Sgt Wiley, his second written statement and the damage to and marks on his car in so far as they are referrable to this accident, considered in the context of his quarrel with Rosemary, his following her in the car and his picking her up on the side of the road.

The judge said the jury should examine the injuries suffered by Rosemary and damage to the car and the marks on it.

He summed up the Crown's contention that the buckling of the rim of the headlamp was not part of the January accident, and the dent and ripple on the bonnet, spot of blood and blood marks on the glass and the headlight and blood marks on the top of the right-hand side mudguard were the result from the impact with Rosemary. He said Hatfield very properly pointed out that there were no marks on the car which could have been caused in an impact with the girl. As to the rippling, the jury may think it could have happened in a dozen different ways.

In regards to the detectives' credibility, he said while John persisted that he was cross-examined or questioned for an hour, the detectives' account that the interview lasted about 20 to 25 minutes added up:

> The obligation resting upon police officers is to put all questions fairly and to refrain from anything in the nature of a threat or an attempt to extort an admission, particularly an untrue admission. But it is in the interests of the community that all crimes should be fully investigated with the object of bringing malefactors to justice. A reasonable amount of persistence is justified.

The judge said the fact that the detectives asked John the questions they said they asked him in the way they said, while virtually holding him in custody, was not enough to treat the admission as otherwise than voluntary.

He said the jury might regard as improbable John's statement that he and Rosemary were about to become engaged yet they argue about a piece of fish, then she decided to walk three miles home and refused his attempts to make up yet said he could bring her things to her the next day.

'That struck me forcibly,' Mr Negus said.

> You may ask yourself whether the other story about the argument, which he declares is untrue, is not more probable – whether he did in fact get fresh with her after the poker game and whether she didn't want any more contact with him that night, but would not be unhappy to see him tomorrow.
>
> You may ask yourselves this question: if the story is true and the accused really only intended to scare Rosemary by driving the car at her as closely as possible, why did he not realise he was getting too close to her, why did he not attempt to apply his brakes or swerve. In the absence of any such attempt, is it probable that all he wanted to do was frighten Rosemary?

After speaking for twenty minutes, the judge told the jury to retire and, after Hatfield spoke to him, brought them back to make three more points.

At 4.40 p.m. the jury filed out to consider its verdict after a week of evidence and a day of addresses by Hatfield and Wilson and the judge's summing up.

It was a nerve-wracking time for John, who was pacing the holding cell in the bowels of the Supreme Court building, his thoughts vacillating between death and his return home. He'd looked at the prison wall as he had been driven away that morning, hoping he'd seen the inside for the last time.

A warder had farewelled him in the same vein. 'I hope I don't see you again,' he said as John was ushered into the police car.

It was a strain, too, for his family, standing around in the cold outside while the jurors discussed and debated the case for three-and-a-half hours.

In weighing up the evidence and their impression of John, the jury did not have the benefit of knowing that John had snapped at Rosemary thinking it was Jimmy. In all his evidence at the *voir dire* and before the jury, John had not thought it important enough to explain that point. He didn't realise that jury members who might understand tension between brothers could misjudge his nature and his love for Rosemary.

At last word came that the jury was ready.

At 8.12 p.m. the twelve members filed in. John Button climbed the stairs to face them, overhearing the instruction behind him: 'Prepare the death cell.'

The clerk of Arraigns stood and faced the nine men and three women:

'Members of the jury, have you agreed upon your verdict?'

'We have, Your Honour,' responded the foreman.

'How say you, is John Button guilty or not guilty?'

'Not guilty, Your Honour.'

Not guilty. John's relief was overwhelming. While part of him had always had faith that truth and justice would prevail and anything else was impossible, the juggernaut of madness had appeared to be charging through reality.

Finally it was over, the jury had seen it for what it was. John wanted to jump over the railings of the dock, tell Hatfield he was better than Perry Mason and run out, free. But obedient as ever, he stood and waited, wondering what happened next, as Ken Hatfield started gathering up his papers. He was elated, as was Kakulas, who gasped: 'Thank Christ for that.'

Eight seconds passed before the clerk asked if it was a unanimous verdict.

The foreman spoke. 'I'm sorry, Sir, I said the wrong thing there. I must apologise, Your Honour.'

'Read that again, will you please?'

'How say you, is John Button guilty or not guilty?'

'Guilty, Your Honour.'
Four seconds passed.
'Of what crime is he guilty?' Judge Negus needed to clarify.
'Manslaughter, Your Honour.'
Eighteen seconds had passed between the foreman's words of 'not guilty' and 'guilty.' Eighteen seconds of relief and celebration changed to disbelief and despair.

The case made front-page news in the *Sunday Times*. 'Jury returns manslaughter' was the huge headline, above a secondary headline 'Verdict in car case', with a photo of Charlie Button, Kakulas and Hatfield leaving the court.

Hatfield was reading the paper in bed the next morning, having his first cup of tea. The girls came in and sat on the corner of the bed to chat, as they often did. Jill wanted to talk about Button. She'd gone to the Court to see as much of the case as possible, joining the people in the public gallery in her lunch hour. She was a telephonist and typist in the commerce branch of the Bank of New South Wales in St Georges Terrace, close to the court, and took an extra long lunch break for this trial.

'See, you weren't right,' Jill said to her father. 'He was guilty after all.'

The man who often teased his daughters and joked around the house as much as he did in public, was very serious. 'I'm telling you, that boy is innocent.'

John left Fremantle Prison for sentencing on Monday, 6 May. Just before 10.30 a.m. he started up the stairs into the courtroom to a call of 'good luck'.

Character references were given by his former employer, Len Boulden, and dance teacher Alan Butcher, both of whom spoke of his honesty, courtesy, shyness and lack of ill temper.

John Button was ordered to stand for sentencing. Mr Justice Negus spoke slowly:

> John Button, the jury has found you guilty of the crime of manslaughter. I have listened to what your counsel has said and the very good things that have been said by Mr Boulden

and Mr Butcher and I have watched you throughout the trial.

I can't understand how you did this thing. I believe that you were fond of Rosemary. I have formed the impression early in the proceedings that looking at your conduct as a whole it was difficult to impute your intention of actually hitting her.

But what you have done is to deliberately drive a car at 35 miles per hour to a position so close to a girl that you made an error and hit her ... to do a thing like that, it behoves you to use extra care to see that nothing happens.

I feel that I cannot take a lenient view of what you have done. The Criminal Code allows me to sentence you for a crime such as this to imprisonment with hard labour for life.

I suppose I must bear in mind all the things that have been said on your behalf and particularly the fact that you picked the girl up, also that, as Mr Hatfield said, you were under strong emotional strain. But taking these things into consideration, I would not be doing my duty if I did not impose a substantial sentence.

I sentence you to imprisonment with hard labour for ten years.

Ten Years' Hard Labour

1963–73

John Button couldn't believe it. He'd really felt it was impossible that anyone could think he had done it. The way he'd been treated in remand reinforced his understanding that the police and prison officers knew he was innocent. The two police who drove him to and from court every eight days had chatted lightheartedly with him, not treated him like a murderer, and trusted him not to run while they bought cigarettes. They'd only ever handcuffed him for the obligatory time while waiting outside the court to be called. And once when he was called and the handcuffs had to be taken off for court, they couldn't find the key. He helped them by just slipping his wrists out – that's how tightly they'd secured him.

He'd been shocked when the preliminary hearing had committed him for trial – he was sure it would be thrown out through lack of evidence. And now a whole jury believed he'd done it. He felt lost, that terrible feeling of abandonment welling up in him. He fell into the deepest despair.

His mother suffered terribly, too, as she fought the panic of facing ten long, bleak years without John. She wept for the loss of her son and the loss of the hopes she had for him. Not only had John been taken away from her, so had all hope of the pride and happiness a mother feels when her child grows up, makes good and marries. She yearned for the lost contentment of seeing John following his father's footsteps in the bricklaying trade, happily settled and bringing his family over for Sunday roast.

The dream had been on the verge of reality – he'd found the right girl and he'd finally taken up the trade. It was all pointing to her quiet, shy son finding his way and settling into a fine trade and happy marriage. And then the grandchildren. Her eldest son, Peter, would marry and have his children back in England, and Margaret would go back to Wagga for the birth of her child. She'd so been looking forward to grandchildren from John. Now it had all been ripped away from her, in such a cruel and unjust way.

Ten years stretched before her as an eternity. They would have moved from middle-age to the beginning of old age. John's youth would be gone. He would be 29, and have to start again with no money, no trade, no girlfriend – none of the happy life experiences of the twenties. What a punishment for something he didn't do.

Not only would his best years be spent behind bars, but ten years' income would be sacrificed to the State as well. What woman would want a 29-year-old pauper, let alone one damned as a murderer? Would her John ever be able to regain everything he'd lost? Would he ever be able to get over this unfair wretchedness?

The pain was constantly there as she carried on with her duties as wife and mother. She was stoic, and didn't show it publicly as she learnt to cope with the constant pain in the middle of her chest, the tight heaviness like a rock sitting there, occasionally changing into a sharp cutting knife as something in the house reminded her of his absence during this living death. She had a constant headache, she was tired and listless, her energy drained, her warm smile changed into dull, patient defeat.

The guilty verdict on the lesser charge meant a move from cell No. 14 in the grim isolation of Death Row into the mainstream prison. No longer on the list for execution, he was Prisoner No. 29050 in cell 43 on C & D landing, the first floor in the Main Division. It was a little bigger and had an iron bed, a small table, a shelf, a water canteen and enamel mug, a tin of floor polish, a sanitary bucket and water bucket. He had his own radio with earphones. It was luxury in comparison. And there was the huge benefit of being able to work. Work – doing something all day at last, feeling useful and mixing with other prisoners.

On his arrival after sentencing, he was taken into the superintendent's office where he stood at attention and replied 'Yes, Sir', 'No, Sir' to the chief's fatherly talk, explaining that if prisoners did the right thing by the officers, the officers would do the right thing by them. On being dismissed with 'We hope your stay here will be uneventful', he was marched out and escorted to his new cell.

Later, the principal officer, Tom Nicholson, called him aside as he walked to parade. He spoke softly to the new long-termer: 'John Button, I know your father. So I'm going to do two things for you. I'll put you in the carpentry shop – there you can learn a trade. And I'll never speak to you again like this.'

It didn't take long for John to understand these favours. The carpentry shop was the best place to work in the prison. It was in a far corner and gave the prisoners some extra freedoms in that they could make hot drinks over the fire and there were extra hiding places for them to stash the tobacco used for trade. And John soon learnt that having a friend among the warders was not acceptable to the other prisoners. Any signs of help or softness from his father's friend would have brought retribution.

Each weekday was the same bleak routine. The cell doors were opened at 7 a.m. The whole building stank from the sanitary buckets in the rows of cells on four levels. Prisoners went out to the yards, leaving the lids of their dixies and their mugs outside their cells and taking their water buckets to refill them at the tap. That's where they washed themselves, summer and winter, apart from shower days. Twice a week in summer and once a week in winter they were allowed the treat of a shower, marched to the ablution block yards away, past the main entrance. Every other day of the week it was a cold water wash in the open air.

On the way back to their cells after their wash, they each picked up a small bottle of milk and a half a loaf of bread. The lids of the dixies had been filled with porridge, 'bargoo' to the inmates, and their mugs with black tea. Breakfast was eaten alone inside their cells, sitting on their bunks next to the sanitary buckets still containing the late afternoon and night's contents. They carefully measured out the milk, which was to last all day, making sure they left enough for their evening cup of tea before pouring it over their porridge. Then they were lined up and marched to work.

They were brought in again at lunchtime, picking up their dixies of food on the way through to their cells, where they ate alone. They left the lids of the dixies outside their cells when they returned to work in the afternoon. They were marched back in at 4 p.m. when, after parade, they were given soup in the dixie lids and locked in at 4.30 to eat their soup and bread alone.

Each week they were given a small jar of Vegemite, honey or margarine in a three-week turnabout, and two ounces of tobacco. There were also the little extras they'd bought with their 'spends', the small amount of their weekly wages they were allowed to spend each week. Lights out was at 8 p.m., leaving nothing but the radio to break the monotony. At 11 p.m. that was turned off, and there was silence apart from the occasional shrieks of men's nightmares or inability to handle the long nights of memories and hopelessness.

It was bearable during the day, when the men were kept busy, with instructions to follow. There was no need to think or to remember the real world. There was no connection between the life John Button was torn away from and this one. But the nights were unbearable, when he was left completely alone in the dark with no distraction. No-one to talk to but the demons inside his head. Every night was the same. As soon as he was locked away at 4.30 p.m. he knew the nightmare was not far off. He could stall it for a while, making a small meal out of the tins he'd bought with his spends and doing a bit of study. But at 8 p.m. he was faced with himself, alone in the dark, suffering eleven hours of ghosts and demons. He couldn't even stand on his bunk to look out the bars at the moon and the stars. Guards paraded the bank, shrieking 'down from the windows' if any prisoner was seen trying to look beyond the blackness of his cell.

At least now John was given something to help him sleep. The sleeping pills didn't work very well, but they helped a little and he needed this crutch. After a month the prison doctor announced he was taking him off them. John dropped to his knees, begging – he couldn't go back to the sleepless agony of those nights in Death Row. The doctor explained that he was just changing the type of pill, taking him off barbiturates because they were habit-forming, on to a liquid sleeping draught.

John relied heavily on the sleeping draught picked up with his meal each afternoon on a prescription gained fortnightly. The prisoners' nickname for Dr Dunkley was Dr Death, but to John he was a saviour who brought him a little sleep at night. He was so dependent on the pink liquid that if he ran out before his next appointment, it was unbearable torture to spend a night without the potion that partially blotted out his painful memories and questions. Necessity taught him to ration his provisions, saving a little of each day's measure in an empty Vegemite jar to cover an extra night, should he not get the next prescription in time.

The first month was the worst, the other inmates told him. After that you got used to it. It didn't work like that for John. It was years of hell. Every night his mind returned to Rosemary, his love, his guilt about the argument and the agony of his loss. His visions of her face, the smell of her hair, the touch of her skin, all deepened the hole in his heart, relieved only by moments of belief that it was all a nightmare and she was alive and he would wake up at home. He thought he would go crazy with wanting Rosemary and wanting the jury to believe him. Every night he saw their faces again, accusing him, refusing to believe the truth.

'Why didn't they believe me?' he kept asking himself. 'What did I do?' he kept asking the jury. 'Just tell me exactly what I'm supposed to have done. Exactly how did I kill her? I didn't do it. I loved her,' his head screamed all night, adding inconsolable grief to his anger and confusion.

He spent the night pacing the floor. Eyes closed, he padded up and down the nine-foot cell, his bare feet shuffling slowly along the floorboards from wall to wall. He could cover the length in four paces, but he wasn't in a hurry to get to the other end, so he slowly took smaller steps, just to create movement, to be doing something to while away the endless night. Backwards and forwards over the same small space. The memory, the pain and anguish, the anger and grief, the questions, the 'if onlys' wouldn't allow him the relief of sleep.

The strain of his sleepless nights showed on his face each morning. Owen, a tough guy doing a long sentence, took pity on him, knowing from his own experience what John was going through. He, too, had known the interminable darkness with no-one to talk it through, no distraction, no escape. He'd devised a good distraction for himself and gave John the same mental exercise to carry out at night. In the yard one day, Owen presented John with a detailed map of Fremantle Harbour and that part of the coast. He instructed John to come up with a plan for building a bridge from Point Peron to Garden Island. He was to work out how much material was needed for the depth and compaction, the cost of provision, cartage and building. John worked at the mental exercise each night, struggling with ideas and calculations until exhaustion overcame him.

Polishing the floorboards of his cell also gave him some relief through the movement and the exercise. Each prisoner was given a small tin of polish and had to keep the boards shiny.

After six months he was moved to cell F52 on E & F landing. There was another landing above his cell and two tiers of cells below. It was further away from the officers' room and John wondered if he'd been put closer to them at first out of concern that he might try to commit suicide. He wasn't suicidal, but he felt so alone and desperately lonely, dragging himself through one day at a time. How he waited for his mother's parcel containing cigarettes, dropped off at the weekend and delivered to him Monday lunchtime, and her letter, which was given out Monday night.

And how he counted the weeks and days until visits. Just half an hour once a month, Monday afternoon. Because Charlie was working, Lilly came with Gwen Andrews from dancing. Lilly faithfully booked their visit each month and John sent her the pass in each month's letter. He was only allowed one letter a month, and that had to be to his parents in order to send the pass. Half-an-hour once a month was not long enough to catch up on all the news and just be with someone who cared. He had to be torn away from them and suffered terribly for a few days afterwards. His desperation for company eventually turned Gwen off and Lilly came alone. No-one else visited him. All his other friends just disappeared.

His defence team decided against an appeal, although they were quite convinced of John's innocence. They had no complaint about the trial, believing it to be fair. It was the jury that got it wrong. But the verdict was still a lot better than it could have been, given the charge of wilful murder and his confession, and it was in John's interests to leave it.

Lilly and Charlie fought on as best they could, maintaining their son's innocence. An appeal to their local member of Parliament brought promises and efforts, but no results.

But Charlie's and Lilly's efforts to convince a sceptical Perth population got nowhere. No-one would listen. Their hearts were broken, they were impoverished and their belief in Australian justice had been shattered.

For months Lilly's constant image of her son was the John she saw in prison – a miserable, lost, defeated boy. She pictured him there in the visiting room, and she pictured him wherever she imagined he was at the time, in that horrible small cell behind bars, lining up for slops of meals, labouring in the carpenter's shop, sitting around the bleak yard.

Then suddenly one night the thought came to her to take him out of prison in her mind – to free him, to bring him back to the carefree son she knew. She tried thinking of John in the house, dancing, washing his car, anywhere but in dull khaki behind dark grey walls – and it worked. She was able to save John's image from the ignominy of prison life, and it eased her ache a little bit, sometimes even brought the tiniest relieved smile.

She didn't know that John also left the prison walls each night. The worst time for him was late at night when he could hear other prisoners – often hardened criminals – crying and screaming. In his head he devised an escape route that became well worn over the years. Each night he lay looking at the wall six feet away, locked in, the only sign of an outside world being a small sliver of moonlight from the barred window high up above his bunk. His body was there, but his mind was not. Each night he broke out of the prison, to find a car and caravan waiting for him. He drove to Yanchep, along the Lancelin road he knew so well from roo shooting, and across the dunes to the beach, covering his tracks as he went. There he set up camp and lived in perfect happiness on the beach for the rest of his life.

The reality was far different as he concentrated on surviving one day at a time.

He was sent to work in the carpentry shop, where the officer in charge, Mr Alexander, told him to learn what he could from Steve, a Polish inmate who was a pattern maker by trade. John spent the first week learning the names of the tools, the second learning how to handle them and finally he started to use them.

He was taken step by step through the correct way to saw, plane and store wood. It was a good apprenticeship with a perfectionist, and when Steve was released after six months, John took over his bench. Inspired by Owen's mental exercise, he enrolled for courses in maths, electrical work and art. Besides a pencil and papers in his cell and magazines to copy from, John was also allowed a palette knife. He had something to open tins and spread his bread with all the time – not like the other prisoners, who had to push their knives out through grooves under the doors at night.

There was no work at weekends, and the prisoners spent the days out in the yards. John gained light relief through the games of chess and the weekly bridge tournament for the prize of two ounces of tobacco. He found two bridge mates, the three of them taking turns at the tournament and one of them showing him how to stack the cards – a trick he was never game to try.

He was amazed at the cats. He soon got used to the warbs – old homosexuals who looked after young prisoners in return for sexual favours, but the cats were a complete surprise. He first saw two as they were coming in through reception. He'd been sent down from the carpentry shop one day to collect his sleeping draught repeat when he saw two beautiful women come in through reception. One had long red hair, the other was blonde. He drank in their beauty, their long slim legs and that feminine walk as they disappeared into the office. The next day they were there in the yards, their hair cut to prison regulations, their shirts open, revealing perfect breasts. It was a shock to realise they were really men – but they and the other cats were treated like the women they appeared to be. They were referred to as 'she' and other prisoners lit their cigarettes for them and stood to give them their seats, just as they would real women.

After John had finished the project for Owen, he lost the opportunity for more helpful ideas from this sympathetic prisoner. Owen was moved to the punishment block for attempting to escape. It was a Sunday morning, when they were all out in the yards, walking around for exercise or sitting under the shade provided by a small tin roof.

'Keep the officer talking.' John looked up to see that Owen had said this to another prisoner before walking off towards one of the three toilets in the back wall. As the prisoner talked to the officer in a position so as to keep his back to the wall, John noticed Owen's friend Johnny, nicknamed Barefoot Bandit, with a rope knotted around four pieces of wood that had been broken off the toilet door. He swiftly hooked the rope over a small drain pipe protruding from the wall above the toilet and climbed up it. He made it up the twelve-foot wall and was grappling with the guard when the rope slipped off the pipe while Owen was halfway up. He fell to the ground, briefly knocked out. Warnings were broadcast to the other prisoners over the loudspeakers as the two hopeful escapees were led away.

The next day the doors were removed from the toilets. John found it impossible to use the toilets in full view of the other prisoners. He suffered, holding it in during the Saturdays and Sundays spent in the yards.

John chose to be given two sets of clothes which he was responsible for cleaning rather than taking one set which was sent to the laundry each week and replaced with another. He couldn't bear the thought of wearing clothes that had been worn by someone else the previous week. Twice a week he put a four-gallon kerosene tin on the fire at the back of the carpentry shop and did his washing. He did his ironing by putting the clothes under the mattress at night.

The dreams of Rosemary had started when he was on remand, and they continued, unrelenting. Always that beautiful feeling of love and happiness and being with her was shattered by reality, turning the dream into a nightmare. He dreamt of walking up the front path of Rosemary's house, full of joy, and knocking on the glass door at the front, expecting to see her – the beauty shattered by her mother answering the door with the most awful look on her face. That dream haunted him for months.

Accepting her death was impossible. Every time the phone rang in the cell block – maybe five times a night, he still expected someone to unlock his door to tell him Rosemary was alive and he could go.

He constantly sketched her, trying to get every detail right, to make his memory and his constant dreams of her more tangible. Finally he achieved the portrait he wanted. Her lovely hair neatly tucked behind her ears, that favourite light green dress with the roses embroidered on the shoulder, a small smile. Pinned on the wall of his cell, it was all he had of her.

A Smart Cookie

1963

The man with revenge and murder on his mind was still walking the streets of Perth, stealing, peering in windows, laughing at the terror he caused. That feeling could come over him again at any time and he knew he'd get away with it again. He felt powerful. The police pressure and the people's panic made his night activities even more satisfying – every housebreak, every intimate moment he saw through a window, every stolen car was now a victory against not only society in general, but particularly the police – and how he loved fooling them. He got away with it every time.

He loved the thought of detectives running around uselessly fingerprinting the houses where his thefts were reported, distracting them from their major task of finding the killer. They were under such pressure – their reputation at stake because of him. Even with the lights left on all night in the western suburbs, they couldn't get him. He was outwitting them all and making a good living out of it: £10 from Elsie Evans at 19 Leonora Street, Como, easily taken from a wallet in her purse in the kitchen after he'd got in through the back door; £20 from 4 Blythe Street, South Perth, from the man's room after he'd snuck through the house while the family were watching television; £10 from 37 South Terrace, South Perth – silly people who didn't take more care to lock up after he'd previously stolen their transistor radio; £8 from the handbag in the bedroom wardrobe in Comer Street, Como – they were lucky he didn't bother taking all those wedding presents; £20 from 396 Walcott Street, Mt Lawley; £15 from 5 Armadale Crescent, Mt Lawley – they must have been annoyed at their key going missing, but they could have found it in the gutter above the light on the front veranda; £9 from 128 Eton Street, North Perth – it was easy getting in the sleepout window; £25 from a purse in the bedroom of a house down the road at 70 Eton Street – no use locking your bedroom door if it can be opened with the key left in the back door; £45 from a wallet in the bedroom of 158 Flamborough Street, Scarborough – that back door was easy, too; £70 from a house in Custance Street, Lathlain Park, after he crawled through an unlocked back window; £8 from 110 Mary Street, Como – they were in bed while he was taking it from a handbag in the kitchen.

Sometimes he took small amounts, laughing to think the people wouldn't even realise they'd been robbed:

The people at 56 Leonora Street, Como, wouldn't have realised. Nor would the people in flat Nos 1, 2, 11 and 13 at 88 Broadway, Nedlands, or at 12 Cunningham Street, Applecross – or the people at 70 Robert Street, Como, though they would have noticed their back fly-wire door had been kicked in.

The couple living in Eildon Court in Thelma Street, West Perth, must have felt sick at losing their £100 and Fijian money – that was a good haul. He went there twice on the same night, first getting in through the back window and leaving the back door unlocked. It was easy to get in again later when the couple were in bed, and take the money from a wallet on the bookshelf. He threw the wallet with the Fijian money on to Plaistowes' roof, above the third window. That was a while ago, but the wallet could well still be there.

He had a way with dogs. He generally avoided places where he knew they were, and had been chased a few times, but he could quieten them when he needed to. He needed to on Saturday 1 June, when he got in through the open sleepout door of 9 Dunbar Road, Claremont, to find four Pekinese inside. There'd been an article in the paper about Valda Dagg's wedding that day – nice-looking bridesmaid, Norma Lloyd. That was the best way to find out if a house would be empty, but he was not counting on the dogs. He managed to quieten them enough to check the house thoroughly without attracting attention. In one bedroom, he found business cheques in a wardrobe and across the passage in the main bedroom, he found wedding gift vouchers. They were no use to him, so he searched further, finally finding a purse. He pocketed £4/19/– and used the telephone before he left. He didn't know that he'd been spotted when he'd prowled around the house previously.

He was seen a few times, but he managed to get away with it. Luckily a couple of times when he was caught red-handed, they were just children. A little girl at 5 Dunkley Avenue, Applecross, mistook him for her father, calling out 'Daddy' while he was stealing a hat, watches and three ten-shilling notes – he had a laugh at the expense of the real daddy, George Fidock. He got away with being mistaken for a father in another Applecross home, too, 9 Tweeddale Road – he could see a woman and children watching television in the lounge room, so he stayed in the kitchen, finding ten shillings there after getting in the back door. A little girl came to the kitchen while he was there, saying 'Is that you, Daddy?' He quickly slipped out the back door but as he ran away, he heard her calling from the lounge-room window 'Are you out there, Daddy?'

There was a close shave at 8 MacKenzie Road, Applecross, when the occupants he'd seen in front of the television in the lounge must have heard him – the woman went to the kitchen and then started heading to where he was in the bedroom. Lucky he'd removed the clip of the fly-wire screen in readiness for just such an emergency. He grabbed a coat from the bottom of the bed and was out the window in no time. Outside, he found £4 in the coat pocket, dropped the coat and ran. Mervyn Wyatt, the manager of the Applecross branch of the Rural and Industries Bank, couldn't find his coat next morning. His wife found it outside the house later that day. When they reported it, the sergeant commented that he hoped it wasn't the murderer who'd gone into their house. If only they knew.

Another close shave came when the young nanny heard him trying to get into her louvred bedroom at the back of Dr Teasdale's house in Ullapool Road, Applecross. She heard him before he'd even put his gloves on, but hearing Delores running from the room sent him fleeing before he could do anything they could pin him for.

He was sprung, too, outside the Como boarding house where four country girls were living. Plenty of opportunity to see attractive women through windows there. He was at the front of 22 Hensman Street one night in April when one of the girls came home with her boyfriend. He was hopeful when they started kissing outside, but then Georgina Moss turned around and spotted him, getting a good look at his face in the moonlight. He had to escape quickly – she'd caught him crouched and spying, before he'd covered his face, so he quickly sprang back behind the house and got away. He didn't have much luck there after that. That girl left the next day and Mrs Ramshaw made certain of keeping the back door locked.

That was close – so was the camera, but he outsmarted it. It was a lucrative place and he'd been back a few times, so someone had set a trap with a camera. He heard the click and worked it out. One smashed camera.

Generally the disguises saved him whenever he needed them – they couldn't see a hare lip under a handkerchief, band-aid or nappy. The nappy he'd taken off the line and tied around his face saved him when the German woman in Orrong Road woke up and called him 'Putze', flailing her arms when she realised he wasn't her husband. She had strong legs, kicking him in the stomach and pushing him into the baby's cot. But he managed to get away.

He especially enjoyed the times he did get caught but managed to talk his way out of it. Too close for comfort, maybe, but an extra laugh against the people who let him go.

Like the time he was caught by SEC engineer Sam Clarkson at 16 Cliff Way, Claremont. He'd cased that street a few times – wealthy people in big houses there. What bad luck, an owner walking around the grounds of his home to check the sprinklers were all off. If only it had been a week later, Clarkson and his wife wouldn't have been there, away on a nine-month overseas trip. But he was spotted about to check out the neighbouring house. He had to change tack, so he displayed bravado and quickly walked away from the low bushes dividing the two houses, heading down Cliff Way towards Richardson Avenue.

Sam Clarkson called out to him: 'Hey, stop. I want to have a word with you – and don't try to run, because I can run faster than you can.' At nearly five-foot eleven-inches, fit from an active life and a good runner, Clarkson felt confident he could outstrip the short man. Cooke knew it too. He had to take this one head-on and hope for the best. He stopped twenty yards down the road and was grabbed by the scruff of the neck: 'What were you doing there?'

Always ready with an answer, he said, 'I just went in there for a piss.'

'I doubt that, but what are you doing around here, anyhow. You've got no business around this area.'

From the appearance of his catch, Clarkson knew he was not the sort of person who belonged in this small exclusive street. He thought the man he held was an unsavoury-looking character, and he took good note of his features – swarthy, dark curly hair, short, a distinctive mouth that seemed as if he had a hare lip and cleft palate – a face he'd recognise again anywhere.

'I've been drinking down at Claremont, and I was walking along trying to find a bus-stop,' came the confident response. 'You wouldn't find a bus-stop around here, and it's a long way to walk up from Claremont. Obviously you've been on the prowl and you're up to no good.' Pulling him up tighter, Clarkson warned him: 'I've had a good look at you, and if I see you around here again, I'll trot you down to the police station. Get on your way.'

Freed, he walked at an even pace down the hill towards Richardson Avenue, too clever to show any panic that could alert anyone that he was more than a prowler.

As he walked back into the house, Clarkson pondered the incident. Then his mind went back to the girl hacked to death in her bed, just two blocks away, a couple of years back. The thought of murder made him wonder about the intentions of the snooper. 'Maybe I should have hung on to him,' he said to his wife, Pam. Now regretting letting him go, he went to the phone and dialled 31 444 to report it to the Claremont police.

Inspector Fred Douglas and the Chief of the CIB, Inspector Cec Lamb (right) thank William and Leila Keehner the morning after Cooke's capture. The Keehners later received a reward of £1000 for finding the rifle.

Eric Edgar Cooke after three nights in the police lock-up. This is the image of Cooke best known to the public. He was usually clean, dapper and well-groomed.

Cooke shows detectives where he threw the first rifle he used into the Swan River, after stealing it from Donald Cornish.

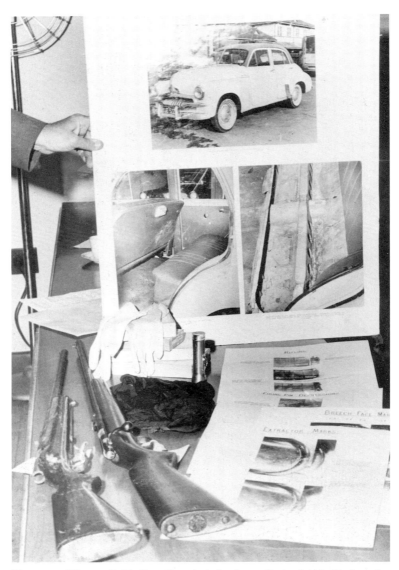

The memorabilia compiled by the police – including the car Cooke stole for his Australia Day weekend shootings, the two guns, the gloves he wore and the back of his car where a cartridge case was found.

Cooke showing Detective Jack Deering, Detective Sergeant John Dunne and Detective Sergeant Bill Nielson where he did a U-turn in Stubbs Terrace to drive back and run down Rosemary. His final statement said he saw her emerge from the subway (left of the photo) and walk towards the Floreat Iron Works, which is where he said he hit her.

11 September 1963: Less than two weeks after Cooke's arrest, he shows Detective Sergeant Bill Nielson (left) and Detective Sergeant John Dunne where Rosemary Anderson was walking in Stubbs Terrace when he first saw her. He later said that was incorrect, and the spot was in fact where he hit her after seeing her turn in to Stubbs Terrace from the subway under the railway line.

Cooke shows the detectives in September 1963 the tree stump near which Rosemary landed after being hit. When this picture was taken, he said it was where he hit her, changing it in December to where she landed in the sand.

11 September 1963: The day after Cooke first confessed to running down Rosemary Anderson, he points to the spot on Stubbs Terrace where he then said he hit her. Detective Sergeant John Dunne (left), Detective Jack Deering and Detective Sergeant Bill Nielson pose with Cooke for the police photographer.

Stubbs Terrace on 11 September 1963: Seven months after Rosemary was run down, the detectives are illustrating the discrepancy between Cooke's confession and the facts. Cooke is pointing to where he said he hit her and Detective Deering is pointing to where the bloodstain was found beside the road.

Detective Deering points to where the bloodstain was found. Cooke said he travelled 20 or 30 yards with her on the bonnet before she slipped up on to the hood of the car and after travelling another 30 yards – about 65 yards in all – she was thrown off the car, landing near a tree stump.

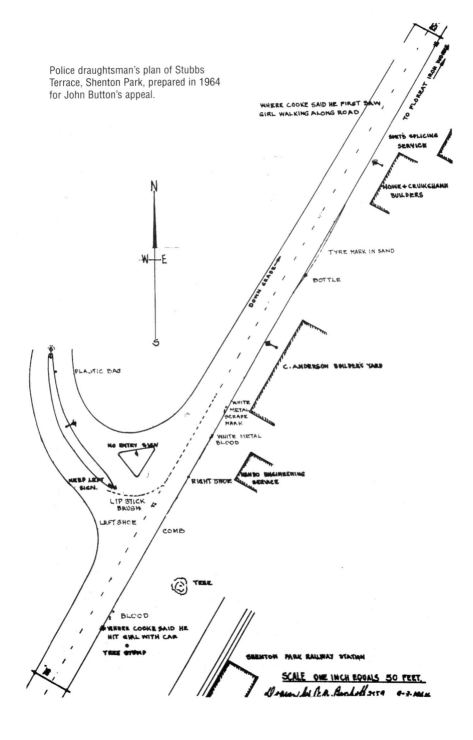

Police draughtsman's plan of Stubbs Terrace, Shenton Park, prepared in 1964 for John Button's appeal.

John's marriage to Helen Featherstone while on parole, in November 1968. The bridal couple are with John's parents and younger brother Jimmy.

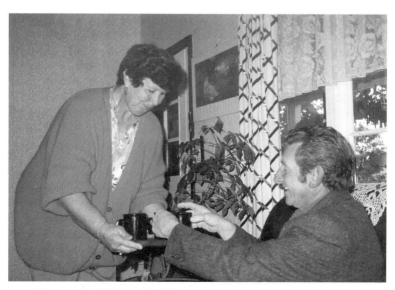

John Button meets Sally Cooke in 1993.

The Button family today: (top) Helen and John, son Gregory and daughter Naomi.

On tenterhooks as the manhunt for the gunman strained every nerve of every Perth policeman, the Claremont detectives rang the report through to Central and very quickly two police cars arrived with detectives from Perth and Claremont. They had an exact description, but a search of the district was fruitless; the prowler had disappeared.

That was not the only life this cat-burglar/killer used up.

He was caught in a headlock in Subiaco one night. He'd seen a couple pull into their driveway at 180 Barker Road about 12.30 a.m. There was a chance of watching them through the bedroom window – maybe even making his way in, once they were asleep. He waited until they were safely inside before starting to snoop around their house, but suddenly a man came out of the house to grab him.

Charlie Burton had noticed a short man walking on the footpath as he waited at the wheel while his wife opened the gates.

He thought no more of it as he prepared for bed, until he heard the front gates click and asked his wife Anne if she'd been out the front. Thinking that someone was trying to steal the car, they both dashed outside to the front veranda, Charlie heading to the right and Anne to the left. Anne saw him first, crouching in the garden opposite the bedroom window. She screamed and Charlie sprang over and grappled with the intruder, the bigger 42-year-old quickly overpowering him. He was pinned down with a foot on his neck and Anne went in and dialled 000.

He had to think of something fast. It was all right, he was just trying to get a drink of water. Charlie let him go, but immediately rued his decision as the man with something in his hand ran for his life along Townshend Road, making it as far as York Street before the police arrived just minutes later.

There was another time he was caught in a house and managed to get away by begging and pleading that he was out of work and was only stealing to buy food for his children. That man gave him food before letting him go.

Despite his close shaves, he remained as audacious as ever. Sometimes the mood took him just to brazenly front up to people, laughing to himself that if only they knew who he was.

A sixth sense told Phyllis Thompson to remain calm. She wasn't the screaming type, but her natural instinct was to call her husband Leonard who was nearby in the lounge. She didn't even do that. Some intuition told her to act nonchalantly and be polite to this stranger who had just walked into the kitchen. He walked by twelve-year-old Neil who was playing at the laundry trough, giving the boy a blank look as he passed, continuing straight into the kitchen. It was about 5 p.m. and she was preparing the evening meal, with another son playing at the kitchen table. She was shocked to be confronted by this uninvited visitor who wore a hat and carried a gladstone bag. She was stunned when the bold stranger asked her if her husband was home. Then he put his bag down and started asking questions about her children. He wanted to know how many children she had, how old they were, where they went to school.

It was clear to Phyllis that there was no way of predicting what this man with the hare lip would do next. Listening to that voice at the back of her head, she answered most politely – four children, three boys and a girl, aged nineteen, fifteen, twelve and ten. When she finished telling him about the children, he picked up the bag he'd placed at his feet and quietly left again. Phyllis and Leonard watched from their house on the corner of Angelo and Wattle Streets, South Perth, and saw him disappear around the corner and down Sandgate Street.

People he knew or worked with weren't safe from his wrath. They might have been nice to him, but they were still a part of the happy world that he'd been cheated out of by the twist of fate that gave him a deformity and a vicious father.

Shirley Hunt's friendship didn't stop him trying to perve on her and her husband. Shirley had lived in the area a long time and sympathised with Eric. She, too, had been an outcast as a youngster, mocked by other children for the way her mother always dressed her as Shirley Temple after whom she'd been named. She chatted with him when they were scoring local cricket games together and when she saw him at the Ascot Picture Theatre or out with the children.

He got a laugh when they were talking about the murders

once and she said: 'It would have to be a madman doing this.' If only she knew.

She was an attractive, bubbly girl – what a pity her husband Brian spoiled his fun by seeing him looking through the bedroom window of their home in nearby St Kilda Road. But he got away by jumping the fence and he knew Shirley wouldn't report him. She didn't, but she couldn't understand Cookie doing this. Nor could she understand the recent incidents of the clothes being taken off the line and stuffed under the house, and some money missing from a jar in the kitchen. She accused her young nieces who were staying, but they adamantly denied it.

Workmate Arthur Reynolds would never know if it was really Cooke who tried to run him off the road when he was driving his parents home to Carlisle from his Rivervale home. Reynolds could have thought the FJ Holden accidentally slid into him on the wet night, but he probably guessed it was on purpose. He had to go right off the road to avoid a crash. It made Reynolds nervous, especially when he told his wife Alma on arrival home, and she said an FJ Holden had been parked out the front of the house for a while before suddenly taking off.

Reynolds suspected that it could have been Cooke. As leading hand on the tractor assembly line at Chamberlain Industries in Welshpool, where Cooke worked, Reynolds often heard him threaten the young blokes when they mocked him. He'd say things like, 'You don't want to get funny with me, otherwise you'll get what's going' – and he'd do things like let down their car tyres.

Cooke had been to the Reynolds' Kooyong Road home one day with his little girl, and they'd asked him in for a cup of tea. Alma didn't like him, getting the feeling that he was looking around. About three months later, their three boys woke up screaming in their sleepout in the middle of the night, saying there was a man standing over them. The next morning sheets, blankets and a bedspread were missing from the linen press on the back veranda. The boys wouldn't go back to the sleepout, insisting on sleeping on the floor inside. Reynolds suspected Cooke of these two incidents, wondering if he'd said anything to upset him at work.

Then there was the Mayfair Theatrette usher whose house he was watching in West Leederville. He checked on what time Bill Waldock got home late at night, walking the two-and-a-half blocks from the bus stop in Cambridge Street to his home in St Leonards Avenue. He hid in his car watching as the usher walked down the centre of the road, frightened not only of the marksman who might strike any time, but also worried about being jumped by other nervous residents who might mistake him for the gunman. Cooke waited in the car several nights, parked by the high galvanised iron fence blocking off the Home of the Good Shepherd convent. This time, he started up the engine and rolled slowly along the street, following Waldock the few yards to his home. Waldock dashed inside. There he was with his wife, looking through the curtains. Then their tiny black dog dashed out the back door, around the side of the house to the front, producing a savage bark aimed at the strange greyish-blue car. With Towser's ferocious warning breaking the stillness of the crisp moonlit night, he started up again and moved off down the street towards the lake. Pesky dog. Still, there was plenty of time. Another night.

Cooke loved his night work. But he needed paid day work, too. He managed to fool his day employers, saying he'd been away up north when he went to get his old job back in April. He succeeded, and was now again one of three truck drivers for the Irvine Street hardware department of Krasnostein Metal and Hardware Merchants.

It was the job he'd left a while ago, telling the hardware manager he needed money and was going north – asking, before he went, if he could have his job back when he returned. The manager had asked Sol Krasnostein, who pointed out they could make no promises. But Krasnostein liked the quiet, loyal driver who was a very good worker. As soon as he arrived at the office of a morning, Cooke was one of the few who would look up and say 'Good morning, Mr Sol'. He was a bit of a loner, but he did a good job. So about nine months later when the manager said Cookie was on the phone, back from up north and asking for his job back, he was re-employed.

The Krasnostein brothers never knew that he hadn't been up north – and Pope Engineering Works didn't know that he'd looked for other work and decided to go back to Krasnostein's during three weeks' sick leave.

And it was only later that the other Krasnostein staff realised what a joke Eric had been playing on them when he said over lunch one day, 'Whoever's doing these murders must be a smart cookie'.

Attack on a Little Lovely

15 June 1963

Exactly four months after he got away with murdering Lucy Madrill, Cooke was climbing through a window into another flat where three young women lived.

Carmel Madeline Read had moved into the Nedlands flat just a month earlier after answering a newspaper advertisement for a third girl to share. The high-ceilinged flat, one of four in the two-storey block at 101 Smyth Road, was perfect for twenty-year-old Carmel – it was within walking distance from the University of Western Australia where she worked and only a few yards from Stirling Highway with its buses to Perth and Fremantle. Her successful interview with the leaseholder, teachers' college student Patricia Murphy, meant she could at last move out of the West Perth boarding house where she'd been staying during her search for permanent accommodation. She didn't know anyone in Perth, being a country girl from Merredin and having completed her final two years' schooling at the isolated monastery school at New Norcia. Two months previously she'd started a job in the faculty of education at the university, doing statistical and clerical work as a general assistant to a senior lecturer in education, Dr Bert Anderson.

Carmel shared the large front bedroom with Kathleen Ferguson, who worked at Stirling Pharmaceuticals in Claremont. Trish Murphy had the small single bedroom to herself. Theirs was Flat C, the northern ground-floor unit at Kumara Flats.

There were more single women upstairs and a couple next door.

Both Carmel and Kathy had twenty-first birthday parties to attend this Saturday night. Kathy was celebrating her boyfriend's and staying at his parents' place overnight, so Carmel would have the bedroom to herself. Carmel rarely went out, but it was her close girlfriend's party and the celebrations continued into the early hours of the morning. It was 2.20 a.m. on Sunday when she was dropped home by her girlfriend's fiance. After escorting her into the flat and seeing that all was well, he left and Carmel prepared for bed.

Trish was already asleep in her room across the hallway from the main bedroom and Carmel was in bed by 2.45, very tired from her unusually late night. A little nervous, she left a small light on in the lounge room and made sure all the doors and windows were locked. The only one she didn't worry about was a small ventilator window in the side wall of the lounge room. It was just two-feet by one-and-a-half-feet, and five feet up. Certain that this one was safe enough, she left it slightly ajar.

Cooke walked around to the back of Kumara Flats. He was in the area where the hunt for him was focused, only five blocks away from where he'd killed the two men in January. It didn't worry him. At night he was more powerful than all those terrified people and the police. At night he could do anything.

He'd been round these flats before, and had discovered a good spot where he could hide behind the neighbour's front brick wall and watch people inside the flats through the side windows. This time he didn't just want to watch. He checked all the doors and windows to look for a way in. At the back, the doors of the ground-floor flats were locked, as were the doors at the top of the steel stairs. But walking right around the outside looking for any other access, he found the small crack he'd been looking for – a window, slightly ajar. It was too high for him, but he wasn't going to be thwarted.

He went back to the area behind the flats and searched for something to stand on. There, among a bit of rubbish, was an old car tyre. That would do. He carried it back and leaned it against the wall under the window. He clambered on to it and heaved himself up, dropping into the lounge room beside the fireplace.

There was a light on in the room, and ever careful of being seen, he switched it off, but not before spying an umbrella by a chair. He opened the front door for a ready escape before flicking on his torch and looking through the flat for money. The pickings weren't good – he found only some shillings in a purse in a bedroom where a woman was asleep. He looked at her shape beneath the blankets as he took the coins and then moved on to the dining room.

Two hours after going to bed, Carmel was woken by a rustling sound in the dining room.

'Is anyone there?' she called out instinctively, her heart racing at the realisation that whatever made the noise shouldn't be there. Silence.

The man wearing gloves and a mask over his lower face heard the woman call out. Another one about to start screaming and wake up the neighbourhood. He picked up the umbrella – the handiest weapon – and went back to her room.

Carmel sat up, straining her ears. Then she saw the figure of a person standing in the bedroom doorway. She only saw him for a second because she was dazzled by a torch shone into her face. She couldn't see anything, but she could tell he had come in and was standing over her. Terrified and still dazzled, she pulled the bedclothes over her head and screamed.

He had to stop that screaming. He stabbed at her with the steel tip of the umbrella.

Carmel felt a sharp pain in her chest. She rolled to one side to avoid a second jab then realised she could do nothing to escape while she was a prisoner in bed. Terrified, she thought fast. She had to get to the door to turn the lights on and either get away or catch him. Trying to throw the blankets at him, she jumped out of bed. It was dark, she could see nothing, but she started running to the door. At five-foot ten-inches and a fit country girl, she thought she might have a chance against him.

She felt a sting on her cheek as he struck, and she could tell from the angle of the punch that he was a short man. Then he ran for it. Dropping the umbrella in the passage, the man ran out the open door.

Screaming and shocked, Carmel ran to Trish's room, to find her lying in bed hiding under the covers. But the couple in the neighbouring flat heard her screams and the thumping on the wall. They ran in to see what was wrong and rang the police.

The police received the call at 4.55 a.m. A patrol car had passed by the flats just a few minutes earlier, on its regular check on the bowling club further up the street. There were soon five police cars at the flats.

They found Carmel with abrasions and severe bruising on her chest and the inside of her right upper arm, and abrasions on the left side of her face, but could find no evidence of fingerprints or anything helpful to identify the attacker.

Kathy Ferguson arrived home later that day to find that her purse containing fifteen shillings had been taken from the foot of her bed, where she'd left it with her sunglasses. The sunglasses were still there; the purse was gone.

When Detective Sergeant John McLernon interviewed her, Carmel begged him not to tell the media, because she didn't want to worry her parents in Merredin. That suited the police. Before interviewing the two other girls, Detective Sergeant Jerry Parker wrote a note to his colleague 'Owen', presumably Owen Leitch, asking him to go and talk to 'the little lovelies' and 'impress on them that there is to be no publicity. There is a blanket ban on publicity by BOSS.'

Another Gun, Another Unlocked Door

10 August 1963

Carl Dowd liked the replacement baby-sitter immediately. As soon as he picked her up from St Catherine's College, he was relieved to find that she seemed a down-to-earth and sensible student. He and his wife Wendy had a regular baby-sitter, but when she took ill during the day, they were assured that another student would be available. The Dowds relied on baby-sitters to care for their eight-month-old son during the many social engagements that helped build and maintain business networks.

Dowd had been transferred from Melbourne four years previously to run the Perth office of the ladies' lingerie firm Hickory, and the Victorian couple had no family in Perth to help. However, they lived close to the university, where students living in the female residence, St Catherine's, were always keen to gain some income by baby-sitting.

Second-year science student Shirley McLeod baby-sat once a week to help her through her university years. She often baby-sat the three Silberstein children and was due to do so this night, but it was cancelled when Dr Silberstein succumbed to the chills of the cold, wet winter. This left Shirley free to fill in for her sick friend at the Dowds' house at 37 Wavell Road, Dalkeith.

Chatting to Shirley after picking her up from St Catherine's, Dowd felt confident about leaving baby Mitchell in her care. He could see that the pleasant, quiet girl was genuine and conscientious. She had a satchel of books with her and told Dowd how she planned to work very hard for the rest of the university year. Her study was very important to Shirley, who had chosen a career in social work despite her father's practical advice that it didn't pay well. She was taking units in anthropology, psychology and zoology, and wanted to gain good grades in her exams a couple of months later.

The baby was asleep when the Dowds left for their party a half-mile away. They went down the stairs to the garage, which was at a lower level than the single-storey house because of the sloping corner block. They locked all the doors except the one leading from the hallway to the top of the garage stairs.

It was a stormy night with rain lashing down outside, but the heavy curtains were drawn, the electric heater was on and it was warm inside. Shirley put on a record, slipped off her shoes and settled into the lounge-room sofa in front of the heater. The eighteen-year-old opened her books and notebooks to study.

Cooke left home at 12.30 p.m., driving his 1956 FJ Holden to Adelaide Terrace and parking outside Fairlanes. It was the Brunswick State Championships and he'd been pleased to have been asked to score. He'd enjoyed scoring for the qualifying rounds of the State championships. But when he arrived, he found that organiser Frank Baden-Powell had instead put him down as an usher. Cooke was a little upset, saying he was too self-conscious for that role. But he carried on, and after the games, he had supper with fellow players Keith Bell and Rhonda Meloncelli and played a game. He left at 7.30 p.m., giving Keith a lift home to Leederville.

From Leederville he drove to Wembley. He went to Doubleview and from there to his favourite area, Cottesloe. He was only half a mile from where he'd shot those three in January, and where the residents were particularly terrified and on the lookout. But that didn't bother him.

On the beachfront, he parked the car at the bottom of Pearse Street and wandered up the hill, taking no notice of the rain, snooping around the houses as he went.

There was a light on in the front of 17 Pearse Street. That meant someone was home. It didn't deter him, even made it more fun – taking these fancy people's things from right under their noses. He crept through the carport to the back, testing for unlocked windows. Success – the back door was unlocked. He opened it quietly and snuck inside to the kitchen. He could see a short woman sitting talking in the lounge. He loved the risk – and knew he could always make a dash out the back door that he'd left open. No-one was going to follow him in this storm. He tiptoed through to the main bedroom, where he looked for money. Opening a wardrobe, he found a .22 rifle. That feeling of power started to come over him as he ran his fingers along the barrel. Now he had a gun again, after all these months. He didn't look any further. He quickly left the house with his treasured find, walking back to his car and driving towards the city along Stirling Highway.

He hadn't gone far, to Bay View Terrace in Claremont, when he decided to look for a place to rob in Dalkeith or neighbouring areas. Again it was near the site of his two murders, and everyone was nervous. If only they knew he was creeping around anyway, watching them through windows, stealing from their houses. He had it all over them.

He turned off the highway and drove to Dalkeith, parking where Circe Circle merged into Carroll Street. He took the rifle and wandered through a small triangular park bordered by Carroll Street, Wavell Road and Brockman Avenue. It was a black night, with lightning and thunder. The heavens were on his side, providing the noise to mask the sounds of a gunshot. It was a good night to shoot someone.

He didn't expect to see anyone outside in this weather. But a woman suddenly ran out of a big corner house in Brockman Avenue. He was hidden by a tree and could watch her unnoticed as she jumped the low limestone wall at the front of the house and ran across the road into the park. Perfect. No one was around and his shot wouldn't be heard. The power consumed him as, steely-eyed, he lifted his rifle and drew a bead on her, waiting for her to stop running so he could get a good shot – neatly in the forehead, like the others.

Bernice Rogers was ignoring her husband's instructions by chasing their runaway dog into the park. Alfred Rogers was very strict about security while there was someone shooting people in the area. He'd been a major in the 3 Field Regiment at El Alamein and was all too familiar with the results of gunfire. So the house at 34 Brockman Avenue was well locked and their two sons had been brought in from their louvred sleepout to makeshift beds in the lounge room.

Although he was 22 and a fit, athletic league footballer who played full back for Claremont, John Rogers didn't mind obeying his father. Neither did his seventeen-year-old brother Paul. They were as petrified as everyone in the Dalkeith/Nedlands area. The drama was brought even closer home when John was treated as a suspect in the Australia Day shootings. The police were looking for the light-coloured car that had been seen nearby that night and John owned a white Ford Falcon. As he pulled up under the palm trees at the front of the house one night, he heard a sharp instruction not to move. After some heavy questioning by the detectives, they finally accepted that he lived in this house and had a genuine alibi for the night of the murders.

Their mother had opened the front door for just a minute. Joe, excited about something outside, dashed out and bounded across to the park. Not thinking, Bernice followed to bring the boxer back. She couldn't catch him, so stopped chasing to stand and call him.

The moving target finally stopped. He took aim. This was it. Another of those wealthy people who had everything would be blasted away. Just at that moment, she moved a little, enough to put a tree in the way. From his hiding place he couldn't get a direct hit. She stood there, shielded by the tree. Thwarted, he put the rifle down and watched, waiting for his next opportunity when she moved again. By the time the dog came bounding over to the woman and she started walking back to the house, he'd lost interest. The power had left him. He walked on.

Bernice Rogers locked the door. She was glad to be out of the stormy weather. Inside, she felt safe, protected from the elements and from the gunman.

Cooke walked north along Wavell Road, then on a whim changed his mind and walked back towards the river. A house on the corner of Minora Road attracted his attention. It was distinctive, all white with a blue roof. It was a single-storey home, but the garage was at a lower level than the house. He walked around the corner and looked into the garage. It was empty. He saw chinks of light through the front curtains. Maybe they'd left a light on, or maybe there was someone in the lounge room. If there was, all the better. He had a rifle and was in a killing mood. He walked through the garage and up the stairs to the door into the house. It wasn't locked. He quietly went inside.

Shirley Martha McLeod had a lot to live for. A top student and prefect at Kent Street High School, she'd won a scholarship to attend the University of Western Australia. She'd also been a successful sportswoman at school, a good basketball player and an A-grade hockey player. At university, she had taken the social step of making her debut at the Graduation Ball the previous year. In a small group of debutantes that included Julie Hogg before she'd met John Sturkey, Shirley had been partnered by dashing law student Julian Grill. She'd looked stunning in her strapless white ball gown with the rose-embroidered lace and long white gloves. She continued to have a good social life, currently going out with a fellow student, a Quaker, but right now she was putting her studies first.

Shirley was the second of Heath and Stella McLeod's three children. She also had two half-brothers and a half-sister, from Stella's first marriage. The blended family was close, all of them suffering the grief of her half-brother John's death in a road accident the previous year. The family had lived in Kensington and, like Cooke before her, Shirley had gone to Kensington Primary School. Although she'd left home to live at St Catherine's College, she was still family-minded, going home every Sunday for the roast and doing her mother's hair each week, as she had from the time she was a young girl. She made friends easily and often brought some with her for Sunday lunch, her father smiling at her lack of concern for creed or colour when she brought home friends from Africa and Asia.

When bus driver Heath McLeod found a suitable house in Shenton Park, the family moved. It was closer to university for their son Denis, who was at law school. Denis, nineteen months older than Shirley, was handy with tools and closed in the back veranda to make bedrooms for himself and his brother Lindsay, six years younger and still at school.

During the summer vacation after her first year at university, Shirley went to New Guinea with her friend Fay, whose father Les Johnson was the Director of Education. It was there that she and Fay heard the news of the murder of their friend John Sturkey. They had been on their way to a picnic with another friend from university, twenty-year-old law student Nicholas Hasluck, who had joined his father, Territories Minister Paul Hasluck, on his tour of New Guinea's educational institutions. The news of the Perth shootings came over the radio, ruining the picnic for Shirley, who shared some of John's lectures and his social circle.

Discussing the murders, they learnt that Nick Hasluck had known the youth convicted of Jillian Brewer's murder. Nick told them about Darryl Beamish at the Claremont Baths and at the Windsor Picture Theatre's Saturday matinees. He remembered the deaf-mute as part of a disruptive gang at the pictures and as a shivering, frightened boy flanked by huge policemen one particular time at the baths. As a law student with a personal interest, he'd sat through Beamish's trial.

Back at home, Shirley learnt of another connection with the shootings – her father had known Brian Weir's late mother, Trudy. Home from New Guinea, she told her parents about her decision to become a social worker.

'There are so many people who need help, and the pay isn't what you get out of a job, Dad,' she replied to Heath's point about the career's limited income.

Cooke stood in the hallway. It was quiet inside, but there were loud thunderclaps outside. Looking through the entrance hall, he could see a young woman sitting on the couch in the lounge room. The rest of the house was dark. She was quite alone.

She was facing him, but her head was lowered. She hadn't seen him. She was either concentrating on the books on her lap or she was dozing. An easy target. He could score another win against all of those lucky people. His face turned colder and harder, his mouth more twisted as revenge took control and he raised the rifle.

Cooke walked back to his car, checking the rifle. He pulled back the bolt and the cartridge case flew out. He rammed home the bolt and picked up the cartridge case. He wasn't going to leave a tell-tale piece of evidence like last time. One used cartridge found on the Louise Street driveway was enough to teach him not to do it again. He threw away that rifle so it couldn't be matched. But he might keep this one – it could come in handy another time. He tossed the rifle and the cartridge case into the car. He took off and went back along Stirling Highway the way he'd come, driving home via Canning Highway. He made a detour and hid the rifle, in a spot where he could retrieve it and use it again. No throwing this one in the river.

He pulled into his drive after 1 a.m.

'I'm home, but it's late,' he called to his wife. He looked and acted as if nothing had happened. But she noticed his clothes were wet.

The Dowds arrived home at about 2 a.m, in good spirits after a late and successful party. From the entrance hall at the top of the garage stairs, Wendy went straight to the bedroom to check on the baby while Carl went to the lounge room to collect the baby-sitter. The teenager was sitting on the settee, her head slumped to one side. The turntable was still rotating with a record that had played out, the heater was on, a cup and saucer was on the small table by the settee, her shoes were on the floor in front of her. He thought she'd fallen asleep over her books, understandable when they were so much later than expected. But then he saw the blood on her face and clothes and the bullet hole in her forehead. She was dead. Her pen was still upright in her hand, an unfinished sentence on her writing pad.

His shock and horror was accompanied by the terrifying thought that the killer was still in the house. Dowd ran into the bedroom, slammed the door and, with his back pushing against it, told his wife that Shirley had been attacked. Not knowing it was too late, and with baby Mitchell gurgling and smiling in her arms, Wendy said she'd go and help her.

'No, no, no,' was all Dowd could say as he pressed against the door, wondering how they would all get out of there safely.

Petrified, trying to work out just where in the house the killer was hiding in wait for his next victim, he took a while to summon enough courage to leave the bedroom and creep to the telephone in the hall to ring the police. In his panic, his trembling hands fumbled with the telephone book, making it difficult to find the police listing. He rang the first he managed to see, the station at Fremantle instead of the nearer ones. Then he dashed back into the bedroom and holed up, terrified of what was out there and counted the seconds until the police arrived. When they did and he felt safe, Dowd phoned his close friend Geoff Bingemann, who came immediately and took Wendy and the baby home with him.

Shirley McLeod's cold-blooded murder caused a further wave of panic. People cancelled outings, baby-sitters cancelled bookings. The latest shooting couldn't be definitely linked with those in January, especially without a matching cartridge case. The hunt for it became the detectives' first goal.

While Cooke was taking his family for a Sunday drive, police were combing the Dowd house and its surrounds for the sought-after piece of evidence. They even enlisted the help of a soldier and an army mine detector.

The Chief of the CIB, Inspector Lamb, was back from leave. He and Inspector Athol Wedd went to the Wavell Road house the next afternoon to take up again the task of the unsolved murders, grimly adding another one. No one had heard anything – except one neighbour, who said he'd heard what he'd thought was a particularly loud thunderclap at about the time Shirley would have been shot.

Then the police found a clue that seemed to be the breakthrough so badly needed – one fingerprint. People who'd visited the house over the previous months were fingerprinted. The police found no match with previous tenants, visitors or tradesman, and were convinced it belonged to the killer. It was their best clue, along with the bullet extracted at the postmortem. It had particular identification markings.

The hunt continued in all directions. Perth's detectives were organised into two twelve-hour shifts focused on tracking down the killer, leaving only suburban detectives to do general work. A squad of 50 detectives worked through Nedlands and Dalkeith, interviewing more than 8,000 residents in what was believed to have been the biggest door-to-door canvass in one area of Australia.

While the police hunted him and Perth lived in fear of him, Cooke lived as usual, working for Krasnostein's, ten-pin bowling at Fairlanes and socialising with colleagues, friends, neighbours and family.

At Fairlanes, he'd made friends with Jennifer Jackson and Julie Shore, following their team and giving them a lift home from time to time so they would be safe from the murderer. He'd told them he lived in a flat in Nedlands and was a relief mechanic for the Police Department.

On 13 August the McLeods buried Shirley, angry that the man dubbed the Nedlands Monster had deprived them of a girl of the highest personal quality and of unlimited promise, and that she would be always remembered in the company of her murderer, forever enslaved to his hateful fame. That night, Cooke and his bowling friend Keith Bell were the two men in a group of five celebrating Jennifer Jackson's twenty-first birthday at the Heidelberg Restaurant.

The Geraldton Wax Trap

16 August 1963

William Keehner surprised his wife by announcing he was going for a walk. He'd woken from his nap about 3 p.m. and the elderly couple had sat down to their regular afternoon cup of coffee. It was their habit to walk along the river every afternoon when the sun shone. The couple, generally known as Pop and Mum, would walk down the hill to the river near their Mt Pleasant home, amble along the bank, check that their little fishing boat was moored properly and chat to friends while they worked in their gardens. It was usually a quiet area – except for last summer, when they were caught up in the thrill of competitors from the Commonwealth Games rowing along this section of the Canning River. Now it was a quiet backwater again.

The Keehners hadn't been on any of their regular walks for a while. It had been cold and wet and 84-year-old Pop had been sick with bronchitis. This was another cold mid-winter's day, but the sun bursting through the clouds inspired him.

'Well I'm coming, too,' Mum said. She slammed the steel doors shut after stoking up the wood fire and slipped a cardigan over her house dress. The couple wandered down their road, Hawkins Street, to the river two blocks down the hill. At The Esplanade they turned left, ambling along the bank of the river towards Canning Bridge and noticing one of the flowering flame trees had broken boughs and car tracks leading to it. Stopping for a closer look, they guessed it had been a light car like a Volkswagen or Prefect and wondered if the driver had been hurt. The rain was holding off and it was brisk and pleasant, but two blocks along the river were enough for a first walk in a while, so at Rookwood Street they turned towards home.

Rookwood Street was steep, cut into the hill with steep overgrown sandy banks leading up to the houses either side. It was a testing climb for elderly people, but the next road along was quite a way off and they were both hardy people from lives of hard work. The banks of Rookwood Street were resplendent with Geraldton wax flowers, those delicate precursors of spring. Halfway up the hill Mum decided to pick some of the pale pink flowers. She had no idea why such an impulse came over her — she randomly selected a top sprig from a bush on the left and reached up to pick it, one knee against the sandy incline. Her eyes on the flowers, she didn't see something on the ground shift a little and slowly start to slide down the slope. She looked down when she felt it touch her knee. It was the butt of a rifle.

Startled, she quickly pushed it back under the bush and just stood there, wondering what to do. She was used to guns, having lived on a farm at Three Springs, but a gun in a suburban street was a shock. Pop, further up the hill by now, couldn't understand the hold-up.

'C'mon,' he called as he turned around to see her standing staring into a Geraldton wax bush.

'There's a rifle here.' He had seen a lot of guns during his lifetime that began in Germany in 1879 but could not imagine a rifle here. He backtracked to have a look for himself. 'We'd better take it home.'

'We can't carry a rifle, we're not licensed,' his law-abiding wife remonstrated. So they left it there.

They walked to the top of the hill, wondering about the rifle. It looked old and rusty, and they figured that some children had been playing cops and robbers through the bushes. It was a popular street with the kids, because it led to a jetty. Youngsters would run down the steep hill, along the jetty and dive into the river. At the start of the kids' run, the top of the street, Pop and Mum Keehner turned towards home. It wasn't until they were home that it occurred to them to call the police. Mum reported the rifle to the nearby police station. Thinking no more of it, she stoked up the fire and started to prepare dinner while Pop went out to his vegetable patch.

A constable from Canning Bridge station pulled up outside 3 Hawkins Street, his motorbike and side car making such a noise that the curiosity of the neighbours was aroused. It was inconceivable that such an upstanding couple could have anything to do with the police. They knew the pensioners to be honest folk who'd worked hard all their lives – Pop on the team building the first north-to-south rabbit-proof fence in the outback before becoming a metropolitan baker, and Mum, twenty years younger than him, raising three children on her own and running an orchard before they met. The police could have no business with such solid citizens.

The officer asked Mr Keehner to take him to the gun, so the old man accompanied him in the sidecar, to the astonishment of the neighbours and the distress of his five-year-old grandson who lived next door. His mother tried to stop the howling, explaining that Poppy was just going to show the nice policeman something, but the boy wasn't happy until the policeman brought him back.

The officer took the rifle from under the bush and put it on the floor of the sidecar to take to the station. Pop sat over it for his ride home.

Mum was still preparing dinner around the disruptions when about 30 minutes later, two detectives knocked on the door of the weatherboard and asbestos house.

Just that morning, the CIB had decided they would take the fingerprints of all men between the ages of fourteen and 60 in the whole metropolitan area, beginning in Nedlands and Cottesloe. Teams of police started early in the morning, going from house to house taking fingerprints, finishing at 7 p.m. Those who were not home were asked to go to the Claremont Police Station.

People were in a panic, the Opposition in State Parliament was calling for experts to be called in from outside the State and a psychiatrist gave a public warning about people developing a mass neurosis about the killings.

Finally there was a breakthrough. The gun the Keehners had found had been used to kill Shirley McLeod.

A huge search around Rookwood Street failed to find any cartridges, but one bullet left in the breech of the Winchester repeater .22 rifle was enough for ballistic experts to confirm the connection. When test-fired, the copper-nosed bullet matched portions of the bullet removed from the victim. The case bore the ejector-extractor marks and the rifle's firing pin marks. It was a surprise result. They had been looking for a single shot Lithgow rifle, the type used in the January shootings.

The gun belonged to Garrick Agnew, the successful company director and former Olympic swimmer who lived at 17 Pearse Street, Cottesloe. He had reported it missing three days previously, on his return from overseas, where he'd been since 29 June. The Winchester .22 bolt-action repeater was stolen from his bedroom wardrobe. Another rifle in a cupboard in the lounge room had not been taken, nor had any money or other portable possessions.

Carl and Wendy Dowd arrived back in Perth to a new round of interrogation from the police. The Bingemanns had taken them away on a trip to the Murchison River to get away from it all, but now they were back among it. Still staying with the Bingemanns, Carl was questioned about how well he knew Garrick Agnew and how often he had been to his house. He hadn't been told about the find, so the implication that he and Garrick Agnew were suspects because of their business association was incomprehensible to him.

Cooke knew Rookwood Street. The Davis couple lived there, the bird people whose business was in the same street in Rivervale as the Davis couple with the wood business, where he worked occasionally. He knew Rookwood Street, too, from one of the bowling girls, who had a boyfriend who lived there. It was a good street for a peeping Tom – the quiet, dark street with no street lights and a view of the river was a popular parking spot for courting couples.

The police had a murder weapon, but they needed the murderer. Whoever had stolen and hidden it probably planned to use it again. They hoped he'd come back for it.

They set a trap. They put the rifle back in the exact spot Mum had found it, fastening it firmly with a 100-pound fishing line. A lookout was set up in the garden of the house opposite, with police watching 24 hours a day.

Eddie and Noreen Davis agreed to this invasion of their backyard and police were a constant presence in their property. The house fronted onto The Esplanade, ran back along Rookwood Street and covered the whole block to View Road. Eddie's bird and hardware business was in Rivervale, just along from Felix Davis's timber yard.

Felix Davis would call on Cooke whenever he needed extra help. He often needed it for his government contract to supply Claremont Mental Hospital. They'd go out bush to Sawyers Valley to collect and chop the wood, and Cooke would also help unload it from railway wagons at Karrakatta Station and truck them to the asylum.

Felix was impressed with Cooke. He was a good worker, quiet and said nothing while they talked about the murders; a sober man who couldn't be talked into a beer when they stopped off at the Sandringham Hotel after work. He and his wife June befriended Cooke, often having him in their home. June's only concern about her husband's casual worker was that he seemed a bit callous towards his wife and children.

Eddie and Noreen Davis and their six-year-old son Kim were sworn to secrecy as police came and went in round-the-clock shifts, watching the Geraldton wax bush from under a bushy gum tree at their side cyclone fence.

It was a bleak, wet August, and the police stood in almost constant rain to watch the bank opposite, day and night. They borrowed an SAS army tent and slung it across a pole, creating a camouflaged pup tent that they erected each night to give them some shelter from the rain. Each in turn had a break in the tent while the other kept his eyes, ears and nerves strained.

The police kept a close watch to protect the Keehners as well.

Sometimes friends came in to warn them there was a police car outside their home. The Keehners kept their silence without lying, saying 'There are police cars everywhere at the moment.'

Inspector Lamb decided to share the secret of the breakthrough with two other people, taking the police reporters from *The West Australian* and the *Daily News* into his confidence. He knew Ralph Wheatley and Jack Coulter very well and knew he could trust them. He needed them to help ensure any publicity on the manhunt did not go the wrong way.

Another person learnt the secret of the rifle by chance. Thanks to Cyril Head, the news didn't slip out by mistake in radio bulletins prepared in the *West*'s news bureau.

Always interested in the news, the *West*'s driver read the first edition when it arrived at the transport office during his night shift in the car pool, and also read the late-night radio news bulletins before delivering them to 6PR, 6KY and 6IX.

One night he was reading the bulletins in the transport office, about to set out on his run, when he was fascinated to see a story about a gun being found. He was thrilled to realise that finally there'd been a breakthrough, with the possibility of the murderer being caught at last. As well as ending the general terror and his concern for his wife, it would mean he'd finally find out if the killer had cycled between Cottesloe and Nedlands, as he'd tested for the *Daily News*. But he was alerted by the word 'embargo' printed across the top of the story. He'd spent enough time in the news bureau, fascinated to see the teleprinters bringing in news from around the world, to recognise that an embargo meant the story was not to be used. He rang the head of the news bureau, Hugh Schmitt, who confirmed it was a mistake. The item that would have ruined the police operation was quietly removed from the bulletins.

The trap set, the secret retained, the police watched and waited.

'We've had a Visitor'

31 August 1963

The sounds of Pat Cannon and the Statesmen drifted across the river, relieving the boredom of Constable Bill Hawker as he stood at his post in Mt Pleasant.

'You rotten sods, having a good time, and here I am,' he thought. He half wished he could be among the revellers at the Manning Hotel. They would have finished their smorgasbord dinner and would now be dancing, while he was spending another cold, lonely night watching for the gunman.

It was a little overcast, with the moon giving off a hazy light through the cloud cover so that it wasn't totally dark for observing the street. Hawker thought it was one of the more pleasant nights he'd had to sit out on watch; it wasn't teeming down with rain as it had been for most of the past fortnight, but it still wasn't how he'd choose to spend a Saturday night.

Constables Peter Skeehan and Bill Hawker had taken up their post at the lookout at 6 p.m., preparing themselves for another bleak Saturday night and looking forward to getting home at six in the morning and spending Father's Day with their families. They scanned Rookwood Street, focusing on the Geraldton wax bush. Hawker shared his theory with his colleague that if the rifle was ever going to be collected, it would be just as the suburb's street lights went out, when the whole area was dark. That would be 1.15 a.m.

It wasn't unusual for them to take turns at keeping watch during the night shifts, allowing each of them to lie down in the pup tent to get a bit of sleep. As he watched, the loneliness of his lot was brought home by the couples who chose that little out-of-the-way street to wander down to the river, arm in arm, stopping occasionally for a passionate embrace. At least the music wafting over the river from the Manning Hotel and a bit of action in the street prevented any chance of him nodding off.

Mary Halliday was having a smoke with her boyfriend Vic on the front veranda of the house where she boarded at 98 Gladstone Road, Rivervale. Mary had met Cooke and Brian Robinson during stays at RPH. Cooke had asked her where she lived, and they'd discovered they were within a block of each other. From then she'd always call out hello as he passed, and he often stopped for a chat about everything from the weather to the latest world news. Mary started to wait for him, looking forward to the routine yarn with the near neighbour she called a good friend.

She was often on the front veranda when he passed by late at night. She assumed that he was a shift worker and when she called out a cheery 'On night shift again, Eric?' he'd say 'Yes'. She didn't know where he worked and wouldn't ask, nor could she guess. He didn't appear to wear a uniform or work overalls, but she noticed he often had on a thick overcoat and sometimes an old cowboy-style hat, pulled low.

The spate of shootings that was terrifying Perth hadn't worried Mary or changed her outdoor preference. She'd stay outside despite Cooke's warning to her to be more careful. She, too, told him to make sure his wife locked the house while he was away on night shift, and asked him if he wasn't frightened of walking around the streets alone so late at night.

He had indeed warned his wife, who was frightened when he went out on night shift. He'd brought the children in from the sleepout to sleep on mattresses on the lounge-room floor and locked up before he left. She had strict instructions not to unlock anything until she heard his whistle.

'Hi, Eric, off to work again?' Mary called as he went by. Cooke ignored her and kept walking, his overcoat pulled up at the collar. 'That's funny, Eric can't be in a very good mood,' she said to Vic. She hadn't experienced that before and was sure Cooke enjoyed their conversations as much as she did. Then he turned and walked back, and Mary thought he must have had a change of heart and was going to say hello after all. But to her amazement, he still didn't speak – instead he suddenly opened the door and sat in Vic's Holden utility parked outside the house, trying to start it. Mary was alarmed at her friend's strange action. It was as if he didn't know what he was doing. Startled, Vic leapt to the road, frightening off the would-be car thief, who walked away again.

Cooke walked back home and took his own car, a greyish-blue Holden sedan. Just a short time earlier, he'd been playing ball with the next-door children. As he left, he told the Simmonds boy he'd teach him how to throw next time.

Now, he headed back to Peppermint Grove and its big luxurious houses through which he'd successfully prowled for four years. From reading papers in some of the houses, he even knew who lived in them — F. Leuba on the corner of Leake and View streets (nice car radio he got from there a couple of years back) and C. R. Bunning on the left side of View Street (he didn't bother with Charlie Bunning's place after a while – the whisky wasn't to his liking). He also learnt about the owners' hobbies from poking around their houses. And he knew the layouts of many of the houses, from plans published in *The West Australian*'s Saturday architecture column that featured interesting designs.

It was late when he had some luck at 41 Irvine Street. The car was gone, the house was in darkness and the back door was unlocked. His gloved hands quietly opened it and he crept in. Searching through the master bedroom, he found £17 on the dressing table. He heard footsteps heading towards the kitchen and stealthily moved on through the house into the rear dining room. He hid there until the footsteps retreated to the bedroom and all was quiet again, letting him safely creep through to the back door to make his escape. It was closed. He'd purposely left it open, as always, for a quick exit. He opened it quietly and slipped out, not bothering to close it again behind him.

From there he wandered down to the river again, to one house in particular in The Esplanade, overlooking Freshwater

Bay. No. 60 had been built only two years before in the front grounds of the original house and had recently featured in Saturday's architecture column. It was dark, apart from a small light in a room to the side. There were two doors at the back, and one was unlocked. He got in easily.

He went from the kitchen and bathroom area at the back to the first bedroom on the right of a hall leading to the front door. He could see a woman asleep in a single bed, and he moved around quietly, not waking her. He continued through the hallway to the front bedroom. It was very light, the open curtains letting in the all-night street lighting. There was another woman asleep in this room, about the same age as the other.

Heading to the left, he went through into the big lounge with huge windows looking right on to the river and was checking around when a car swung into the driveway. He sprang out the back door which he'd left open, around to the side of the house and watched, trying to see who had disturbed him halfway through the job. From the dark of the bushes he looked into the side room with the light on, then went up to the window and peered in. It was a young woman. He watched as she walked to the bathroom at the other side of the house and listened, and when he could hear that she was under the shower, he went back in. This time he went straight to the side room that he'd seen from the outside. It wasn't a bedroom, more like a sitting room – and there on the couch was the young woman's handbag and, nearby, an overnight bag. Still hearing the shower, he searched through both bags, taking some money from the handbag and a transistor radio from the other, and quietly left through the back door.

It was late. The street lights would soon be off in Mt Pleasant. It was time to retrieve the gun.

Bill Hawker tensed a little when it was time for the street lights to go out. If it was going to be tonight, it would be soon. He had already faced two weeks of waiting and false alarms. But this morning's story in *The West Australian* might just make a difference. It just might be the night. He smiled at the ploy. Let the *West*'s trustworthy police roundsman Ralph Wheatley and the *Daily News*'s Jack Coulter in on the find and get their cooperation to announce that the police were turning their efforts to the Mt Pleasant–Applecross area at the end of the week, giving the gunman five days to worry about the security of his hiding place. This morning's front-page story praising the local people for cooperating with the fingerprinting was another reminder of police activity in the area.

His thoughts were interrupted by low snoring from the tent. It was gentle enough not to disturb him, so he didn't wake the sleeper – until a car pulled up slowly below the lookout, opposite the bush.

'Oh bloody hell, someone's going to have a session,' was his immediate reaction, based on his experience of couples choosing this street, of all streets.

Hawker kept his eyes on the Holden, seeing, because of the elevation, not much more than the roof. After a while, he heard the driver's door open and could see it held slightly ajar. That put him on full alert. After a few moments, the door opened wider. The eyes of the watching policeman also grew wider, and the hair stood up on the back of his neck.

When he saw the person get out of the car and stand, remaining cautiously within the doorway, Hawker was half-convinced that this was their man. He went over to the tent and roused Skeehan, and quietly moved back the few feet to the fence. By then the person had crossed the road and reached the bush.

Hawker knew he had to act quickly. If the man discovered the gun was tied down, he'd be back in the car and away. Without stopping to see if his partner was with him, Hawker leapt the fence and bounded down the sandy embankment, as the man bent down beside the bush. Crouched there, he turned to look back on hearing the footsteps. As he turned Hawker saw something shining in Cooke's hand and for a horrible moment thought he was heading straight towards a gun. But it wasn't going to stop him. Hawker reached the man and grappled with him, with Skeehan just seconds behind.

They had him.

As he felt around to handcuff his quarry in the dim light, Hawker wondered what sort of misfit he had. The man was mumbling incoherently and his hands felt smooth and soft, not like a man's skin at all. About to click his handcuffs into place, Hawker decided to make doubly sure there was no escape. He took his colleague's handcuffs, putting one half through his and attaching the other to the galvanised fence alongside the lookout property.

'If this bugger's going to run, he's going to take the fence with him,' he said.

With the gunman safely anchored, Hawker was anxious to get the news through to base. He knew there was a patrol car around the corner, hidden in the backstreet driveway of their hosts' house and always at the ready to give chase. But he knew this news was too important to put over the car's radio, which could be intercepted. He went back up the embankment and knocked to wake up Eddie and Noreen Davis, asking to use their phone. They knew not to ask why, but they could guess.

Hawker rang through to Duty Sergeant John McLernon. 'We've had a visitor.'

McLernon radioed for Detective Ivor Thomter, out on the eastern districts patrol, to bring Cooke in. Thomter's driver swung around and sped to Rookwood Street. When the car arrived at the scene, its lights gave Hawker a good look at the small man in the big overcoat. The shiny thing he had seen was a pencil torch. The man's hare lip explaining the mumblings, and he could see what had caused the strange feel of his hands. Cooke was wearing gloves – women's gloves. He also had a pair of women's panties in one of his pockets and in the top pocket of his jacket was part of a newspaper's social column dated 12 July. He'd underlined an article about a wedding on 31 August and written an address over it, with three more addresses, some with phone numbers, in the margin.

Thomter sat in the back of the car with Cooke while the driver took them to headquarters. Inspector Lamb also sped to central. He'd received the long-awaited news at 1.30 a.m. He trembled as he reached for the phone, knowing it meant success or failure.

Hawker's part was over. He and his partner had done their job. Now it was for his seniors to take over the inquiry. Hawker had a blinding headache and all he wanted to do was go home. When Inspector Lamb arrived at headquarters, the constable thought that's what he'd be able to do.

'Boss, you don't want us around,' he started his request for him and his partner to go home.

'Yes, I do, wait.' They waited.

Detective Sergeant Bill Nielson moved fast to get to headquarters. He'd been called in about the same time as he'd been called to the last murder. Any grim thought that there must have been another death was ousted with the joyous news that every police officer in Perth had been waiting for.

At CIB headquarters, Cooke was acting differently from how he had on the other occasions he'd been arrested or questioned. Normally he was cunning, not giving anything away until confronted by the evidence. Tonight he was chatty, readily telling them about the number of houses he'd broken into that night and freely admitting that the £22/18/– on him was his booty for the night. CIB headquarters was abuzz. Detective Sergeants Bill Nielson, Roy Balcombe and John Dunne were there, as were Hawker and Skeehan. Inspectors Fred Douglas was with the Boss in his office on the opposite side of the corridor.

But they were getting nowhere. Cooke was denying any connection with Shirley McLeod's death, insisting that he'd arrived home at 8.15 on the night of her murder and had not gone out again. He told them he'd spied the gun the previous Thursday and had come back to take it and sell it. He said that he'd seen it when he'd stopped his van to adjust the load. He changed his story when the absurdity of doing so on the steep Rookwood Street hill was pointed out to him. They kept on with the questions, but all they could get was confessions of his housebreaking that night in Claremont, Peppermint Grove and Mosman Park.

Inspector Lamb decided to bring in Detective Sergeant Gordon Moorman. If anyone could get anything out of Cooke, it was Moorman, who had dealt with him on many occasions and had established a good relationship. The phone rang about 2.30 a.m. and at first Moorman didn't understand when the boss asked him if he'd dealt with Cookie. He suggested another officer, thinking the boss was referring to another Cooke who was also a good thief.

'Spargo's the one you want, Sir, he knows this boy better than I do.'

When it was pointed out that it was Eric Edgar Cooke and that he should come in, Moorman quickly made it to headquarters. He'd been involved in the murder hunt earlier in the year but had later been assigned to other duties. He was pleased to be in on it again at the end.

Detective Sergeant No. 2136, Gordon Moorman, was one of Cooke's favourites, probably because he sensed that the 44-year-old detective actually liked him. Moorman had first picked him up after the teenager had stolen a money box from the South Perth church people, then later after he'd stolen a car. The detective didn't like what Cooke did as a hardened criminal, but he found him all right as a person. He knew bullying didn't work on a man who'd had to cope with bullies and scorn all his life. He believed that to get anywhere with Cookie, you had to treat him nicely. 'Baldy' Moorman was a kindly man, so friendly, polite treatment of offenders came naturally to him. And Cooke responded, calling him by his first name and caring enough to convince him to give up smoking – the former naval man realising that this criminal really was probably saving him from lung cancer. The two sometimes met by chance at football matches, the Perth-supporting detective who'd played a few games for Perth A-grade and the Swans-supporting burglar having a chat during the game. Moorman approached Cooke this night with the same friendliness and courtesy as always. But he was surprised to find that he was the man they'd been chasing – he hadn't thought Cooke could be so cold and so callous.

While the questioning continued, Thomter and officers from the scientific bureau searched Cooke's car at central police yard. In the back of the Holden they found an empty .22 cartridge case.

After working right through the night, they took a break from questioning at 6 a.m., when all, including the suspect, had some breakfast.

Hawker tried again. 'Are you sure you want me, boss? There's nothing I can do.' Then it was explained. In that night of glory for the police force, the boss wanted to go out to the scene to see it for himself. Hawker rang home to tell his wife Mary that he wouldn't be in at the usual time.

'There's either been another murder or you've got him,' this experienced police wife said.

'Well, there hasn't been another murder,' he replied, officially maintaining security on the night's success.

'Thank God for that,' came the reaction.

Hawker accompanied the chief in his car back to the scene, the early morning light piercing the mist over the river as they drove along the freeway. Before they left, Inspector Lamb picked up the phone and dialled 64 2026, explaining that he had to get Ralph Wheatley there. The ruse had worked and he had to keep his side of the bargain, to give either of the two journalist confidants first go at the story. With no *Daily News* on a Sunday night, Wheatley was the lucky one to get the story for Monday's *West*.

Ralph Wheatley woke at 6.30 a.m., early for a Sunday. Remembering it was Father's Day and he could expect breakfast in bed from stepsons Gavan and Dion, he decided to get up and make the tea anyway rather than wait. He rolled out of bed quietly and switched on the kettle, then went to the front lawn to pick up the *Sunday Times*.

It was about 7 a.m. and he was bringing the first cup of tea to Nancy when the phone beside the bed rang. A voice at the other end spoke rapidly: 'Meet me at the Raffles in ten minutes with a photographer.' No name was given and none was needed. Wheatley recognised Cec Lamb's voice.

Wheatley hurriedly phoned the *West*'s chief photographer, Doug Burton, to arrange a cameraman. He didn't know what was on – they were probably cordoning off the area with a gunman in the middle. He then dressed quickly, reassured Nancy that she wasn't in danger if she heard shooting – it would be down the hill, far enough away from home – and drove his Holden at high speed to the Raffles Hotel. Watching Canning Bridge from the carpark, he had to wait just a few minutes before a fleet of police cars crossed it and stopped along The

Esplanade. Wheatley drove across the highway and pulled up behind the fleet, getting out to meet Inspector Lamb.

'Bloody good show. Congratulations,' was the Englishman's response to Lamb's news.

'Come on, I'll show you the set up. Where's the photographer?' he asked, just as Maurie Hammond pulled up.

It was an excited group of police who examined the scene, Inspector Lamb and Inspector Douglas at the lead. Sergeant Ron Gillies and Maurie Hammond photographed the scene – the tent, hidden above the street behind the fence, the gun hidden under the branches and flowers, the group on the road by the bush. Then it was off to the Keehners in Hawkins Street to give them the good news that their imposed silence was over and to thank them for their cooperation.

Though relieved, it wasn't such a surprise to Mum and Pop. Their son Bill, who lived next door at 1 Hawkins Street, had been out the previous night. When he came home late he went next door and woke his parents, saying they must have caught someone up the road because it was all lit up. Despite the interruption to their sleep, the elderly pensioners were up at 5 a.m. as usual. So they were dressed and had finished their toast when there was a knock on the door about 7.30 a.m. Mum asked Inspector Lamb about the man they'd caught. When she heard he had a lot of children, her heart went out to them. She guessed they'd have little presents for him for Father's Day and he wouldn't be coming home. The kindly mother of six was worried for those kiddies and it showed in the newspaper shot of Inspector Lamb thanking the Keehners at their front door.

It had been a long night's work for Hawker and as he finally drove home at about 10 a.m. on Sunday, the relief and excitement at what they'd achieved starting to sink in. It called for a celebration. He stopped to see a publican he knew, explaining that he didn't have any money but he needed half a dozen bottles of beer. The publican gave him credit and he arrived home exhausted, but happy and ready to call a few close friends and ask them over for a drink.

After filling the bath for a long soak, he lay thinking about Cooke and the gloves, torch, panties and social pages: he put two and two together. As a detective attached to the Inglewood Station, his district included the up-and-coming new suburb of Dianella, where there was a spate of break-ins at the homes of the brides on the wedding day. Could it have been him? He'd learnt from the newspaper's social pages which houses would be empty during the wedding.

He also remembered the house where a cheque book was stolen and a cheque used to buy parts for a Holden. He and his partner went to the spare parts dealer and spoke to the salesman, who remembered the customer quite well. He'd bought all the parts necessary to overhaul that same model Holden the gunman had been in tonight and asked for a 15 per cent discount. But it was the salesman's description that pointed to the offender being a cunning Cooke. He'd had a plaster over his top lip, saying he'd got into a bit of a blue at the John Barleycorn pub on the Saturday night. This information had sent the two detectives out to the pub in the hope of a further lead on the wedding night burglar. But now Hawker realised that the plaster had probably been used to hide a hare lip.

He was lying in the bath, his head full of thoughts of the night's catch, when he had a surprise visitor – a friend who was a printer for the *Daily News* dropped in and the constable, still sworn to secrecy, talked cautiously to him from the bathroom.

'How are you going, Bill?'

'Not bad,' the thrilled constable replied.

'Are you getting any closer?'

'No, not yet.'

'Oh well, see you later.' Hawker realised his friend would soon regard him as the biggest liar of all time.

Thomter, too, had to lie to keep the secrecy ordered by the boss. Straight after finishing work in the morning, he and his young family drove to Busselton to see his parents for Father's Day. His mother and brother were later furious that he hadn't told them about his important night's work, letting them carry on a long conversation speculating about who the killer could be.

Early on Sunday morning in Peppermint Grove, Tony Manford had a word to the live-in baby-sitter about security. When he and his wife Toby had come home to 41a Irvine Street from their evening out, they'd found the back door open. But Delores denied it, declaring the opposite – that she had found it open in the middle of the night and had closed it. She said that one of the three children had woken and wanted a drink, she'd seen the door open when she went to the kitchen and had closed it before going back to bed.

It was a mystery until the phone rang about 7 a.m. Detective Sergeant Nielson was on the line, asking if the Manfords had money missing from the dressing table. On confirmation that £17 was gone, the detective informed them that during the night they'd caught a man who had told them he'd been in their house and hidden while someone went to the kitchen.

John Button awoke to another routine Sunday at the prison: cells open half-an-hour later, out to the yard to empty the bucket and wash, pick up the porridge, back inside the small cell to eat breakfast, then out in the yard for the day.

But today was Father's Day, the day when he would bring Charlie his favourite eggnog in bed, hassling Jimmy to help, trying to make their father feel a little bit special. He could do nothing for him this year but say 'Happy Father's Day' on the next visit. John sat in the yard, glumly, thinking about his father. He recalled his first memory of him, the time when Lilly was having Jimmy. John, three years old, wasn't allowed into the hospital to visit his mother. Left sitting alone in the car while his father went in with Margaret, he felt abandoned, so wanting his father to come and get him.

Now, at nineteen he felt just as abandoned and wanted to see his Mum and Dad. But he also felt miserable at the pain and humiliation he was causing them. For the next few years all he could do for his father was drag him down to Fremantle on the occasions he could get away from work – and put him through the depressing procedure of entering the thick limestone walls for a half-hour talk and an emotional grip of his arm.

In the Cooke household in Rivervale, seven little children were waiting expectantly for their father to come home. They'd made a gift for him and had hidden it. Now they were up early, gleefully looking forward to the thrill of his finding their offering in the game of treasure hunt.

When there was a knock at the front door at 8.15, they squealed with delight and raced each other to open it. But it wasn't their father. When they ran back to tell their mother Sally there was big man at the door with a hat on, she knew immediately it was a detective and that her husband was in trouble again.

Detective Sergeants Nielson and Dunne told her at the door that they had Cooke for breaking and entering and had a search warrant. She was used to the police, but there hadn't been a search warrant before. She knew his theft must have been something big this time, and wondered if he'd broken into a bank. They sat her down in the lounge room and asked her whether she was pregnant before breaking the news.

They wanted to check his alibi that on the night Shirley McLeod was shot he'd been at the bowling alley until 8 p.m., gone home and stayed there. Sally had been asked by her husband to give him an alibi once before, on the night of Jillian Brewer's murder. But she hadn't been questioned by the police, and anyway, it had nothing to do with Cooke – Darryl Beamish had done that. Knowing he was suspected of murder, she didn't have to think about it, she readily told the truth and gave a written statement. He had come home late.

When the detectives returned to central and showed Cooke Sally's statement, Cooke said he didn't believe it was her handwriting. He told Moorman he wouldn't say anything before seeing her. She was brought in. She was a loyal wife despite the torment he'd given her, but she was also intensely moral. She told him that she had written the statement.

'Why did you do it?' he asked.

'Because it is the truth, Eric, and you know it.'

'What do you think I should do now?'

'That's up to you, Eric.'

Detective Sergeant Max Baker had his first Sunday off for months, and was finally able to get to his beloved Claremont Football Club. He was a former footballer, playing in his youth in the country town of Waroona and later making it into Victoria's Gippsland League. When he joined the police force at the age of twenty he was based at Claremont station and played League scratch matches and reserves for Claremont. He kept playing throughout his career. When he finally gave it up, he served on the committee and was chairman of recruiting.

The club was entertaining some country recruits this Sunday and Baker was pleased to get there at last after the months of long hours of duty in the hunt for the killer. He had just arrived at the club when he was called in to work. Like Moorman, he'd had previous dealings with Cooke and Cooke liked him.

Baker knew how to deal with Cooke; he knew he'd have to sit and talk and wait. With Cooke, there was no need for some of the methods detectives used to get fellows to cough when they were absolutely certain they had the right person but not enough evidence. With Cooke there was no need for a bit of rib-tickling to persuade him it was far better if he told the truth. With others it was very difficult not to add a little bit to the interview like 'I'm glad it's all over', or use more drastic methods like dangling the suspect out the window of the CIB interview room, two storeys up. Baker remembered the time he and another detective were doing this, hanging a suspect out the window. He and the other detective looked down to see a group of people looking up at the fellow who had a pair of arms around him and who was shouting blue murder. They hadn't realised a new bus stop had been put in Beaufort Street, right outside the window. Baker rushed downstairs and ran under the window, yelling up from the pavement for the observers' benefit: 'For Christ sake hang on to him, don't let him jump.' They told the others, too, that the suspect had rushed over to the half-open window to try to get out. There were many things done that weren't in the Evidence Act, which was going out of bounds a bit, but it was better to have criminals off the street and the cops were there to do that – the end justified the means.

But not with Cookie. If Cooke was the one, he'd eventually say so. Not if you asked directly – he'd deny it. You had to sit and chat and eventually produce some evidence. Baker had heard it before.

'Not me, Mr Baker, no no, you don't think I'd do something like that, no no.' It wasn't until some evidence had been put to him and he'd finally decide the game was up that he'd reach into the detective's top pocket for his pen and say: 'All right, what do you want to know', ready to write out a confession.

Baker left the football club, went home and picked up Richie Benaud's book *Spin Me a Spinner*, then went to central to see Cooke in his cell. Knowing you couldn't rush in with Cooke, he didn't even ask him anything. He gave him the book and chatted, and waited.

The scientific team under Leo Murphy and Jimmy Woods worked quickly, testing the cartridge case found in the car. By the end of the day they were able to prove that it came from the gun that had killed Shirley McLeod.

Cooke's game was up. He took Moorman's pen out of his pocket and wrote out his confession, admitting to shooting McLeod, but claiming a partial blackout or grey-out.

Late Sunday Cooke was charged with the wilful murder of McLeod.

Ralph Wheatley was in Inspector Lamb's office that night with the other inspectors, Athol Wedd and Fred Douglas. The sergeants' door across the narrow passageway opened and the sergeants came out with Cooke. Detective Sergeant Des Ayres, who'd overseen the rifle testing during the investigation, walked down the passage with Nielson and Dunne as Cooke was brought past.

'Hello Mr Ayres, how are you?' the man charged with murder said to the detective whom he'd not seen since he charged him with car stealing eight years before.

'Goodnight, goodnight, goodnight,' Cooke called out cheerfully to anyone else in earshot as he was led away.

Lamb declared that they all deserved a drink – and the officers and the reporter followed him down the stairs, past the lockup where Cooke had been taken and across the yard to the wet canteen where some ordered scotch and water, others beer.

The pressure of the past seven months was finally lifted. At last they had their man.

A Cooke's Tour

3–20 September 1963

News of the capture in Monday's newspaper brought enormous relief and happiness all around Perth. It brought shock and disbelief as well to those who knew Cooke.

None was more amazed than his employers, Sol and Jack Krasnostein, who couldn't believe that their hard-working, quiet truck driver wouldn't be turning up for work as usual. Sol Krasnostein was reading the paper over breakfast.

'There can't be two of them,' he exclaimed as he read the name. He quickly dialled the warehouse and spoke to the sales manager. He didn't need to ask the question.

'Frank.'

'Yes, it's him.'

If the police had come to Sol Krasnostein and said they thought he had a murderer among his staff, Cooke would have been one of the last he'd have thought of. Only when the police came to look around later did he learn more about his employee. A cache of violent magazines was found hidden behind one of the outer stores, where Cooke would sometimes eat his lunch on his own.

A mile away, Jack Krasnostein's wife Norma gasped. He'd recently been in her home, and she'd entrusted her son to him. Their first daughter was getting engaged and they were celebrating with a huge party at home. Needing to hire equipment for the hundreds coming, Sol suggested that a truck driver from the firm could help with it. They chose a helpful, trustworthy one – Cooke. He went off with their young son to collect the equipment and set it up at the house. Norma made him a cup of tea, and, as it started to get dark, he reminded her to be sure to lock up and be very careful because of the murderer still on the loose.

All of Perth was curious to see the Nedlands Monster. Channel 7's cameraman joined the crowds at the Perth Police Court. But they caught only a glimpse. It was a quick appearance, at which Cooke was remanded in custody for eight days. He was hidden as he was led to and from court.

Cooke was taken back to the CIB for further questioning. To be totally triumphant, they had to get him to crack on the five Australia Day weekend shootings. Even though the murders were done with a different gun, it was clear that they were Cooke's work, now that they knew what he was really capable of.

They took Cooke around the western suburbs, continuing their questioning as they drove. Cooke, seated in the back between two detectives, happily told them about his many break-ins. But they were getting nowhere on the other murders.

Penelope Ritson missed the news of Cooke's arrest, leaving Perth early to return home to Boyup Brook. The occupational therapy student was on holidays at home, but had gone to Perth for a friend's kitchen tea, staying overnight with her twin aunts in The Esplanade, Peppermint Grove. Elizabeth and Margaret Evans, totally unaware of the other visitor they'd had that night, joined the rest of the people of Perth in relief at the end of the months of terror.

On Monday Elizabeth Evans went to work and Margaret set about the usual Monday washing. About mid-morning there was a knock at the door. Margaret opened it to a detective who wanted to talk to her about the intruder. She explained that the man they had previously reported for hanging around the riverfront had been identified as a local with a mental disability and returned to his father's care. She couldn't think of anything but this; an intruder on Saturday night meant nothing to her. When the confusion was cleared, she was dumbfounded to hear the intruder's accurate description of her house, her sister and her niece. But neither she nor Elizabeth had lost any money or a transistor. That part wasn't accurate.

While the detective was with her, she rang Penelope, the niece who had stayed overnight in the garden room, and asked if she'd lost anything. No, she hadn't, was the teenager's surprised reply – until she went and checked her bag and purse. Yes, about ten shillings was missing, along with her transistor. As well, Penelope told her, when she got in from the kitchen tea, she thought she'd heard something outside. Peeking through the curtains, she didn't see anything, so decided she just had the jitters about the murderer at large and forgot about it while she had a long shower.

It was a shock to discover that someone had come in and stolen from their home without their knowing it. But that was nothing compared with the news of who the intruder was. The detective said he had Cooke in a car outside and asked if he could bring him in to check his description, advising her to get on with her work and ignore him. Margaret was fascinated but didn't dare look at him. She stayed in the laundry while Cooke walked through the house again, showing the police where he'd gone and what he'd done. Before they left, the police handed back Penelope's transistor and money.

The police continued their efforts on Tuesday. They had confessions to many burglaries and car thefts, but they couldn't break him on the Australia Day weekend shootings.

It had been a long morning driving around the streets of the western suburbs. Nielson was in the front of the car and Cooke was sandwiched between Baker and Moorman in the back. They took a break for a counter lunch at the Albion Hotel, a regular haunt for the detectives on Stirling Highway in Cottesloe. There, over his curried chicken and rice, Cooke finally gave in to the efforts of the two detectives.

Baker, certain that Cooke was the culprit from the way he'd reacted as they drove past the houses where people had been shot, had produced a powerful argument. 'Cookie, you're going to hang, there's no two ways about that. You'll go to the gallows as a bloody coward for the way you shot these people. Your wife and your kids are going to be reading history about you as a cowardly mongrel who went to the gallows without letting the people know exactly what you've done. So what are you going to do, Cookie – go like that or go there like a bloody gentleman and clear the air and let's all know about it?'

Cooke didn't finish his curry and rice. He reached over to take the detective's pen from his pocket, indicating he was ready to give a confession.

The game was over. He'd played it to the limit to get back at the society that had shunned him, to overcome his powerlessness against his father, to be a winner. Now he would clear his conscience.

They went to Garrick Agnew's house, then drove five blocks north up Marine Parade, turning into Napier Street to the base of the Cottesloe Civic Centre wall where Cooke confirmed the details.

Certain that Cooke was ready to tell all, they went back to the CIB office in Perth to collect the police photographer. Sergeant Ron Gillies had been busy these past months at the scenes of the crimes. Now he was to return for more photos, this time with the perpetrator showing how he'd done them. Cooke was prepared to have photos taken as part of his confessions, despite his no longer looking his dapper self. He still wore the dark striped suit he had on for his Saturday night out when caught. But he had a couple of days' stubble and looked dishevelled after two days in the lockup, especially compared with the detectives in their three-piece suits and hats.

Cooke's tour began.

Cooke directed the detectives over the Narrows Bridge to 30 Karoo Street. A Holden, registration UHK 268, was in the driveway. He told them that was the car he'd taken to get to Cottesloe on Australia Day. Going in to see the owner, Henry Threlfall, Nielson learnt that he had never known his car had been stolen – but he had wondered how the interior light globe had gone missing. An insurance assessor, Threlfall had parked his cream-and-yellow Holden in the garage at 11 p.m. and gone upstairs to bed. At 8 the next morning he saw it there in the garage just as he'd left it. It wasn't until Monday evening, when he next took it out in the dark, that he noticed the interior light wasn't working. Thinking the globe had blown, he removed the cover to find it gone. He thought it was very strange, but didn't believe it was worth reporting to the police.

They drove back the way they'd come, over the Narrows Bridge. The back-seat passenger stopped them near the middle of the bridge, telling them he'd thrown the gun into the river near light pole No. 324. Detectives who described Cooke as having a memory like a bull elephant still marvelled that he could quote the number on a light pole seven months after noting it. Leaving the car, Cooke showed them how he'd thrown the gun.

From there they went back to Agnew's house for photos of the wardrobe where he stole the Winchester, Napier Street for photos showing how he shot at August's car, then around the corner to Broome Street for photos illustrating the shooting that had taken the useful life of Brian Weir. After that they went to Vincent and Louise streets for exact details of how he'd shot John Sturkey and George Walmsley. He posed for photographs at each place, readily showing how and where he'd held the gun to destroy so much talent and promise.

'Why?' they kept asking.

'I just wanted to hurt somebody,' he kept saying.

It was late in the afternoon when they'd finished hearing the details of those five shootings and drove Cooke back to the CIB. He wanted his wife present before he gave his final confessions. There, before his wife, Sergeants Nielson, Dunne and Moorman, he used Moorman's pen to write out confessions on each one. When he came to Sturkey, Nielson again asked him why he'd done it. Cooke became quite emotional.

'I didn't have any reason. He was so young and never had a chance. I will never meet him because he will be up there and I will be down there. I'm just a cold-blooded killer.'

Late on 3 September he was formally charged with the wilful murder of John Lindsay Sturkey and George Ormond Walmsley, the attempted murder of Nicholas August and the unlawful wounding of Rowena Reeves.

The next day he was in the Perth Police Court to face these

charges. Magistrate K. H. Hogg was face to face with the man who'd brought so much heartache to his daughter. With the other new charges, he remanded Cooke for eight days on the wilful murder of Sturkey.

Later that morning Nielson and a ten-man diving team from the underwater recovery squad went to the Narrows Bridge. Nielson stood by light pole No. 324, raised his arm the way Cooke had indicated, and with an overarm action, threw an old model rifle of the same calibre into the river. The divers slid into the Swan River, heading for the area where the gun had just fallen. The idea worked. It took only three hours for Constable John Dyke to find the murder weapon in the muddy riverbed. The .22 calibre Lithgow single-shot rifle, serial number 58572, lay embedded about 30 yards east of the bridge. He raised the barnacle-encrusted weapon to the cheer of a crowd watching from the bridge.

The rifle and six rounds of .22 calibre Remington-Peters ammunition collected later from 5 Norton Street were handed to Sergeant Murphy. They proved the accuracy of his earlier judgements on the type of weapon and ammunition used. The rifle's owner easily recognised his weapon from the strap he'd put on it. Donald Cornish, the proprietor of Cornish Furniture Works, was horrified to discover what it had been used for. He'd last used it the previous Easter and had only realised it was missing in June, when asked by the police to produce it. He'd owned it for seven years and knew it was a little faulty. Just as Murphy had detected, the bolt was loose and there was a blow-back.

The relief around Perth was immense. People could start living normally again. Carl and Wendy Dowd could finally leave the Bingemanns' hospitality and go home. To many, it provided possible answers to unsolved crimes.

Kathleen Bellis and her family had moved back to Melbourne. Five years after being run down, she was still suffering from her injuries. She had constant pain in her knee and couldn't walk normally. She had a permanent limp and partial deafness in her right ear, on the side of her body that took most of the impact. Phil's mother mentioned in a letter that Perth's murderer had finally been caught and everyone could relax at last. As soon as he learnt that Cooke lived in Rivervale not far from where they had lived in Belmont, Phil decided that this must have been the person who'd run down Kathy. There was no mention of this murdering gunman doing hit–runs, but Phil was certain. Uncle Albert put the same thought into words at the next family gathering and everyone started wondering, watching the press for an announcement. But there was no mention of any hit–runs.

In Applecross, out of the blue, Lucy MacLeod said it might have been Cooke who'd caused that head injury to her daughter Mollie. A preposterous thought – how could that be? How could he have got in? Why would he have done it? Why hadn't he killed her then? It didn't make sense, it was impossible, so the off-hand remark was forgotten, never to be raised again.

Sam Clarkson and his wife, back from their overseas trip to a completely changed Perth, immediately recognised the murderer's photo in the paper. It was the man who'd been prowling around the Hughes' place. He remembered how he'd humiliated the prowler and warned him off. He wondered if his actions had really frightened him off or, because of their trip, he might never have had the opportunity to retaliate.

When Phyllis Thompson heard that the murderer had a hare lip she immediately recalled that frightening time when the twisted-mouthed stranger had walked into her kitchen. A newspaper photo confirmed her suspicion that it was the same person and she thanked the power behind the intuition that had warned her to remain calm and polite.

Perth was never the same again. Never again would doors be left unlocked and keys left in cars. No longer would people enjoy the safety of a big country town where everyone could be trusted. Perth had grown up to become a city of suspicion and locked doors.

While those who knew Cooke were stunned that this charming, helpful man could have such an evil side to him and the rest of Perth was moving freely at night again, Cooke was telling the police about all his crimes. Kept in custody in the Perth lockup,

Cooke spent the days of the next two weeks driving through the suburbs pointing out premises and giving minutely accurate details of crimes he had committed over the past five years.

Cooke's memory was extraordinary. He could provide detail that seemed impossibly trivial, which often proved he'd entered a house when the occupants had no idea they'd been burgled. Many Perth householders were startled to be approached by a detective who described the interior of their homes. Sometimes they'd remember losing some money from a purse or wallet – having previously thought they'd just overspent or silently accusing someone else in the house of having taken it.

Detectives compiled a list of 30 burglaries Cooke told them about. But the list could have gone on and on and taken forever for them to investigate, because Cooke admitted to entering around 250 houses. Some of the 30 they were able to confirm; others could not be verified because there'd been no report or the owner was not aware of a break-in or anything missing. In the end, they made do with the twenty they could confirm, and Cooke was officially recorded as committing only those.

The amazing detail Cooke gave the detectives included even precise amounts of money stolen from each place. The detectives were sometimes less accurate, ticking Cooke's confession of stealing £7 or £8 from 10 Waterloo Street, Mt Hawthorn after breaking a piece of leadlight window to get in, but listing the owner as 'not known', even though the theft at Robert James McPhail's house had been reported and investigated by his friend Constable Ralph Featherstone, who'd been present socially when the burglary was discovered.

The attack on Mollie MacLeod was listed only as a break and enter, not as an assault. Cooke told detectives he went to 55 MacLeod Road, Applecross, walked down the right side to the back, got in through a sleepout arrangement, went to the kitchen, stole a few bob, went outside to relieve himself and when coming back in, the back door slipped out of his hand, waking up a girl aged about sixteen. He said he hit her with something handy. The detectives ticked this on the list of his confessions, adding the misspelt name McLeod to it, but did not record this as an assault. Nor did they advise the MacLeod family, who continued to think Mollie had fallen out of bed.

Cooke confessed to attacking women while they were asleep on four other occasions over four years. These were thoroughly investigated as assaults causing bodily harm.

He made the first confession to this type of crime on 10 September. He took the detectives to Bellaranga Flats, at 93 Stirling Highway, in Nedlands. Sitting in the car outside the block, he pointed to the upstairs middle flat, No. 3, and told the detectives that he'd assaulted a woman who awoke in her bedroom when he was raiding the flat three or four years earlier. He couldn't remember the date, but he could remember exactly how much he'd stolen from her purse – £6, including one £5 note. He said he hit her on the head, near the temple, but he couldn't remember if there was anything in his hand or not.

Four days later Cooke wrote out his confession by hand and signed it. The police found Alix Doncon, the former trainee nurse who still suffered severe epilepsy from the attack four years previously. Confirming with her that he'd remembered exactly the amount stolen, they informed her that the identity of her assailant was Cooke.

At 5 p.m. on 10 September, Cooke and the detectives were parked near Hampden Road in Nedlands after a long day of confessions, including the serious attack on the woman in Bellaranga Flats. The detectives were now ready to finish, but Nielson checked if there was anything more before returning their prisoner to the lockup.

'Is there anything else on your mind that you feel like telling us about?'

'Yes, I have committed two crimes for which two men are now serving sentence of imprisonment.'

This was a surprise to the detectives. The previous week he'd told them that no-one had ever been charged for anything he'd done. On that occasion, they'd been in a car outside a house and Nielson was seeing the householder. During the conversation between Dunne, Moorman and Cooke, Dunne had said, 'It is a wonder that some poor devil has not been taken on for one of your jobs.'

'You can be assured Mr Dunne that no one has been charged or is doing time for any job I've done.'

Nielson now asked him which crimes he was referring to.

'The killing of Jillian Brewer and the girl Rosemary Anderson.'

Nielson asked who Rosemary Anderson was. 'She was Button's girlfriend. He was sentenced to ten years for running her down in a car.'

Nielson asked if Cooke was sure he knew what he was talking about, and Cooke said he was. Since it was such a serious matter at the end of a big day, Nielson said they would see him for the details first thing next morning. They returned Cooke to the Central Police Station lockup.

Cooke had committed the Brewer and Anderson murders! But men had already confessed to those and were in prison. This was serious. There were nuisances who confessed to things and caused the police a lot of extra work, but those crazies were sifted out. This one had proved he was well capable of committing the horrendous crimes.

Nielson, Dunne and Moorman picked up Cooke from the central lockup the next morning. Referring to his confession on Rosemary Anderson, Nielson asked him to detail his movements on the night of 9 February.

'Yes, I can take you and show you where I got a car from and how it happened.'

Cooke directed the detectives to 1 Leonora Street, Como and told them how he pushed a Holden car backwards out of the driveway, rolled it down the road, started it and drove off at about 8.30. Then he took them through the city to Subiaco, through Wembley to Scarborough and back to Graylands and Shenton Park. Travelling at the speeds Cooke directed, Nielson noted that the journey took about one-and-a-half hours.

In Stubbs Terrace, Shenton Park, he pointed out a position near the Floreat Iron Works. 'It was here I first saw this girl walking along the road. She was on my right on the extreme edge of the road. I drove up towards the telephone box and made a U turn in the wide part of the road there. I drove back.

I hit her as she walked off the edge of the road in the sand opposite the Shenton Park Railway Station. She was scooped up on to the bonnet of the car between the right hand headlamp and the centre portion of the car. She dented the bonnet and came up over the top of the car. I was doing about 40 miles per hour when I hit her.'

Having driven up to the phone box at the junction of Cunningham Terrace and Nash Street, they stopped at the railway station and drove on as Cooke directed them. 'I drove straight ahead to Mengler Avenue, turned right and then left into Brockway Avenue and parked with the left-hand-side wheels up on the footpath. I stopped here for about five minutes, had a good look at the damage and rubbed a few blood spots off the top of the car with my handkerchief. I then returned to where I had hit her but could not see either her or anybody else about at the time.'

They continued on, following the route Cooke was telling them. 'I then drove under the subway and up to Kings Park where I rammed the car into a tree. I left the car there and walked through the bush behind the caretaker's cottage and up to the corner of Hay and Thomas Streets where I used a free phone to call a taxi and drive home in it.' He pointed to the tree he was referring to – it showed no damage at all.

Nielson asked him at what time he reckoned he struck the girl. 'About 10.15. I was home by about 11 o'clock.'

The next morning, on 12 September, the three detectives collected Cooke again. This time they had Ron Gillies with them for photographs, as well as the detective involved in charging John Button with Rosemary Anderson's murder, Jack Deering. Deering had also been involved in the interview of Darryl Beamish over Jillian Brewer's murder.

They took Cooke to the site of Rosemary Anderson's attack. They asked Cooke to show them where the girl was when he first saw her walking up Stubbs Terrace. Cooke squatted and with a piece of yellow chalk wrote 'F' on the road at the point. Still squatting beside the road, with Nielson standing to one side among the dandelions and Dunne on the road beside him, he looked up at the camera and pointed, as Gillies took a photo.

They drove 635 feet up the road until they came to the place where Cooke said he had struck Rosemary with the stolen car. They got out of the car and Cooke wrote 'H' at the spot. With Deering and Dunne looking down at him and Nielson leaning against the police car, Cooke again squatted and pointed for the camera. Then they all stood for a wider shot. Then another shot from the side, in the foreground the tree stump near which John had found her body. Next Gillies took photos of Cooke standing and pointing to the 'H' he'd marked on the road as the spot where he'd hit her, with Deering standing pointing to where the blood stain had been found. The distance between them was less than two car-lengths.

They went back to the detectives' office in Perth where Cooke wrote out his confession:

> On the day of 10th February 1963, I left home at about 2 p.m. catching the local bus and alighting in Adelaide Tce. outside of Fairlanes Bowling Centre. I met some people there and stayed playing bowls until about 5.30 p.m. After having a snack at the Centre I caught another bus and went out to my parents' house in South Perth 31 Pitt St.
>
> I stopped there about half an hour and walked up to the Hurlingham Hotel, had a beer and walked up to the Como Hotel where I had some more to drink. After leaving the hotel I prowled around some house in Norton St South Perth. I went into a house in that street and took some money which was in a bank book. The bank book was in a dressing table drawer, the amount I took was £20, 2 ten pound notes and a bit of loose change in the kitchen. I think the time was about 7.30 p.m. After leaving that house I prowled around some more and finally ended up in Como. At the corner of Saunders and Leonora Sts. I took a Holden sedan car, two tone in colour, it was parked in the driveway of this corner house.
>
> The keys of the car were in the ignition and I drove it out of the driveway, along Mary St. up to the Narrows Motel turned into Melville Parade and drove along the parade to the Narrows Bridge. After crossing the bridge I went up Spring St. and Malcom St. through Subiaco-Wembley to Double

View. In Double View I turned off the main road into Grant St. along till Ewen St. to Sydenham St., along this street to Scarbro Beach Rd. Again along the main road to St. Bridgets Tce., along this terrace to Weaponess Rd.

I went along Weaponess Rd. into Wembley Downs to a street on the right which I turned into this was Purdom St. I turned left off this street into Buxton and went along here till I came to Ken St. At Ken St. I stopped the car and went back to prowl around some houses I had seen, which were in darkness. I decided not to break into these houses as my wife's brother-in-law had told me a detective lived a little way up Buxton Rd. The length of time I were away from the car was about 10 minutes. I got back into the car and drove along Buxton Rd. till I came to Empire Rd. into which I turned and drove until I came to Alyth St., this street led to the Boulevard, Wembley. I drove along the Boulevard till I turned right into Brookdale St. over Cambridge St. to Stephenson Ave. I drove along this Avenue until West Coast Hwy where I turned left.

I drove along West Coast Hwy to Alfred Rd. in the suburb of Mt. Claremont – all the time, well within the speed limit. Along Alfred St. through Graylands, as I neared the intersection of Alfred Rd. and Stubbs Tce. I saw walking towards me a woman and a man with a little child in between the two. I drove down Stubb's Tce past the Shenton Park railway station, I saw a young woman walking towards me, but on the right hand side of the road, she was between Smit's Splicing Service and Wembley Iron Works. I have indicated to detectives the spot where I had first seen her. She was walking at a normal pace towards Graylands, I drove past at 35 m.p.h. and down to the intersection of Cunningham Tce and Stubbs Tce where I did a U-turn, my intention to go back in the direction I had come was to run her down. I can remember wanting to hurt someone and so I decided on this girl I had seen.

I completed my U turn and drove back in the direction I had first come, my speed was at about 40 m.p.h. when I started up towards the walking girl. I didn't stop the car on my way back, the girl I had seen previously was still walking in the same direction and on the same side of the road and at the same pace. I saw her about opposite the Shenton Park railway station, I drove half way off the road straight at her. The left hand wheels were off the bitumen on the verge and I made a sudden swerve to the left to hit her. The car struck her, she was tossed on to the bonnet and bounced onto the hood and over the back of the car. I did not hear any noise apart from the first impact – no scream or that.

I struck her with the front right hand side of the car, in between the right headlight and the centre of the grill. I were doing about 30 m.p.h. when she was tossed over the car and I picked up speed – at no time did I stop or turn around to have a look, I looked in the rear vision mirror, but saw nothing. I don't know how she was dressed, but I have a recollection of something in one of her hands. I continued on till I came to Mengler Ave. where I turned right until Brockway Tce I turned left in to Brockway Rd and stopped the car about half way between the next street.

I drove the car up on to the side of the road and parked it with the left wheels on the footpath, stopped the car, turned off the light and got out to survey the damage. The damage to the front of the car was on the right hand or drivers side of the grill – it was pushed in a bit. I remember thinking that there wasn't much damage really. Where she had struck the bonnet there was a dent and on the hood of the car were a few blood spots. These blood spots I removed by wiping away with my handkerchief. I can't recall if the car was equipped with a sun visor or not. I looked around the outside of the car carefully and couldn't see any more blood or any more damage. I was parked there not more than 5 minutes. I have since indicated to detectives where I had parked this car and also where I estimated I had hit her on the road.

After looking at the car I got in and drove back towards where I had struck the girl – on the way to the scene I passed a couple of cars travelling towards me. My speed was about 35 m.p.h. When I got to where I thought I had hit the girl I slowed down to have a look – but there was no trace of her. When I never saw her lying on the ground I thought some one must have picked her up and taken her to the hospital annexe opposite.

I then drove under the subway along Nicholson Rd. to Rokeby Rd, where I turned right and drove across Thomas St. into Kings Park. I drove along and turned left into May Drive and along on the wrong side of the road and picked out a tree into which I drove the car. This tree was on the right hand side of May Drive as you travel towards the War Memorial, I have shown the detectives this tree, which I had deliberately driven the car against. I were travelling at about 20 m.p.h. when I hit this tree. When I had looked at the car earlier in Brockway Rd. I saw what part of the car had been damaged and so I aimed this portion at the tree. My idea was to cover up any damage caused by me in the hit and run to look like it was due to the crash into the tree.

I jumped out of the car through the left hand door, my reason being to make believe there were more than one person in the car and also to jump clear of the soft sand and thus leave no footprints. I walked towards Thomas St. until I reached the gardeners house turned left and along a fire break until I came to a foot path. I walked along this path till I came out near Kings Park Rd. and walked up to the Children Hospital and caught a taxi home. I never have owned a watch and estimate the time I drove around, from the time I picked up the car until I hit the girl would have been approximately 1 & three quarter hours, that made the time of the hit and run about 10.15 p.m. I arrived home at about 11.30 p.m.

The following day I read about it in the paper and later on during the week read more details where she was found in Stubb's Tce near the Shenton Park railway station and that a car driven by her boyfriend whose surname was Button. The girl's name was Rosemary-Something-Anderson and that she lived in Alfred Rd. Graylands.

My reason for running down the girl was just to inflict injury and pain on her. I never knew her, the reason I left this statement until I were arrested on other matters was:

First:- When it happened I didn't want to be charged with this crime

Second:- Now that I have been arrested on other matters and have so much more against me this bit can't hurt me and I'd like to see an innocent person like Button free.

Cooke signed and dated his confession and Nielson witnessed it. Then Nielson and Dunne went to check Cooke's facts. They found the report of the vehicle stolen from 1 Leonora Street. Cooke's account of stealing a car from there and crashing it into a tree in Kings Park fitted the report.

The detectives went to Swan Barracks to see Arthur Lindsley James' car and check exactly where in Kings Park it had been found. They examined his Holden sedan UKN 547 in the parking area, looking particularly for any signs of damage to the sun visor or hood. They detected no damage of any kind in the car, which had been repaired since the incident. Then they asked James to show them where his car had been found. He accompanied them into Kings Park, but he was unable to select one of the hundreds of trees in May Drive as the one he and his wife had identified the day after the theft. All the memorial trees looked the same, and it was seven months ago. James thought Kath might be able to help them; when the detectives asked her to point out the tree, she took them straight to it. She remembered the soldier's name, Longmore, on the tree, because of her classmate Peggy Longmore. Nielson inspected the Longmore tree. It showed damage consistent with a car having hit it. But Cooke was wrong again. He didn't point to the right tree at all. Among the hundreds of memorial trees in Kings Park, he was wrong by three trees.

At 5 p.m. Nielson, Dunne and Moorman talked to Cooke again, Nielson pointing out to him the discrepancies between the positions he'd indicated and. Deering's positions, which had been produced and proved at Button's trial. It didn't matter that there were similar discrepancies in Button's confession – he also had said he'd hit her opposite the Shenton Park railway station, an impossibility proved by the police plans. But Cooke didn't know that.

'I don't understand it. I am sure I killed her. I can prove it. I didn't drive straight on to Brockway Avenue after hitting the girl, I drove up to the driveway of Lemnos, turned and came to have a look and saw a black European model car at the scene with both doors open. I then went down past the scene and made a U-turn and went up to Brockway Avenue and inspected the damage to my car then.'

Nielson continued: 'From the position you showed us where you reckoned you first saw the girl to where you say you struck her with the vehicle is a distance of about 200 yards. Considering the pace you say you were travelling and the distance you say you covered from the time when you first saw her to where you say you hit her, it appears impossible that these circumstances could have occurred. We have carried out tests and even a person running at a fast rate could not have been where you say she was hit. Moreover, there would have been tyre marks seen in that area by the investigating detectives in the loose sand where you say you hit her. You say she came up over the bonnet and over the top of the car. We believe she was carried on the bonnet some distance before she skidded forward on to the road. Also, certain articles belonging to her were found some distance back from where you say you hit her. Also, you are a way out on your timing, considering the route you say you took that night and the speed you said you travelled. According to your reckoning you must have arrived at this scene about 10 p.m. or shortly afterwards when in fact this girl was hit around about 10.45 p.m. I believe you are telling us lies for some reason only known to yourself.'

Cooke wrote out a retraction:

I, ERIC EDGAR COOKE, states: On Tuesday afternoon whilst at Hollywood with Det. Sgts, Nielson, Moorman & Dunne I were questioned as to whether I had any other matters on my mind which could be cleared up. At the time I had no other thoughts in my mind but Rosemary Anderson & Jillian Brewer who were killed. They were so prominent in my mind that I were perfectly willing to swear on a stack of bibles that I were the culprit of these crimes. And that the two men subsequently serving prison for them could be released. I decided to confess to both of these crimes for that purpose. I now know by visiting the scene in respect to the crime in relation to Rosemary Anderson & having had the facts & positions pointed out to me I find they are the opposite to what I had said earlier. When I admitted to this crime I firmly believed I were the person responsible.

By reading all the available papers on this crime & remembering where it took place & the person involved I were able to describe, what I believe – & what I believe I did.

Having read some books I get so engrossed in them that I project myself & believe I'm the person in those books. Having given further thought to my admissions to the detectives I'm now of the opinion that I couldn't have been the person associated with the death of Rosemary Anderson.

I recall by reading the papers of events leading up to the time when she was killed about the argument concerning the fish & chips – of his parents going out & leaving Button & his brother home with Rosemary Anderson, how they were playing cards & won some articles of clothing off her & how she got into a huff & started to walk home on her own. I also remember by reading & remembering where Button lived it was in Redfern St. Subiaco. Also where the doctor was that young Button took Rosemary Anderson to. His name is Quinlivan & he resides in Alfred Rd. Graylands & she lived in Alfred Rd. as well. In further thoughts I can't remember if I were in Stubb's Tce. or not on the night that Rosemary Anderson was killed. I know that I were in a stolen car that night & that I got this car a Holden sedan, two tone in colour from outside a house on the corner of Saunders & Leonora St. Como of that I'm positive. I know for sure where I finished up with this car, by ramming it into a tree in May Drive in Kings Park. It was nearly 11 p.m. when I did this – I walked away, after crashing the car, through Kings Park & out on to Thomas St. Subiaco. I walked up to the Children's Hospital & caught a taxi home. I got this taxi by phoning through on the free phone & waiting about 6 minutes for it to arrive. I know for sure that I were home by 11.30 p.m.

I cannot positively remember where I went in this car, though I had it for a couple of hours at least. I know that I did use it for the purpose of prowling around somewhere.

> I give this statement of my own free will & it is true & correct in every detail & is given without threats, promises or inducements.

Cooke signed his retraction and Nielson witnessed it. There was no explanation of how Cooke knew such detail about Rosemary Anderson's death. Did he know just as much detail about any other hit–run death? He hadn't claimed he'd killed Alice Kathleen Bennett, who was run down on a crosswalk in Canning Highway on 16 May 1961. The case remained unsolved.

The next day, they picked him up again, this time with Detective Sergeant Leitch, to go through the detail of his confession on the Brewer murder. Before they started, Nielson asked him if he was satisfied with the previous day's investigation, and the sergeant recorded this response, 'Yes, I would like to apologise for what I have done and the inconvenience I have caused.'

The detectives then pointed out to him the discrepancies between his confession of murdering Jillian Brewer and the established facts.

Nielson asked, 'Does this satisfy you that you were mistaken about the whole affair?'

The recorded response, 'Yes, as I said before to you and Mr Dunne and Mr Moorman, I read something and then I seem to live the part in the story. I can see now I couldn't have done it but I had it proved to me one way or another. It seems so real to me sometimes but I see now I couldn't have done it. I am satisfied now, but why do I feel like this about things?'

Again, his memory on Jillian Brewer's 1959 murder had been very detailed. He didn't claim any knowledge of the unsolved murder of Shirley May Williams, whose body was found buried in a shallow beach grave. He didn't claim this one as well, only of Anderson and Brewer.

Nielson suggested Cooke might like to see Inspector Lamb about these two matters and took him into the chief's office, where Inspector Hagan was also present.

'Sergeant Nielson has mentioned to me that you confessed to the Jillian Brewer and Rosemary Anderson killings and now that you have retracted these confessions.'

'Yes, that is right, Mr Lamb, I did not do them. I am sorry if I caused any trouble.'

'Are you quite sure that you did not commit these crimes?'

'Yes, I am quite sure, I am sorry I caused you all this trouble.'

The detectives collected Cooke the next day to continue the trip through the suburbs of Perth. On 13 September he continued telling them about break and enters and they kept surprising householders with accurate descriptions of the interiors of their houses, remembered by Cooke.

There were more serious ones, too, more of the attacks on women like the one at Bellaranga Flats he'd told them about three days earlier. He took them to 8 Hawkstone Street, Cottesloe, and told them about the attack on a woman who woke while he was in the front sleepout.

He also took them to 124 Broadway in Nedlands and pointed out flat No. 2. Cooke described in detail how he'd stolen a piece of towelling from a clothesline in Fairway and tried to strangle and rape a woman asleep in the flat, tying one arm to the bedhead with a stocking when she started to come to. He wrote out these confessions and signed them.

On Saturday he took the detectives to the industrial part of Bayswater and showed them where he'd driven at a girl walking along the road late at night.

A hit–run! When he'd told them about the Anderson hit–run, it had seemed quite out of character, just not his style. Now he was telling them it was. Cooke gave them the details of how he watched this girl walking along the road before coming up behind her and running her down. He showed them where he'd stolen the car from Gardner Street, Como, and where he'd abandoned it on the corner of Munt and Irvine streets.

Then another hit–run. He took them to 210 Ewen Street in Doubleview and described stealing a big Chrysler or Dodge car, driving it out to Queens Park and running down three girls who were walking home from the station. He showed them where he hit the girls and where he abandoned the car just over the Oats Street crossing.

On 14 September he wrote confessions to these two hit–runs, and also the assault he'd told them about earlier, on the girl asleep in No. 3 of Bellaranga Flats.

On 16 September they collected Cooke from the lockup and he continued with the details of his violence as they drove around. He told them about three more hit–runs and another assault on a sleeping woman.

At 101 Smyth Road he pointed out Flat C and described stabbing at a woman with an umbrella when she awoke during his prowling. He showed them a spot in Hill View Terrace, Bentley, where he'd run down a woman cycling alone at night way back in September 1958. It was the first time he'd used violence, he said.

He showed them the house he'd stolen the Consul from in Mackie Street, Victoria Park, and where he'd abandoned it. At a block of flats in Leonora Street, Como, he pointed out another carport from which he'd taken a Morris Minor.

Then he took them to Daly Street, Belmont, and described how he'd seen a girl leaving a bus late at night and walking down deserted Daly Street. He told them how he ran down the girl and left the car bogged at the site. Moorman had been involved in this investigation and he was finally getting the solution. Another hit–run: Cooke pointing out a driveway in Coode Street, Como, where he'd stolen a utility with a Geraldton number plate and driven to Homewood Street, Belmont, where he ran down a woman after she'd got off a bus and abandoned the car at the Neptune garage in Oats Street. Cooke hand-wrote and signed confessions to all these.

There were five hit–runs and five attacks on women in their beds. All the details fitted the crimes that had been reported at the time. Thorough investigations through police records and with the people involved all checked out accurately.

All the hit–runs were solidly established as Cooke's doing; Cooke was recorded as the perpetrator and the files closed. There were a few little errors in his confessions, but these weren't cause for retractions. He was out by a few streets on where he abandoned the car on the first hit–run; he got the name of a street wrong in the fourth hit–run and on the second, he was one-and-a-half years out on the date. He said the

Homewood Street, Belmont, hit–run had been in April 1960, when it had been on 27 December 1958. These slips of memory didn't matter, even though his memory was generally infallible. Everything else was so spot-on, with details that no one else could know, that the detectives were totally satisfied.

All that concern about a maniac driver on the loose, running down women, and now they knew it was Cooke. Despite all the attention given to the hit–runs in the media at the time, the police did not make a media announcement that it had been the murderer, attacking women far earlier than had been realised. The Perth public wasn't told that Cooke had run down six women on five occasions, nor about the retracted confession to another one.

The assaults were also established as his – all of them at first, but then they decided that he was too hazy on some of the detail of the assault on Alix Doncon, despite his precision on the amount he stole. They said he was very vague and hesitant about the location of the flat and where the girl was sleeping, as well as how he assaulted her and how he entered the flat. They didn't advise the victim of this change of mind, but noted this as a false confession on Cooke's record. Officially the attack on Alix Doncon of 9 August 1959 remained unsolved.

While not telling Alix Doncon that they'd decided it wasn't Cooke after all, they didn't tell Mollie MacLeod about her attack by Cooke at all. And, despite being ticked off on the list of offences, it was not listed as a fifth confession of assault occasioning bodily harm, merely as a break and enter. While the detectives knew what had happened to Mollie, the mystery was never solved for her or her family, who continued to believe she'd fallen out of bed.

Anne Melvin, still traumatised and terrified of the dark, read some more headlines about Cooke one morning before heading off to the real estate agency where she now worked. It suddenly dawned on her that this must have been the man who had attacked her, and she confidently told her father that she expected the police to be in touch. She was right. That day, Brennan and Nielson went to Joseph Charles Learmonth Duffy in St Georges Terrace and took her to the privacy of the manager's office. There they read Cooke's confession to her.

She didn't believe all of it. She was certain that he'd been watching her from under the street light and didn't believe he'd entered her flat to steal. She wondered, too, if he'd been checking her previously, maybe seen her at work in the coffee lounge and followed her. But she felt no resentment, just sorry for such a sick person. Brennan was surprised at her compassionate response when he suggested she'd be glad to see him executed.

It was a beautiful sunny day and Dick Cleak, a keen gardener, was out the front working among his roses. His daughter Jennifer was with him, chatting as he worked.

Jennifer saw it first. A Holden pulled up outside the house, in it four of the biggest men she'd ever seen, surrounding a little man in the back seat. She thought he must have done something very unusual to warrant all that attention, when one of the officers in the back seat got out and spoke to her father. She was astonished to hear the officer ask if he'd had a car stolen five years previously, in 1958. After some more questions and answers she heard the policeman say they had apprehended the culprit.

Dorothea Dagg was surprised when a detective knocked on her door and asked if she'd reported some money being stolen from the house a few months before. She told him that her daughter Hillary's purse had gone missing with £4/19/– in it on 1 June, but her daughter hadn't mentioned it at the time because there'd been a wedding and a lot of people through the house and they didn't want to cast suspicion on all the guests.

She told the detective that the people next door had lost a lot of money that night, too. When she asked who had told them about it, she was told to wait a minute while he went to the car to get a piece of paper. Curious, Dorothea followed him to the car and was stunned to see Cooke sitting in the back, flanked by detectives. She went to say something but was stopped by the detective who read to her Cooke's confession, describing the house as the one with the Pekinese dogs. He said he'd known there was a wedding from an item in the *Daily News* about the bridesmaid. Dorothea was stunned, remembering coming home from daughter Valda's wedding to find her four dogs looking frightened and huddling in a corner instead of asleep in their two baskets in the bathroom. And she still had the newspaper article about Norma Lloyd's trip home from New Zealand to be bridesmaid. It all fitted. Then she remembered too, Hillary telling her and her husband Bob just a few nights before the wedding that she'd seen someone with a torch going along the side of the house and next morning had found the gates open.

Maureen Rogers was working at the Metropolitan Markets in West Perth, invoicing for fruit and vegetable packer J.F. McNamara. She'd returned to Perth the January after her hit–run attack and found a job, giving up on finishing the commercial course that had been interrupted by her injuries. Many of her co-workers at the markets remembered Cooke from when he worked there in the early 1950s, and couldn't believe that the kindly workmate could do these terrible things.

One day she got back to her quarters at the YWCA to be told by the matron that two men from the CIB had been to see her that morning and they'd be coming back at 5 p.m. She nervously wondered what trouble she could be in. When they returned they asked her to go to CIB headquarters to check something for them. It was all a worrying mystery until she got to the office and was taken to see Nielson. He told her someone had confessed to running her down and they wanted her to verify the confession. The confession was exactly right.

Terese still wouldn't believe it, even though she was assured by everyone that Cooke had all the details. But it was all in the paper, the fifteen-year-old was protesting. But Cooke had far more exact detail – the driveway he took the car from, where he hit them, where he abandoned the car. And he told of one of the girls trying to flag him down, which wasn't in the paper. Only the three girls and the driver knew that Georgina had tried to get a lift, thinking the car was a taxi.

Georgina Pitman was still suffering from back pain, migraines and a paranoia that someone was out to get her. But she'd tried to put the attack behind her, had married her jive partner and was living in Geraldton with her husband and six-month-old son. She was surprised to answer the door one day to two policemen. They told her they now knew who had run her down and went on to give her the news that it was Cooke.

She was stunned and asked how the police had found her, at a different address and with a different name. The detectives had previously knocked on the door of her old address and spoken to her mother, Anne, telling her that it would ease her mind to know that Cooke had confessed to the crime.

When Jess Connell read about the murders and noted that the murderer lived so close by in Rivervale, she suspected that he was responsible for running down Jill. She rang the CIB and asked if Cooke had run down her daughter. She was told to take Jill to the CIB that afternoon – they would talk it over.

Jill was baby-sitting a boy that day, so the three of them went to CIB headquarters in James Street. Jill noticed a big safe and some papers on Nielson's desk as he told them that Cooke had confessed to running her down and he had the confession in writing. As he read out the confession, Jill tried to read the other papers on the desk, but could only make out the name Glenys Peak. Nielson told them that Cooke had taken the police back to the scene, showing them where he stole the car and exactly where he hit Jill; they'd checked it all out and it fitted exactly – apart from making a mistaken reference to Aberdare Road. Jess then realised that it was most likely Cooke who'd been in their backyard, running away from the car through the houses under construction and across their backyard on his way home to Gladstone Road.

Jill was elated at finally having the answer and proving to her mother that it wasn't any friend who'd turned nasty. But then she heard nothing more. When she told people, they didn't believe her. She rang Nielson and asked when she'd be going to court – a court case and Cooke's conviction would convince everybody. But the detective explained that there'd be no trial on Jill's case. Jill had mixed emotions – angry that a man could be seen as guilty before he'd been tried, but mostly, she felt cheated.

She wanted her day in court. She wanted the public verification that she, too, had been a victim of Cooke's – with the lifelong legacy of a nine-inch scar up the front of her leg and years of physical and emotional pain. There was no court case, so when she told friends about her case finally being solved, they didn't believe her. How could they? Cooke shot people, he didn't run them down on the road.

The Reverend Sullivan went to see Cooke in the Perth lockup as soon as he was able. Pres Sullivan had known him for twelve years, since Cooke had started to attend the main Wesley Church in Perth, and he'd officiated at his wedding.

It was 18 September when he spoke to Cooke in Nielson and Dunne's presence. Cooke told his minister that he had killed others, but he wouldn't give names.

Pres Sullivan made another visit two days later, again accompanied by the detectives. He talked about it again. 'With regard to that matter I spoke to you about the other day, these gentlemen have convinced me that I did not do these killings.'

Dunne asked the Reverend Sullivan to interview Cooke and express an opinion on whether he was telling the truth. An interview was arranged for 31 October.

The three-week Cooke's tour of Perth was over. On 20 September Cooke was transferred from the police lockup in Perth to Fremantle Prison, to await his fate in the solitary confinement of Death Row.

Defence of the Nedlands Monster

OCTOBER–NOVEMBER 1963

A little more than four months after defending John Button, Ken Hatfield was appointed to represent Cooke by the WA Law Society, which offered free representation through its legal aid scheme. Hatfield accepted the case in his usual style of supporting the underdog, seeing Cooke as a 'poor wretched fellow'. He was not optimistic of Cooke's defence having any chance of being fairly presented and did not think there would be any result other than the death sentence.

The junior counsel appointed by the Law Society was a 33-year-old solicitor, Des Heenan, from his uncle's Terrace law firm E. M. Heenan & Co. Heenan willingly accepted the assignment. He felt privileged to be asked to take on such a challenge. He'd previously defended another controversial criminal, Mervyn Fallows, who'd been executed for raping and strangling an eleven-year-old girl. Cooke caused even greater outrage with his multiple random murders. Heenan was also delighted to have the opportunity of working with the highly regarded Hatfield.

Unbeknown to both the junior and senior counsel appointed to Cooke, they had prior connections with him. Heenan had once rented the house in which Shirley McLeod was shot. He lived in 37 Wavell Road for six months in 1959 when he was newly married, and so had been one of the first to volunteer his fingerprints.

Hatfield had represented the Motor Vehicle Insurance Trust against Nel Schneider in her claim for compensation for her epilepsy resulting from the hit–run. She had succeeded in gaining some compensation, despite Hatfield's efforts to claim she was feigning some of her epileptic symptoms. In acting for the MVIT, Hatfield was representing the unknown driver of the car that hit Mrs Schneider – Cooke, as it turned out.

The chief crown prosecutor, Alan Dodd, had also come across Cooke before. At 11.30 one night he'd had a call from the Fremantle Police Station because his articled clerk had been picked up on a drink-driving offence. Dodd collected him from Fremantle and took him back to his unit behind the OBH, took off his coat and boots and put him to bed to sleep it off. Returning to his car parked in the OBH carpark, he was just approaching his blue Mercedes, when he saw a figure spring away from his car. The man ran to a Holden parked 30 yards away and drove off. Dodd thought no more about it until he was talking to Cooke after having learnt all about his break-ins and thefts around the Cottesloe area.

'Were you ever in the OBH carpark?' he asked the lithe man.

'Oh yes, the blue Merc,' Cooke immediately replied.

As soon as the defence team was appointed, Heenan consulted Hatfield. They had a twenty-minute meeting in Hatfield's office at 8.30 a.m. on 19 September. The first task was to talk to the accused, and Heenan immediately rang Fremantle Prison to arrange a 10 a.m. meeting. The young lawyer was curious to see what Cooke was like and as he sat in the taxi alongside his secretary, Miss Dalton, he wondered what kind of man could change the whole style of living in Perth.

At Fremantle they were led through all the clanking gates to the bare disinfectant-smelling cell where Cooke had been placed. Heenan was surprised to find him smaller than expected, pleasant and polite. They sat with Cooke for two hours, Miss Dalton taking formal notes and Heenan scribbling the first-hand account of Cooke's life and his crimes over pages of plain foolscap.

He started with the first murder charge, Shirley McLeod. But Cooke told him he could not remember killing the baby-sitter and had suffered a blackout when leaving the house.

Getting Cooke's account was a long, arduous task requiring six visits. Sometimes Hatfield accompanied him, the three discussing Cooke's defence; at other times Heenan was alone, taking further details on Cooke's activities over the past few years. Cooke went on and the lawyer continued writing, his neat hand deteriorating into a scribble, as the list of serious and petty crimes seemed endless.

Despite little formal education, Cooke was quick, with a remarkable memory. Addresses, descriptions of interiors of houses, street names, suburbs, amounts of money, makes of car ... they tripped off the tongue easily. His lawyer sat in the stifling bare cage hunched over a small table getting it all down.

Suddenly one address attracted his attention: 17 Kildare Road, Floreat Park. Cooke had finished prowling for the night and needed a car to get back to Rivervale. He found one in the open garage, with the keys in the ignition. Heenan thought of his friend Alf McDonald, who lived at that address and who sometimes gave him a lift to work in his 1960 white Holden FB with the tan flash. The Heenans lived in Roscommon Road, Floreat Park, with their three young children. Heenan's wife usually had the car, and the city lawyer caught the bus to work, from the No. 80 terminus in Louth Road. But McDonald often gave him a lift, dropping him off at the GPO in Forrest Place. This was the car Cooke was saying he'd stolen. The Death Row prisoner asked Heenan to give a message to the chairman of the Egg Board and former Claremont ruckman: 'Tell him his accelerator's stuffed. I wanted to get home but had to dump it in Subiaco, the motor was racing.' Cooke said he'd abandoned the car behind a business and thrown the keys over the fence of a nearby house.

On his way home that afternoon, Heenan dropped in on McDonald with the news of Cooke's confession. And sure enough, his friend confirmed it. His car had been found in a rear lane in Subiaco and the car keys were returned much later, after being found in a garden bed by the lane. McDonald laughed at mention of the accelerator. It had been only a problem with the floor mat – it used to slip down under the accelerator, causing it to stick.

Cooke's audacity and memory astounded Heenan. He believed that what Cooke was telling him was accurate, and a lot of it was borne out independently. Cooke was a cunning, clever burglar. He was equally successful in his violence, evading discovery by the police over five years, as well as by people who knew him and professionals who treated him. And despite the best efforts of the police, he was only caught through an incredible chance.

Now in custody, Cooke was telling them how he'd outwitted them even more, saying he'd committed more murders, as far back as 1959, by means other than shooting. They were the stabbing of Pnena Berkman and the strangling of Lucy Madrill. During Heenan's six visits in the latter half of September, Cooke told him about another two murders he'd confessed to – Rosemary Anderson's and Jillian Brewer's. Just over a week after retracting these confessions to the police, Cooke told his lawyer the confessions were true. But right from the outset, none of the police believed him.

Hatfield was excited when his junior brought him the news that Cooke had admitted to running down Rosemary Anderson. He and Bart Kakulas had always been convinced of John's innocence. The jury's decision had really upset the QC; he had been particularly upset by the foreman changing the verdict after those long seconds of deep relief at the first 'not guilty' announcement.

The CIB had not informed Hatfield, as either Cooke's or Button's defence, that Cooke had confessed a week earlier to killing Rosemary Anderson and then withdrawn it. Hatfield needed copies of the confession and retraction, and wanted to know the circumstances under which it was withdrawn – not only for the sake of John Button and justice, but for a more complete picture of what his current client was saying and doing in order to assess his mental state.

Heenan requested copies of the statements. On 25 September Nielson told Heenan that Inspector Lamb was not prepared to make the statements available before the court hearing. Nielson, however, was prepared to discuss them with him.

On 25 October Cooke was charged with two of the four other murders he'd confessed to – the wilful murders of Constance Lucy Madrill and Patricia Vinico Berkman.

On one visit, Cooke had told Heenan he wasn't too sure if he had done these, though he'd confessed. He said he'd certainly been in Berkman's flat stealing. This sort of confusion on these two murders hadn't affected the police's acceptance of them as it had with the Anderson and Brewer murders.

The day before they were preferred, Dodd rang Heenan to advise him of the new charges, and at the same time, Dodd said the police were 100 per cent satisfied that Cooke had not killed Rosemary Anderson or Jillian Brewer. He said they were satisfied that he had committed the five hit-runs he'd confessed to, but no further action would be taken on them.

Further confessions on the Anderson and Brewer murders did not move the police to change their minds. Cooke talked about it again when the Reverend Sullivan visited on 30 October. It was a long talk between minister and parishioner, and Cooke told him quite specifically that he had killed the two women. He said his reason for changing his earlier statement and denying the killings was that he was ashamed of them. He gave his minister a long and detailed account of what he had done.

Cooke's counsel, however, were kept in the dark about what their client was saying. They were frustrated and Heenan applied to the chief crown prosecutor on 5 November:

> In the course of our conferences with Mr Cooke, Mr Hatfield and I have learnt from him that he has signed a written statement in which he admits having killed Rosemary Anderson earlier this year and has also made oral confessions as to the killing of Jillian Brewer. As you are aware, Messrs Button and Beamish respectively are serving terms of imprisonment relating to these two murders.
>
> As we consider this aspect of the matter to be of importance in the conduct of Cooke's defence, we shall be obliged if you will confirm as soon as possible that in fact our client has made confessions in respect to the above matters. In addition, we shall appreciate a copy of each and every written

confession he has made and particulars of every other confession that he has made since his arrest in September.

Your urgent attention to the matter will be appreciated.

The information was not forthcoming. Crown counsel Ron Wilson replied:

> I regret that I am unable to comply with your request. I think it would be contrary to public policy to discuss details of police investigations in relation to offences which have not yet been the subject of preliminary proceedings for committal for trial and which are still wholly the responsibility of the CIB.
>
> You may be assured that at the trial the Crown will do everything it can to facilitate the production in evidence of such documents as may be relevant and admissible.

On 21 November, with only three days until the start of Cooke's trial, Hatfield appealed to the Government in an effort to get copies of these statements. He wrote to the Attorney-General that 'failure to produce them made Cooke's defence a mockery. If any question of Cooke's mentality arose at the trial, the statements he made in connection with these crimes were vital'.

Access to Cooke's confession on Rosemary Anderson's murder was finally agreed at a conference between the prosecution and defence the next day, the Friday afternoon before Cooke's trial began on the Monday. It arrived at Heenan's office later that afternoon with a covering letter from Wilson stating restrictions to their use, including that 'they were to be used only in connection with the defence of Cooke in the present proceedings, were not to be copied and were to be returned at the conclusion of the trial'.

The defence was not given copies of Cooke's confessions on the other hit–runs. But at least Hatfield could now see exactly what his current client had said about the crime attributed to his former client, John Button. Although Cooke had withdrawn the confession under police questioning, he had since insisted to Heenan that he'd been confused by the police – he had in fact run down Rosemary Anderson. Hatfield saw that Cooke had not said in his retraction, 'I didn't do it.' He'd said, 'I can now see I couldn't have done it.'

The confession's relevance to John Button's conviction had to be put aside for the time being, as Cooke's counsel prepared for the trial.

There was no denying the crimes or disputing the facts. Even though Cooke kept saying he didn't remember shooting Shirley McLeod, he had confessed and was not denying those confessions. Insanity was his only defence. And his two counsel found enough background of psychopathic behaviour to be convinced he was insane.

They studied Cooke's medical, psychological and social history. Heenan went to his house and spoke to his wife and children. Her story seemed to support the possibility of schizophrenia – she told him that he was never worried after the murders, and ate and slept normally. Heenan also went to Cooke's parents' house and interviewed his mother. He took down what she told him:

> Eric did not have a happy childhood. He always felt that the other boys were laughing at him. He had a lot of operations and was in and out of hospital. I sent him to a speech therapist but people then did not do as much for children as they do now.
>
> His father would not really accept him. He was an unattractive child. He was a nice little boy, it was just that he wasn't normal like other children and my husband never seemed to be able to accept this. He treated him very badly. He used to beat him up for no reason at all. He just didn't seem to want him. He has been beaten with belts, sticks and bare fists.
>
> If you publish this I am going to get into an awful lot of trouble. I have to live in the house with my husband and he is a very cruel man.
>
> The poor thing – I don't know what comes over the boy. When he was young he used to suffer from blackouts and he had a tumour of the brain. I think Mr Ainslie removed it.
>
> When he was a young lad, about 16 or 17, my husband

accused him of something. My husband was under the influence of drink. My husband bashed him in the head with his fist and Eric's temple hit a light switch which was on the wall between the kitchen and dining room. He had to go to hospital. I think there was a fracture or something. I think that is why Dr Ainslie had to operate on him.

Since Eric has been arrested I have been forbidden to go and see him by my husband. He is wallowing in self-pity and drinking himself to death. I am sorry for the boy and I wish there was something I could do. I only think he has done what he did because he wanted to be a big shot. I believe he shot the people in question because he said he couldn't stop himself from shooting, but I do not believe that he admitted to strangling the girl or anything like that. I think he has just wrapped everything up in a neat little parcel for the police and presented it to them. I think he is just wanting to hit back at the world or something. I can't believe that he is a deliberate killer.

A couple of years ago my husband attempted to murder me. He was put on a bond by the Police Court. I was taken to hospital. I had a compound fracture of the ribs and one of them was piercing my lung. I was on the danger list and a detective stayed with me. I wouldn't charge my husband because I was afraid. He works at Sydney Atkinsons in the spare parts section. I have had to work all my married life because my husband doesn't keep me – ever since the children were at kindy. I am not leaving him now because I have worked for the home and I don't want to leave him to it. On three occasions I have taken him to court for separations. On the last occasion Charles R. Hopkins got a separation for me. This was about ten years ago. I have not worried about it since, but I have been beaten up regularly. The police won't interfere.

The essential element was, however, psychiatric assessment. Hatfield understood that psychiatrists in private practice generally appeared to be unsatisfactory witnesses, but he did not believe it was satisfactory to rely on the opinion of a psychiatrist employed by the Government's Mental Health Services

Department. He applied to the Crown for a medical opinion from a psychiatrist in another State. It was refused. He then requested that Heathcote psychiatrist Ian James be granted access to Cooke for psychiatric assessment. At first consent was given, then it was withdrawn. At this point, Hatfield, who'd been pessimistic about a fair trial, knew they were in trouble.

The Crown refused access to someone junior to the Director of Mental Health Services, Dr Aren Samuel Ellis MB, BS, DPM, the State's most senior mental health practitioner. Dr Ellis examined Cooke, considered his hospital records at RPH and Heathcote and obtained evidence on his mental state from personality tests, an EEG, X-rays and social case history. He found Cooke fit to plead.

Dr Ellis reported that he did not believe Cooke lacked the capacity to control his actions, noting that 'all actions surrounding the event were ultimately directed at concealment' and that there was no evidence of delusions at any time. His report continued:

> I think this man's antisocial reactions can be traced back to his early childhood and his resentment at having been born with a hare lip and cleft palate. The children at school picked on him and he regarded himself as the freak of the family. His persistent stealing, arson and finally murders all seem directed towards satisfying his craving for power over others – in fact he says that 'After I had shot him and I was walking towards the car I felt as though I was God or some person who was untouchable'. He learnt to shoot in the army and found that he had a flair for accurate and rapid shooting and in this way he was able to satisfy the urge for domination. He seemed totally deficient in emotion. He has no remorse for his actions and he has a complete inability to put himself in the place of others or to imagine that they have any rights or feelings. He has been in prison many times, but is obviously not capable of learning from the experience. He admits that his actions are wrong, but having with his own statements committed the murders in January, he took no steps to give himself up or to report the matter to the police. Apart from his antisocial

actions he has managed his personal life reasonably well. He appears to be a good husband and father and although he has had frequent changes of work seems in the main to have provided adequately for his wife and family. The presumption therefore must be that despite his emotional immaturity and inability to learn from experience, he is essentially of sound mind, aware of the nature, quality and expected results of his actions, aware that he has done wrong and although lacking in proper emotional response, must therefore be considered responsible for these actions.

One of the personality assessments on which Dr Ellis based his opinion was compiled by psychologist Leon Blank at Dr Ellis's request. The psychologist had visited Cooke over three days in October to conduct tests. The test findings were summarised in a report:

The general picture is of a person of bright normal intelligence who has a psychopathic character disorder. Beneath a facade of conformity and compliance, pretentious intellectualisation and harmlessness, there is quite a preoccupation with the immediate gratification of his egocentric needs. Primarily he needs to be in a dependent relationship in which he is given love, support, acceptance and a continual building up of his shaky self-esteem. In order to gain these, he exploits everyone with whom he has contact, but the need is so great that it can never be fully met and the resultant frustration finds an outlet in antisocial outbursts. These outbreaks, in terms of his need, can only be directed at people who are unknown to him. The tests show the characteristic sexual naivety, extremely sharp sensitivity to the impression he creates on others, over-alert watchfulness, resistiveness to reflection and introspection and incapacity for deep emotional awareness or involvement which are found in psychopathic character disorders. No evidence of disturbed thought processes or of distorted perceptions of objective reality was found.

Test Behaviour:
The prisoner was most cooperative at all times. He was eager to help in any way possible, stating that he knew that he was going to hang but did want to understand why he had committed the murders. He was remarkably sensitive to the mood of the examiner – e.g. on the barest non-verbal indication he said I must want to get on with the testing and terminated his discussion. He took in every detail of information available in the situation, even reading the labels on the test materials and drawing on his broad range of general knowledge and apparently excellent memory to show off his intellectual and cultural accomplishments. Actually his comments were invariably at concrete or functional level with embellishments which gave a superficial spurious air of abstraction. His manner was forthright, open, engaging and frequently cheerful, with only two or three brief breaks in his composure when talking about his love for and concern about his wife and children.

He was most at ease with the intelligence test where he was working with relatively familiar material, though with the other tests, especially where he could get no indication of what his responses meant, he was less cheerful although still cooperative.

Test Report:
Intelligence and thought organisation: The prisoner's performance on the Wechsler Adult Intelligence Scale indicated he was functioning at a bright normal intellectual level. Full scale IQ = 113, verbal scale IQ = 110, performance scale IQ = 115 – i.e. he is functioning at a level that is better than that of 75% of people in the age range 25–34 and worse than 9% of them.

Comparison of relative achievements on sub-tests and detailed consideration of his performance shows a deferent, ingratiating, conscientious manner mixed with loosely integrated knowledge and pretentious guessing. There does not however appear to be any basic disorganisational breakdown of communicative ability. He manifests a keen, rapid, overalert grasp of situations and his grasp of conventional judgments is appropriate to his general level and cannot be considered impaired. However his concept formation is restricted to a concrete and functional level, never rising to the abstract level one might expect from his general level of functioning. Learning efficiency is also relatively poor, reflecting an impairment of concentration which he overcomes to some degree with conscious effort. His independent creative thinking is on a primitive level, closely tied to concrete observable detail. He is characterised by a noteworthy resistiveness to reflection or introspection, which has its origins in low anxiety tolerance.

Emotional factors:
He presents an excessively polite, orderly and compliant front which does not appear to be conscious play-acting. In ordinary everyday situations he keeps his feelings under strict control and adopts a relatively passive but watchful role. The passivity, compliance and conformity is seen as his mode of coping with a real inability to cope adequately and directly with any emotional impact. Behind the facade of socially acceptable behaviour, there is a preoccupation with egocentric needs and feelings. In general, these needs and feelings are controlled by unconscious denial, reaction formation, isolation and intellectualisation. When these defences prove inadequate, the primitive urges (especially aggression) come to the surface and are carried out completely in ego-syntonic fashion. That is, awareness of the commonly held ethical and moral code is simply put aside for the moment, and the only consideration for others is in directing his actions away from the people whom he has found to meet his pervasive needs for love, acceptance, support and self-esteem. Thus, in effect, he can only vent his hostility on people who are personally unknown to him, and even then he has little awareness of his emotions.

Conception of reality:
The crux of the problem appears from the tests to lie in his conception of the world around him and of his place in it.

This conception is dominated by his dependency needs which are so strong as to be insatiable and he has built up a fund of frustration. People are divided into those who can or should meet these needs, and the others, with whom he has no social contact. His relationships with people are essentially exploitative. His intellectual capacity is largely taken up in a sharp awareness, sensitivity and grasp of situations necessary so that he can, without incurring any hostility, exploit them for his immediate needs. He both needs people and fears them – the latter because they might decide not to accept him as he wishes to be accepted. Several of his T.A.T. stories show a preoccupation with the theme of breaking away from dependent relationships into a bad way of life which leads to punishment, isolation and dejection, followed by forgiveness and re-establishment of dependency relationships. That is, he is quite aware of the distinction between right and wrong, but this is not as important in deciding his actions as the immediate satisfaction of his needs for gratification. To some extent he can satisfy these needs in conscious fantasies, daydreams of a concrete nature in which he can see himself as important, successful, dashing, suave, devil-may-care, with no ties or responsibilities – but this is a very stop-gap measure. Actually, for all of his having seven children, he is sexually naive and afraid of women who might conceivably test his sexual adequacy. The only safe woman for him is the mother.

On receipt of Dr Ellis' opinion, Hatfield requested a second opinion. This was denied him. He enlisted Dr James, giving him all the material he had on Cooke and seeking the doctor's assessment, without his having the opportunity of interviewing Cooke.

Case 11106 began in Court 2 of the Supreme Court on Monday, 25 November, before Mr Justice Virtue.
    Eric Edgar Cooke sat in the same dock as John Button six months earlier, charged with wilful murder. Two of the counsel seated in front of him were the same as those for Button – Hatfield was defending him and Wilson was prosecuting. This

highly successful prosecutor had been made a Queen's Counsel four months earlier, one of the youngest barristers in Australia to receive the honour and the first who had come through the Crown Law Department's clerical staff. Beside their leaders were different junior counsel – Heenan for Cooke and Kevin Parker for the Crown.

Beside and behind Cooke were police officers. To his right were the eight men and four women of the jury. To his left was the crowded press bench, reporters hunched over shorthand notebooks and *The West Australian*'s artist Norm Aisbett sketching his profile, skilfully portraying the low parting of his dark wavy hair, the big nose, the grim down-turned mouth. Upstairs behind him was the crowded public gallery. The man everyone was gazing at was dressed smartly in a dark grey suit with a white pocket handkerchief.

Hatfield's first move at the preliminary hearing was to try to save his client from public scrutiny. He immediately sought to have the hearing held in camera – an application rejected by Magistrate A. G. Smith. Cooke wasn't required to plead, remaining seated and guarded by a police officer as a special ten-foot table was brought into the court for the exhibits, which included a barnacle-encrusted .22 rifle labelled 'Cottesloe-Nedlands', a dressing gown and a blood-stained shirt with a bullet hole in it.

Witnesses detailed the results of his rampage. There had been no explanation, though, of why he did it or his side of the story. No defence at that stage, only the Crown putting its case for the magistrate to decide if there was a strong enough case to send Cooke to trial.

There was. The next day, Smithy, as the magistrate was known to everyone, committed Cooke for trial on the charge of wilfully murdering John Sturkey. He was remanded for a further eight days on the other charges.

On 25 November the public gallery heard the voice of the so-called monster when he pleaded not guilty to the wilful murder of John Lindsay Sturkey at Nedlands on 27 January.

The opening day moved quickly, the Crown completing its

evidence after calling only two-thirds of its 21 listed witnesses. Very few of them were cross-examined. The accused had confessed to the murder and the defence was not questioning the facts of what he'd done but whether he could be considered sane enough to be held responsible.

The defence's angle became clear even before Hatfield's opening address, through his cross-examination of Nielson on Cooke's medical history. On Hatfield's questioning, Nielson revealed he'd been told of the violence Cooke suffered at home and that he'd been admitted to hospital with a facial fracture after a fall and that he had been a patient at the Heathcote Reception Hospital. He stated that inquiries at both hospitals had not indicated brain damage or any mental abnormality.

The report of the much-awaited trial was pushed off the front page of *The West Australian* by the murder of President Kennedy's assassin. There was a big front-page picture of Jack Ruby lunging towards Lee Harvey Oswald a split second before the shooting. The half-page single column item headed 'Murder Trial Moves Quickly' in a far less prominent spot on the right.

On the second day, people heard from the man himself why he did it. The crowded public gallery heard about the feeling of power that came over him, the very strong power as though he were God and had power over life and death. All eyes were on the small man describing how he only approached the car in Napier Street to be a peeping Tom, but the feeling of power came over him as he neared it. The power did not leave him until after he had shot George Walmsley, when he felt deflated, like a pricked balloon. He told the court he knew what he had done, but it was too late. He could not make amends for it.

'Were you able to combat that power?' his attorney asked.

'No, Sir. I wish I had.'

'Did you feel any change come over you in your outlook?'

'I felt these people in the car were not people in the sense of the word.'

'You did not regard them as human beings?'

'No, Sir.'

The story went on, on from the shooting of the couple in the car through to the rest of that night, the power leaving him after he'd shot George Walmsley and was walking back to his car.

'Were you able to prevent yourself doing this shooting?'

'No, Sir. The power was so great in me that I could not, even if I had wanted to, have stopped myself.'

He asked if he could say something else. 'Since I have been arrested I have thought I had 50 bullets. What a blessing it was I hadn't used the other 45 bullets.'

As well as his explanation of what happened that night, they heard the facts of his miserable childhood – the teasing, the brutality, his continuous sinus problem, the blackouts and greyouts.

His story over, he was cross-examined by Wilson, whose job it was to convince the jury that Cooke was sane and able to take responsibility for his actions. Wilson scored a point when he asked why he'd taken the bullets from the Norton Street house, Cooke's reply negating an earlier answer that he didn't intend to use the gun in a hold-up: 'What use is a firearm without bullets?'

Cooke was also able to understand what would happen to him if he gave himself up. He told the court that afterwards, when he read the details, he realised what dreadful things he had done. Wilson asked him why he didn't come forward for treatment.

'I knew I would have to stand trial,' Cooke said.

Wilson also drew him out on the lies he'd told. Cooke admitted to not being wholly truthful in his statements to the police, saying that in every statement some details were true and some were incorrect. He mentioned that while he wrote each statement himself, each was condensed more than he wished it to be.

Then he referred to his other confessions. 'I told Sergeant Nielson other true things which he disbelieved anyhow.'

The Medical Superintendent of RPH gave evidence on his many admissions and medical investigations into his headaches and blackouts.

His wife gave evidence that he was a good husband and father. She said the trouble was she couldn't keep him at home.

The defence's linchpin was Dr James attesting to Cooke being schizophrenic. Dr James told the court it was extremely difficult to distinguish between schizophrenia, which was a recognised mental disease, and a psychopathic state, which was not. He said a psychopath was often said to have no conscience and to be unable to tell right from wrong. With schizophrenia, a sufferer might be unemotional and unresponsive and feel that his actions and thoughts were being influenced from outside. This type of schizophrenia was very hard to diagnose.

Dr Ellis maintained in his evidence that Cooke did not suffer any mental disease.

The packed public gallery also saw Cooke's mother and heard her story about her son. Christine Cooke was so frightened of her husband's reaction that she had to be sedated before giving evidence.

The next day's newspaper report was also full of the aftermath of President Kennedy's assassination – Cooke's trial took second place to the haunting picture of three-year-old John Kennedy Jr saluting his father's casket. But the story spilled over three pages inside, giving a detailed account of the day's proceedings.

The eight men and four women took just one hour and five minutes to find Cooke guilty of wilful murder.

'I have no doubt that was the right verdict,' Mr Justice Virtue told them before they filed out.

'Have you anything to say?' he then asked the convicted man.

'No.'

The judge ceremoniously put a black cloth on his head and pronounced the death sentence.

The condemned man said, 'Thank you, Your Honour, thank you.' He said it almost jubilantly. He winked at Nielson and smiled at the detectives behind him as he was led away.

Murray Drayton, in the Police Transport Section, drove Cooke back to prison after sentencing. Now he'd be taken to cell No. 12 in Death Row, the Condemned Cell. Drayton had driven the infamous prisoner to the preliminary hearing, but this time the task was grimmer. It would presumably be his last trip, the first stage of the journey to the gallows. He wondered what Cooke would say.

Cooke's words took him by surprise. 'Good day, Mr Drayton. Whereabouts do you live?'

The unexpected question alarmed Drayton. Like everyone, he'd been very wary until Cooke's capture, especially since he'd been brought up in the Nedlands area and knew all the murder sites. But the question put him on edge again.

'If this guy ever gets out, he's going to come looking for me,' he said to himself. To the prisoner, he quickly said 'Angove Street, North Perth', not letting on his true address in Claremont – just in case.

With the sentence of death achieved for Sturkey's murder, other charges were held in abeyance.

Hatfield could not understand Dr Ellis' certainty on Cooke's sanity and did not give up seeking another opinion. He was adamant that in such a capital case and on such a complicated diagnosis, one opinion was inadequate. He was equally adamant that Cooke's mental condition justified at least a consideration of commuting the sentence. Three days after the death sentence was passed, he wrote to the Premier, the Minister for Health and the Minister for Justice. Hatfield asked that the sentence not be enforced because he and Heenan still had the gravest possible doubts as to Cooke's mental condition, and again requested that Dr Ian James be allowed to examine Cooke, given that justice and human life were involved.

The request was rejected. Eric Edgar Cooke would hang.

A Beggared Imagination

29 November 1963–22 May 1964

Cooke was not going to stand trial on the other charges. Despite a call by the *Daily News* editor for the 'fullest inquiry' into Cooke's other crimes so that the details were made public, it was not State practice to pursue further trials once a person had been convicted of wilful murder.

With the trial over and no more to prepare for, it was time for Hatfield and Heenan to pursue the matter of their client's confessions to the two other murders.

A day's respite from the trial, and Heenan was back at Fremantle Prison on 29 November to discuss with Cooke an appeal against his conviction. The man in the condemned cell was still as calm as when the death sentence had been passed, accepting the inevitable, and willingly paying the price to society for his crimes. Cooke specifically instructed his solicitor that he was not to appeal against his conviction; he had committed these crimes – he did not know why – and he was prepared to pay his debt to society.

Then Cooke spoke again of Rosemary Anderson and Jillian Brewer and offered to write out his confessions to murdering them, as he had done for the police two-and-a-half months earlier. He said he had been in two minds about whether to raise these matters again, but he wanted to clear his conscience before his execution. He was worried that Button and Beamish might blame him for their misfortunes and retaliate against his family, but his need to face God unencumbered outweighed this concern.

Having confirmed that Cooke was prepared to put in writing what he'd told him on several occasions before his trial, and with the written instruction to contact Button's and Beamish's solicitors, Heenan went back to his office and did so. It was Friday afternoon. After Heenan's call, Bart Kakulas immediately rang Fremantle Prison to make arrangements to talk to Cooke first thing Monday morning about Rosemary Anderson's death.

The public learnt about Cooke's other two murder confessions for the first time when they opened their newspaper on the Saturday morning after he'd been sentenced to death. It was the lead story in *The West Australian*:

> Convicted murderer Eric Edgar Cooke (32) is alleged to have told the police that he was responsible for the deaths of two women for which two men are now in prison. Subsequently he withdrew the claims.
>
> This was revealed last night by Justice Minister Griffith in a statement related to crimes with which Cooke was charged. Mr Griffith said that senior police officers had been satisfied after a thorough investigation that Cooke was not responsible for the two deaths . . .

Readers who read on despite the claims' seeming lack of substance learnt the names of the victims and the convicted men, and that relatives and legal representatives of the prisoners concerned would be allowed to interview Cooke and obtain statements. In the same statement, the minister announced there would be no further trials, but inquests would be held into the Berkman, Madrill and McLeod murders.

On 2 December Bart Kakulas sat at the table in the Death Row visiting cell where a few months previously he'd interviewed John Button about Rosemary Anderson's death. The lawyer looked at the convicted murderer across the table and thought of old times, when they were primary school pupils together.

Cooke was a couple of years older than Kakulas, but Kakulas knew him, as everyone at the school did. He was the target of all the school bullies, and he was always in trouble. Battles were often a part of playground life for the pupils at Highgate Primary School. Kakulas remembered one in particular when the playground divided into two gangs hurling berries at each other. It was all-out war, no one able to tell which side was winning, but it didn't matter, it was fun – until a teacher was seen striding towards the battlefield. The teacher picked out two children, one from each side. Eric Cooke and Bart Kakulas were marched up to the sixth-grade form master, Mr Jones, and stood side by side holding out their hands for six cuts each. On the way back to their classrooms, Cooke, well experienced in getting the cane, gave the first-timer a tip on how to cool his hands by placing them on the cast-iron bars across the underside of his desk.

Now the two schoolyard combatants were on the same team preparing for a different battle – to gain a retrial for Button so that a jury of his peers could weigh up his confession with the benefit of Cooke's confession also before them. Cooke had greeted Kakulas by asking where he lived. After giving his Floreat Park address, the lawyer was relieved to be told, 'No, I haven't been in your house.' But he discovered Cooke had been in the house of one of his friends. Telling the solicitor about his Floreat Park break-ins, Cooke mentioned 31 Oceanic Drive, detailing how he got in through a back window and stole £10 from a sports jacket in a wardrobe. Recognising the address, Kakulas told his friend, 27-year-old radiographer Angelo Anastas, who lived there with his parents. At first Anastas said Cooke must have made a mistake. After thinking about it for a few days, he recalled once missing some money and blaming his mother for putting it in the wash and destroying the paper note.

Anastas had a story about Cooke to tell Kakulas, too. Working at RPH, he'd taken the X-rays of Cooke's skull six weeks back for neurologist Dr Mercy Sadka to analyse, along with an EEG. Cooke had asked the Greek radiographer, who looked a bit like his Greek friend, 'Are you a Kakulas?'

That surprised Anastas, but he was more surprised by the jocular reply to his explanation to his patient that he had to put a band across his chin to immobilise it for the X-ray, 'There'll probably be a tighter one later.'

Their introductory chat over, it was down to the serious business of Cooke's confession. In front of Kakulas, he wrote out his confession by hand, each page witnessed by the prison's deputy superintendent, Ivan Thorpe, a Justice of the Peace:

I Eric Edgar Cooke now of Fremantle Prison say. On the 10th (sic) Feb. 1963 between 9 and 10 p.m. I stole a Holden sedan car, a two Tone, blue. This car was parked in the driveway of a house on the junction of Leonora & Saunders St. Como. The keys were in the lock, I removed the dome light globe. This car I drove over the Narrows Bridge & into the western suburbs. When I arrived in Double View, I parked this car in Vera Street in a service station yard. I then prowled around in that area for a little while. After getting into one house & seeing no other opportunities I went back to the car. This I drove through Wembley Downs & along to Perry Lakes Stadium. I turned right into Stevenson Drive & drove towards West Coast Hwy. From there I drove to the junction of West Coast Hwy & Alfred St. Mt Claremont. Here I turned left towards Graylands, after driving down Alfred Rd., near the junction of Stubbs Tce & Alfred Rd. I saw on my left walking on the road towards me a man & woman. In between the two was a little girl in a white dress. As soon as I saw them I decided to run them down – But after seeing the little girl in the middle I didn't. For I thought of my little kids at home & how I would of felt if that had happened to one of them like that. Turning into Stubbs Tce., I drove towards Shenton Park subway (Nicholson Rd.) when I were near the subway I saw a scooter driven towards me, on it were a man & woman, the man was driving I then decided to run these two over as I saw they weren't wearing safety helmets. When I turned around & started after them they were quite a fair way in front of me & I just overtook them in Graylands on the hill in Alfred Rd. When I were just about to hit them a car was coming towards me, in the other direction. So I waited a bit longer for another try, then after doing a right hand signal the scooter turned into Davis Rd & went in the direction of Claremont Mental Hospital. I then drove up to Mt Claremont where I turned around again towards the subway in Shenton Park. When I reached the subway I was obliged to stop for a car, which was on my right hand side. This car carried on in Selby St & while I were waiting for the traffic to clear, I saw a young girl walking from under the subway on the side of the road. After being cheated of two chances before I decided that I wouldn't be cheated again. I made a U turn in Cunningham Tce & parked the car, near a telephone booth & watched her walk up the road. She was walking up Stubbs Tce. towards Shenton Park railway Station. I can recall she had a handbag in her hand, a flat satchel type. I waited for a few minutes for a few cars to go past her & me, then I started the motor & drove up toward her. When this girl was near a factory (Wembley Wrought Iron Works) I drove the car straight at her, at the time I struck her I were doing 40 M.P.H. I struck the girl with the right hand part of the front of the Holden car, she was scooped up onto the hood for a couple of seconds & then thrown over the bonnet. My left hand wheels were then on the gravel & sand verge of the road. When I slowed down a bit I made a right turn into Lemnos Hospital drive & back again towards where I had struck the girl. As I drove up, I saw in the approximate position where the girl landed, a Simca car, with both left hand doors open. I can't recall the colour of the car, when I drove past I saw a man bending over the girl I had hit. This was right near a tree stump, opposite the railway station. I drove back to where I had first made a U turn near the telephone box & made another U turn, then drove back towards the railway station along Stubbs Tce. As I drove past where I had hit the girl I saw on the road a few bits of cosmetic stuff, which usually is in a woman purse I thought it must of come from this girls purse. Near the tree stump where the girl had come to rest there was no sign of anything & the car which I had seen before was no longer there. I drove up to Graylands & into Mengler Ave & turned into the first street on the left, this street leads to Lock St. Station. Half way up on the left hand side of the street, I parked the car with the left wheels on the footpath. I got out of the car & had a look at the damages, the right front grill was stove in – between the right head light &

the centre of the grill. On the hood was a dent & on the bonnet or roof were about 4 spots of blood, which I wiped off with my hanky, I then got back into the car & drove the way I had come. Going under the Shenton Park Subway I drove up Nicholson Rd to Rokeby Rd. there I turned right & drove the car into Kings Park. I turned left into the Drive & after going about 40 yards I picked out a tree & drove the car up against it. This was to give the impression that someone had used the car to joy-ride & lost control of it I jumped out the car through the left hand door & walked through the bush onto a path & through to Thomas Street near the Home of Peace. I walked up to P.M.H. & rang for a taxi which I took home to Gladstone Road, Rivervale.

I confirm that the above statement is true to the best of my recollection.

Cooke's confession was the breakthrough the Button family had been waiting for. Margaret was back in Perth with her family, her husband having gained a compassionate transfer to Pearce airbase so that their baby daughter could give Charlie and Lilly some joy. She was at her parents' home when Kakulas brought Cooke's confession for them to see. He was so excited, and so were the Buttons. Finally the mystery was solved and their belief in John's innocence was vindicated. Everything fitted – the proof was there, especially in Cooke's mention of the tree stump. John had told them he'd found Rosemary lying by a tree stump, but it had never been mentioned in any newspapers, courts or anywhere, and at John's trial there'd been John's confusion over her position in the sand. Now there would surely be a retrial, the next jury having the benefit of both confessions.

Kakulas couldn't help thinking how different the verdict on Button would have been if Cooke had been apprehended earlier and Button's jury had been able to choose between the two confessions. He was convinced that no jury would have convicted Button. The next day Kakulas made the necessary arrangements, going back to Fremantle Prison to see Button and to get his signature, and lodging a Notice of Application for Extension of Time within which to Appeal and Notice of Application for

Leave to Appeal. He requested a new trial on the grounds of the fresh evidence of Cooke's statement admitting responsibility for the death of Rosemary Anderson.

The hearing was set for February and April 1964, in tandem with Darryl Beamish's similar application regarding his conviction for the wilful murder of Jillian Brewer.

Christmas Day in prison was miserable for Button. He awoke in his small, hot cell and gave in to the eruption of tears. On top of his constant feelings of isolation and loneliness, he suffered a wretched longing for home and everything that Christmas meant. His head was full of memories of Christmas with Mum and that wonderful last one with Rosemary.

This year his company was a group of inmates, all trying to take their minds off traditional Christmas days as they played a special bridge tournament. His only company for Christmas dinner was Richie Uziel, a seventeen-year-old who'd shot his mother. But in comparison with the past ten months, it was a treat to eat in any company. Only on that one day of the year could prisoners eat with another inmate instead of being confined to their cells at meal times. The doors were unlocked and they could join another prisoner for lunch. John went down to Richie's cell, C&D27, on the landing below. It was lighter on that side of the prison as the sun swung around in the afternoon and Richie was his friend from their Death Row days. They ate Christmas dinner sitting on Richie's bed, balancing their dixies on their knees.

The kitchen staff had made a special roast dinner and plum pudding. But for John the best treat was the two boxes he'd received the day before. One was full of the goodies he'd chosen from a Christmas list with an extra allowance of spends. The special Christmas choice was packed for the prisoners and presented to them with a box of tinned food that each family was allowed to provide for Christmas. There were Mum's treats and the wonderful tins of ham, strawberries and peaches John had bought. He'd managed to make custard in the carpentry shop with the milk he'd traded cigarettes for, thanks to Mum regularly sending him extra packets. John mixed the fruit and custard and tucked in. It was a long time since his stomach had experienced anything but plain prison food. He spent Christmas night with his head over his sanitary bucket, vomiting violently.

On Death Row Cooke received two little treats from warders on Christmas day. One gave him some apples, oranges and bananas in the morning and another gave him a packet of barley sugar in the afternoon. Apart from those gifts and ginger beer with lunch, Cooke had a routine day – folding his blankets at 9.35 a.m., having a wash at 10, lying reading before dinner, reading and sleeping after dinner, exercising from 3.38 to 4.08 p.m. and having tea of bread, jam and a cup of tea at 4.30.

The Christmas visit from his wife had been two days earlier.

Just before that visit, Cooke silently joined in the Bible reading given to his fellow Death Row inmate, Brian William Robinson. Cooke stood at the grille of his cell with his Bible in his hands, following Robinson's reading.

There was a lot of work to do in preparing the case, requiring Kakulas to see Cooke several times. There were four affidavits to prepare, including Cooke's. Cooke's first effort was a draft affidavit before writing the final version. There were some differences in detail, including the addition of another girl he'd attempted to run down that night but who walked into the Lakeway Drive-in.

Kakulas could understand differences in the retelling of an event, but Cooke remained adamant about the essential fact – he had stolen a car and run down Rosemary Anderson in almost exactly the same way as he had run down those other women. Cooke ended his draft with mention of the detectives:

> 11. I was arrested by the Police in relation to other matters on the 1st day of September 1963. I was questioned about many matters and I made a statement to the Police in relation to this matter. Approximately 10 days after I gave them my statement the Police took me over the route I told them. When we got to the scene of the accident I asked them to stop the car and we went over to a spot on the left side of Stubbs Terrace going towards Karrakatta and there I pointed out where the girl was when I struck her. I made a mark with a yellow chalk and I

was photographed pointing to this mark. We then went further up the road and near the tree stump. I pointed out the approximate position where the girl landed after being flung off the car. This was marked and photographed.

12. The Police said I was incorrect. Detective Deering and Detective Sergeant Nielson said I was a liar. I ask them why and Detective Deering said I was out in the times and in the distance in which she fell after being struck. After being told this Detective Sergeant Nielson said to me:

'You are only trying to make a big fellow of yourself and trying to get someone else in the shit – you've read so much in the paper you believe you were involved.'

I have quoted to the best of my recollection the words Detective Sergeant Nielson actually used to me but I do so with respect to the Court. I thereafter signed a further statement.

13. What I have said here is the truth relating to the matters referred to.

Cooke also wrote an affidavit confessing to murdering Jillian Brewer.

Cooke was brought face-to-face with the prospect of his fate on 8 January, with the confirmation that Robinson was to be executed twelve days later.

Robinson was woken at 1.20 p.m. to be told the date had been set for Monday, 20 January. His mother, Shirley Mucklow, had been certified under the Lunacy Act. His father told the media, 'I think he'll be better off dead. There never was any hope for him. I don't want to see him reprieved. I haven't visited Brian or been in touch with him in any way and I don't want to.'

With the gallows on his mind, Cooke again spoke of his other two murders – this time to warder Seiler, who recorded that at 9 p.m. Cooke was at the gate of his cell talking about the seven murders he had done, adding that 'two prisoners now in Fremantle prison are doing time for crimes that he had committed'.

During the lead-up to the death of his fellow inmate, Cooke suffered a personal blow with the sudden death of his eldest son.

Nine-year-old Michael drowned on 15 January. The mentally retarded boy had been in weekend care, enjoying a picnic by the river at Sandy Beach in Bassendean. He had been allowed to eat too much and had gotten into trouble in the water.

Cooke was very upset when prison officials told him that evening, commenting that the boy would have been ten in May.

'I will go that way, I have no fear,' he said. The man who was soon to follow his son cried and talked about Michael during the night and next morning. His wish was to be buried beside his son's ashes.

Five days later Brian William Robinson went to the gallows. He was hanged at 8 a.m. and buried in a public grave in the Anglican section of Fremantle Cemetery three hours later.

Cooke and Robinson were not friends. Robinson used to bait Cooke, heckling him about just being a cold-blooded sneak whereas he at least had killed a cop. But Cooke was very quiet on the day leading up to Robinson's hanging and on the day of execution. As Robinson was led away early in the morning, Cooke sat by the grille gazing out. He spent three hours there and more later, gazing through the grille. The observing warders noted that he was 'in deep thought'.

An ironical side-effect of Cooke's desire to wipe the slate clean before his death was that the legal process, now started, would delay his own execution. Although he'd refused an appeal on his own case because he didn't want a delay, once the opportunity arose through Button's and Beamish's appeals, he made the most of it. It was a fluke opportunity – if his first confessions in September had been accepted, there wouldn't have been delays in starting the appeals.

There was a disadvantage, too, in living a little longer. It gave him time to worry, and Cooke sat in Death Row increasingly concerned about how Button and Beamish might retaliate against him or his family once they were freed. Isolated in Death Row, he'd never met them to get any idea of what kind of people they were or how they felt about him. He raised it with Kakulas, who tried to reassure him about Button's quiet nature and total absence of any violence in his life. But it continued to play on his mind in the lead-up to the first anniversary of Rosemary's death.

On 7 February 1964, two days before the anniversary, he asked the observing warder for pen and paper, and on the lined paper, headed 'Trial, Remand and Debtor Class, Fremantle Prison', and wrote to Heenan:

Dear Sir,
I am writing this letter in a state of some mixed feelings. Firstly, I have been contacted on several occasions by Mr B. Kakulas in connection with the Button case. When he interviewed me last Tuesday he, Mr Kakulas, said that he would be returning to have me sign the sworn statements I have made to him. Could I have your advice on this matter, or should I just carry on in this manner?

I spoke to Mr Kakulas of my fear that if and when Button and Beamish are released, as to the state of their feelings concerning my immediate family. My fear Sir, is that one of them or both may decide to take vengeance against me in the form of punishment against my wife and children. This is my greatest fear and I would like some assurance that this position will not eventuate. I realise Mr Heenan, you personally cannot give such an assurance to me. But please Sir, could you please in some way give me some peace of mind on this subject. For the way I am feeling at the moment, the fate of these two I have mentioned is indifferent to me, in as much as my family are first and foremost. I have confessed all of my crimes to the authorities and it is now in their hands, and this has cleared my conscience a little.

I spoke to Mr Kakulas of my fear and his answer was to get in touch with you on this matter. I don't think I have thanked you enough for the way you conducted my trial and your attitude towards me. Once more thank you.
I remain yours faithfully,
E.E. Cooke

His solicitor could give no such assurance. He had not met either man to assess their personalities. Heenan wrote back:

> I am unable of course to give you any firm undertaking as to what will be the actions of the two above-mentioned should they be released, because I will have no control over them. However I should think it most unlikely, if they were released, that they would take vengeance against you or your family. There are two very good reasons for this. The first reason is that both Button and Beamish have already served sufficient time in prison not to risk being sent back there by carrying out the type of action that you contemplate. The second reason is that they will at last owe their release substantially to the fact that you have confessed to the crimes of which they were convicted.
>
> Of course you have a duty to God, yourself and everyone else to state the truth in these matters. The consequences of your telling the truth are really immaterial, but you can be assured that by doing so you can only improve the situation for yourself and your family.
>
> I hope that the above is of some assistance and I thank you for your expressions of gratitude.

Sunday 9 February was Button's twentieth birthday, the first anniversary of his loss of Rosemary. It was a searing hot day, 101.5 degrees in the shade. But Button, out in the yard as always on a Sunday, couldn't sit and take advantage of the small shaded area. He couldn't stay still and he couldn't chat or concentrate on any of the games. Despite the heat, he paced up and down the hot bitumen enclosure. He needed movement to give some physical relief to the emotional torture.

The Andersons marked the occasion by placing a notice in the 'In Memoriam' section of Monday's newspaper: 'In loving memory of darling Rosemary, who passed away Feb 10 1963. A beautiful star called to heaven. A cluster of beautiful memories sprinkled with many a tear. Always in our thoughts, darling. Fondest love, Mum Dad Helen and Jim.' Nanna and Grandad did the same, as did Laraine and Frank, adding the name of their new son, Peter.

In his cell on Death Row, Cooke was also aware of the anniversary. He broke up the monotony of the day by looking at family photographs, reading the Bible and playing patience. At 6.15 p.m. he said to Warder H. A. Harris: 'It's one year today since I knocked off my first job.' Then he went back to playing patience. Rosemary Anderson's hit–run death was not his first job, but the anniversary was on his mind. He'd made no reference to his 27 January shooting spree on that anniversary a fortnight earlier, though he hadn't been able to sleep. He'd read all night, including the Bible, only getting about an hour's sleep after 3 a.m.

The anniversary of Rosemary Anderson's murder and the Belmont murders and manhunt passed unnoticed by the general population. They had another shocking crime to think about. They woke to the news in the *Sunday Times* of a university lecturer murdering his mentally retarded son. Dr Maurice Benn had shot his four-and-a-half year old son Bernard on 8 February. It started a controversy about the difficulties of coping with a mentally retarded child and the rights and wrongs of mercy killing. Dr Benn was later convicted of wilful murder, his death sentence commuted to ten years' imprisonment.

It was Cooke's birthday on 25 February. He received two birthday cards and a visit from his wife. His birthday lunch was roast beef, cabbage and potatoes, with a dose of cough mixture.

Cooke signed the affidavit for Button's appeal, again with a few changes, on 11 February. Button's appeal before the Court of Criminal Appeal began on 27 February when, along with Beamish's appeal, preliminary consideration was given to the procedure to be followed and some submissions were heard. Beamish's appeal was adjourned until 17 March and Button's until 7 April.

Cooke was in a temper in his Death Row cell on the day Beamish's appeal got underway. He refused to shave, citing regulations that he was to have someone shave him. Warder Patterson was given the job in the bath cell.

His concern for retribution against his family played on his mind again as the appeal progressed. On the second day, 18 March, Cooke became upset on hearing a news report about the previous day's proceedings, and told the warder that he was worried that Beamish might do his family some harm. He cried, sniffed and talked a lot about Beamish the next day, too.

'He seems to have a fixed idea that Beamish may cause injury to his family should he be released from custody,' the warder noted.

On 20 March Cooke gave evidence at Beamish's appeal. Dressed in a suit again, he was driven to court at 9.15 a.m. and returned at 4.35 that afternoon.

Cooke was also agitated as Button's appeal neared. The day before it started, he refused lunch, cried and punched the wall of his cell until both hands bled. The day the appeal hearing began, he started a week's fast, refusing all meals, saying he wasn't hungry. He only had a cup of milk each morning.

The Court of Criminal Appeal hearing of *John Button v. The Queen* began on 7 April before the Chief Justice Sir Albert Asher Wolff, Justice Lawrence Walter Jackson and Justice John Evendon Virtue over three days. Although officially an Application for Extension of Time within which to Appeal and Application for Leave to Appeal, it was in fact treated as an appeal.

Button's request to be present at his appeal was refused. On 7, 8 and 9 April he was behind the walls of Fremantle Prison while his future was being decided, wondering if the God who wouldn't tear the walls down for him last year would now finally bring him justice.

Button's counsel went to the appeal not knowing the details of Cooke's other hit–runs. On Hatfield's request to the court for copies of any relevant actual confessions, Crown counsel said there were such confessions but no charges. The Chief Justice asked Crown counsel to prepare a statement on the matter.

Stating his case to the court, Ken Hatfield said there was fresh evidence – Cooke's confession – that would have had some impact on the minds of reasonable men or women trying Button. There was no witness to the crime, no witness who saw the vehicle strike the girl, nobody who identified any person as the driver of the car that struck her. The only credible evidence was Button's statement to the police, after his repeated denials.

The absence of blood marks and damage to the front of Button's car proved almost conclusively that it was not the car that hit the girl. There were no signs of damage or blood, flesh or fibres that might be expected if this car had struck the girl. He had made his confession after stoutly denying for hours that he was responsible. What was the evidence? Boiled down, it was the belated, indoctrinated statement Button made to detectives the morning after the accident.

Crown counsel Ron Wilson said Button's confession was sustained by facts and that fresh evidence from Cooke was suspicious and unreliable.

Wilson said the evidence against Button was very strong, and must have been so to have survived a trial of that length and the vigour of the defence. There was Button's written confession, which was deemed to have been voluntary by the trial judge, which had been tested most thoroughly. This was supported by the general conditions and by the position of blood spots on the headlight of the car. If they had got there after Button put the girl in the car, one would have expected to find them also on the steering wheel and on the door handle. It would have been very difficult for the blood to have dripped on to the headlight because of the way in which the mudguard overhung the glass of the headlight. This indicated that it had splashed from the road when the girl was hit. There had been an argument and the girl had insisted on walking home and had rejected attempts by Button to apologise. Button was seen at the scene of the impact in Stubbs Terrace immediately after the impact by people travelling in two cars that arrived there within a very short time. This confirmed the general situation and supported Button's confession.

The Crown presented eleven affidavits: from Sergeant Nielson, which included Cooke's original confession of 12 September; Sergeant Dunne, in support of Nielson's affidavit; Inspector Cecil Lamb, referring to Cooke's retraction and apology; prison officer William Steele, attesting to Cooke's statement in the exercise yard that he had killed five people; Desmond Heenan, describing Cooke's confessions to other murders and Rosemary Anderson's and Jillian Brewer's murders; Constable Harold Inkster, saying he heard Button say in the charge room

'I did not mean to do it'; City Motors' foreman panel beater Barry Harvey, saying there was an imprint of a tree in the centre of the bumper of James's car and bark from a tree adhering to the damaged portions; spray painter Peter Brown saying the dent on the hood of James's car was not there when he painted it in February – he was sure he would have noticed it if it had been; Kathleen James, saying there was damage to the bark of the tree and skid marks leading to it, and that she did not see any dent on the car afterwards; Cooke's mother Christine, reporting her son saying 'nobody in Australia has committed as many murders as I have'; and the Director of Mental Health Services, Arch Ellis, saying Cooke was not suffering from any mental disease but would go to any lengths to bolster his self-esteem, leading him to exaggerate facts and to tell lies.

The judges also studied Cooke's retraction of his confession and Judge Negus's reasons for admitting Button's confession.

There were four affidavits for Button: from Cooke confessing to running down Rosemary Anderson; Arthur Lindsley James stating that on the return of his vehicle approximately ten days after the theft, he noticed a small dent on the left-hand side of the roof approximately seven to eight inches from the drip mould and almost centre of the left-hand front door; from Ernest Head, confirming James's car was removed from his driveway on 9 February; and from Kakulas, attaching details of the repairs James's car required.

Two witnesses were called. James remained adamant that he'd seen the dent on the hood when his car was returned from City Motors. That night, he complained to his wife that the Crown was trying to put words in his mouth. Mrs James, who'd given the Crown affidavit that she hadn't seen a dent, did see one when it was pointed out to her later. But her sighting of the small dent which was only evident in a certain light was too late for Button's appeal.

The main witness was Cooke, who appeared on the second day.

On 8 April Cooke was dressed and taken to court in Perth just after 1 p.m., having left his lunch untouched.

Cooke faced Wilson again, as he had done at his own trial and at Beamish's appeal, while the prosecutor went through the detail of his affidavit, trying for specific accuracy on what time he stole the car, whether he pushed or reversed it from the drive, and the details of the people he planned to run down that night.

Cooke admitted to deliberately leaving out pertinent details originally, so as to delay his execution by needing to give evidence at the appeal, agreeing with Wilson that he was playing it shrewd. He admitted that not everything was true – not the part about going to Buxton Road in Wembley Downs. But he denied the prosecutor's suggestion that by adding his planned hit–runs on other people earlier that night, he was adding a bit more ornamentation or elaboration to make a better story.

'I was playing it shrewd because, Mr Wilson, the police never believed me from the onset. As soon as I opened my mouth about these the police said I was telling a pack of lies, and from then on I thought that the best thing for me to do is to shut up and see my solicitor when he came to see me and then inform him and he could tell the proper people.'

'Then why tell the police other things, take them right out to Scarborough?'

'So would you if you were stuck in a cell nine-foot by six-foot, 24 hours a day with people watching you all the time. You would like a bit of fresh air too, wouldn't you?'

He said that where he had originally told the police he had first seen Rosemary Anderson walking in Stubbs Terrace was actually the place where he had hit her. He had in fact seen her coming around the corner from the subway and had hit her outside Floreat Iron Works, a little more than 75 yards further on. He now said that the position where he'd told them he'd hit her was in fact where she had landed, by a tree stump.

'Why has your story changed in these respects?'

'From the outset, I knew that they never believed me. From the first moment I told them about that I knew they never believed me.'

'They hadn't said so, had they?'

'Yes, they had.'

'Why did you lie to them?'

'Because they never believed me, so why should I worry about them.'

'Whether they believed you or not, was it not just as easy for you to tell the truth, as to where you saw the girl, for example?'

'When a person, or several people do not believe you from the outset, you – or I, myself, if someone doesn't believe me from the outset, I get annoyed with that person and from then on I do not cooperate as fully as I should.'

Mr Justice Virtue asked, 'You wanted to help these people, did you not, who were in gaol for crimes they had not committed?'

'Yes.'

'Did you think you would help them by telling a pack of lies that could be shown, demonstrated, to be a pack of lies; make a confession which was most obviously a fabrication? How were you going to help them by doing that?'

'As I said before, I thought the best thing I could do was wait until I saw my lawyer, and then tell him about the facts.'

'Did you think that by making a lot of contradictory statements that was going to help them?'

'No, not very much. It got me off the hook at that particular moment.'

Wilson resumed. 'You say you got annoyed with the detectives. In fact, you have a very high regard for them, have you not?'

'That is quite so. I have a high regard for my children, too, but I get annoyed with them.'

A few questions later, 'Why did you not tell them straight out, at that stage "Well, look, I am sorry, I have told you the wrong positions"?'

'But Mr Wilson, what was the good? They never believed me from the outset. Why should I say "I made a blue; it was further off"? They would say "oh, no".'

He went on with his sworn testimony. 'The poor girl, she was walking on the sandy part the whole time, and I took at least three-quarters of the width of the car off the road in order to strike her.'

He described her being about six inches off the road, and how he gradually went off the road as he came up behind her.

He travelled 20 or 30 yards with her on the bonnet, then she slipped up on to the hood of the car. He was travelling at 40 mph, not slackening speed, with the girl on the bonnet about eighteen inches from the windscreen. He didn't know what caused her to go over the hood, whether it was vibration or wind or what. He didn't think there was a sun visor on the car. He'd travelled about 200 feet before she was thrown off the car. He went to Lemnos Hospital, turned around and drove back, and saw a Simca car there with both passenger doors open.

Sir Albert Wolff questioned Cooke about his telling lies to the police, asking several times if in fact he was helping himself rather than Button.

'How can I help myself? I cannot help myself in any way at all. I am finished.'

He denied Wilson's suggestion that he did not mean to hit the tree in Kings Park. He said he drove into it at about 20 mph, the only noise caused being a 'plop'. A Ford Pilot car went past as he walked off in the bush.

Wilson intimated that he'd changed the points of where he saw and hit the girl to where he hit her and she landed because of Deering pointing out the discrepancies. Cooke denied it, again venting his frustration at the police. 'That is immaterial, about misleading the police. They misled me plenty of times; why not me mislead them?' He went on, 'I know where I struck the girl. Near the Floreat Iron Works.'

He again vented frustration at the police. 'Mr Wilson, they are ramming down my throat the argument constantly that I knew nothing about it (they said a few more words) and was making up a pack of lies . . .'

Cooke claimed that the statement he had made retracting his confession on Rosemary Anderson had been mostly dictated to him. He said he'd wanted to write, 'I believed myself infallible as to the time and the distance', but somehow wasn't asked to put it in. He said the part where he said he was of the opinion that he couldn't have been the person was not true. The statement was not a true statement.

'Well, why did you write it?'

'You write many things when you are under – I cannot say arrest because they never did – but when you are under pressure you write anything.'

He went on. 'They weren't interested in the truth at the moment. They were interested in a retracting statement from me about this crime.'

'But you didn't have to go along with what they wanted, did you, if it wasn't true?'

'I am afraid, Mr Wilson, that you haven't been in the hands of the police.'

He said that while the part about him getting involved in books he read was correct, it wasn't the reason for these confessions, just as it wasn't for the Sturkey and Walmsley confessions – he'd read about them, too. The reason he withdrew the statement about Anderson was to get the police off his back. He went on that he'd not explained it all in truthful detail to Heenan at first because he wanted to look after his own case. He had in fact been of two minds about coming forward.

Then it was Hatfield's turn, and he homed right in on Cooke's other five hit–runs, asking if he had attacked other people with vehicles and when the last time was. Cooke told him he had done so on five other occasions, but while he could remember the occasion of the last time, he could not remember the date.

'Have you confessed those crimes to the police?'

'Yes, and they have proved that I was the culprit.'

He detailed where he had stolen the car and where he'd hit the women in each case.

Wilson asked if he'd at any other time taken steps to cover the damage caused by the collision with the people.

'Only once. When I had run down the lady in Belmont with the Holden utility I abandoned the car at the rear of a garage and I placed it as though it had been struck against a post.'

The questioning was over. The witness asked if he could say something. His request was denied by the Chief Justice.

It was the first time the public had heard any detail about Cooke committing hit–runs. But there was still no media reference back to the spate of serious hit–runs that had concerned the police in 1960 or the fact that the police had absolutely established them as Cooke's doing. Readers only learnt that Cooke claimed to have done other hit–runs.

The West Australian's headlines ran 'Cooke Claims He Ran Down 7 With Cars': 'Eric Edgar Cooke (32) claimed in the Court of Criminal Appeal yesterday afternoon that he not only ran down Rosemary Anderson (17) in a car but he ran down six women and girls on five previous occasions and had made written confessions to the police about these incidents.' The article went on with other information about the appeal.

The Chief Justice was not convinced. When Hatfield explained that Cooke claimed he made five confessions and the confessions were found to be correct, the Chief Justice said, 'Supposing what he says here falls down in the central features, does any amount of bolstering up like that help it?'

Sir Albert noted that there was little damage to the car Cooke had stolen that night. When reminded by Hatfield that he'd driven it into a tree to mask the damage, the Chief Justice said, 'It was not damaged very much when he ran into the tree. He is a vicious man. He might also like to destroy property.'

The story was going around town that Cooke was confessing to everything but the Great Train Robbery. This belittling of his confessions fitted in with his mother's testimony that he wanted to go down in history as being greater than Ned Kelly. People laughing at the joke, however, were not privy to the crimes he had confessed to and how many had been established as his – and how few were not proved as his, mostly because householders weren't aware of a theft and couldn't confirm it. The police had taken it upon themselves to decide what he had and hadn't done. Cooke wasn't actually charged with any of the break and enters for a court to judge. The one of his four assault confessions they hadn't accepted hadn't been put to the test of the courts, either.

Cooke confessed to twenty murders and attempted murders. The only ones the police didn't believe were the Anderson and Brewer murders and one attempted murder. If Cooke had wanted to claim as many murders as he could, there were two other unsolved murders in Perth he could have tried to notch up, such as the 1958 killing of nursing aide Barbara May Williams and the 1961 hit–run of Alice Kathleen Bennett.

After giving evidence at Button's appeal, Cooke was handcuffed and driven back to Fremantle Prison – the last time he could expect to see the world outside the cells and exercise yard of Death Row. He arrived back at his cell at 4.45. He had done all that he could.

'I won't eat till I hang,' he announced.

The next morning, he refused breakfast, taking only a cup of milk. At lunchtime he handed back his food and refused to go out for his exercise. At 3.30 he handed back his tea and at 4.30 refused bread and soup.

The next day, 10 April, he accepted only a cup of milk again for breakfast, refused a mid-morning walk, left his dinner of potato pie and carrot untouched and said to his guard, 'All my troubles will end when they hang me.'

His wife visited him in the early afternoon. He told her he did not want to see his mother again because she'd asked him if he wanted to be Al Capone or Ned Kelly. After her visit, he asked for a black-and-blue pullover and told the guard, 'It's a pity my wife got tangled up with a bastard like me.' He refused his tea.

The next morning he again had only a cup of milk and refused exercise. His mother was still on his mind as he talked to the warder about his row with her before going on to talk about the welfare of his family, and later to name the owners of some of the houses he'd broken into, including those of the Premier, David Brand, and the Chief Secretary, Ross Hutchinson.

At 11.35 lunch was placed on his pillow. He refused it. 'I'm not hungry,' he said. At 3.25 he was asked how many pieces of bread he wanted for his tea. 'None.'

It was the same the next morning when asked how many pieces of bread he wanted for breakfast. 'None,' he said and accepted only a cup of milk. After exercising that morning, he told the warders he did not want any dinner. Later, asked what he wanted for tea: 'Nothing.' He spent some time that afternoon reading the Bible and looking at family photos.

The following day he wanted only a cup of milk for breakfast.

At 11 a.m. he asked Warder Harris: 'Do you think I should start to have my food?' The warder replied that it was up to him, it was his fault if he didn't have his food – it was offered to him.

At 11.30 he broke his seven-day fast by eating lunch, the first he'd eaten since a slice of toast and honey at 7.30 p.m. on 6 April.

A month later, on 7 May, he suffered the anguish of his second son's birthday. The boy turned nine, and was now the man of the family. Cooke couldn't see him, but he did what he could – he organised for the boy to have his most treasured possession, his Bible. He wrote a dedication to him inside it: 'To my son . . . may God bless you and reward you. Dad.' He knew his execution would be over by the boy's next birthday.

In Main Division, John Button waited for the court's decision, counting down the days till his release. It wasn't just his freedom he wanted, but to have Rosemary's parents believe him at last. Difficult as it would be to sit at Rosemary's kitchen table without her, he so wanted to talk to them, have them understand his pain, knowing that he didn't deprive them of their daughter or himself of the one he loved.

Hatfield told him that his appeal was most likely to go the same way as the Beamish appeal. If the judges believed Cooke on that, they would on Button's. This gave John some extra hurdles to overcome. All the judges on the appeal bench were involved in Beamish's case. The Chief Justice, the presiding judge on the appeal bench, had been the judge for Beamish's original trial, so granting the appeal would be overturning the decision of a trial he'd presided over. As well, the other two judges, Justices Jackson and Virtue, had been on the bench that dismissed Beamish's original appeal. Also, he believed that Beamish's having a police record made a difference, whereas John didn't.

The decision was set for 22 May. John hoped this would be a good omen. It was six years to the day of his arrival in Australia.

Beamish's appeal was dismissed. The judges refused to take into account Cooke's confessions to other murders, saying similar facts would not be admissible at a retrial for Beamish – even though it would not be Cooke on trial, but Beamish. The appeal judges decided Cooke was an inveterate liar, and that his confession to Brewer's murder was not compelling fresh evidence.

This alone was bad news for John Button, but there was worse in the Chief Justice's written Reasons for Judgement. On page 50 he referred to the Button appeal:

> It is as well to size up the situation which the Court is asked to accept, viz., that on two different occasions and on dates widely apart he, Cooke, was on the scene and was responsible for two separate killings to which two men have separately confessed their complicity . . . and in the case of Anderson, if Cooke is speaking the truth, he must have done the killing seconds before Button appeared on the scene, and, what is more, he claims to have had little damage to the car he was driving and what little damage there was resembles in some measure that which was found on Button's car. Is it possible to imagine such a set of circumstances arising merely out of coincidence! The mathematical odds against such a coincidence beggar the imagination.

John felt that if such imagination-beggaring odds never came up, no one would ever win their fortune from a charities ticket. Cooke was a liar, but can't a liar sometimes tell the truth? And he did have a very good memory, but it wasn't perfect.

The Chief Justice continued about the discrepancies and changes in Cooke's confessions:

> Having seen and heard him trying to explain these discrepancies, he emerges, not unexpectedly, as a low, cunning liar who, when cornered, will say anything to try and escape from a denouement. It is clear that he thinks that the more confusion he creates, the longer will be his chances of clinging to life. In fact, when asked in cross-examination why he had lied in regard to certain important matters he said that he had done it with that purpose. It is clear too that he is still trying to win support for his theory that he is the victim of compulsive insanity.

Sir Albert's rejection of the evidence of the 'similar acts' of Cooke's other murders was another bad portent for Button:

> The evidence would not be admissible if Cooke were put on trial for the murder of Brewer, yet it is urged that it should be accepted on the appeal because all the crimes were similar as being wanton killings without motive – no legal basis is propounded for its admission. That is a very handy stick to beat a dog but where, as here, the evidence points unmistakably to a fabricated confession, Cooke's complicity in other crimes cannot logically have any bearing.

Judge Jackson did not believe Cooke, either:

> It has been amply demonstrated that Cooke himself is a witness of no credit at all. It is not merely that he suffers the discredit of being a convicted murderer who has confessed to, and has been accepted by the Crown as guilty of four separate homicides amounting in each case to wilful murder, in addition to the murder for which he has been convicted. It is that he has been shown during his cross-examination to be a palpable and indeed a self-confessed liar.

And later in his Reasons for Judgement:

> in this as in the other cases in which I heard him give evidence, as his examination continued, his conduct, demeanour and the content of the answers to questions put to him portrayed him as a palpable and unscrupulous liar whose lack of veracity became more evident as his testimony progressed.

Button's appeal was similarly dismissed: the judges didn't believe Cooke, and the evidence of similar offences was ruled out.

The Chief Justice began his written Reasons for Judgement by noting that Button had not originally appealed his conviction within the prescribed time and that, although Cooke had first confessed in September, Button's application was not made until December. He obviously didn't know that the police had not informed Button's lawyers of the September confession, nor the difficulty Cooke's defence had encountered in getting this information from the police in November.

Sir Albert went through in detail the differences, additions and omissions of the various versions of Cooke's confessions, finally stating:

> As in the case of the Brewer murder, it would be possible to go on and instance many other criticisms of Cooke's statements and of his evidence under cross-examination, but it would serve no useful purpose. It would not be necessary to go beyond the various statements made by Cooke to determine that his whole claim to have killed Anderson is a fabrication. Cooke has been caught in the web of his own lies.

Sir Albert ended his reasons with reference to the similar offences:

> In this case as in the Beamish appeal, we were urged to accept evidence of what were referred to as 'similar acts'; acts wherein Cooke was the driver of a car and ran down women on five separate occasions on and from the 12th of September 1958 to and including the 20th May 1960. One of these incidents concerning running at three women walking together on the road and he hit two of them, and on another occasion when he knocked down a woman he returned and stole her purse. While the applicant's Counsel deny that this evidence is introduced to prove the applicant's case by establishing a propensity, I cannot help thinking that despite the denial that is the tenuous ground on which it is sought to introduce it. In the result, that would be the only 'evidence' (if it could be called by that name) to establish the applicant's case; the claim made by Cooke to have killed the girl Anderson is so bad at its core and so obviously fabricated, that the admission of the other unconnected acts could not help the applicant against whom the evidence is very strong. As in the Beamish case these other alleged instances must be regarded as an open question so far as this Court is concerned, and the fact that the

police have been willing to accept the evidence as implicating Cooke depends, of course, on the investigation of these cases, and the general remarks made in considering similar evidence in the Beamish appeal apply with equal force here.

Justice Jackson also dismissed any consideration of Cooke's other five hit–runs:

> The applicant sought to rely on Cooke's admission that he had, while driving stolen motor vehicles, intentionally run down and injured a woman or women on no less than five occasions during 1958 and 1959, and that his confessions to these offences have been accepted by the police as substantially true. But these assaults, in the absence of some special common feature, are of no probative worth in considering whether Cooke also ran down Rosemary Anderson. And the fact that the police may have believed his confessions to these five attacks cannot serve to strengthen his credit as a witness, for he is patently a man disposed to tell lies whenever it suits him and to invent fanciful stories. What is important is that the story he tells is itself beyond belief by reasonable men. It is for that reason that this fresh evidence, being itself worthless, cannot avail the applicant in his claim for a new trial.

Justice Jackson did differ from the Chief Justice on one important point. Whereas Sir Albert had decided that the case against Button was very strong, Jackson saw that it had hinged only on Button's confession: 'If his second written statement were put aside, the rest of the evidence against him would scarcely have warranted his conviction. The strength of the case for the prosecution really depended on the probative value of his confession.'

Justice Virtue did not provide written Reasons for Judgement.

The decision was devastating for John, who saw nine years of loneliness and pain stretching ahead of him. His heartbroken parents vowed to fight on. So did Hatfield. They lodged an appeal with the highest court in the land, the High Court.

The Highest Judges in the Land

11 September–25 October 1964

The High Court travelled from its Sydney base to hold a sitting in Perth in September 1964. Button's appeal was set to follow Beamish's appeal.

The Application for Special Leave to Appeal from the Judgement of the Court of Criminal Appeal of Western Australia was listed as No. 8 of 1964 in the Western Australian Registry in the High Court of Australia. Mr K. W. Hatfield QC and Mr B. P. Kakulas appeared for the applicant and Mr R. D. Wilson QC and Mr K. H. Parker appeared for the Crown.

It was mid-afternoon on 11 September when Mr Francis Burt finished speaking for Beamish. At 3.50 p.m. the four arguing the Button case stood before five justices of the High Court – the Chief Justice, Sir Garfield Barwick, with Sir Frank Kitto, Sir Douglas Menzies, Sir William Windeyer and Sir William Owen. They had before them the thick buff-bound tomes 'Papers for the Judges'.

Ken Hatfield rose to address them. As he encapsulated the facts again, he was interrupted by questions from the judges. The Chief Justice asked whether there were independent facts verifying Button's confession; Justice Owen asked whether there were any marks on Button's car indicating a collision.

Hatfield submitted that it was not correct for WA's Chief Justice to say there was a strong case against Button, because it rested entirely on his subsequent admission – and that the court should accept Mr Justice Jackson's summary of the case when he said that the only evidence against Button in substance was his own confession.

There were further questions from the judges, including if the hit–run happened at a time when other traffic might be expected to be there, the interval of time between Button seeing Rosemary turn into Stubbs Terrace and his account of finding her – and if Cooke had run down other people.

Hatfield continued:

> We submit with respect that it is not really the function of the Court of Criminal Appeal to say 'We disbelieve him' out of hand . . . 'we as judges, we as lawyers, we think he is an incredible person; he has no general credit at all; he is a known criminal, a braggart, a boaster.' It would have been more satisfactory to the applicant, your Honours, if in fact the Chief Justice, who gave the leading judgment, had directed himself to the problem promulgated and faced and dealt with by the two learned judges I have just referred to.

Hatfield said the kernel of the problem was whether the evidence of Cooke's confession and his evidence at the trial would have any impact on the minds of reasonable men and perhaps removed the certainty of conviction of guilt that existed before they notionally heard his evidence.

He argued that while Mr Justice Jackson had referred to this problem, the Chief Justice and apparently also Mr Justice Virtue did not apply themselves to it. The Chief Justice, in applying himself to his own personal assessment of the character, conduct, reliability, cogency of Cooke's evidence, did not apply himself to whether it would have any effect on the minds of sensible men, when taken in conjunction with the evidence given on Button's trial.

Hatfield had been on his feet for three-quarters of an hour when, at 4.35 p.m., the proceedings were adjourned until 10.30 a.m. on 14 September.

Resuming after the weekend, Hatfield referred to Cooke's retraction:

> This was not a matter of saying 'What I have been saying is a pack of lies, it is untrue'. He was persuaded by some logic based on the hypothesis that he was wrong on his various remarks, positions and facts and that therefore his statement must have been incorrect. At no time had Cooke agreed with the detectives' proposition that he was telling lies. He did not say 'yes, I am, I made this all up'.

Hatfield continued that it might have been a hopeless case if, in the retraction, Cooke had said 'it is a pack of lies, I made it up to get out of jail or have a holiday', but it was a matter of the logic and impelling persuasion of Nielson, which was really inexorable. Not only was Cooke persuaded, but strongly persuaded.

To Barwick's statement that the evidence of the damage to Button's car exactly fitted what was described, Hatfield raised the point that if he had struck Rosemary with the car, he would know exactly where he hit – yet his statement was that 'it was in the front and I think it was on the left-hand side. She came up on the bonnet and I carried her for a few yards on. It all happened so quickly.' He pointed out another part of Button's confession that was 'nonsense' – that he had caught up to her when she was nearly opposite the Shenton Park Railway Station – because the police's composite plan made it quite manifest that she was nowhere near the station when she was struck.

'That is about as big a discrepancy as Cooke made in his description to Detective Sergeant Nielson.'

He went on that Button's statement that she was carried a few yards on the front of his vehicle was completely exploded by the police plan.

'But,' interjected Barwick, 'a jury has accepted this. This is a very great factor when you come to ask for special leave to appeal. The jury has in fact accepted it.'

Hatfield repeated the basis of his submission:

> I am putting that the evidence of Cooke combined with the evidence at the trial makes this confession far less valuable than before. By itself the jury could agree with it. As to Button's confession which was the sole evidence against him at the trial, he said when he denied the statement for so long, denied the complicity, the circumstances in which he made this statement, apparently . . . but these details were manifestly unlikely.
>
> We say that if the fresh evidence had been discovered, that combined with the evidence of Cooke's confession, combined with the unsatisfactory nature of the details of Button's confession as to his complicity and the striking of the girl, in those circumstances the Court could readily say that in all these circumstances not to grant a new trial, with this fresh evidence, is a miscarriage of justice.

Barwick brought the hearing to a close: 'You begin by saying that the Chief Justice put the case too strongly against Button.'

'Yes, Sir.'

'For that reason you call attention to these discrepancies, for that reason you say that insufficient effect was given to what Cooke said.'

'That is so, Sir.'

'And that this also weakened the criticism of Cooke's discrepancies.'

'That is so.'

'That adds it up?'

'That is correct, your Honour.'

The hearing ended with the Chief Justice advising that they had no need to hear the other side's arguments. Barwick told Wilson that they did not wish to hear him.

The High Court's rejection of Button's appeal was immediate, the judgment delivered by Barwick that the court was of the opinion that there was no ground for granting special leave.

John Button learned of the failure of his last chance at justice from the radio news. His counsel couldn't get to Fremantle to tell him before the journalists filed their stories. Hatfield and

Kakulas were as upset as John and his family. They had no doubt at all that Cooke had killed Rosemary Anderson. They believed that despite Cooke's little inconsistencies, looking at the evidence as a whole, the slight changes between his confessions made very little difference. John's counsel were convinced that if there was a trial where both of them were accused of the murder, each blaming the other, the court would find that Cooke was the murderer and Button was not. There were too many things Cooke said which he couldn't possibly have known about and too much of a coincidence that he was in that stolen car that night and rammed it into the tree.

Beamish's appeal was also dismissed by the High Court of Australia. His counsel decided to take it to London's Privy Council.

On 25 September Vivian Cooke surprised his son with his first visit to see him, accompanying his wife Christine to Fremantle Prison.
 'This is the first time I have seen you for thirteen months,' Cooke said at the sight of his father. Orderly conversation followed for a while. But the visit ended angrily.
 Vivian Cooke said to his son, 'I have been told that you would have shot me if you could have found me. But it would have taken a better man than you, unless you had got me in the dark like you did the others. You never gave them a chance, that is why I feel so bad about it.'
 Cooke swore at his father, finally shouting 'go and get fucked'.
 The prison officer ended the visit. The warder escorted his parents out of the cell while the prisoner shouted, 'Open this door and let him in, I will murder him.'
 Then he called his farewells. 'Thanks for coming, Mum.'
 And to his father, 'Goodbye, I will see you in hell.'
 He remained agitated and hysterical, blaming his father for where he was. He told the observing warder that he should have adopted that attitude to his father earlier, saying he'd always persecuted him and he'd just accepted it.
 The officer told Cooke he should have been ashamed of his

language. That sent Cooke into a rage. He charged around the cell, repeatedly hitting his head against the wall. Two officers restrained him until he was given a sedative.

On 14 October the State Government announced its decision to go ahead with Cooke's execution. It was thirteen months since his capture. All the processes of law had been completed. It was a month after Button's and Beamish's appeals had gone to the highest court in Australia and had been dismissed. There was no reason to delay.

The Executive Council issued a Minute Paper signed by the Minister for Justice, Arthur Griffith. The execution date was fixed for 8 a.m. on 26 October.

Cooke was advised at 4 p.m. by acting prison superintendent Thorpe, accompanied by the prison chaplain, the Reverend Ralph Thomas. He seemed troubled after they left, talking to the warders about his family. Then he opened his Bible and read the 23 Psalm aloud.

The Reverend George Jenkins went to see Cooke early next morning and his wife went mid-morning. She'd learnt of the decision on the radio news and already knew when a detective sergeant had gone to her home to tell her. When she arrived at his cell at 10.45, Cooke asked her if she'd heard the news. She said 'yes' and the event was not spoken of again during her twenty-minute visit.

He had curry and rice for lunch but didn't have any supper, saying he wasn't hungry. On the 11 p.m. news, he heard an item referring to a stay of execution for a retrial. He said he'd commit suicide if that occurred.

His mother visited the day after, with one of his sisters, June. At night he read the Bible for a while and looked at photos of his children. He was in a jovial mood, talking and laughing and telling the warder that he was not afraid to die – hanging was better than spending all his life in prison.

On Saturday he was measured and weighed for the executioner's calculations.

On Sunday he read the Bible several times during the day, as usual, and was quite cheerful in the early evening. The countdown of his last week of life was beginning. This time next week it would be his last night. He tossed and turned through the early hours of the morning. The Reverend Jenkins visited him briefly the next morning, providing further solace and preparation for the following Monday.

He had trouble sleeping the next night, too.

The Reverend Jenkins was involved in a church conference during the week, but the Reverend Thomas visited him on Tuesday morning. Cooke had a bad day. He cried for a while in the afternoon, and spent some time gazing at the photo of his wife and children, asking for a pencil to write on the back of it and showing it to the warder. He had another sleepless night.

On Wednesday he replied to a letter he'd received from a Don F. Simpson, offering to engage another solicitor for him. 'This I definitely refuse to grant and don't want any more interference concerning my case or my family. The less said about me the better as I'm at peace now. Thanking you. Eric Edgar Cooke.'

On Thursday Des Heenan visited in the afternoon to say his final goodbye.

The Reverend Jenkins went in to see him on Friday morning, spending half an hour with him in prayer. They discussed his execution and Cooke acknowledged to his minister that the decision to hang him was just. He told his minister he had one major concern, though; he was worried that two men were still being held in prison for crimes he had committed.

Without any prompting, Cooke took the Bible from the Reverend Jenkins and said: 'I swear before God I did these two.'

After the minister left, Cooke looked through his letters and photos and asked for a tablet and a letter form. At 11 a.m. he had his last visit from his mother and sister, who were accompanied by his wife. His father did not visit, but instead told the *Daily News*: 'It will be a good thing when the whole episode is over – perhaps then we will be able to settle down to something like a normal life.'

Christine Cooke and June said their final goodbyes to their son and brother 55 minutes later. Cooke was quite cheerful after his curry lunch, reading, talking about the Olympics, and looking through the Bible and his children's photos.

On Saturday, with two days to go, he woke at 5.35 a.m. and read, later asking for playing cards and talking, seeming cheerful and relaxed. After lunch of corned beef, he signed the necessary official forms and spent the rest of the day reading the Bible and looking at the children's photos and letters. That night the sleeping draught worked and he slept well.

His wife made her final visit on Sunday, staying 45 minutes. She knew she would never see him again, alive or dead, having been refused her request for his body for a family burial. She'd written to Superintendent Thorpe six months earlier, on 6 March:

Dear Sir,
If he does die I want to know whether I can claim his body as both Eric and I want him to be with my little boy. I have asked the funeral directors to hold Michael's remains until I wrote to you about Eric. It's important as I was told I had to claim the body before anything happens. Please could you write to me and let me know how I go about it.
   Your sincerely, with thanks,
   Mrs S. Cooke.

The superintendent wrote on the bottom of the letter that it was noted and that Mrs Cooke had been informed to contact the Comptroller-General, Mr Waterer, about claiming of the body, should the execution be carried out. The Comptroller-General of Prisons was the one in charge of all execution arrangements, including the funeral. Mrs Cooke was given a verbal refusal.

A few hours after the Government announced the execution date, a private member's Bill for the abolition of capital punishment was put before the State Parliament. It was the fourth attempt in twelve years by the Labor member for Balcatta, Herb Graham, to end hanging in Western Australia. It suffered the same fate as his previous attempts.

Darryl Beamish's conviction and life sentence remained controversial. But John Button was forgotten. When Cooke's execution date was set, the *Daily News* ran a story headlined 'Cooke Sticks To Story Of Murder', saying that he still insisted he murdered Jillian Brewer, with no reference to his equal insistence that he also murdered Rosemary Anderson.

The Labor Opposition in the Western Australian Parliament worked on Beamish's behalf, asking a series of questions in Parliament and calling for a retrial.

On 21 October Police Minister Jim Craig answered a question about the offences Cooke had confessed to and what had been ascribed to him. It was the first time there was public confirmation of the five other hit–runs and three of the four assaults. But this announcement was too late for Button's and Beamish's appeals.

The Opposition made a last-ditch effort for Beamish, seeking to have Cooke's execution delayed until the case could be resolved. The Leader of the Opposition, Bert Hawke, rose at 6.02 p.m. to move a resolution calling on the government to introduce a Bill to grant Beamish a new trial before a judge and jury. He went on that because Cooke would be a vital witness, his proposed execution should be deferred. Hawke argued that although Cooke was a liar, he did sometimes tell the truth – as shown by the police acceptance of most of his other confessions – and that Beamish's case should go back to a jury to decide.

The debate finished at 12.30 a.m. on 22 October, and the vote was taken. The House divided, all members voting along party lines. The motion was defeated by one vote.

Eight members were paired and so did not vote. Twenty Labor members of Parliament voted to delay Cooke's execution for a Beamish retrial. Twenty-one Liberal and Country Party members voted against the motion, giving the go-ahead for Cooke's appointment with the hangman on Monday morning.

Before the Executioner

26 OCTOBER 1964

'How long have I got?'

'You've got ten minutes,' The Reverend Ralph Thomas quietly but firmly told Cooke. The chaplain was resolute and his voice didn't waver as he answered the 33-year-old standing in the bare, narrow holding cell behind the gallows. But the weight of his matter-of-fact reply hit him, wrenching at his insides.

He'd lived and worked by the maxim that you always gave a man hope, no matter what. He'd comforted a lot of dying men during his war years as chaplain to the AMF and AIF, encouraging them with visions of a future after they'd pulled through – until their last breath ended the lie. Now, as Anglican Rector of Fremantle and Chaplain of Fremantle Prison, he faced a man dying under such different circumstances. There was no pretence against the State's methodical killing. He desperately searched for words to soften the honesty required by the condemned man's direct question and to provide some comfort over the next ten minutes.

'But don't worry, I'll be with you.'

The small, handcuffed prisoner had come to know the churchman over the past few months since he'd taken over as chaplain. He'd called for the Anglican to provide solace on several occasions, seeking some understanding of the reason why he'd killed and injured so many people. But Ralph Thomas wasn't his own type, not Methodist – and a Methodist could parry with Anglicans. He often made the Anglican cleric laugh.

'You're on my list, too, Rev,' he'd once quipped. 'That would make headlines – mass murderer kills prison chaplain.' This one made Ralph Thomas a little nervous. The charming, jocular prisoner was, after all, a serial killer. But now the murderer was himself facing death, and the chaplain felt nauseated at the reality of a man about to be killed in cold blood. He received sympathy from the most unexpected quarter – the condemned man himself, relieving him of the horror of witnessing the deed.

'No, you don't have to be with me. You don't have to see a man swing. Go to the chapel and say a few words for the missus and the kids.'

The clock ticked steadily towards eight. It was time for some formalities. He hadn't been chaplain long, so he made his own rules, going through the questions he believed a prison chaplain should ask.

He faced Cooke square on. 'Did you have a fair trial, Eric?'

'Yes.'

'Is this all as it should be?'

'Yes.'

'Do you have a last wish, Eric?'

'I wanted to get a bike for my eldest boy's next birthday. Could you organise it for me?'

The minister's difficult task this morning was over. He had spent the last one-and-a-half hours with Cooke, seeing him through his last daybreak. These final ministrations to a man about to be executed were stressful, but he'd shared the load with another clergyman, the prisoner's religious adviser from his own Methodist denomination.

It was fourteen years since the Reverend George Jenkins had taken the troubled, wayward eighteen-year-old under his wing after his first convictions. The teenager had readily absorbed the spiritual guidance and was an active part of the church and the youth groups, but these efforts had not succeeded in countering the damage from his father's brutal loathing and other children's cruel taunts. Now George Jenkins was an honorary prison chaplain helping his charge face the hangman. The young man who'd originally sought attention by petty thieving and arson was about to be hanged for wreaking havoc on the society that had ignored his needs.

At 5.30 a.m. two warders arrived at the main gate of Fremantle Prison to start duty one-and-a-half hours before the normal early shift. Accompanied by the officer from the main gate, the only one to hold keys overnight, they went straight across the parade ground into the administration block. In the chief's office they picked up a newly made set of prison clothes – the Death Row version with tapes instead of buttons. Accompanied by the deputy superintendent and the night officer who opened each division's door and locked it behind them, they walked towards Death Row where Cooke had spent his last night sleeping on a mattress on the floor with the cell light blazing. There were to be no suicide attempts in a darkened cell on the night before an execution.

For the past thirteen months he had been closely watched 24 hours a day through the open bars of cell No. 12, the Condemned Cell. Ever since he'd arrived at Fremantle Prison on 20 September the previous year, warders had sat outside the bars in eight-hour shifts, observing him day and night and noting in the occurrence book every ten minutes or so exactly what he was doing, even when he was asleep. This was the careful observation of every condemned prisoner – the system was scrupulous in ensuring a Death Row inmate didn't cheat the hangman, even more so since Leonard Charles Jackson managed it with a razor blade and a table knife in 1947. Now there were no buttons for him to choke on, no knives and forks he could harm himself with. Meals were eaten with a spoon that was passed in and out through the bars with the plate. Toilet paper was passed in every time he wanted to use the bucket in his cell and passed out afterwards, as were pencils when he wanted to write. His cell was searched every time he was escorted out into the small segregated exercise yard. It was standard procedure. But they were particularly on alert with this one. As he was being taken through to Death Row from reception on his arrival at the prison, he'd pointed to the No. 1 post:

'Is that guard an accurate shot?'

'I know nothing about the officer,' his escort replied.
'What should I do to make the man fire?'
'Why would you wish for such a thing?'
'It would be a good way of getting over my troubles.'

The attention prison officers paid to every minute detail succeeded. During the last week, prison officer Tom Straiton noticed that Cooke's pack of cards wasn't fitting perfectly into the box. An attempt to push the cards in failed, so he pulled them out. At the bottom of the box was a cache of pills. Straiton didn't check what they were, but guessed them to be phenobarbitone, the light sedative that Cooke was taking several times a day, prescribed to keep him calm. But a big dose would be fatal. The canny Scotsman quietly removed them and placed them on the desk of his chief officer, reporting that he'd found them in Cooke's cell. Nothing more was said about the incident. He would never know if the prisoner was preparing to cheat the hangman or to kill himself if there was a last-minute reprieve.

Straiton had a good relationship with Cooke, as did most of the warders. They would play cards with him and would banter with him, such comments as Straiton's 'Cookie, before you go, will you tell us where you've hidden half the stuff you've pinched', eliciting an equally light-hearted reply. Cooke could even jokingly raise a concern that he would be too light to make the gallows' trapdoors fall open. Principal officer John Lees, popular with colleagues and prisoners for his sense of humour, told him not to worry, he was organising a pair of heavy diver's boots for him to wear. It remained a joke between them, Cooke reminding Lees about his diver's boots whenever he saw him. But the prisoner's weight and height had been measured and noted in good time for the necessary preparations – height: 5 foot 6½ inches; weight: 8 stone 13 pounds. Even during this grim formality, Cooke cracked a joke, offering his neck size – a 14½ collar.

Cooke's eyes fluttered awake for the last time at 5.45 a.m. on 26 October 1964. He lay on his back for three minutes before turning on to his left side. Another three minutes and the officers would arrive to start the morning's proceedings.

His last meal hadn't been anything special – the normal tea of two slices of bread and jam with a cup of tea at 4.15. Sunday's breakfast had been identical, arriving ten minutes after he'd woken up at 8.10 from a sound sleep. His last day had been much the same as most days, apart from seeing his wife and religious adviser, the Reverend Jenkins. He'd been given some medication after breakfast, and had been taken over the corridor to the bathroom for fifteen minutes to empty his bucket, wash and shave. At 9.55 a.m. Sally made her farewell visit, escorted out at 10.40. He was depressed when she left, spending the next hour talking about her and his family.

Lunch distracted him for a while – his last real meal, a roast followed by plum pudding. After lunch he sat on his blanket on the floor, listening to the radio, lying down after fifteen minutes and continuing to listen and doze, chatting occasionally to the warder. The Reverend Jenkins arrived at 1.55 to conduct a half-hour communion service. After communion, Cooke requested toilet paper and took another tablet, then was led outside into the exercise yard for an hour. Back in his cell at 3.45 p.m., he stood at the bars talking to the warder for a few minutes before sitting down and continuing to chat. He asked for a drink of water at 4.03, had tea at 4.15, put the dishes away at 4.35 and sat by the grille reading. He stood by the grille listening to the radio for ten minutes before making his bed by the grille at 5 p.m. and lying on his back on the bed. He fell asleep within 25 minutes, turning over three times as he slept a little. At 7.20 he awoke and asked for more water and then sat by the grille listening to the radio, looking over papers and books and reading the Bible. Occasionally he chatted to the observing warder – nothing of note, just general topics. At 8.40 p.m. he wanted another drink of water, and five minutes later asked for a pencil to write his farewell letter. He sat writing for one-and-three-quarter hours, handing the pencil back through the grille at 10.33 p.m. Seven minutes later he asked for toilet paper to use the bucket, and afterwards lay by the grille reading his mail again. He took a tablet and sleeping draught at 11.25, lying on his back by the bars, resting and chatting generally while he waited for them to take effect. At 11.45 he sat up and read the Bible. He was asleep by time the clock ticked over into his day of execution and he slept soundly through his last night.

At 6 a.m. the officers walked through the wire cage surrounding Death Row cells to the end one. They arrived at No. 12 and the night officer opened the locks. It was an emotional, awkward time for the officers. How can you say good morning to a man about to be hanged? Cooke broke the ice for them.

'Is it time?'

'Well, Cookie, I'm afraid so,' David Campbell confirmed.

The two officers escorted Cooke out of his cell across to the shower. He quietly showered and dressed in the new set of khaki, put on his shoes which were always kept outside the cell and submitted to the handcuffs. When he was ready, it was time to move to the holding cell in the punishment block just behind the gallows. The peep-holes of all the cells along the route had been taped over, to ensure no prisoner saw the procession.

The two officers led him out of Death Row in the New Division towards the gallows in the Main Division. They marched through the dark stillness of the concert hall, past the sombre rows of locked cell doors of number four division, into number three division. Cooke walked firmly, past the observation cell and segregation cell, turning left out past the gallows and the old flogging triangle, into the punishment block at the back. His last one-and-a-half hours were to be spent in one of the cells where wayward prisoners suffered a month's solitary confinement. He was led to the first on the left, purpose-built 110 years previously with a concrete floor – not even a chance to do self-harm by prising splinters from floorboards.

Cooke went in through the double doors to meet the two clergymen and wait, the two escorting officers taking up their positions just outside the open cell doors. Cooke spent the time chatting with the officers, talking calmly with the clergymen and watching for the first strains of light through the small high window facing east. He declined the offered nips of whisky. The man with just 90 minutes to live appeared as cool and calm as he had been each time he had raised the rifle. He faced the taking of his life in the same way as he had taken others' lives. He knew he had done wrong, he had a debt to pay to society and to God and he accepted it.

In the gallows building, the witnesses were gathering. The

Comptroller-General of Prisons, the superintendent and deputy superintendent. The prison's medical officer and the officer in charge of the prison hospital arrived to witness the execution and attend to the body. Another nine officers were entering the gallows – some stoically accepting it as being part of the job, others detailed against their will. The four with the grim task of acting as cornermen took up their positions on the two black planks placed over the trapdoors. They would be only an arm's distance from the prisoner, close enough to steady him if need be. When the trapdoors fell, they would be standing over the pit, looking down on the result of the hangman's work.

The six-foot, two-inch man with grey hair and glasses left his makeshift overnight accommodation in the boardroom and walked down to his appointment. He'd slipped into Perth from Melbourne under the false name of L. Wilkinson. From Perth Airport he'd caught the airport bus to Ansett's city terminal, considered to be a safer meeting place than the airport under the strict secrecy of his arrival. Flight and payment arrangements had been made previously between the Comptroller-General of Prisons and the Sheriff of the Melbourne Law Courts, as had been done each time 'Mr Wilkinson' had provided the same 'special service' for the Western Australian Government. He had left his home in Melbourne and flown into Perth as 'Mr Wilkinson' four times previously – to hang Carol Tapci in 1952, Robert Jeremiah Thomas in 1960, Mervyn Fallows in 1961 and Brian William Robinson nine months earlier. The man with his own city pharmacy had also followed his father's trade as hangman. Prison officials could now recognise him, no longer needing the description of what he was wearing.

The government was paying him £150 this time, triple his usual fee, as negotiated when he was over for Robinson in January. It also provided the £244 return air fare and £94 in other expenses.

Mr Jones had entered the prison through the women's section on Saturday night and had immediately set about his preparations. A prisoner weighing 126 pounds in his clothing required a length of six foot eight inches. Mr Jones was known to work swiftly and quietly, not wanting any interference as he set about to ensure an expedient hanging – a fast, neat broken neck, not a slow strangulation or the ghastly decapitation that had occurred at the execution of Chas Odgers 50 years previously. He followed exactly the 'Instructions for carrying out details of an execution' published in a confidential circular in December 1891 and updated in March 1905.

On the Sunday night, he'd tested the gallows with a bag of sand that would stretch the rope with a force of 900 foot-pounds. It was a new rope for the occasion. He left it suspended all night to ensure the stretch was taken out.

At 6 a.m. on Monday, as Cooke was being met by his escorts, the hangman was at the gallows continuing the preparations. He raised the bag of sand then dropped it again. While it was suspended, he measured off the rope length and made a chalk mark on the rope, as well as a plumb line chalk mark on the scaffold. He worked quickly to allow the rope time to regain a portion of its elasticity before 8 a.m.

It was just past 7.45. With his time nearing, Cooke wanted to clear his conscience one final time. The Reverend Jenkins noted that he was in a calm and controlled state of mind as, with between ten and fifteen minutes of life left, the murderer made his final confession before the Anglican and Methodist ministers. Just as he'd taken the Bible out of the Reverend Jenkins' hand on Friday and said before God that he'd killed the other two women, he again took the Gospel from his minister's hand. His dying confession was: 'I swear before Almighty God that I killed Anderson and Brewer.'

John Button and Darryl Beamish were close by, sitting in the yards with the rest of the prisoners. The routine work day started later when there was an execution. Button had learnt the sign alphabet so that he could communicate with Beamish. But the two who were linked by a strange fate were not communicating now. They were grimly imagining what was going on in the punishment block just the other side of the wall.

Shortly before the minute hand reached the top of the clock, the executioner arrived at the holding cell and faced the condemned man. Quickly and quietly he manacled his ankles with leather-covered chains, long enough to allow him to walk. He slipped a white canvas hood over his head, lifting the front flap back so that he could see. Then he led the prisoner out for the short walk to the gallows.

'Take care of your Missus,' Cooke farewelled Campbell as he left the cell, accompanied by the chief officer and two escorts. His last walk required only 47 steps – around to the front of the punishment block, past the flogging triangle and along to the door of the gallows with its three steps up and in. It was the same route taken before him by the 42 men and one woman hanged since the Swan River Colony's convicts had been forced to build the gallows in 1888. Cooke walked briskly and silently.

The chief officer and two escorts joined the group of witnesses to the left. Cooke was led on to the thick jarrah trapdoors, to the chalk mark in the centre. The straps on his legs were tightened. The thick rope noose, hanging from a heavy rafter adzed by the convicts, was fitted over his head by the hangman, the knot placed securely with the metal eye forward in front of the angle of the lower jaw.

The hangman started to pull the flap of the hood over Cooke's face. Only then, as the calm, shackled prisoner looked directly at cornerman Straiton facing him a few feet away, did a tear start to form. In an instant, the flap had covered his face and while the hangman still appeared to be adjusting it with one hand, he pushed the lever, withdrawing the pins under the trapdoors quicker than the prisoner would have expected. It was all over in less than a minute from when Cooke left the holding cell.

The pigeons' startled flight from the gallows roof notified the other prisoners.

The prison's medical officer, Dr Charles Dunkley took the thirteen steps down to the dank limestone pit and confirmed that the extreme penalty of the law had been carried out.

For the loved ones of the murder victims, Cooke's death was a relief, despite some being intellectually opposed to capital punishment. There was no more he could do to add to the pain they were already suffering. There was no chance of release or escape, no chance of ever being confronted by anything new about him. There would be no anguish of thinking about him in the present tense. They could get on with dealing with the non-existence of their loved ones without having to cope with thoughts of his continued existence.

For Sally Cooke, it meant the end of ten years of hell. She had been a dutiful and loyal wife to the man who'd won her love with his magnetic charm before enslaving her with his viciousness. She was left in peace to raise her six remaining children, though with a permanent concern and sadness for the victims' families.

For Vivian Thomas Cooke, it meant he had escaped any responsibility for the monster he'd helped create through his part in the cycle of domestic violence. The son he treated so brutally would cause him no further embarrassment.

As Dr Dunkley and the officer in charge of the hospital, Ted Winter, carried out their duties, the other warders filed out of the gallows into the chief officer's office. They signed the form, finalising their role of witness, and several of them accepted the invitation of a brandy as a steadier before going back to work. Straiton had a nip of brandy after being the third last to sign. Despite believing his face was the last thing Cooke had seen, he didn't think he needed it. He'd seen many people killed in action during his years with the Seaforth Highlanders, and he firmly believed that a job was a job and you couldn't let the likes of prisoners hear that you were sentimental and needed a drink. But a good Scot never declined such an offer.

The Reverend Jenkins slipped out through the side of the prison. He generally took things in his stride, but didn't want to face the waiting news media or the single protester opposed to this generally popular execution. He had a quick word with his colleague, Pres Sullivan, who'd come to offer support, then hurried home to the nearby manse in Ellen Street. A short break with many cups of tea, he was back at his 80-hour-a-week job. As well as honorary prison chaplain and minister of the Fremantle Methodist Church, in Cantonment Street, this devout and dedicated clergyman was president and secretary of the Prisoners' Aid Society, a member of the Prisoners' Classification Committee, chaplain of the Citizen Naval Forces and chairman of Kingswood College Council.

He routinely went through his duties for the day, remaining absolutely silent on his morning's duty. He didn't involve his family, but the look on his face and the seemingly endless cups of tea were a giveaway. Nor did he let his family know of the secret burial he had to preside over the next day. He didn't explain when it was obvious that his daughter Joan had guessed why he was dressing in his clerical robes so early in the morning. She too knew that it was a subject not to be spoken of.

'Is today an important day?', the question her only means of expressing empathy for her father.

The minister, a prison official, the cemetery board secretary, a grave digger and three staff from Arthur E. Davies funeral parlour moved up the main drive of Fremantle Cemetery. Up in the distant sandy section they turned left into the far Methodist portion. There were just a few graves dotted around this isolated back part. At the base of a weeping willow was a pile of sand and an iron number. These identified the public grave that had been reopened to receive the body of Prisoner 21649. Grave No. 409 had first been dug 55 years previously, for the coffin of another prisoner who had taken that same final walk to the gallows – Martha Rendell, a 38-year-old convicted of murdering her three stepchildren, the only woman ever to be hanged in Fremantle Prison on 3 October 1909. She was buried seven feet down in grave 409. Cooke, the last man hanged at Fremantle Prison, was buried two feet above her.

As the coffin was lowered to the five-foot level, George Jenkins committed Eric Edgar Cooke's body to dust and his soul to God.

The Reverend Jenkins and his wife Ethel went to see Mrs Cooke, taking her a bunch of Peace roses. Mrs Cooke hadn't been told of the funeral, despite having asked for his body for a private burial and an anonymous Adelaide businessman offering to pay for it. She was officially informed the next day, when she was told that she could put flowers on the grave.

George Jenkins told her that he was now convinced that Cooke had killed Rosemary Anderson and Jillian Brewer. 'He was virtually on the gallows; it wasn't going to delay his hanging at that point,' the minister told Mrs Cooke. 'He had nothing to gain, only the opposite. He was terrified that Button and Beamish might try to take it out on you and the children.'

He had laid Cooke to rest, visited the new widow and reported the calm acceptance of his death and his final confession. There was nothing more he could do but pray for the souls of the tormented killer and of his victims – and for all those left to try to put together their broken lives.

Epilogue

On 16 June 1965 John Button was transferred to a minimum security prison farm at Keysbrook.

At Karnet Rehabilitation and Training Centre he worked on the construction gang, in the gardens, in the welding shop and as a cleaner. He studied various subjects, particularly welding, receiving excellent reports. He kept to himself, associating with only one other prisoner, Max, a man his age, sharing the same fate. He also had been charged with the wilful murder of his girlfriend, found guilty of manslaughter and sentenced by Justice Negus to ten years with hard labour.

Parole was introduced in WA on 1 January 1965, the first Parole Board Chairman being Button's judge, Justice Negus. Button was included in the program involving a series of assessments from which he was recommended by the prison superintendent as suitable for release on parole for the maximum period.

On one report, the assessing officer described Button as a pleasantly disposed youth who, however, still denied that he committed the offence. The officer reported: 'Quite a few attempts have been made over the last fourteen months to trick Button into admitting his guilt. He has resisted valiantly.'

Another reported that Button was able 'to express remorse for whatever he did that night which was responsible for her death. He cannot say "I killed Rosemary".'

Button's only misdemeanour during his whole prison term was to make an extra cup of tea in his cell at night by the ingenious method of putting a wick in the tin of kerosene-based floor polish, setting it alight and boiling a cup of water over the flame. It was the Saturday after Cooke's execution. Brought before the magistrate, he was sentenced to the loss of sixteen marks, suspended while he remained on good behaviour.

John Button was released on parole on 20 December 1967 after having spent nearly five years in prison. A condition of his parole was that he was disqualified from driving for the remainder of his sentence.

After the prisoners' farewell ritual of being thrown fully clothed into a bath of cold water, he said sad goodbyes to Max and took his seat in the prison van for the drive to Perth and freedom. Jimmy picked him up from the Victoria Park Post Office and drove him home for the family welcome. Home was then a rented apartment in Swanbourne, his parents having had to sell their Subiaco house to pay for his defence.

Margaret and Jimmy had their own families: Jimmy was married with a son. Margaret had three children and was living in Sydney.

The monetary system had changed to dollars and cents.

His first wish after his reunion with his parents was to visit Rosemary's grave. He did so, alone, the next day.

With the aid of the Parole Board, he found employment as a second-class welder at S. W. Hart & Co, enrolling in a welding course at night school.

He resumed his ballroom dancing at Alan Butcher's Studio. On the studio's annual Easter trip to Geraldton, three months after his release, Alan Butcher asked Helen Featherstone to look after John, who was having difficulty adjusting. Helen and her elder sister Margaret had known John at the studio before his imprisonment. Helen willingly agreed to help and soon afterwards took him home to meet her parents. Her mother Peg and father, Sergeant Ralph Featherstone, welcomed John into the family. Featherstone told the parole officer that he believed John was innocent.

John Button and Helen Featherstone were married on 9 November 1968.

Despite a supportive wife and psychiatric treatment, John suffered a series of deep depressions and mental breakdowns for nine years after his release, as he struggled to accept the injustice and to adapt to life beyond prison walls – and to cope with the memories that cast him into a well of heartache and self-pity.

In 1977 his car sped out of control across a paddock when he fell asleep while driving alone late at night, heavily sedated. Something within him told him to pull left. That action took him back up the embankment on to the road, where he fell asleep out of harm's way. When he awoke in the car next day, he retraced his tracks, discovering the car had knocked down three guideposts, slid sideways down the embankment and sped across the paddock, returning safely to the road. Believing God had kept him safe, he joined Helen at her church soon afterwards and finally found peace. Since then he has become deeply involved in the church.

On 19 November 1995 John Button was ordained as a Ruling Elder of the Westminster Presbyterian Church. His parents, Charles and Lillian Button, returned to England in despair at the Australian justice system. They have since died.

John Button still suffers from the loss and the injustice, and has regular nightmares of being in prison, unable to get out. He has written to premiers over the years asking for his case to be investigated.

Detective Sergeant John Pearson Wiley rose to become chief of the CIB and, after three years in that position, attained the rank of Assistant Commissioner (Operations) in 1982. He took early retirement in 1984.

Detective Jack Michael Deering was transferred to Bunbury six weeks after Button's trial, returning to Perth as a detective sergeant three years later. He rose through the ranks of detective inspector and senior inspector, becoming a superintendent in 1985, four months before he retired.

Detective Sergeant Bill Nielson was promoted to inspector in 1966 and superintendent in 1970. He retired in 1972.

Detective Sergeant John Dunne resigned from the police force in 1966.

Detective Sergeant Owen Leitch rose to the top position, being Commissioner of Police from September 1975 to February 1981.

In 1969 prosecutor Ron Wilson was appointed Solicitor-General in Western Australia and in 1979 he became the first Western Australian to be appointed Justice of the High Court of Australia, where he sat until 1989.

He was the President of the Human Rights and Equal Opportunity Commission from 1990 to 1997. As such, he headed the commission's National Inquiry into the Separation of Aboriginal and Torres Strait Islander Children and their Families. He was President, Australian Chapter, World Conference on Religion and Peace from 1991 to 1996, Deputy Chairman of the Council for Aboriginal Reconciliation from 1991 to 1994 and President of the Assembly, Uniting Church in Australia from 1988 to 1991. He is opposed to capital punishment.

In 1978 he was made a Companion of the Order of St Michael and St George (CMG) for services to the community. In 1979 he was made Knight Commander of the Order of the British Empire (KBE) for services to the law. In 1988 he was made Companion in the General Division of the Order of Australia (AC) for services to the law.

Sir Ronald delivered the Australian Bible Society's 1988 Olivier Bèguin Memorial Lecture, titled 'Searching for a Just Society'. In it he said: 'The search for justice is as old as humanity. It is not an activity confined to any particular group of human beings. Indeed, the longing for justice is characteristic of all that is best in human nature.'

In 1988 John Button was attending the Bible Society's annual general meeting with his daughter, when he recognised the guest speaker as the prosecutor at his trial. He approached Sir Ronald Wilson and introduced himself.

'I want to say two things,' he told the man whose role 25 years earlier had been to present the case that John had committed wilful murder, and was now the Commissioner for Equal Opportunity.

'First, you were wrong – I didn't do it,' John Button said to Sir Ronald. 'Second, I now understand it was part of God's plan for me and because of what I went through I turned my life over to God and He has blessed my life and my family. I want to thank you for the part you played in God's plan.'

As for the women who survived Cooke's attacks, Nel Schneider still lives in the same house with her husband Jan. She was granted compensation after a difficult court battle in which it was claimed she was faking her epileptic attacks. Ken Hatfield's strong defence on the part of the Motor Vehicle Insurance Trust had Nel Schneider in tears and neurologist Mercy Sadka writing to him in complaint. Mrs Schneider bears no grudge against Cooke, believing in God's will. She had three more children after the attack, losing one as a baby. She is a content grandmother but is still on strict medication for epilepsy.

Mollie MacLeod has a successful business involving the Art of Speech in which she excelled at school, running courses to help people feel confident about speaking in public. She and her family learnt that Cooke had attacked her only when I contacted her 38 years after the event. Although Ern MacLeod was very upset to think he hadn't been able to protect his daughter, Mollie is grateful for the explanation of what happened, because it explains repressed memories she has experienced during the intervening years.

Kathy Bellis, recently widowed, lives in Queensland. She has suffered permanent pain and a limp.

Alix Doncon married and raised a family and lives with her husband on a farm. She suffers severe epilepsy.

Glenys Peak married and had four children. She lives in the WA Wheatbelt with her husband, Malcolm.

Jill Connell married and had four children. She lives with her husband in a Perth suburb and helps care for her grandchildren.

Maureen Rogers married and had two children. She lives in a Perth suburb with her husband, Richard, and is the proud grandmother of triplets. Her memory suffered from the attack and she suffers pain in her leg. but despite this, is a keen bootscooter.

Georgina Pitman married and had two sons, one now a police officer. She lives in a hills suburb of Perth, is still a very keen dancer and enjoys her three grandchildren.

Terese Zagami married, had two children and a career as an accounts clerk. She still lives in the same area and, after meeting Georgina again, has maintained social contact with her through dancing.

Anne Melvin stayed in New Zealand where she married and had two sons.

Peggy Fleury never recovered from the trauma of Cooke's attack, and died of cancer five years later, on 16 April 1968.

Carmel Read married and had one child. She lives with her husband in a hills suburb of Perth. It was a long time before she could talk about the attack, but she has suffered no serious consequences.

Sally Cooke did not move or change her name. She successfully raised her children on her own, losing the newly married youngest to cancer. Her eldest son received the bike for his ninth birthday. He knew it had something to do with his father, but did not know it was his last wish until informed by the author.

In 1966 Melbourne University's Professor of Jurisprudence, Professor Peter Brett, published a 57-page booklet, *The Beamish Case*, strongly pleading the case of a grave injustice perpetrated against Beamish. Brett refers to Button at the end of the booklet: 'There must also be anxiety concerning the position of Button, convicted of the Anderson killing, in view of Cooke's known propensity to commit crimes of the same nature. I cannot, however, speak of this case, since I have not had the opportunity to consider the evidence against him.'

He concludes: 'The important and immediate step to be taken is the pardon and release of Beamish. The judicial processes have failed and the Executive should now intervene ... The judges, Crown Law officers, and police who participated in the sorry proceedings which I have described can be left to live with their own consciences.'

Professor Brett publicly offered to conduct a similar inquiry for Button. Charles and Lillian Button declined the offer, fearing it may upset the authorities and prejudice their son's chances of parole.

Amendments to the Road Traffic Code in the mid-1960s made it illegal to leave the keys in the ignition of parked cars.

Videotaping of interviews was introduced in Western Australia in November 1996. Section 570D of the Criminal Code states that a confession to a serious offence will not be admissible unless the evidence is a videotape recording (except where there is a reasonable excuse for there not being a recording or in other exceptional circumstances).

Instruction OP-30.14 of the Commissioner's Orders and Procedures manual also requires members of the Police Service to be careful to protect the rights of people with special needs, including those with physical, intellectual or psychiatric disabilities. It states, among other things: 'Care must be taken when interviewing a person with special needs to ensure that any confession is voluntary. Members are to be aware that any admonishment to speak the truth has the same effect as holding out of a threat, promise or inducement.'

In 1992 the Australian High Court (in McKinney and Judge) ruled that a charge should not proceed if the only evidence against a suspect was a challenged confession obtained by agents of the state.

Capital punishment was abolished in Western Australia by the Burke Labor Government on 22 August 1984, twenty years after it was used for the last time on Cooke.

I met John Button on 17 February 1992 and took up the case. The original publication of *Broken Lives* in October 1998 brought a strong public, political and legal reaction.

On 10 November 1998 an Urgency Motion by the Hon. Tom Stephens, the Leader of the Opposition in the Western Australia's Legislative Council, resulted in the Attorney General seeking the advice of Western Australia's Solicitor General.

Epilogue

On 14 August 1999 the Western Australian Government granted Button a new appeal before the Court of Criminal Appeal – a rare event and unprecedented in a case 36 years after the conviction.

On 21 December 1998 Darryl Beamish's sister, Mrs Frances Grenville, approached me, asking for help in having Beamish's conviction re-examined. While previously declining to have any part in *Broken Lives*, Beamish and his family changed their minds as a result of the Government's action on Button.

In January 1999 former Chief Justice of Western Australia and former Governor of Western Australia, Sir Francis Burt, wrote that the Beamish case had shattered his belief in the judicial system. According to him, *Broken Lives* had revealed a good deal of fresh evidence about John Button and that the judges of that time, no doubt unaware of the information, must have been infected with the community opinion that Cooke was incapable of telling the truth about anything.

In June 2000 the Western Australian Government granted Darryl Beamish a new appeal before the Court of Criminal Appeal.

Solicitor Jon Davies and barrister Tom Percy QC agreed to act for Button and Beamish *pro bono*.

In February 2000 a world expert in crash reconstruction, Rusty Haight, was brought from America by Bret Christian and reconstructions of the events leading to Rosemary's death were carried out in Perth. Haight reconstructed the Crown case by driving three times into a biomedical dummy with Simcas and reconstructed Cooke's version of events in a Holden. Each of the Simcas received a big dent on the bonnet. When hit by the Holden, the dummy's actions fitted exactly Cooke's confession, hitting the bonnet and causing a big dent, before being flung over the sun visor and on to the roof, and falling on to the road on the passenger side.

In April 2000 former police officer Trevor Condren told me that as the police fatal accidents vehicle examiner who examined Button's car, he had never believed that Button's Simca had hit a pedestrian and that it was not the car that hit Rosemary Anderson. On 16 August 2000 Condren signed a statutory declaration to that effect.

In September 2000 Dr Alister Turner, who as a young orthopaedics resident attended to Rosemary Anderson on the night she died, said that he never believed that John Button had committed the crime: 'I believed that the patient's internal injuries and the injuries to her head and body were too severe to have been caused by a car that had been gutter-crawling and driven at her to scare her.'

John Button's appeal got underway in August 2000 with a series of Directions hearings. The hearing is set for the 2001 sittings of the Court of Criminal Appeal.

The Verdict

John Button's groundbreaking appeal made Australian legal history when it went before Western Australia's Court of Criminal Appeal in May 2001.

    Never before had a new appeal been granted on such a longstanding conviction, which had previously exhausted all legal processes and avenues of appeal. Recognising its historic importance and the public interest, for the first time ever in the state the Chief Justice of Western Australia, David Malcolm, allowed media cameras and tape recorders inside the Court to record the opening moments.

    The Chief Justice presided over the hearing, which was held before himself, Justice Henry Wallwork and Justice Neville Owen and which lasted for four days. Extra bench space was made available for the large media contingent and the public gallery was packed with people wanting to hear the evidence of the appellant's twelve witnesses. They included Rusty Haight, the crash reconstructionist who came from the USA for the hearing; Trevor Condren, the Police Force's Fatal Accident Vehicle Examiner who examined Button's vehicle; six of Cooke's seven surviving hit–run victims; and Cooke's widow, Sally Cooke. The Crown produced no witnesses to give evidence counter to the author's claims, and there was no car crash expert to oppose Rusty Haight.

    Acting pro-bono for Button were Tom Percy, QC, and Jon Davies, aided by Bill Chestnutt. I acted as legal clerk and sat with solicitor Bill Chestnutt behind the main two, with Bret Christian taking this role for Haight's evidence. Acting for the Crown was Simon Stone, whose parents Ron and Abigail took in the eight-year-old son of Cooke's first murder victim Pnena Berkman, when Simon himself was eight years old. Mr Stone was assisted by Amanda Forrester.

The judges reserved their decision.

It was a bright, sunny 31-degree (Celcius) day on 25th February 2002 when John Button walked into the WA Court of Criminal Appeal in Perth, flanked by his wife and children.

Mobbed by television and press cameras outside the Court, he faced more cameras inside the Court: two television cameras, two cameras for a proposed film and a press photographer.

After a tense wait for the Button family, the voluntary legal team and a packed public gallery, the two judges present bowed. Justice Neville Owen, busy in Sydney with the HIH Commission, did not appear.

The Chief Justice, David Malcolm, started to read. Emotions rose and fell during the 35-minute reading.

The Chief Justice said that on a majority of two to one, Cooke's confessions were not admissible. He said the evidence of crash reconstructionist Rusty Haight, as far as it went, was compelling and convincing. It was corroborated in relevant respects by the evidence of Mr Condren.

> In addition, there is now the primary evidence of four of the victims which reveals a striking coincidence of fact and detail between the primary evidence of the victims and the confessions by Mr Cooke leading to a conclusion that the same person was involved in each of them and in the incident involving Ms Anderson, leading to the conclusion that there was, at the least, a real possibility that the same person was involved in each of them, namely, Mr Cooke. The evidence of Mr Cooke matched the accounts given by the respective victims. …The relevant evidence of the hit-run victims, coupled with the evidence of Mr David Priest regarding the Morris Minor stolen by Mr Cooke in May 1960, all lends credence to Mr Cooke's confessions.
>
> …The fact that Mr Cooke maintained his guilt in relation to the death of Ms Anderson in the 'gallows' confession on 26 October 1964 shortly before he was hanged takes on some additional significance against the background of the other matters to which I have referred.
>
> All of this material needs to be considered against

the background of Mr Button's youth at the time, his actions in taking Ms Anderson's still living body immediately to the nearby doctor, his persistent denials when questioned and his confession only after several hours in police custody all combine to lead me to the conclusion that the verdict must be regarded as unsafe and unsatisfactory on the ground that there has been a miscarriage of justice.

As it became clear that the day John Button had dreamed of all those years had finally arrived, a tiny smile appeared, his lip quivered and he fell into the arms of his wife.

Uproar broke out in Court, supporters in the public gallery clapped and cheered as John and Helen Button clasped each other and cried. The legal team had to contain its jubilation on the counsel benches but were all smiles. The Chief Justice hid the smile on his face, but not in his voice as he said: 'I hope you will refrain your further enthusiasm until the adjournment of the Court.'

He continued: 'For these reasons I would allow the appeal and quash the conviction for manslaughter. There could not and should not be an order for a re-trial.'

The other two Justices agreed. It was unanimous. After the adjournment and the bows, the joy was uncontainable. Handshaking, backslapping, hugs, kisses, laughter and tears filled the court.

Button was totally exonerated – a free man.

Outside the court, his junior Counsel Jonathan Davies read a statement to the media:

> It is with profound joy on behalf the defence legal team, myself and my colleagues and friends Bill Chesnutt and Tom Percy QC, that I congratulate John Button and his family on the success of this Appeal. It has been our great privilege to act for him. He is a man of great courage and dignity. Mr Button has led an exemplary life and has raised an excellent family. One can only admire the fortitude with which they have borne the burden of his unjust conviction for the past 38 years.
>
> That this appeal has been possible is due to the insight, energy, and years of dedication put in by Estelle

Blackburn. But for her efforts and sacrifice, and those of Bret Christian, the new evidence which has made this appeal possible could not have come to light. The defence team did not have the enormous resources enjoyed by the Crown in running this appeal. Everyone who contributed their time to Mr Button's cause did so on a voluntary basis. Our thanks therefore go to the small army of volunteers.

The success of this appeal so many years after the conviction is a poignant and fundamental reminder that justice has no 'use by' date. ... Justice failed Mr Button because of inadequacies in the system of criminal investigation and prosecution. There is no guarantee it could not happen again. ... A thorough and proper investigation and an impartial prosecution are the starting points of fairness in our system of Criminal Justice.

During the proceedings which led up to the hearing of this appeal we were surprised and disappointed by the reluctance of the Crown to concede the merit of the appeal notwithstanding the growing body of evidence which pointed to John Button's innocence.

It is to be hoped that a fresh look at the confessions of Eric Cooke will encourage the Crown to support an appeal in the matter of Darryl Beamish whose 1961 conviction, for the murder of Jillian MacPherson Brewer, continues to trouble the legal community and now clearly deserves the closest of scrutiny.

Our thoughts and sympathies are also with the family of poor Rosemary Anderson whose tragic death so many years ago at the hands of Eric Cooke led to this extraordinary chain of events. There is of course no consolation for them from these proceedings, but at least they may now know the truth behind the loss of their loved one.

John Button, a 58-year-old grandfather, spent five years wrongfully imprisoned and 39 years carrying the burden of Rosemary Anderson's murder. He can now finally live the remainder of his life as an innocent man. Eric Edgar Cooke has left behind so many victims – not only those he killed but those who lived with his legacies of fear and permanent injury, and those who paid the price for his crimes.